GUIDEPOSTS

IN

MODERN JUDAISM

Guideposts

in

MODERN

JUDAISM

An Analysis of Current Trends

in Jewish Thought

by

JACOB B. AGUS

New York
Bloch Publishing Company
1954

Printed in the United States of America

by The Polyglot Press, New York

Dedicated to my children
ZALMAN
EDNA
ROBERT
DEBORAH

TABLE OF CONTENTS

Part Two:

NEW PATHWAYS FOR JEWISH LIFE

Preface

In this volume, I aimed to do no more than set up guide-posts to help the intelligent reader find his way in the restless and variegated domain of contemporary Jewish thought. It is addressed to the searching men and women in our midst who seek answers to the following three questions—What do the several interpretations of Judaism really teach? How do the central ideas of the Jewish faith stand up in the light of modern thought? What should be the fundamental philosophy of the Jewish community as a whole?

The first part of this volume charts the map of American Jewish thought, describing the living ideas in the camps of the Orthodox, the Reform and the Conservative. The second part consists of essays dealing with the three central pillars of Judaism which the Zohar declares to be one in essence—the idea of God, the meaning of Torah and the concept of the Jewish community.

Standing on the threshhold of the fourth century of Jewish life in America, we cannot evade the task of taking a fresh look at our heritage and our surroundings, especially since we face a world new in many ways. Our generation has seen the rise and fall of the most vicious antisemitic conspiracy in history, the total liquidation of the "heartland" of Jewish people in modern times, the opening of the American century in world affairs, and the rise of the state of Israel. What is the import of these events for us of the American Jewish community?

1

Traditionally, earnest soul searching and philosophical reflection concerning the fundamentals of faith have been compared to an adventurous exploration of a mysterious garden. So twisted are the paths in the garden and so intertwined are the precious plants with the inevitable weeds that one must tread with extreme caution in order to "enter in peace and leave in peace." Yet, this adventure in all its ardor and travail is the inescapable duty of all who pretend to leadership.

No people is as sensitive to fluctuations in the intellectual climate as we are. Whatever affects the convictions and habits of the upper intellectual crust in the general community strikes deep among us. For our very existence as a people is proof of the Divine assertion "that man does not live by bread alone." In the study of Jewish life, philosophical and sociological considerations go hand in hand with hardly a boundary between them.

In examining the varied strands of the current ideological pattern, I find many a dynamic surge, a happy insight, an openness of mind, a buoyancy of faith and a generosity of spirit, but no rounded, self-contained, all answering systems. Modern Judaism, by and large, follows Amos in basing the whole Torah upon the principle, "seek me and live," rather than Habakuk who declared "The righteous live by their faith."

In the second part, I expound the doctrine of God as the Self of all selves, thus reasserting the so-called "personal" conception of the Deity. I do not claim to have found the "way—" only a few guideposts, which others may examine and use. Throughout my researches, I follow the broad highway of reason and universal experience, skirting the easy impetuosity of sudden illumination or the pale detachment of mystical wonderment.

In the essays dealing with Divine revelation, I offer a Conservative philosophy of Jewish law and a program of action based upon it. The paradox inherent in the nature of revelation is exposed to view and the implications of this paradox are developed. Out of this discussion, there emerges a dynamic and consistent Conservative ideology.

The nature of the overall Jewish community is examined in three lengthy essays. The attempt is made to uncover the enduring worth of Jewish existence, its purpose and significance. The argument is pressed that American Jewish life is amply validated in its own terms; that its purpose is not to preserve the patterns of the past out of filial piety or to serve the blind "survivalist" instincts of the Jewish "nation"; that it is to regard itself not as a colony cast amidst "alien corn" nor as a "beleaguered minority" but as a "creative minority" within the American people. Throughout that discussion there is developed the concept of a pervasive Jewish spiritual tradition, apart from our strictly theological heritage. And the nature of this tradition is exemplified by contrast with the philosophy of the outstanding Protestant theologian of our day.

Nearly all the essays included in this volume were published previously. The lengthy review of the contemporary theological scene was published substantially in its present form, in a Yiddish translation, as part of the fourth volume of the Yiddish Encyclopedia. The other essays appeared in "Conservative Judaism," in "Judaism—A Quarterly Journal of Jewish Life and Thought," and in "The Menorah Journal." The chapter on "The Meaning of God in our Experience" is published here for the first time. The chapter "Pluralism in Law" was given as a lecture at the Graduate Institute of the Jewish Theological Seminary. The extended review of Prof. Kaplan's works is reprinted from "The Jewish

Quarterly Review." I wish to thank the editors of these publications for their kind cooperation. To the members of Beth El Congregation, I am deeply grateful for their kind encouragement of my literary efforts and their sustained devotion to the ideals of Judaism.

April, 1954
Baltimore, Md.

GUIDEPOSTS

IN

MODERN JUDAISM

Part One

CURRENT TRENDS IN JEWISH THOUGHT

1

The Impact of American Culture

Even as American civilization consists of a new blend of the ancient cultures of Europe, the spiritual face of American Jewry taken as a whole is a novel and completely unparalleled expression of the deathless genius of the Jewish people. It appears that the mere act of physical translation transforms a religious culture and effects a rearrangement within it of its constituent values and institutions. For while the message of religion is directed to the individual in the name of eternally valid truths, the language and symbolic structure of faith are inevitably affected by the ubiquitous pressures of the living cultures of the day. Frequently, too, the very substance of faith is radically altered, though the ancient dogmas continue to be pompously trotted out, reverently dusted off and ceremoniously reaffirmed, as if nothing had changed. Thus, according to a newspaper report of this year, a Methodist minister learned to his chagrin that out of a hundred and fifty regular attendants of his church, only two believed in the innate sinfulness of human nature, the rest subscribing to the prevailing doctrines of liberalism, though he had preached the dogma of "original sin" proudly and vociferously for 20 years. In the same manner, the progressive Catholic circles of America, mellowed by the pervasive tolerance of democracy, shudder at every demonstration of the ruthless logic and fanatical consistency of their brethren in Spain and South America.[1]

Should we not then expect a similar development in the

---

[1] Commager, *The American Mind,"* p. 162.

case of Judaism, especially since our faith had been built of old after the pattern of Abraham's tent in the desert, with hospitable doors opening to all sides?

Accordingly, we propose to analyze the contemporary trends in American Judaism by describing first the prevailing winds of the American spiritual climate, tracing then in some detail the varied religio-cultural heritage of the Jewish community and outlining finally the massive processes of transformation to which the component institutions and trends appear to be subject.

* * *

The American mentality has been variously described both by native scholars and by distinguished foreign visitors in terms which vary all the way from pedantic jingoism to the cold contempt of an old aristocrat looking down his nose upon an aggressive parvenu. Apart from the inevitable subjective bias of all such essays, the analysis is rarely relevant to our theme. For an understanding of the manner in which the heritage of Judaism is even now being molded into an American pattern, we must learn to recognize the ideas and circumstances which bear upon the emergence of a specific *organizational structure* of American Jewry and those characteristically American sentiments and ways of thinking which are bound to affect the *pattern of ideas* in Judaism. In a sense, the structural organization of a group is related to its ideology as the body is to the soul. Nevertheless, it is important for us to envisage clearly and separately the play of ideas, on the one hand, and the pressure of social factors, on the other hand, which together make for the eventual emergence of typically American interpretations of Judaism.

Perhaps the most fundamental factor in American society is the absolute separation of church and state. While in European countries this relegation of religion to the domain of private conscience has been achieved sometimes slowly, sometimes violently, but always in conscious opposition to a long and honorable national tradition, in America the foundation of national life was laid out in accordance with the inviolability of this principle. Thus, as Americans return ever and anon to the basic principles of their heritage, they renew their contacts with the great liberal tradition of the eighteenth and nineteenth centuries. What has been a revolution and a protest to the older countries of western civilization was here a beginning, an axiom, the cornerstone of a brave new society. To be sure, in actual practice Americans frequently temporize with this principle, as in the singing of Christmas carols or in the teaching of Scriptures in schools. Every year we are certain to hear of a community leader arousing a storm of protest by calling attention to this flagrant deviation from principle. Yet, these perennial protests have proved to be of no avail, for radical consistency is rarely to be found in any human institution. At this writing the national community relations agencies are divided on the manner in which the problem of religion in the schools is to be handled, with the N.C.R.A.C. advocating public protests and the A.D.L. counselling acquiescence. The American conscience is likely to resolve this issue, not by eliminating the Christmas festivities, but by introducing the celebration of Hanukah and other festivals into the extracurricular program of the schools. Insensibly and irrevocably, the inner values and outer forms of Jewish observances are likely to change in accord with the need of conveying a significant message to a non-Jewish society. The ethnic factors and folk elements of the festivals are likely to recede into the background, making room for the growth of the universal values implied in their observance.

Organizationally, the impetus of liberalism makes for a progressive lessening of social pressure in behalf of any kind of conformity. Its basic implication is that any one religion is as good as another, the social validity of creeds varying in direct proportion to their tolerance of other faiths. The one "unforgivable sin" is intolerance. In a liberal atmosphere it becomes difficult to maintain any kind of rigid orthodoxy. Fundamentalism tends to be confined to the uneducated and the provincial, or it may in practice follow policies of conciliation and accommodation which it rejects in theory, or it may hide beneath a smoke-screen of multitudinous equivocations. In the face of implacable fanaticism, it is easily possible and indeed inevitable to oppose the equally inflexible assertion, "my faith and mine alone is right," but in the face of good-natured ridicule the rigid stance of orthodoxy is bound to soften and melt.

* * *

In America, the liberal attitude has not resulted at any time in a wave of conversions to any form of the Christian faith. Reverence for religion, which is an intrinsic element of American liberalism, certainly includes reverence for one's own inherited faith. Indeed, in a competitive world, it is distinctly a supreme virtue to blow one's own horn and to make the most of one's heritage. As to the underworld of prejudice and social snobbery which scorns the Jew as a scion of a lesser breed, conversion to Christianity is likely to be of dubious efficacy in providing a safe escape. Thus, assimilation in the full and final sense of conversion was not ever and is not now a grave and massive threat to the existence of the Jewish community.

While American liberalism does not offer aid and comfort to the escapist elements in the Jewish community, it does definitely weaken the cohesive forces of the community. In fact, American Jewry is scarcely organized on the basis of community-loyalty, which formed the basis of Jewish collective existence throughout all the centuries of life in the Diaspora. None of the forms of communal structure in European countries affords an exact parallel to the total lack of this all-inclusive base in American Jewry. While the Federations and Welfare Funds of some communities seek to embrace in their purview all of the non-sectarian areas of service, they still remain mediating agencies, not basic units of identification. The substitution of the congregational unit of organization for that of the community is, of course, an outgrowth of the liberal tradition of America and its emphasis upon the complete freedom of the individual. If there be a pyramid of values in American culture, the sovereignty of the individual constitutes its apex. It is not at all taken for granted that the individual is to be regarded as part of any community, axiomatically and automatically. As the focus of all values, he is at liberty to choose out of the organic cluster of values and institutions that is Judaism whatsoever may appeal to him and reject whatever does not suit his fancy. In consequence, the American Jewish community is actually a loose association of organizations, ministering to one or another Jewish or general ideal.

Corresponding to the free individual is the congregation in its complete independence and virtual self-sufficiency. While the various national associations of synagogues along ideological lines endeavor to act respectively as Orthodox, Conservative and Reform "movements," they are actually free associations of more or less like-minded congregations which can rarely be induced to follow any one policy. Nor are the lines of demarcation in the domain of doctrine identical in all cases with the actual lines of congregational affiliation. The open and competitive market of a free society is reflected in the frequent crossing of ideological lines for the sake of traditional loyalties to a national theological seminary or because of incidental advantages of one sort or another.

The effects of the American exaltation of the individual are not confined to the organizational pattern of American life. If the source of all values and the goal of all ends be the contemporary man or woman, then all forms of group-existence must be judged ultimately by the effectiveness with which they minister to the needs or respond to the ideals of the individual. On the organizational plane which we discussed up to this point, the powerful impact of this emphasis was clear enough. But its implications for the future development of American Judaism are even more profound and enduring. For in the long run this pervasive tendency is likely to undermine the purely ethnic loyalties of the Jew. Traditionally, Judaism consisted of a blend of religious and national loyalties, the proportion varying in accord with the temper of the individual thinker and the spiritual atmosphere of his day. In America, there is little or no opposition to the cultivation of minority cultures, but the pervasive individualism of the dominant civilization tends to dissolve the loyalties of the immigrant to his specific culture. The same Poles who have resisted violently the imposed process of "Russification" find themselves caught up in the freely accepted process of "Americanization" to the point of seeing no reason for the continuance of their Polish culture. For several generations they may render lip-service to their inherited loyalties which are doomed to slow attrition and eventual extinction, precisely because they are not opposed. When emphasis is shifted with the unquestioned certainty of an axiom from the group to the individual, and the individual finds his legitimate needs and aspirations satisfied within the framework of the general civilization of the country, he cannot see any useful function in his own life for the minority loyalties which he inherited. Cultural pluralists may succeed in preserving for a time the unique "folkways" and arts of America's immigrant groups, trotting them out like so many museum-pieces at public functions, but the roots of these sub-cultures in the life of the American individual are bound to wither and die. Likely to endure, then, are only those elements of Jewish loyalty and culture which are absorbed into the organic pattern of Judaism.

The process of denationalization is even now visibly at work in the Jewish community, though, for a generation, it had been slowed down and almost brought to a halt. The rise of the international conspiracy of antisemitism stimulated the ethnic consciousness of the American Jew and led him to reassert his will to live through the various agencies of anti-defamation and the movement for the upbuilding of the homeland. The will to live of the Jewish group, challenged as it was on a purely ethnic basis, asserted itself in ethnic terms, bringing about a massive revival of nationalistic sentiments. But, with the establishment of the state of Israel, the zeal of American Zionism was spent and the movement is presently being slowly deflated to minor proportions. To American Jews, Zionism was but a means of helping their unfortunate brethren in other lands, not a personal philosophy of self-fulfillment and self-redemption. The rise of Israel served to "normalize" the American Jew's conception of his own status. Like the American of European ancestries, he too now has a homeland whence he came, in spirit if not in body. This "homeland" is entitled to sentimental nostalgia and a fair share of philanthropic effort since it represents for him the background of his spiritual life and the challenge for his Utopian idealism in the building of a good society. But the sense of oneness of destiny, which is the true source of Zionist energy, is slowly fading away from his consciousness, permitting him to yield to the general pattern of American assimilation.

By the same token, the battle of anti-defamation is waning into insignificance, primarily for lack of antisemites to combat. To be sure, there is no telling when new demagogues might arise to peddle their foul wares and to arouse once again the ethnic will for self-preservation. However, we may point to objective factors which make such an eventuality improbable. There is, firstly, the undoubted fact that the antisemitic ideology as it was fostered by Nazism is now utterly discredited. Secondly, the rise of the state of Israel robs the ideology of antisemitism of the appearance of universality that clung to it, on account of the ubiquitous presence of the harassed and homeless "wandering Jew." The Jew is now "normalized," no longer a mysterious alien "here and everywhere, now and forever." In relative freedom from the virulent sting of mass antisemitism, we may expect the pattern of Jewish loyalties to shift ever more decisively from the pole of ethnicism to the one of a personal faith.

*   *   *

The exaltation of the individual in American society is likely to affect the Jewish religion in itself, in addition to constricting the ethnic loyalties contained in it and clustering about it. With the living individual as the goal of all values, it is no longer sufficient for a religion to be "proved true" in terms of the absolutes of logic and ethics. Religion must be approved not only in relation to abstract universals, but also in the light of what it actually accomplishes for the anxiety-ridden, confused and groping individual worshipper. It is no longer consistency with Aristotle or with Darwin or with the impersonal majesty of science that is decisive, but suitability for the supreme goal of the individual's happiness, his "peace of mind" or his "peace of soul." The vague arts of psychiatry have come to occupy the center of the stage, serving as the final arbiters in all questions of truth and goodness.

This popular emphasis may in time be redeemed through its blending with the Jewish ideal of the "perfect man" ("ho-odom hasholaim"). If the individual is to be the source of all values, then we must not take him as we find him, in all his empirical vulgarity, but in his potentialities for ideal perfection. However, concerned as we are with the forces playing upon the heritage of Judaism in American civilization, we must recognize American individualism for what it is presently, apart from what it might eventually become.

Another corollary of American individualism is its thoroughgoing pragmatism and its impatience with mere ideologies. It is scarcely possible to exaggerate the pervasiveness of this fundamental bias, that it is not what ideas are that counts, but what they do. Since Judaism takes on the color of its intellectual environment, we may expect the earthy genius of pragmatism to permeate the Jewish tradition, which, in the pre-philosophical era, had many points of contact with it. As the Jewish movements of Russia in all their variety, ranging from revolutionary socialism to cultural Zionism, were alike in being profound and impassioned, bursting with messianic fervor, in keeping with the dark pathos of the Russian soul, and even as the Jews of Germany were meticulously orderly and systematic, guarding against the slightest "impurity" of ideological inconsistency, American Judaism is likely to unfold the happy insights of the pragmatic approach, which frequently scandalizes the philosophical purist in its bold defiance of mere logic, its brave optimistic surge, and its determination to stay close to the realities and ideas of common sense. The isms which presently divide American Jewry are only faintly ideological and largely practical—such as, wearing of a hat, mixed pews, organ playing, etc. There is no attempt on the part of the Orthodox groups to discourage intermarriage with the Reform or Conservative wings. The lines of demarcation are inchoate, indecisive, and ignored not infrequently. While strong opinions are held concerning practical questions, the ideologies of all three groups are kept flexible, open at the upper end, unrounded and unfinished. The characteristic ambition of German Jewish savants to tie their ideological boat securely to one or another anchorage in classic German thought is conspicuously absent in this country. The great founder of the American Conservative movement, Solomon Schechter, entitled his profound study of Talmudic thought "Aspects of Rabbinic Theology," in the belief that a complete and rounded system was neither desirable nor possible. Contrast this attitude with the classic attempt of Prof. Mauritz Lazarus to demonstrate that Jewish ethics is but an explication of Kant's ethics of "the pure will!" Schechter's conception was as typically American as Lazarus' system was typically German. The place of Kant and Hegel in German Jewry is largely preempted here by the pragmatists and the experimentalists, notably William James and John Dewey.

* * *

In describing the characteristic spiritual atmosphere of America, it remains but to add that the institutions of religion form a central focus of the cultural and social pattern of American life. Religion is not so much a set of convictions as a body of experience and aspiration, growing naturally out of the national culture, like fine fruit out of fertile soil. The quality of "moral optimism" which distinguishes the American temperament is easily projected into the infinite universe, forming the buoyant mood of monotheistic faith, "that underneath are the everlasting arms." With the impetus of individual initiative looming so large and importantly in our society, people are not disillusioned by the lack of absolute certainty in the sphere of religion, responding readily to the conception of faith as a brave and adventuresome decision to live "as if" our noblest insights were rooted securely in the infinite reaches of the dark unknown. Philosophers cannot prove or disprove the theistic belief; hence, it is legitimate for the "will to believe" to tip the scale for faith. This argument, which was developed by the most representative thinker of America, William James, articulates the living impact of its vibrant culture, for this "will to believe" is a powerful impulse in the national tradition and the character of the people, to be felt in every robust beat of the national pulse.

Thus, American churches by and large are short on metaphysics and long on all forms of social service. Not mere dogma but the human equation in all its ponderous perplexity is the theme of all liberal pulpits, and the church is the social center of the community, not merely the isolated refuge of comforting holiness. By the same token, the American synagogue is able to embrace under its wings every cultural and uplifting interest of the Jewish community, taking on quite naturally the role of a synagogue-center. The inclusion of a massive program of athletic and recreational activities within the budget of a synagogue is now a commonplace. The very conception of a synagogue-center, which makes room for social, recreational, and all kinds of cultural activities within the walls of the same institution, is distinctly American. And the implications of this conception are far-reaching. For it reflects the belief that religion is not a static body of dogmas, but the upward surge of the human personality in all its fullness. Translated in Jewish terms, the message of the American synagogue reads today, "nothing that is Jewish or human is alien to me."

17

Summarizing the continuing impact of American culture upon the heritage of Judaism, we take note of the persistent liquefaction of Orthodoxy through the prestige and power of the liberal tradition. At this particular moment, there is a revival of neo-orthodoxy and neo-supernaturalism among Protestants and a renewed aggressiveness among Catholic Thomists, but this development is scarcely more than an ephemeral reflection of the despair and frustration of the war era. In the long run, the enduring tradition of America is liberal humanism, enshrined as it is in the basic documents and heroic saga of the nation. Secondly, the individualism of the American temper makes for a progressive dissolution of ethnic ties and national sentiments, shifting the emphasis of residual Jewish loyalty steadily in the direction of religion and the congregational unit of organization. Thirdly, the same fundamental bias makes for a steady substitution of psychology and the goals of happiness for philosophy and the abstract ideals of truth and rightness. Fourthly, the pragmatic quality of American thought is evidenced in a characteristic impatience with mere ideology, a downright contempt for rounded systems and a keen concern with practical issues and results. Finally, the central place of the religious institution in the context of American culture is likely to be reflected in a continuous expansion of the synagogue, so as to embrace an ever wider area of cultural interests and activities.

These influences have been at work for many generations. But since most American Jews have been until recently immigrants or sons of immigrants, the full effect of these factors is still to be felt. Manifestly, too, the Reform and Conservative groups have been permeated more deeply with the American spirit than the Orthodox communities, which still consist for the most part of recent immigrants. It does not follow from this circumstance, however, that the progressive Americanization of the Jewish community will lead to the emergence of a uniform type of American Judaism. For each of the groups is sufficiently virile, thoughtful and tenacious to deal with the challenge of modern life in its own terms. In the spiritual atmosphere of America, the factors making for variety and growth are likely to prevail over the seductive appeals of unity and uniformity. The vistas of the future, so far as we can see them, reveal a number of confluent but not commingling streams, flowing upon the wide bedrock of the same tradition.

2

The Orthodox Stream

American Orthodoxy has not yet matured to the point of assuming a definite cast of thought or pattern of practice. Consisting of many strands which vary in the timber of their orthodoxy and the degree of their resistance to the modern temper, its texture is still unfinished and uncertain. On the whole, it may be fairly stated that, apart from popular tracts and collections of sermons, Orthodoxy has not yet settled down to the task of rendering an intelligent account of itself in the American idiom of thought and culture. Among its thoughtful adherents, we may distinguish disciples of the three trends in Orthodox Judaism—the supernaturalism of Kabbalah, the mysticism of Hassidism, and the transcendental rationalism of western neo-Orthodoxy.

Kabbalistic supernaturalism continues to function as an effective, living faith, largely in the form which it has taken in the "mussar" movement of the Lithuanian Yeshivoth. While the various Hassidic dynasties and notably the HaBad school of Liubavitch occasionally conduct energetic campaigns with the aid of a tight little band of ardent disciples, they remain an exotic and outlandish phenomenon, hovering uncertainly on the shadowy periphery. HaBad literature consists of endless variations of the old Kabbalistic themes, symbols and terms, without any attempt to take note of the modern world, save on the level of elementary education. The "mussar" movement, on the other hand, has influenced the teachers and students of the great Lithuanian Yeshivoth, so that it may be regarded as the philosophy of

Orthodoxy's elite. Echoing the world-view of the thoughtful exponents of the movement, the "mussar" ideology is vastly more important than might be surmised from the paucity of its literature. In the domain of speculation, Orthodox rabbis were extremely reluctant to publish their reflections, contenting themselves with oral admonitions to their students. Thus Rabbi Hayim of Volozhin allowed his classic little volume, "Nefesh Ha-Hayim," to be published only after his death. The literary output of Rabbi Israel Lipkin of Salant is amazingly meager. In large measure, the successors of the founding masters share this characteristic reluctance to entrust to the printed page the delicate task of tracing a safe pathway in the danger-filled, forbidding domain of the "garden of metaphysical thought." Accordingly, we have to rely for the most part on secondary sources and on the published notes which the students took of the "conversations" ("sihoth") of their masters.

As formulated by the unique genius of the aforementioned Rabbi Israel Lipkin, the "mussar" movement was, in its early stages, thoroughly uninterested in metaphysics. Its principal concern was to deepen Jewish piety and to project the ideal of the perfect Jewish personality. Unlike the Hassidic movement of Poland and the Ukraine, which directed its message to the masses of the people, the Lithuanian pietists appealed to the chosen few. The mussarists aimed to develop great spiritual personalities, in the belief that the masses reflect in varying degrees the piety of their spiritual heroes. Thus, the mussar-movement set its sights high, far above and beyond the fixed norms of the "Shulhan Aruch." While the Hassid was encouraged to feel that he is part of the holy community of Israel, if he identified himself with it emotionally by so much as sharing in the "tsaddik's" meal, or in the merry-making and the whiskey drinking of the pious, the mussar-man was taught to recognize his complete unworthiness, even if he devoted every ounce of energy to the study of the Torah. The Hassidim learned to serve God in joy, to sink their individuality with utter abandon in the total community of Israel, which is assured of salvation by the unbreakable word of the Covenant. In contrast, the "mussar"-men were asked to ponder in fearful anxiety over the fate of their own soul, to envisage the tremendous difficulty of meeting fully the demands of the Torah and to worry ceaselessly over the urgency of achieving the complete perfection of their souls, ere the curtain of death ended the possibility of growth. The keynote of "mussar" was persistent and deeply anxious self-analysis and self-criticism. Before the bar of Divine judgment, the individual stands in total isolation, mindful only of his sins and failures, pleading tearfully and with anxious trembling for the undeserved boon of salvation.

For a while, the "mussar" movement organized "sh'tib-lach," small rooms for solitary meditation and penitent crying, which contrasted with the busy, noisy and merry "klauses," the gathering places of the Hassidim. Gradually, however, the movement withdrew from the lay-community and confined its teaching to the great Yeshivoth, where it constituted the official interpretation of the faith.

The individualistic emphasis of the "mussar-movement" may be understood in the light of the powerful inroads which were made by the rise of "Haskalah," the move-ment of humanistic and secularistic enlightenment. In the last decades of the nineteenth century, the Jewish com-munity of Russia was no longer dominated intellectually and socially by pious believers, whose central concern it was to achieve the bliss of salvation in the hereafter. While the masses of Russian Jewry were still in the tenacious grip of tradition, the intelligentsia was swept along by the powerful storm-winds of the new liberal and revolutionary faiths. The naive uniformity of belief and practice which prevailed uninterruptedly for so many centuries was now broken up, and even the conviction of the faithful remnant lost in depth and tenacity. Perforce, the Jewish individual became the center of attention since the empirical community was no longer identical with the ideal congregation of Israel (K'nesseth Yisroel), which is the counterpart of the Divine Presence ("sh'chinah"). If the community as a whole no longer merited to be "saved," selected "men of perfection" were needed to serve as the bearers of "the yoke of Torah and mitzvoth."

The "mussar"-movement construed the challenge of "Haskalah" as a psychological, not a philosophical, problem. They did not attempt to refute the arguments of the modernists, point by point, in the belief that dialectical fencing was only a subtle defense-mechanism. To the faithful, arguments are superfluous, and to the unbelievers, the most consummate apologetics will be of no avail. For faith dwells below the level of the conscious, in the domain of will and feeling, where the soul freely submits to its Master or rebelliously turns away from Him. Hence, the problem of religious education is to reach down to "the unconscious feelings," "Hargoshoth Kaihoth," of the people and to build there an impregnable foundation for the superstructure of faith.[1]

In turn, this task of subjugating and conquering the vast domain of the unconscious can be achieved by the two complementary methods of fear and love. The primitive mentality, which underlies and controls the thought-processes of even the most civilized of men, is moved only by coarse and selfish concerns. Hence, the need of dramatizing the varied punishments of hell and dwelling upon the delights of heaven. These central pillars of naive piety were brought into the foreground by the "mussar"-teachers,

[1] *"Tnuath HaMussar,"* by Dov Katz, Vol. 1.

in order to arouse and mobilize the feelings of fear and anxiety which are rooted in the lowest reaches of the human soul. At the same time, they sought to compound out of the maxims of our vast religious literature the image of the spiritually perfect Jew, which they presented as the ideal worthy of emulation to the idealistic youth of the "Yeshivoth." What is a more fitting goal for the edification of the young than the achievement of perfection in the qualities of character and the wisdom of Torah, in humility and piety, in sympathetic understanding and in the love of truth? The foundations of heaven and earth are firmly founded on the merit of Torah students. The world would be returned to chaos, they believed, if the loyal few failed to meditate in the Torah day and night. Thus did the humble "yeshivah-bohurs" persuade themselves that, like Atlas, they carried the whole sinful world on their frail shoulders.

In the subsequent development of the "mussar"-movement, two schools of thought emerged, which stressed respectively the two contrasting emphases in its teaching. The followers of Rabbi Yitzhak Blaser and of Rabbi Yosel of Novarydok devised a system of instruction and training which aimed at the cultivation of the fear of God, in all its gradations, from the terrifying specters of hell fire and brimstone to the noble sense of awe and reverence of the philosophers.[2] To the austere, sensitive conscience of these teachers, it seemed that no man could ever mature spiritually to the point of outgrowing the level of fear-consciousness, so as to feel altogether confident of Divine favor. Characteristic of this mood is the following episode in the life of Rabbi Yitzhak Blaser: Asked to address a group of Yeshivah-students, he told them an allegory concerning a group of men who were lost in a forest. After days of

2 *"Or Yisroel,"* by Rabbi Yitzhak Blaser.

wandering, they encountered an old man and implored him to show them the way out of the forest. But the old man replied to them, "You have been lost for only a few days. I have been lost for many years. How can I help you?" Applying the parable to himself, he concluded, "You are young men and you feel perplexed for only a short time. I have been lost for a long, long time. Let us cry together. Perhaps the Almighty will help us." [3]

The awareness of perplexity is itself the way out, if it leads to fear and trepidation, for fear is the beginning of all wisdom and its end as well.

More influential in the long run, especially upon the American scene, was the stream of "mussar"-teaching which appealed to the sentiments of love and aspiration and set up the ideal of the perfect personality as the goal of piety. Growth toward ever nobler ends is the positive pole of all psychical impulses as fear and anxiety constitute their negative pole. Thus, Rabbi Simha Zissel Ziv of Khelm and his disciples aimed to transform piety into an all-embracing ideal of perfection that would appeal to the healthy, outgoing instincts of Jewish youth, shunning no exercise or discipline that makes for growth of the spirit. While the other "mussar"-teachers, including the founder, Rabbi Israel Lipkin, opposed the introduction of secular studies into the curriculum of the Yeshivoth, for fear that the students might be influenced by the manifold errors of modern thought, Rabbi Simha Zissel himself established the "Beth HaTalmud" of Grobein, a school where secular studies were taught with the aim of synthesizing Orthodoxy and modern culture so as to produce a new type of Jewish gentleman. His example was not followed by the heads of other "Yeshivoth" of Poland and Lithuania, but the founders of the great Yeshivah University, which

[3] *"T'nuath HaMussar,"* vol. 2, p. 250.

laid the ideological cornerstone for American orthodoxy, were certainly encouraged by his pioneering effort.

To Rabbi Simha Zissel orderliness was the basic quality of the ideal personality, enabling "the pure and rational soul" to prevail over the body, "which is more ugly, repulsive and disgusting than the bodies of all other animals." Self-control can be effective only when it is habitual. Thus, he demanded of his pupils that they devote time to quiet reflection and self-examination day by day. "Not one day should be allowed to pass without habituation in the practice of reflection, for it is the key to wisdom, the focus of all the faculties, leading to the attainment of the whole man."[4]

Since reflection is the key to perfection, man must strive to allay anxiety and to acquire the capacity to be calm, poised and unperturbed at all times. "In the quality of inner rest, all perfection is included." His disciples were asked to undertake a series of exercises so as to achieve the state of calm confidence which is the necessary prerequisite for pious reflections on the nature of God and the destiny of the human soul. However, he cautioned, the goal of inner peace and imperturbability of spirit must not be interpreted as implying disinterestedness in other people. On the contrary, impulsive charity, the unquestioning and unreasoning love of our fellowmen is essential to the attainment of perfection. For the love of people serves to overcome our native selfishness and it is also the one sure way to God.[5]

The emphasis on reflection in the Khelm branch of the "mussar"-movement was bound to reawaken the metaphysical interest, which was initially sidetracked. The "mussar"-teachers shunned the disciplines and methods of modern

4 *"Tnuath HaMussar,"* Vol. 2, p. 161.
5 *"Tnuath Ha Mussar,"* Vol. 2, pp. 153, 154.

philosophy, seeking authoritative answers to the baffling questions of faith in the sacred literature of Kabbalah. While the intricate details of Kabbalistic theosophy were studied only by the consecrated few, the Yeshivah-teachers sought to uncover the inner impetus and essential thought of Kabbalah for the benefit of their students. In this process of unconscious selection and interpretation, a new quality of thought is inevitably introduced.[6]

The following world-view is blocked out in a series of "mussar"-lectures that were given in the European Yeshivah of Tels and later edited and published in America.[7]

The authors present as a truth of Kabbalistic revelation the fundamental generalization of Plato's that all the things and events which we encounter in this sensible universe are only shadows of ethereal essences that inhere in the upper realms of eternity. The eternal patterns, which constitute expressions of the Divine Name in the first realm of Emanation, become progressively "coarsened" as the chain of worlds descends link by link down to our own earthly realm. The more of value, beauty and goodness things possess, the closer they are in the chain of being to their counterparts in the domain of Emanation.

"One range of existents is realized in all the worlds, and in every world the same thing assumes a different form in keeping with the nature of that world."[8]

In this cosmic chain of being, the Torah fulfills at every level the function of soul to the body of the corresponding world, the Torah constituting a series of coarsening expressions of the Will of God, and the universe a parallel descending series of His Work. While the early Kabbalists,

---

[6] *"Pishai Sh'arim,"* by R. Yitzhak Hover is a typical outline of the intricate Kabbalah-system of the nineteenth century.

[7] *"Shaiurai Daath,"* New York, 1949.

[8] *Ibid,* p. 11.

battling for recognition, loved to contrast their "hidden wisdom" with the plain meaning of the Torah, the "mussar"-men, unaware of the surge of conflicting ideas in the long history of Jewish thought, saw the Kabbalah as an integral, organic phase of the revealed Torah.

"In the wisdom of the Torah and the reasons of the commandments, the revealed and hidden reasons are not unrelated. In reality, they form one reason, the hidden one being the root and soul of the revealed explanation. He who understands any motivation literally knows only the garment, but the Torah has a garment and a body, and a soul, and a soul to a soul, rising ad infinitum." [9]

In the days of the Messiah, the higher expression of the Torah will take the place of the one we now possess.

"For the Torah which is given to us in this our world is of no account in comparison with the Torah which is going to be revealed in the days of the Messiah." [10]

Because of this vertical and infinite dimension of Torah, the faithful student senses the quality of endlessness and eternal truth in its study.

"For the holy Torah is a long chain which reaches from this lowly earth to the loftiest heavens. When a person contemplates truly the reasons of the Torah, he moves this chain, as it were, so that he feels and hears a ring above which authenticates and ratifies the truth." [11]

The meaning of Torah in this connection is, of course, the totality of "halachic" and "aggadic" literature. As new discoveries in Torah-reasoning (hiddushim) are made, the nature of the universe is fixed accordingly. "For the act of voting (in the Synhedrin or Academy) and the establishment

9 *Ibid*, p. 13.
10 *Ibid*, p. 66.
11 *Ibid*, p. 23.

of the 'halachah' by the vote of the majority fixes the nature
of creation." [12] Naturally, this concession to the notion of
growth in Torah does not imply the possibility of modifying
any rabbinic enactment in accord with the needs of the
times. "For whatever has been set into "halachah" remains
part of creation forever and is no longer subject to change."

As the sequence of events in nature is not one which could
be deduced rationally but is only to be known by experience,
so the reasoning of the Torah may frequently appear irrational. In reality, its seemingly absurd distinctions and
seemingly trivial ritual niceties correspond to important
heavenly counterparts or "roots" in the higher world.

But, if reason is powerless to comprehend the logic of
the Torah, the student of Torah acquires after a while a
"spiritual stature" ("shiur Komah") which enables him
to discover new insights or to arrive at right decisions in
new situations, with the aid of the Spirit of Holiness, ("Ruah
haKodesh") or by the gift of prophecy. Indeed, the Torah-
scholar is exalted fantastically to a central cosmic role in
these discourses. [13] In a world of indifference and neglect,
the remnant of the faithful "carries the burden which was
designed for many others." [14] It is for them to fulfill the
purpose of all human life—to wit, "the uplifting of the
low forces of matter in the human soul and in creation
generally, bringing them back to their roots." [15]

In such a supernaturalistic ideology, tailored to fit the
measurements of a literalist Orthodoxy, miracles are of
course the order of the day. In fact, there is no line of
demarcation between the natural and supernatural orders.

12 *Ibid*, p. 29.
13 *Ibid*, pp. 22, 26.
14 *Ibid*, p. 157.
15 *Ibid*, p. 198.

Speaking of the power of the saints, the authors maintain, "that the forces of fire and water were limited along with the other powers of matter, so that they might not affect superior individuals, who cleave to God in their thoughts." [16]

It remains but to add that this bold assertion of supernaturalism goes hand in hand with an extreme idealization of the past, so that the mysterious intricacies of the hypothetical higher links in the chain of being were presumed to have been known by the ordinary men and women of the past. "Just as to us the processes of sowing, growing and harvesting seem simple and natural, so to them, all these high and exalted matters were simple and natural." [17]

This idealization of the past is an essential component of any literalistic Orthodoxy, and, in the "mussar"-school, it is carried to the extreme of absurdity. If the mantle of sanctity is to cover indiscriminately every phase of the tradition, the builders and keepers of the faith in every generation must be accorded the status of divinely inspired men. Also, the acceptance of the legendary lore in the Talmud at face value cannot be squared with the assumption that the Sages were simply men of flesh and blood.

One example of this interpretation may be cited in illustration. The Talmud tells of a rabbi who had a wonderful son and a beautiful daughter. Once he found a man climbing a fence in order to look at his daughter. Said the rabbi, "my daughter, your beauty will lead men to sin. Return to your dust." Whereupon, the daughter died. The son of this rabbi was once faced with the necessity of providing a meal for workingmen. By a miracle, he caused a fig tree to bring forth figs, which the workers ate. When the father heard of the miracle, he ordered his son to

16 *Ibid*, p. 85.
17 *Ibid*, p. 162.

"return to his dust," for having caused his Maker undue trouble." [18]

This gem of ancient folklore may be enjoyed as a farcical treatment of the realistic observation that one may be too good or too beautiful. But, in the humorless literalist bias of "Mussar," this tale is cited as an illustration of the occult powers of the ancients—how the rabbi knew the heavenly "roots" of the acts of his son and daughter and thus knew that they deserved to die.

The self-sufficient supernaturalism of the "mussar"-school, in all its dry dogmatism and scornful repudiation of the great wide world extending beyond its narrow tradition, constitutes even today the living ideology of many "Yeshivoth," from "Torah V'Daath" in Brooklyn to Tels in Cleveland. The Hassidic institutions, notably those of the Liubavitch organization, are not essentially different, for the original, creative elan of Hassidism was dissipated long ago, its pristine mystical dynamism having yielded in the course of time to the beguiling seduction of a safe and staid authoritarian tradition. The living ideas of Hassidism were absorbed into the mainstream of Jewish life so that the distinction between "Hassid" and "mithnagid" is no longer significant or relevant.

The most luminous representative of Orthodox mysticism and the real heir of the great Hassidic heritage was doubtless the late Chief Rabbi of Palestine, Abraham Isaac Kuk. While his visits to the United States were relatively brief, the influence of his personality and his writings was extensive. Through his work, the complex of ideas and sentiments in the Mizrachi interpretation of Zionism was articulated and dialectically justified. The moderate Orthodox elements that favor cooperation with non-Orthodox groups draw their inspiration from his life and thought.

[18] *"Taanith,"* 23b.

Kuk was primarily a mystic, in the genuine, psychological sense of the term. Doubt and certainty were to him not opposing poles on the field of thought but all-embracing experiences in which his soul was tossed about as a helpless boat on a raging sea. He felt the onset of doubt as the ebb of his vital forces, giving way again and again to the triumphant flow of Divine Grace, which infused his being with buoyancy, certainty and, as he felt, truth. Generalizing from his own mystical experiences, he saw the world as presenting two faces to man—a happy, God-centered face, bearing the beneficent lineaments of the Torah, and a melancholy, grey face of indifferent force, shadowed by doubts of the historicity of revelation and ringed about with the bitter, Satanic darkness of moral chaos, universal meaninglessness and total frustration. Thus, doubt was not an intellectual problem so much as a psychic let-down, appearing on the scene of consciousness along with multiple contradictions and deepening despair whenever God decides to hide his face from mankind. When in His Wisdom we are taken back into His favor and are uplifted joyously upon the crest of the current of love issuing from His Being, we speedily behold the clouds of doubt vanish in the distance and we glimpse the Truth, in all its infinite depth and healing power.

From his scattered and unsystematic writings, we gather the following description of the mystical experience of the "nearness of God." One is overwhelmed by an exquisite, consuming longing for the Divine Presence, "an intense thirst, pleasing in the extreme . . ." which slowly deepens into "pure fear, the intensity of holy trembling." The mystic feels that he had been touched with a holy flame, wakening within him an unearthly yearning to break out of the confining bounds of the sensible universe and to sink his being into the Divine Reality, which extends beyond "the walls of deed, logic, ethics and laws." And in this heavenly yearning there is already a kind of fulfillment, so that the mystic wills to express to others his paradoxical experience in which delight and anguish are commingled. But his vision is doomed to remain stubbornly incommunicable. "I am not one of God's elected heroes that found all the worlds within them and did not care if others their riches knew or not." [19]

As this first pulsation of the Divine current fades away, the mystic sinks back into the gray and tasteless world of conflict, contradiction and doubt. "Because of the narrow receptive faculty of man, one datum contradicts the other datum; one feeling combats the other feeling, and one image pushes out the other; but, in truth, one datum fortifies the other datum, different feelings vitalize each other, and the several images in one's mind complete each other. The more a man is uplifted, the wider his faculties expand, until he comes to find within himself the satisfying fullness of inner peace and the consequent consistency between all data, feelings and images." [20]

Having once seen the veil of contradiction lifted so as to reveal the organic unity of all existence, the mystic looks forward to the reappearance of the vision, the distinguishing mark of which is "the view of all things together."

"The gates are opened, the King of glory enters . . . The worlds are united, the hidden and the revealed are commingled, body and soul are merged, the 'lights' and the 'vessels' are linked together. And an exquisite sweetness, an inner, intense and highly exalted pleasure is uncovered in the source of the rejoicing soul. Then power and light from above appear unto thee with all the ornamentation of their many lights. Thou wilt recognize thy power and the

[19] *"Banner of Jerusalem,"* p. 131.
[20] *"Banner of Jerusalem,"* p. 132.

intensity of thy exaltation; wilt know thy humbleness and thy unworthiness, the unworthiness of all creatures. . . ." [21]

Thus, the alternation of faith and doubt in the human psyche is due to the continuous ebb and flow of the Divine current. The mystic, who has once sensed within himself the assurance of Divine reality, knows that holiness is the very core of being, and that truth is grasped to the extent to which one feels the "nearness" of the Supreme Being. Furthermore, the Jewish mystic finds that the Torah is the immediate channel of Divine light and grace. While the mystical vision does not contain precise and specific messages as did the state of prophecy in the view of tradition, it does lead to the development of a taste for the quality of holiness.

"Though we do not perceive articulate letters and distinct words, we regard our secular and Torah studies as intended solely for the purpose of obtaining as much as possible the clarity of words out of the exalted sound which beats constantly in our inner ear, that we may present them to ourselves and to others in a form that leads to action and to properly ordered and systematized reflection." [22]

To the Mussar-men, as we have seen, the Torah in its static perfection is the luminous ladder of God's Will, assuming concrete shape in this lowly world. To Kuk, heir of the mystical tradition, the flow of God's Will is conceived, not as a series of precepts, but as a vital current of inspiration, kindling in the hearts of men the "lights of holiness." Kuk's conception was essentially dynamic, enabling him to appreciate modern and unconventional forms of holiness and to delight in all that is novel and creative.

While Kuk achieved his mystical states through the practices of Kabbalah and interpreted their varying character

[21] *Ibid,* p. 135.
[22] *"Banner of Jerusalem,"* p. 192.

in terms of its complex theosophy, he learned to correlate his intimate experiences with the concepts of general philosophy. The "lights of holiness," in his ideology, played virtually the same role as the elan vital in Bergson's last book ("The Two Sources of Morality and Religion"), inspiring creative achievement in the arts and sciences as well as in the life of piety. Thus, the secular world was, in his view, the marginal manifestation on the surface of life of the pulsating current of holiness in the heart of things. The "light of the Messiah," which is the vibrant process of redemption, is manifested in the efforts of all "who labor for the perfection of the world" ("shichlul haolom") and the ennobling of the human personality.

In the same integrating spirit, Kuk saw the force of modern nationalism as a noble impulse, akin to religion, implanted by God for the sake of Messianic perfection. Jewish nationalism he regarded as a supremely holy movement, even if its exponents proclaimed from the housetops its total independence of religion. Every one who lends a hand to the up-building of the Jewish people in its homeland is working for the revival of the "sh'chinah," for the national genius of Israel is peculiarly suitable for the cultivation of true religion. And the physical health of Israel is a prerequisite for its spiritual growth.

"The Holy Spirit and the light of God cannot come to Israel so long as a debilitating sense of fear continues to poison the Jewish soul. This sorry product of exile and persecution prevents the 'shechinah' from resting on the soul of Israel. . . ." [23]

In Kuk's view, the national genius of Israel was peculiarly organic and distinctly mystical, so that the atheistic pioneer and the Kabbalistic hermit constituted part of one organic

[23] *"Banner of Jerusalem,"* p. 209.

society. The "physical exercises of Jewish youth . . . perfect the spiritual power of the esoteric saints. . . ." [24] For both activities constitute supplementary phases of the one process of redemption. "Mystical reflection is the freedom of Israel, in other words, the soul of Israel." [25]

With all his pietistic involvement in the idiom of Kabbalah, Kuk became the saint and prophet of the liberal wing of Orthodoxy, which identified itself wholeheartedly with the Zionist enterprise, recognizing as their brothers in spirit and destiny the zealous nationalists who denied the sanctity of Torah. In thought, Kuk advanced at times to the Conservative position, as when he suggested that even the secular creations of Jewish people, produced as they were by the peculiar genius of Israel, constituted Torah, or holy teaching. Thus, he declared, "And the congregation of Israel is itself Mosaic tradition from Sinai." [26]

From this principle it would follow that not only the "four ells of Halachah" but Jewish culture, in all its manifold expressions constituted the substance of the living faith of Israel. Yet, he did not himself throw the mantle of sanctity over the reborn secular culture in the land of Israel, maintaining that most of its achievements were not products of the pure genius of the Jewish soul, but only unconscious imitations of the Gentile world.

In summary, the mystical humanism and the spiritual nationalism of Kuk reflect the vital currents of thought and sentiment of a considerable section of contemporary Orthodoxy. His writings are still read as guideposts pointing the way toward a synthesis between the Orthodox tradition and the values of secular humanism.

Some of the noblest authorities in Judaism were neither

[24] *Ibid*, p. 210.
[25] *Ibid*,
[26] *"Banner of Jerusalem,"* p. 211.

philosophers, nor mystics, nor masters of the esoteric lore of Kabbalah. Dedicated to the arduous pursuit of religious truths, they found their satisfaction in study and action "within the four ells of Halachah." (Jewish Law). Does Judaism, then, contain a purely "halachic" stream of thought, that takes account of the fundamental questions of existence even while it skirts the pathways of philosophy and mysticism? Historically, there is no question that many illustrious masters of Talmudic lore considered their learning of the Law to be utterly self-sufficient, with no legitimate room left either for the insidious doubt of speculation or for the excessive ardor of Hassidism. But, is this attitude tenable? Can Halachah get along with the one dogma of revelation, ruling out of consideration all that was not included in the peculiar structure of Jewish Law?

Dr. Joseph B. Soloveitchik, Professor of Talmud and Religious Philosophy at the Yeshiva University, champions the view that Halachah contains a characteristic structure of ideas and sentiments which derives from a fundamental attitude of the human spirit. It articulates a psychic complex of ideas and values of its own and it does not stand in need of validation from any outside source. Founded on the solid data of Divine Revelation, Halachah has grown in continuous awareness of the tensions and paradoxes of human nature, which it sought to resolve and to integrate in its vision of the ideal personality.

Dr. Soloveitchik develops his thesis in conscious alliance with the neo-supernaturalistic school of Protestant theology. He ridicules the liberal-humanistic theologians who identify man's rational aspirations for the good life with the living "still, small voice" of God, and he spurns with equal decisiveness the romantic attempts to represent religion as an idealized refuge from reality. Theologians like Karl Barth and Soren Kierkegaard come closest to the understanding of the nature of faith when they point out the succession of "crises" in the human soul, that seeks vainly to grasp the fleeting rays issuing from His Presence and recognizes ever more deeply its "creaturely" failure, its inveterate "sinfulness," its utter nothingness. On this interpretation, the trial of Abraham was not intended to teach that God does not desire human flesh on His altars, but to prove that God's will and thought are incommensurate with man's intelligence and conscience. The man of piety must learn to defy his reason and his moral feeling for the sake of God. Thus, he cites approvingly and in the name of a Midrash Kierkegaard's interpretation of the trial of Abraham—that God wanted Abraham to oppose the scruples of his conscience and the light of his human reason. For, had he not fought from the beginning of his mission against the practice of human sacrifice? Yet, the Lord demanded that he bring Isaac as a "burnt offering." The usual interpretation of this story in Jewish literature stresses its happy ending—the Will of God is indeed identical with the voice of conscience.

The "man of Halacha" is similarily aware of the tension and the "crisis" in the human personality. The passion for pure knowledge in our makeup finds satisfaction in the far flung researches of science that are aimed at the dissolution of the novel and the mysterious elements of experience into a system of unvarying law. At the same time, our religious consciousness heightens our sense of wonder at the very quality of lawfulness that holds the entire range of existence in thrall. With masterful erudition, Prof. Soloveitchik dwells on this dichotomy of the human spirit, alternating between wonder and comprehension, the sense of mystery and the self-assurance of the man of science. Halachah, the author asserts, provides the Divine answer to this human dilemna.[27]

[27] *"Talpioth,"* 1944, pp. 652-660.

The "man of Halachah" approaches the mystery of existence armed with "a priori concepts," with the aid of which he erects a satisfying image of the universe. Having received his principles and laws at Sinai, he comes equipped with "a body of teaching which points out to him the way to the nature of being. There is no phenomenon, event or thing which a priori Halacha does not approach with its ideal measurements." [28] The term, a priori, is used by the author in a dogmatic, not a philosophical sense. To the Orthodox mentality, not only the Sinaitic Covenant but the whole body of Jewish law as it was hammered out by diverse factors in two thousand years of history is literally God-given, and hence as axiomatic as the principle, "twice two equals four." While the religious consciousness centers around the awareness of a numinal realm supervening behind the realm of existence, the Halachist takes this circumstance for granted and proceeds to apply the principles deriving from the divine realm to the sanctification of this earthly dominion of existence. He can afford to be intensely and whole-heartedly oriented toward the temporal world, because he knows himself to be in full control of the "channels" which bind the realm of eternity unto this temporal universe. The Halachist does not engage in a continuous battle against the "flesh," for the laws of the Torah are sober, life-affirming and altogether sufficient for a law-abiding citizen of God's world. Nor does the Halachist storm the heavenly heights of transcendental reality in his yearning to escape from the temporal, for his "God-given mitzvoth" enable him to build eternity within the earthly world—yes, the Halachist, in all his humility, is supremely self-confident, since he is in possession of norms and principles which hold all existence in thrall and to which even the Lord Himself is subject, as it were.

[28] *Ibid,* p. 661.

The piety of the Halachist, then, is expressed in the elaboration and progressive refinement of the eternal norms, or laws, which have been given to his custody. With this dogmatic assurance of absolute mastery, the Halachist is able to rise above the torments of anxiety and the sense of awe. In control of the principles of metaphysical legislation, he is able to fix standards and norms for the amorphous and fluid, tempestuous and unpredictable "feelings" of religion.

"The Halachah which was given to us at Sinai is the objectification of religion in the shape of fixed and lucid molds, in clearly outlined laws and definite principles. It converts subjectivity into objectivity and into a fixed pattern of lawfulness." [29]

Thus, Soloveitchik disapproves of the Hassidic emphasis on religious enthusiasm and feeling, citing the words of rebuke which his father addressed to a "hassid" when the latter was overwhelmed by pious awe during the "shofar"-blowing ceremonies on Rosh Hashono: "Do you tremble and cry on "Sukkoth," when you shake the "lulav?" Why then do you cry when the "shofar" is blown? Aren't both observances equally commandments of the Lord?" [30] Though the purpose of the "shofar" is to arouse the feelings of repentance and that of the "lulav" to express the feelings of gratitude on the Feast of Ingathering, the Halachist takes note predominantly not of the feelings involved but of the actual performance of the ceremony, in all its detailed exactitude. For the significance of the "Mitzvah" is independent of the feelings it arouses or fails to arouse, consisting solely in its being a divine, immutable law. This legalistic emphasis does indeed subdue the stormy surge of religious feeling, but it compensates for this loss of inwardness and depth

29 *"Talpioth,"* 1944, pp. 688.
30 *Ibid,* p. 689.

by the development of a joyous sense of dedication which accompanies the performance of all "mitzvoth."

"The Sages of Israel know nothing of the ceaseless battle against the Evil Desire, such as we read about in the lives of Christian saints. . . . While the faith of the Catholic fathers was won through a struggle and by an inner compulsion, the faith of our Sages was a free and serene growth of the spirit." [31]

This sober restraint of the Halachist is by no means due to the modesty of his purpose. For, in truth, the masters of the Law were animated by the dynamic ambition to be ceaselessly creative. In the domain of social life, the rabbis sought to bring about the realization of the utopia of Halachah, and, for the guidance of the chosen individual, they evolved the lofty goal of prophecy. The ideal personality is the prophet, his qualities of mind and heart having become perfected and balanced to the point where the Divine Presence actually rests upon him. "Every person is called upon to renew his being in accord with the ideal pattern of the prophet and to engage in this creative process until he attains the final consummation of prophetic achievement, the readiness for the reception of Divine Grace." [32]

Through the practice of continuous self-analysis, self-criticism and self-building by way of repentance, the worshipper uncovers new sources of strength within himself, advancing thus by degrees to the lofty eminence of prophecy.

At this point, Dr. Soloveitchik abandons the attempt to picture the Halachah as a self-contained domain, preempting for his purpose the disciplines of philosophy and Kabbalah. Within the strict limitations of Halachah, the ideal of prophecy was never set as an actual goal for the observant Jew. Traditionally, prophecy ceased with the last of the

[31] *"Talpioth,"* 1944, p. 692.
[32] *Ibid,* p. 729.

biblical prophets and it was not to be renewed until the generation of the Messiah. In the philosophy of Maimonides, the ideal of prophecy was reinstated as an actual possibility for the religious Jew, corresponding to the mystical goal of Medieval Aristotelian philosophy. But, to Maimonides Halachah was not a metaphysical reality, only a social in-instrument for the creation of the good society, in which philosophers might be nurtured and encouraged to attain the heights of mystical perfection. Thus, Maimonides arrived at the goal of prophecy by the subordination of Halachah to the disciplines of pure, metaphysical reflection. In Kabbalah, the quest for prophetic mysticism found expression especially in the erratic career of Abraham Abulafia, who considered himself to be a disciple of Maimonides.[33] As to Halachah, its very nature as a rationally ordered system of law pre-cluded the disturbing intervention of prophecy, so that the growth of Halachah, following the reforms of Ezra, nar-rowed the range of prophecy and eventually eliminated it altogether, save as part of the Messianic hope. Well-known is the historic debate between Rabbi Eliezer ben Hyrkanos and Rabbi Joshua ben Hananyah, when the latter refused to accept heavenly signs and testimonies, saying, "The Torah is not in heaven." [34]

In general, Dr. Soloveitchik fails to establish the inde-pendence and self-sufficiency of Halachah, in spite of the brilliance of his exposition. The "man of Halachah" did not live in an intellectual vacuum, and, when he reflected on the truth or purpose of revelation, he found the ramparts of his faith either in the domain of general philosophy, as did Maimonides, or in the shadowy realm of Kabbalah, as did Elijah Gaon and Rabbi Hayim of Volozhin, foremost Halachists of Lithuania, or in a synthetic combination of

[33] See A. J. Heschel, "Ha-heemin Ho Rambam She-hi-g-i-a lin-vu-a?"
[34] "Baba M'tsia," 59b.

Kabbalah and philosophy, as did the foremost Halachic authority of Ashkenazic Jewry, Rabbi Moses Isserless.[35]

By no stretch of the imagination could Halachic principles, in all their naivete and particularity, be regarded as a priori constructions. Through Halachah, fine and consecrated religious personalities were evolved, but this result attests neither to the truth of Halachah nor to its enduring significance. We admire the great masters of Jewish Law, albeit we recognize that it was inevitable for them to take for granted the narrow limitations of dogma which delimited their spiritual world and channelized their yearnings for the "nearness of God." A prominent exponent of modern Orthodoxy writes: "The authority of the Torah is as self-evident to the uncorrupted Israelite as is the existence of

[35] The Kabbalistic teachings of *"Nefesh Ha Hayim,"* the posthumous book of the Rabbi Hayim Volozhim, differ in no distinguishable respect from the standard principles of this "hidden wisdom." The Kabalistic philosophy of Elijah Gaon is dry and dogmatic, as may be seen in his own commentaries on the Zohar, and in the systematic exposition of his disciple, Rabbi Isaac Hover. The Gaon did, however, question the accuracy of some of the manuscripts of the Lurianic Kabbalah. The reflections of Rabbi Moses Isserless are contained in his mystical-symbolic work, "Torath Ha-Olah," where he explains the "mitzvoth," especially the order of sacrifices in the Temple, by means of the principle of parallelism which the revival of Platonism made popular. The Holy Temple in Jerusalem was in all its portions a perfect symbolic counterpart of the universe, and the altar was situated on the highest spot in the world. Rabbi Isserless took his geographical "facts" from the Talmud, of course. As the Temple was a representation of the universe, so the sacrifices symbolized the destiny of man's life in relation to the universe. The organic nature of the cosmos was represented in the animal that was brought as an offering, which recalled also the "creaturely" character of the universe and its eventual disintegration. The wine-offering was to symbolize the flow of Divine Grace, the meal offering to indicate the atomic nature of all physical things. While Rabbi Isserless speaks with the greatest reverence concerning the "hidden wisdom" of Kabbalah, his thought runs generally along philosophical and quasi-philosophical lines. Thus, he writes that the Kabbalah was "derived from the mouth of the prophets, beginning with Moses our teacher." Yet, he refuses to accept the basic axiom of Kabbalah that the actions of men on earth could cause a blemish in the "Sh'chinah," or the S'firoth above. (*Torath Ha-Olah* II, 4, 16; III, 4.)

God." [36] But, once "corrupted" by doubt, the "man of Halachah" can hardly find his way back to faith, through the instruments and arguments of Halachah alone. As to prophecy, Dr. Soloveitchik brings in through the back door what he had previously expelled through the front door, characterizing all efforts to experience the immediacy of the Divine Being as the dark vagaries of romanticism and the dangerous dynamism of mysticism. For in the Maimonidean sense, prophecy does not differ from the achievements of the great mystics. It is largely a human adventure, aiming at unity with the Divine Will, and God rarely withholds His Grace from those who are worthy of receiving the gifts of prophetic inspiration.

In the total complex of American Orthodoxy, the elements deriving from the thought and tradition of Western Europe are of particular interest. Designated on occasion as neo-Orthodox, the stream of romantic piety and inflexible zealotry which is associated with the name of S. R. Hirsch is represented on the American scene by a very small number of congregations. However, its influence is likely to increase in both scope and depth as the tightly packed colonies of immigrants in the great metropolitan centers are permeated ever more fully by the spirit of western culture. Actually, the term neo-Orthodox does not betoken any essential departure in dogma or practice from the Orthodox pattern of faith.[37] Unlike the Protestant neo-supernaturalists who interpret the assertions and tales of the Bible as myths and symbols of eternal principles, the neo-Orthodox in Judaism affirm the dogma of Sinaitic revelation in utter literalness, permitting the freedom of allegorization only along the well-trodden pathways of Kabbalah. Yet, neo-Orthodoxy is distinctly and vividly a new interpretation of tradition, reflect-

[36] Leo Jung, *"Talpioth,"* 1944, p. 736.
[37] *See* Wieman, *"American Philosophies of Religion,"* pp. 85-93.

ing the genteel norms, universalist aspirations and this-worldly emphasis of western culture. Carried along by the passion for consistency and the narrow logic of absolutism, the exponents of this school, for all their urbanity, are frequently more rigid and unyielding in practice than the unpretentious and unsophisticated, unsystematic and altogether "natural" saints and sages of Eastern Europe.

The most recent and most thorough expression of west-European Orthodoxy may be found in Isaak Breuer's impressive volume, "Der Neue Kusari."

The author, trained in the German classical tradition, was painfully aware of the deep frustrations of modern man. As an idealistic philosopher, he regarded the realm of appearance which our senses convey to us as being a product of two entities, the "meta-physical" and the "meta-ethical." These hypothetical realms are themselves outside the space-time world, inhering beyond the reach of the iron laws of causality. The physical universe consists of influences and forces deriving from the "meta-physical" realm, and these are ordered and molded, fashioned and "willed," by the subconscious will of man, which is the same in all men and independent of the vagaries of thought and sentiment that supervene on the surface of consciousness. If we designate this unconscious will as the "meta-ethical" phase of the human personality, we recognize the physical universe as the fleeting surface of contact between the "meta-physical" and the "meta-ethical" domains of being.

From this analysis it follows that truth is not to be discovered by the simple analysis of and generalization from the restless surge of phenomena on the surface of existence. Somehow, the inner will of man, dwelling in the realms beyond our conscious reach and manifesting itself in the alternation of fearful anxiety and bold decision, must provide the answer. But how?

To dramatize his solution, the author describes a young Jewish intellectual, who was launched on his way back to "Torah-true" Judaism by his persistent anxiety over the question, "how should I live my life?" Any sentimental or humanistic answer was to him unsatisfactory, for in his deadly earnestness, he needed detailed guidance for living, not remote ideals and vague generalities. Caught in the swirling currents of modern history, the young philosopher felt an inner certainty that the word of God was somehow conveyed in the unseen handwriting on the broad canvas of human history. But, history is the record of the struggle of the nations, and our hero could not but read this record from the standpoint of the Jewish people, "who live among the nations but are not of them."

In Breuer's interpretation, the lesson of history is two-fold—the inevitable frustration of all human efforts and the existence of the Jewish society as a kind of super-historical or "meta-historical" people which provides the answer to the dark groping and infinite tragedy of mankind.

"Does not the history of the nations prove that people cannot liberate themselves by their own efforts from the power of evil?" [38]

Again and again gifted and inspired nations have risen upon the stage of history only to stumble and sink back into failure and despair. Always it is an ideal, a vision of the Kingdom of God on earth, which lifts a nation or a group of nations to leadership and power, but these ideals cannot bring about the final consummation, since they are only human and partial visions of the Divine image. To the keeping of the Jewish people, however, the Torah, which constitutes the genuine pattern of the "Kingdom of God," has been given, so that the Jewish people have been lifted

[38] Isaak Breuer, *"Der Neue Kusari,"* p. 159.

by the covenant of Sinai above the ebb and flow of human history and charged with the task of representing the reality and truth of the goal to those that are still on the way. So long as the nations are still engaged in the struggle for power, they are distinguished by the qualitites of language, the possession of land and a temporal government. The Jewish people have given up this struggle for national power long ago, substituting the Divine Law, the Holy Tongue and the Holy Land for the temporal values of nationhood.

This removal of Israel from the normal arena of national struggles, even while it is maintained as an "eternal people," is attested by the entire course of Jewish history. "The voice of the meta-historical wonder of the Jewish nation resounds not a bit less loudly than the voice of God at Sinai. . . ." [39]

The author, writing in the late thirties, as the devastating tide of Naziism was gathering for the final burst of total destruction, saw the entire, timeless fate of Israel revealed in the stern predictions of Moses: "And the Lord shall scatter thee among all the peoples, from the one end of the earth unto the other. . . . And among these nations thou shalt find no ease, neither shall the sole of thy foot have rest; but the Lord shall give thee there a trembling heart, and a failing of eyes, and sorrow of mind. . . ." [40] "And upon them that are left alive of you, I will send a faintness into their hearts in the lands of their enemies; and the sound of a shaken leaf shall chase them. . . ." [41]

In these and similar verses, the author saw proof of the divinity of the Torah and of the peculiar destiny of Israel.

"Do the antisemites, do the Jews themselves, know that antisemitism, which reaches from Babylonia-Rome to post-

[39] Breuer, *"Der Neue Kusari,"* p. 89.
[40] *Deuteronomy*, XXVIII, 46-67.
[41] *Lev.* XXVI, 36.

war Germany, is an incontrovertible proof of the meta-physics of prediction?" [42]

To be sure, the recognition of the "meta-historical wonder" of Jewish life presupposes a certain receptivity of mind. One must learn to recognize "the negation of world-history" and to experience inwardly the "Jewish protest" against it. Identifying himself completely with the divinely constituted "congregation of Israel," the Jew senses the unique destiny of his people, even "as the artist grasps a historical personality, as a friend understands a friend, as the lover chooses the beloved. . . ." [43] Through a "living experience" of this kind, the individual Jew knows himself to be a miracle and a witness, "not merely the object of this divine wonder of history, but one who himself lives this history and therefore experiences God hourly. . . ." [44]

It is through the Sinaitic covenant that "K'nesseth Yis-roel," the Congregation of Israel, was constituted. Hence, only those who are absolutely and meticulously loyal to the divinely fashioned community are truly Jews. All others, even those Orthodox people who are personally observant but who belong to a community which includes the non-Orthodox or the non-observant, are "traitors" to "the nation of God." [45] Since it is through the sense of oneness with the community that the Jew discovers his relationship to God, the community in question must be a spotless exemplar of "Knesses Yisroel," lifted, in the serenity of its perfection, above time, chance and circumstance. The author is particularly incensed at the Zionists, whose ideology consists in a conscious rebellion against the "meta-historical" destiny of the Jew.

[42] Breuer, *"Der Neue Kusari,"* p. 75.
[43] *Ibid*, p. 85.
[44] *Ibid*, p. 86.
[45] *Ibid*, p. 103.

Yet, with all his impassioned exclusiveness *vis-à-vis* divergent interpretations of Judaism, the author reveals a powerful universalist trend of thought. The purpose of Jewish "meta-history" is to bring mankind to the goals of individual perfection and social harmony. In its role of "the people of peoples," Israel is "the herald of God's righteousness" and "the symbol of the meta-historical goal of humanity." It was God's will that the Jews be scattered among the varying nations of the globe, in order "that the meta-historical people learn to love and cherish the peculiar characteristics of each nation." [46]

This entire world-view is founded like an inverted pyramid upon the one fulcrum of literal revelation at Sinai. But, on what grounds is this dogma to be accepted? The answer is that this dogma is "willed" by the one who identifies himself with "Knesseth Yisroel" utterly and without reservations. "The final truth cannot be grasped through thought, but only by the will," for in actuality "to know and to will is one." [47] An event that happened only once in history cannot be proven, in the usual sense. Furthermore, to the believer, the Torah is the one source of truth, all other knowledge being secondary in character. "An unconditioned truth is, according to its essence, unprovable. All these proofs lead the unknown back to the known. How could the unconditioned truth be unconditioned, if it must be proven or led back to that which is itself conditioned? . . . The divinity of the Torah is in no wise different from the divinity of God Himself. Not proveable is God, but proving . . . The Torah is essentially a quality of God. Whoever denies it separates God from His quality, denies God. . . . [48]

The ideology of Breuer is precise and clearly-etched. In

[46] Breuer, *"Der Neue Kusari,"* p. 159.
[47] *Ibid,* pp. 267, 270.
[48] *Ibid,* p. 263.

this respect, it is distinctly untypical of American Orthodoxy, which is pragmatic and flexible, changing rapidly step by step even while insisting loudly on its sameness. Thus, a goodly proportion of the congregations affiliated with the Orthodox Union offer family pews, use a microphone on the Sabbath and holidays, and include the reading of English prayers in the liturgy. The balcony for women is becoming a rarity, the "m'hitsah" separating the women's section is beating a fast retreat, the "Bimah," which rabbinic assemblies in the nineteenth century solemnly declared to be indispensable, has long been moved out of the synagogue. As to personal life, there is no counting the "mitzvoth," the negation of which does not disqualify one from accounting himself a member of the "Torah-true" community. There are no clearly marked and easily distinguishable barriers among the lay adherents of the varying interpretations of Judaism, so that Orthodoxy is largely a matter of formalistic dogma—a surface-belief in the literal revelation of the Law. In regard to this dogma, we may expect that there will always be men and women who will accept it as the one "unconditioned" truth, the fundamental axiom of thought and life. For fundamentalist religion is more than a heritage from the past; basically, it is a response to the psychic needs of certain character types.

3

The Reform Movement

Unlike Orthodoxy, the Reform movement has by now acquired a definitely American cast. At the turn of the century, Reform was powerfully entrenched in all the major communities of America, enjoying the overwhelming support of the German-Jewish population. While some few German Jews remained staunchly Orthodox, the majority drifted into the Reform camp, so that the differences of ideology were added to the then existing chasm between the American German Jews and their East European brethren. The residual Orthodox and Conservative German Jews of every community were generally forced to choose between loyalty to their social class and faithfulness to their religious convictions. Except in such big centers as New York, Philadelphia and Baltimore, the ideology of Reform operated as a welcome barrier, separating the immigrant Eastern Jews from their happily situated and keenly class-conscious German "co-religionists." As the massive flow of immigration continued to build up the numerical strength of the East European Jews, there were developed in almost every community two sets of philanthropic and social institutions—the one serving the German Jews and their Czech and Hungarian affiliates, the other serving Polish and Russian Jewry.

Gradually, this social cleavage is being bridged. Through the steady rise of Russian Jews to affluence and influence and through occasional "mixed marriages" with the children of the "Yehudim," the social line of demarcation is being blurred. Also, since the rise of Hitler, it became steadily more difficult for German Jews to be inordinately proud of the vaunted culture of their Vaterland. In the irresistible advance of the process of Americanization, the memories of "old-world" antagonisms are steadily yielding to the blandishments of the rising civilization of the New World. The eventual disappearance of this factor is already apparent as a distant light in the far-off horizon. It would now be hardly conceivable for a Reform rabbi to preach against "mixed marriages" with Russian Jews. As a matter of fact, most Reform rabbis are descendants of East European families and the membership of the temples is constantly being replenished by new converts from the Russian Jewish camp.

Yet, even now it is impossible to understand the spiritual complexion of American Jewry without taking account of the German heritage of the Reform movement. The fact that until recently instruction in the German language was included in the curriculum of the large and prominent K'nesseth Israel Temple of Philadelphia, while the study of Hebrew was pointedly excluded, can scarcely be understood apart from this amazing pride of cultural heritage on the part of the German Jews.

*   *   *

The founding fathers of the American Reform movement were the immediate disciples and banner-bearers of Abraham Geiger and Samuel Holdheim. Men like David Einhorn, Max Lilienthal, Samuel Hirsch, Kaufman Kohler, and Samuel Adler came to America fresh from their eager battles against Orthodoxy in Germany and Hungary. Here, they found a fertile field for their efforts, principally because they were not hampered by the restraining power of an overall community organization. While the Reform movement in Germany was in most cities compelled to effect an uneasy peace with the Conservative group so as not to break up the central institutions of the community, the American Reformers were leaders of independent congregations, entirely free to translate their principles into action. Furthermore, insofar as Reform implied the negation of the value of ritual observances, the movement was aided by the general tendency of immigrants to drop all cultural impediments in their upward climb to material success. Did the early settlers, who frequently formed but a tiny island in the midst of an alien and hostile majority, need any theoretical endorsement of their practice of working on the Sabbath, shaving their beards or eating "trefa" foods? Manifestly, the ideologists limped pathetically behind the people, who were actually impelled by the harsh pressures of business, on the one hand, and, on the other hand, attracted by the prospect of achieving the blessing of inconspicuousness through the complete transformation of their distinctive heritage into a pattern that would in no wise be distinguished from the prevailing mores in American life.

*　　*　　*

The principles of the American Reform movement were first formulated in a brilliant and lucid manifesto that was drawn up by a conference in Pittsburgh, in the year 1885. In the words of the leading historian of the movement, David Phillipson, the Pittsburgh Platform, as this declaration came to be known, was "the utterance most expressive of the teachings of Reform Judaism."

1. "We recognize in every religion an attempt to grasp the Infinite, and in every mode, source, or book of revelation held sacred in any religious system the consciousness of the indwelling of God in man. We hold that Judaism presents the highest conception of the God-idea, as taught in our Holy Scriptures and developed and spiritualized by the Jew-

1 Phillipson, *"The Reform Movement,"* p. 93.

ish teachers, in accordance with the moral and philosophical progress of their respective ages. We maintain that Judaism preserved and defended amidst continual struggles and trials and under enforced isolation, this God-idea as the central religious truth for the human race."

2. "We recognize in the Bible the record of the consecration of the Jewish people to its mission as the priest of the one God, and value it as the most potent instrument of religious and moral instruction. We hold that the modern discoveries of scientific research in the domain of nature and history are not antagonistic to the doctrines of Judaism, the Bible reflecting the primitive ideas of its own age, and at times clothing its conception of divine Providence and Justice dealing with man in miraculous narratives."

3. "We recognize in the Mosaic legislation a system of training the Jewish people for its mission during its national life in Palestine, and today we accept as binding only its moral laws, and maintain only such ceremonies as elevate and sanctify our lives, but reject all such as are not adapted to the views and habits of modern civilization."

4. "We hold that all such Mosaic and rabbinical laws as regulate diet, priestly purity, and dress, originated in ages, and under the influence of ideas, entirely foreign to our present mental and spiritual state. They fail to impress the modern Jew with a spirit of priestly holiness; their observance in our days is apt rather to obstruct than to further modern spiritual elevation."

5. "We recognize, in the modern era of universal culture of heart and intellect, the approaching of the realization of Israel's great Messianic hope for the establishment of the kingdom of truth, justice, and peace among all men. We consider ourselves no longer a nation, but a religious community, and therefore expect neither a return to Palestine, nor a sacrificial worship under the sons of Aaron, nor the

restoration of any of the laws concerning the Jewish state."

6. "We recognize in Judaism a progressive religion, ever striving to be in accord with the postulates of reason. We are convinced of the utmost necessity of preserving the historical identity with our great past. Christianity and Islam being daughter religions of Judaism, we appreciate their providential mission to aid in the spreading of monotheistic and moral truth. We acknowledge that the spirit of broad humanity of our age is our ally in the fulfillment of our mission, and therefore we extend the hand of fellowship to all who cooperate with us in the establishment of the reign of truth and righteousness among men."

7. "We reassert the doctrine of Judaism that the soul is immortal, grounding this belief on the divine nature of the human spirit, which forever finds bliss in righteousness and misery in wickedness. We reject as ideas not rooted in Judaism the beliefs both in bodily resurrection and in Gehenna and Eden (Hell and Paradise) as abodes for everlasting punishment and reward."

8. "In full accordance with the spirit of Mosaic legislation, which strives to regulate the relation between rich and poor, we deem it our duty to participate in the great task of modern times, to solve, on the basis of justice and righteousness, the problem presented by the contrasts and evils of the present organization of society."

Proceeding now to the analysis of the ideas and trends of thought that were reflected in this declaration of principles, we note first that the Reform movement did not tear itself away from the rest of the Jewish community to the point of becoming a separate and identifiable sect. The Pittsburgh Platform was not intended to be a "creed," but a set of guiding principles. The Reform ideologists looked upon themselves and their followers as the vanguard of the entire congregation of Israel, believing sincerely that their interpretations of the faith were likely to be universally accepted on the American scene. Their program was to become, "minhag America," the American form of Judaism. Thus, in 1899, at a banquet celebrating his eightieth birthday, Isaac M. Wise declared, "Within twenty-five years, all the world will have accepted Reform Judaism." [2] Nor was there ever, in America, a distinct line of demarcation, separating the Reform from the traditionalists. The proponents of "radical" Reform, such as Rabbi Emil G. Hirsch of Chicago, pointed toward a possible exit from the Jewish community, while the right-wing of the movement shaded off gradually and imperceptibly into the Conservative camp. There was always a wide range of interpretation and practice within the movement, which was constituted by loyalty to some general principles rather than to a specific program of thought and action. The following may be considered the leading ideas of Reform:

A. The Principle of Development.

The first principle of Reform is the assertion that Judaism is an evolutionary faith, which is capable of indefinite development and expansion. Thus, in this Platform, the authors speak of the "God-idea" as "being developed and spiritualized by the Jewish teachers, in accordance with the moral and philosophical progress of their respective ages." They also maintain that the Bible "reflected the primitive ideas of its own age" and that only its "moral laws" were binding today.

This principle was variously interpreted within the movement itself. Geiger had emphasized the quality of *continuity* in the process of change, maintaining that the dynamic factor was contained in the very concept of tradition.

"Tradition is the developing power which continues in

[2] Julian Morgenstern, *"As a Mighty Stream,"* p. 120.

Judaism as an invisible creative agent, as a certain ennobling essence that never obtains its full expression, but ever continues to work, transform and create. Tradition is the animating soul in Judaism, it is the daughter of Revelation and of equal rank with her . . . Tradition, like revelation, is a spiritual energy that ever continues to work, a higher power that does not proceed from man, but is an emanation from the Divine Spirit, a power that works in the community, chooses its own ministers, manifests itself by its ever purer and riper fruits, and thus preserves vitality and existence itself." [3]

In this context the term "tradition" stands for the institutions, loyalties and sentiments that lend structure to the communiy, especially for the willingness of people to follow the leadership of their scholars. This dynamic factor is made effective in every age by the authority vested in the scholars of every generation to examine, organize and adapt the religious insights and values of the past. The power to legislate new "takkanoth" for the "strengthening of the faith" made for a continuous progression "from precedent to precedent," ruling out any sudden or violent break with the past.

Thus, Geiger favored the continued application of the methods of Halachah, modifying old laws, creating new forms, but maintaining the validity of the law. Persuaded that the Jewish people were endowed with a "national genius" for religion, Geiger thought of Reform as the slow crystallization of new ideas and attitudes, arising among the representative spokesmen of Judaism. Only occasionally, as in the case of circumcision, did he advocate the radical step of abolishing the rite altogether. Even Holdheim, who opposed "the principle of tradition" to "the tradition," took account of the need for continuity. Thus, he wrote of "the principle of eternal youth, the principle of continuity, con-

[3] "Judaism and Its History," pp. 86, 87.

stant development and growth out of the primitive genius which God Himself placed in Scripture."[4] Rabbi Isaac M. Wise, who did most to fashion the organizational structure of American Reform, at one time favored only the kind of changes that were compatible with Halachah.[5]

In the Pittsburgh Platform, there is no mention either of Halachah or of the modifying process of "takkanah." Even the word Torah is rigorously avoided. The preservation of "historical identity" is urged, but not the continuity of the stream of tradition. The so-called "mitzvoth maasioth," "precepts of action," are designated as "Mosaic legislation" and spurned unceremoniously if they do not accord with the "views and habits of modern civilization." Not only are the Dietary laws declared to be no longer "binding," but the observance of these laws is deplored and stigmatized as an unspiritual action—a deed "that is apt rather to obstruct than to further modern spiritual elevation." The year 1885 marked therefore a radical break in the development even of Reform Judaism.

In the succeeding years, this tendency gained momentum. The requirement of circumcision was dropped for proselytes officially at the convention of the Central Conference in 1892. However, for children born within the faith, circumcision is ordained. As to the authority of Talmudic literature, the Conference in 1895 agreed that "the whole post-Biblical and patristic literature, including the Talmud, casuists, responses and commentaries, is and can be considered as nothing more or less than 'religious literature.'"

The new ideas were reflected in successive revisions of the Prayer-Book, with the result that the Union Prayer-Book is now used in virtually all Reform temples. In its latest editions, it stresses social-mindedness and tolerance. Among the

[4] Phillipson, *"The Reform Movement,"* p. 66.
[5] Moshe Davis, *"Hayahduth HaAmerikaith B'hitpathuta."*

liturgical practices characteristic of Reform temples is the employment of an organ and mixed choir, from which Gentiles are not excluded, worship with uncovered heads and without the "tallith," the disappearance of the daily "minyan" service, the abolition of the practice of calling to the Torah, the substitution of the Confirmation ceremony for the Bar Mitzvah, and the non-observance of the second day of Rosh Hashono and of the three festivals. In recent years there has been a marked return to tradition. Most Reform temples now make Bar Mitzvah optional and some are planning to reintroduce the regular daily service.

The clean break with tradition, which the Pittsburgh Platform crystallized, was only in part an extension and application of "the principle of development." In large part, too, it reflected the eagerness of western Jews to "de-orientalize" the Jewish faith, so that it might be taken to be an integral element of Western civilization.

Speaking of the first generation of Reformers, Julian Morgenstern notes:

"A marked tendency to limit the functions of the Hazzan and even to do away altogether with the cantillation of the services manifested itself. Not improbably, a prime consideration here was the feeling that this was purely an oriental mode of worship, and therefore offensive to modern occidental tastes . . ." [6]

Motivated by this aspiration to achieve complete at homeness on the American scene, the Pittsburgh Conference called for the inauguration of Sunday morning services to parallel those of Saturday, a step which led virtually to the abolition of the Saturday-Sabbath in many temples. Sinai Congregation of Chicago, a leading and radical Reform Temple, discontinued Saturday services as early as 1887.

Of revolutionary significance too was the call for participa-

[6] *"As a Mighty Stream,"* p. 127.

tion in the solution of social problems on the basis of "justice and righteousness." No longer painfully self-conscious and preoccupied with internal problems, the American Jew was able to turn his attention to the problems of the community. Many Reform rabbis achieved great distinction in their valiant battles on behalf of humanitarian causes. Thus, for example, Rabbi Stephen S. Wise of New York and Rabbi Henry Cohen of Galveston, Texas, to mention two contrasting types.

B. *The Enduring Essence.*

If Judaism is an evolutionary faith, changing in accord with "the views and habits" of every age, what is its enduring core? Manifestly, if there be in it no such core of permanent, time-transcending significance, there is no reason why the so-called "spirit of the age" should not be substituted for it altogether. In the Pittsburgh Platform, the "God-idea" is represented as the living essence of Judaism. Yet, not the "God-idea" as it is taught in the Bible, but this concept as it is formulated "in accord with the moral and philosophical progress" of every age.

The choice of the term "God-idea" rather than the simpler designation, "the idea of God" reflects the vagueness of this conception in the minds of the Reformers. The term, "God-idea," stands for a block of experience, while the idea of God is an intellectual concept. Kaufman Kohler thought of God in Kantian terms, as revealing His Will in the "still small voice" of conscience. "God appears actually to step into the sphere of human life as its moral ruler." [7] There is no reason to assume any mystical experiences or the possibility of miracles. "The whole cosmic order is one miracle," and all the wonder-tales of the Bible are illustrations of God's power and goodness. The principles of "ethical mono-

[7] *"Jewish Theology,"* p. 36.

theism" may be summarized as follows—that God is one and ethical in essence, that mankind is one in responsibility and destiny, that the human soul is immortal, and that the perfect society of peace and justice will ultimately be founded.

But, are not these conceptions part and parcel of modern Western thought? Especially since the "God-idea" is formulated anew in every age in accord with the prevailing trends of the contemporary intellectual climate, what is there that is peculiarly Jewish about it? Geiger's answer was that the Reformers gloried in the complete identification of Judaism with the modern spirit, maintaining that the impetus of Christian thought, its insistence on "original sin" and "salvation by faith," was essentially anti-modern and anti-liberal.[8] The Pittsburgh Platform studiously avoids any invidious comparisons, terming both Christianity and Islam as allies in the advance toward the Messianic goal. Not all thinkers of Reform concurred with Kohler's identification of the essence of Judaism with a set of true ideas. Geiger, it will be recalled, pointed to the psychological state of piety as the living essence of Judaism. "Religion is not a system of truths; it is the jubilation of the soul conscious of its eminence and at the same time its humble confession of its finiteness and limitations. . . ."[9] This conception of religion as primarily an experience of the human personality is further elaborated and refined in the latest exposition of Reform theology:

"At its root, religion is an awareness of the sacred, an inner illumination and an enthusiastic espousal of the Divine ideal. It comes as an inspiration. Suddenly the heart of reality is bared to us and we feel ourselves standing on holy ground."[10]

[8] *See* appendix to Geiger's *"Judaism and Its History,"* p. 392.
[9] *"Judaism and Its History,"* p. 21.
[10] Samuel Cohon, *"Judaism—A Way of Life,"* p. 9.

C. The Adulation of the "Spirit of the Age."

A potent factor within the Reform movement was doubtless the enthusiastic acceptance and even adulation of the "spirit of the age." Children of the nineteenth century, the Reformers were utterly persuaded of the inevitability of progress. Since it was the liberal movement in European politics which brought about Jewish emancipation, they embraced the cultural philosophy of liberalism with complete abandon and even religious fervor. Many of their spokesmen were disciples of the Hegelian school of thought, believing that they stood at the "end of history" and that the spirit of their age was achieving the consummation of all historical truths. Thus, the Pittsburgh Platform speaks of "the modern era of universal culture of heart and intellect" as approaching the realization of the Messianic Kingdom. Similarly, the protocols of the Reform conferences in Germany are filled with lavish encomiums concerning the exalted "consciousness of our age." As Gotthold Solomon put it, "The age is also a Bible through which God speaks to Israel." [11] Even Julian Morgenstern, in an address on "The Achievements of Reform Judaism" given in 1929, betrays this breathless rush to catch up with the "spirit of the age," which was presumably ahead of us even then.

"Whether we have completely closed the break which three hundred years of enforced standing still put between the world and us, we cannot tell yet. Whether we have caught up with the world entirely or not . . ." [12]

In its heady intoxication with the promise of liberal humanism, the Reform movement not only treated traditional values and institutions with impatient scorn, but it also overlooked one of the most important functions of religion. The custodians of faith must strive to rise above the ideas

[11] *"Protokolle,"* p. 91.
[12] *"As A Mighty Stream,"* p. 159.

and ideals of the contemporary age and from their high vantage point to assay the relative limitations of the absolutes of the moment. While religion is indeed a dead burden, if it fails to keep abreast of the times, it is a useless appendage if it merely approves and blesses the prevailing notions. As human beings, religious teachers may not be able to rise above the seeming axioms of their day; yet, if the tradition they represent is of the highest worth, they are in possession of a platform from which they might undertake an independent survey of popular shibboleths. If they cannot be prophetic geniuses, they can endeavor to see all things against the challenge of the Infinite, as it is reflected in their massive tradition, and preach to their contemporaries the supreme virtue of metaphysical humility, which is so imperative for the spiritual balance of every age.

Unfortunately, Reform absorbed the tenacious optimism of the late nineteenth century in the very marrow of its being, so that it was ill prepared for the harrowing debacles of our own generation. Children of the Emancipation Era in all its beguiling promise and Messianic aura, they sought above all to fall in step with their contemporaries. The processes of history, they were certain, made for the continuous improvement of the world "day by day and in every way." As Geiger, whose shadow extended clear athwart the American scene, wrote, "What the spirit of history wherein God reveals Himself also, removes and has buried, no human skill can reawaken and reanimate." [13]

How were the Reformers to know that, in the very birthplace of their movement, the "spirit of history" was to reverse itself with tragic consequences to their own people?

D.   The Anti-nomian or Anti-ritualistic Bias.

The brief reference in the Pittsburgh Platform to the

13 *"Nachgelassene Schriften,"* **V, 190.**

tendency of dietary ceremonies "to obstruct rather than to further modern spiritual elevation" points to a powerful trend of thought within the movement. The builders of Reform keenly sensed the Christian critique of Judaism as overly "ritualistic" and "legalistic." In the abstract, they were compelled to recognize the real danger inherent in the excessive employment of religious symbols—i.e., the possibility that the external rite might draw to itself the devotional energy which properly belongs to inner piety and ethical actions. Also, within Judaism itself they found recurrent protests against the overemphasis of ritual, protests which were voiced by the great prophets in their battles against the sacerdotalism of the priests and the superstitious fear of the people. "Prophetic Judaism," then, came to be the slogan of the Reformers in their anti-ritualistic crusade. Thus, Geiger wrote in 1890, "that the real contrast is not between naturalism and supernaturalism, but between religion and legalism." [14]

Holdheim was even more passionately anti-legalistic. In his introduction to the prayer-book of the Berlin Reform Temple, he stated it to be the central purpose of the movement . . . "to appreciate the kernel at full strength and to sense it by breaking the shell." [15]

This conviction that the kernel is strengthened when the shell is broken appears very frequently in the polemical literature of Reform. We encounter again and again references to the presumed contrast "between inner religiosity and outer formalism" or between "the principle of sincerity" and "empty formalism." [16]

Kaufman Kohler, doubtless the most influential exponent of Reform ideology in America, held the spirit of legalism

[14] *"Nachgelassene Schriften,"* p. 29.
[15] Quoted by Phillipson, *"The Reform Movement,"* p. 253.
[16] Phillipson, *"The Reform Movement,"* p. 43.

responsible "for the stifling of the ethical and spiritual elements in Judaism."[17] In the vehemence of polemical passion, many Reform spokesmen came to take it for granted that "the spirit of rabbinism" had indeed overcome and "stifled" the spirit of "piety" in Judaism.

The opposition of the Reformers to "legalism" and "formalism"was motivated in part at least by the circumstance that this aspect of the Jewish faith reflected the motives of nationalism and communal exclusiveness. In the interpretation of Christian scholars, the universalism of the prophets was hampered and eventually negated by the racial arrogance of the Pharisees, who required complete amalgamation with the Jewish nation as a prerequisite to admission into the Jewish faith. And the rituals from circumcision to the Dietary laws, were the national customs of the Jewish people. This utterly distorted view of the religion of the Pharisees and the Talmud was the vogue at the beginning of this century. The Christians inferred it simply from the polemics of St. Paul, whom they interpreted with naive anachronism as a crusading liberal theologian, and Jewish scholars found support for this view in the writings of Spinoza and Mendelssohn, who interpreted the ceremonial laws as "national legislation."

Since the reformers opposed the national motif in Jewish piety with the utmost vehemence, they naturally extended their condemnation to Halacha generally. Thus, Holdheim wrote:

"Rabbinical Judaism has converted into religious ideas and tendencies all the exclusive national ideas and tendencies of the Bible which were intended for entirely different conditions and circumstances, and has thereby given them eternal validity. The rabbis have perpetuated as religion the temporary past of Mosaism, the symbolism and particularism of theocracy, and, on the other hand, they misconceived and

[17] "Jewish Theology," p. 352.

neglected its eternal element, the ideal of universalism, which was in truth the real purpose of the theocracy. Hence, the irreconcileable conflict between rabbinical Judaism and the spirit of the modern age." [18]

E. *The Repudiation of Jewish Nationalism.*

The express declaration in the Pittsburgh Platform, "we are no longer a nation, but a religious community," echoes one of the pivotal issues which the Reform movement brought to the fore. Since its creative period took place at a time when the Jews of Western Europe were struggling for the final consummation of complete emancipation, the movement absorbed the anti-nationalistic bias with its first breath upon the stage of history. In western Europe of the nineteen century, the reactionaries, Jesuits and antisemites interpreted the history of Judaism in nationalistic terms. The Jewish religion in all its ritualistic complexity was nothing but a sublimation of intense ethnic pride. The Pharisaic insistence on the rites of Judaism, as against the "freedom in Christ" of the early Christians was due to the drive for self-isolation from the "impurity" of the Gentiles and to the chauvinistic ambition to confine the glory of salvation to their own people. While the Christians thought in terms of universal humanity, the Jews, all through the ages were misanthropes, intent only upon self-glorification. This "nationalistic" interpretation of Jewish survival meant in effect that the Jews were a super-nation. While the reactionaries of Prussia were willing to extend equality of rights to the Poles within their borders, they considered the Jews to have raised their national survival to the rank of a religious faith and to have become an ingrown, overheated nation, incapable of joining hands with the rest of mankind. Interpreting the tenacious battle of the Jew for survival in terms of ethnic pride, they pro-

[18] Holdheim, *"Das Ceremonialgesetz,"* p. 123.

fessed to doubt his capacity to live and act as a citizen of a modern state. Thus, Jewish "nationalism" was in a class by itself, serving as a convenient weapon in the hands of the reactionaries and antisemites.

In opposition to this exaggerated emphasis on Jewish ethnicism, the liberals maintained that the era of Jewish nationhood was ended long ago. Outside of a residual remnant of Orthodox die-hards, the repudiation of nationalism was virtually axiomatic among all Jewish groups down to the end of the nineteenth century. But, the Reform movement endowed this principle with religious sanction and fervor.

In 1897, the Montreal Conference took note of the Zionist Congress in Basel with a resolution of "total disapproval" of the attempt to establish a Jewish state.[19] In 1911, this principle was extended to cover opposition to secular organizations within the Jewish community that reflect the national motive. Thus, the resolution read, ". . . we discountenance any movement in Jewish communities on other than the religious basis, which would violate this principle and tend to create the impression that the Jews are an 'imperium in imperio.' " In 1917, as the Zionist movement was building up toward the triumphant climax of the Balfour Declaration, the Conference resolved by a vote of sixty-eight to twenty that "we look with disfavor upon the new doctrine of political Jewish nationalism, which finds the criterion of Jewish loyalty in anything other than loyalty to Israel's God and Israel's religious mission."[20] After the Declaration had become an accomplished fact, the Central Conference continued its adamant opposition to Zionism, insisting that,

"We are opposed to the idea that Palestine should be considered the homeland of the Jews. Jews in America are

[19] *"Yearbook,"* IX, 12.
[20] *"Yearbook,"* 1917.

part of the American nation . . . The mission of the Jew is to witness to God all over the world." [21]

All through the turbulent twenties, the impassioned opposition of the Reform rabbinate to the Zionist movement was broken only by the revolutionary stand of a few stalwart souls, such as Judah L. Magnes, Gustav Gottheil, Stephen S. Wise and Abba Hillel Silver. Gradually, the inexorable logic of events forced a modification of this anti-nationalist principle, which had constituted a chief pillar of the Reform edifice for nigh unto a century.

F.   The New Fervor and Dedication to a World-Mission.

No survey of classical Reform in America dare ignore the undoubted fact that the movement brought about a renewed sense of dedication among its adherents. Released from the need of preaching on ritual niceties, the rabbinate was able to evoke fresh fervor in behalf of the central ideas of the Jewish faith. Knowing himself to be in the vanguard of the progressive advance of mankind, the Jew dared to look forward to the time when his faith will become the "universal religion" of humanity. The "deviations" of Christianity from the truths of theistic humanism were certain to be corrected, with the progress of enlightenment, so that the Messianic Era, "when the Lord was to be One and His Name One," seemed to be the natural terminus on the broad and sunlit highway that led into the future. Kaufman Kohler, for many years the outstanding theologian of the movement, struck a popular chord when he rhapsodized on this theme:

"Religion humanized and humanity religionized—that is the aim, the beginning and end of Judaism, as Reform understands and expounds it. . . . Nowhere has Judaism better chances of becoming the pioneer of a humanitarian religion, nowhere can the Jewish faith venture to be the advocate of

[21] C.C.A.R. *"Yearbook,"* XXVIII, 133.

the broadest truths concerning God and man, and form the golden chain to embrace all religions and sacred books, and blend them into one religion of humanity than in this blessed new world." [22]

Thus, the Reform movement did not undercut by any means the Jew's feeling of being "chosen" for the sacred task. On the contrary, while the movement steered clear of nationalism in the sphere of politics, it stressed the unique ethnic qualities of the Jew. The Creator had implanted within the heart of the Jew a special "genius" for religion, as was made manifest by the glorious succession of prophets and rabbis and by the endless martyrdom of the entire Jewish people. The Jew possessed "an instinct for religion," or a special bent for the appreciation of the "purity" of ethics, or a unique predisposition for a "spiritual" philosophy of life. Hence, the sacred "mission" to bring mankind unto God. In their various ways, all these interpretations directed a ringing appeal to the Jew qua Jew—an approach which balanced somewhat the one-sided emphasis on the "idea" of Judaism.

Then, too, the American Reform Jew did not suffer from the malady of a split soul, so familiar to us in "Haskalah" literature, the poignant feeling of being rent apart by unresolved conflicts. Having achieved an inner synthesis between tradition, as he saw it, and modern values, he was not plagued by any guilt-feelings arising from the contradiction between an inviolate code of religious demands and the actual pressures of life. He was relatively free of the danger against which Prof. M. Lazarus had warned:

"The decay of a religion, as well as of every spiritual society, must ensue if a large, yea, a very large portion of its confessors no longer observe hundreds upon hundreds of its injunctions; no longer recognize their validity in their hearts,

[22] *"Yearbook,"* 1935, p. 194.

but nevertheless permit them to stand as injunctions of the faith. . . ."[23]

To be sure, the Reform synthesis, which appeared to be a triumphant success at the turn of the century, developed signs of weakness as the tide of liberalism began to recede. With the resurgence of Zionism, the consolidation of Orthodoxy and the rise of Convervatism, the Reform movement became a small minority within the Jewish community and its one-time halcyon hope of becoming the "religion of humanity" faded out of sight. Its rigid rationalism and its "eternal verities" lost their appeal, as the years wore on, and its adherents were totally unprepared emotionally to withstand the shock of the rising tide of antisemitism in the thirties. Tailored in straight lines to suit the cold abstractions of the modern mind, it failed to take account of the mystical, romantic and historical elements of religious experience. A revision of the original principles of the movement was now due, so as to reckon with the deepened folk-consciousness of the people and the mentality of East European Jewry generally, and in 1937 American Reform adopted a new set of principles, which came to be known as the Columbus Platform.

G. *Criticism of the Pittsburgh Platform in the Thirties.*

The Conference of 1935 brought to a climactic crescendo the tide of criticism that had been rising steadily within the movement. A number of factors combined to evoke this reaction—such as, the rise of Hitlerism and the awakened sense of Jewish unity, the rise of Conservatism and Reconstructionism and the emergence of a romantic nostalgia for mysticism, which might be called neo-Hassidism.

Thus, leading rabbis criticized classical Reform as being concerned more with the *clichés* of "the hour" than with

[23] Quoted in Phillipson's *"The Reform Movement,"* p. 486.

the values of eternity. Religion, Prof. Samuel Cohon contended, was not an ideological essence so much as "the growing spiritual experience of a people."[24] A complaint was registered against the architects of Reform, because "they forgot the sense of historic continuity of which the people is symbol and fact, and they created a gap between Jewish universalism and its particularism."[25] A plea was heard for a renewed emphasis on the racial worth of the Jew. Calling for a return to Geiger's doctrine of the racial "genius" of the Jew, Dr. Felix Levy declared, "If I be permitted a generalization, the Jewish people had an instinct for God . . . That intuition can only be explained as the result of historic forces, which the Jews could aver were set into motion by God himself."[26] A new note of appreciation for the legalistic aspects of Judaism, as an excellent means of communal training in reverence for the Divine laws of the spirit, was heard in Dr. Samuel Schulman's summation, "Israel was chosen to teach the world the necessity of law in the lives of individuals and communities—the Law of God."

The spirit and accents of Ahad Ha'am were reflected in a bitter address by Rabbi A. H. Silver, who maintained that the unconscious, national "will to live" of the Jews was the source of all the spiritual values of Judaism. Even the "mission"-ideal arose "in response to a desperate national emergency, out of the indomitable will to live of the race. . . ." It is in the blood of the nation, that the dynamic source of creativity inheres as a dormant, unconscious force, while ideas and ideals are nothing but the surface reflections of this irrational life-stream. Therefore, the primary sin in Judaism is the denial of national unity, and of this sin, classical Reform was guilty. To Silver, Reform participated in the error

[24] *"Yearbook,"* 1935, p. 232.
[25] *Ibid,* p. 234.
[26] *Ibid,* p. 236.

of St. Paul, who sought to level the barriers "between Jews and Gentiles, Greeks and Barbarians."

"But Paul, a product of the culturally diluted Hellenistic Diaspora, entertained views which, centuries later, Reform rabbis in Germany and America were to entertain. The sense of belonging to a Jewish nation and the desire to preserve that nation and to establish the Kingdom of Israel were hardly present with him. Race had no significance. . . . But, with Paul, the mission was a race to save the world. With the Reform rabbis, it was rocking-horse race." [27]

Quite apart from this intemperate treatment of both Reform and St. Paul, this passage is a perfect example of the complete about-face that was now advocated within the movement, in regard to nationalism. Having started out with the axiom that the essence of religion was the relationship of the individual to God, the movement now was told that the individual counts only insofar as he shares in the psyche of the nation, while even the idea of God is but a "projection" of the national "will to live." As Rabbi Brickner put it,

"What is religion but the collective representation of a people throwing out a standard by which it measures the totality of life? As formal religion, based on revelation, begins to lose its hold, the Jewish people project a new ideal in which the whole of life is subsumed. We call it spiritual Zionism. In it, we have God, we have religion and all the values that religion participates in. . . ." [28]

This central principle of Reconstructionism placing the people rather than God in the vital center of Judaism, was now proposed as the basis for a new statement of guiding principles.

A more moderate and balanced critique of the Pittsburgh Platform was developed over the years by Julian Morgen-

[27] *Ibid,* p. 336.
[28] *Ibid,* p. 352.

stern, president of the Hebrew Union College for nearly a generation. He thought that the framers of the platform in 1885 sought to "transplant German Reform Judaism to America." Their ideology was too abstract and formal, not "American" enough. It dealt "with beliefs rather than with life and action." "In fact, the name, America, occurs not once in the entire platform." Also, it was too "universalistic," its framers believing that they were indeed living in the millenium. They had "little comprehension of the meanings and processes of history, or what the full course and development of a historic religion must be; and Judaism is above all else a historic religion. . . ." [29] The course of history had brought it about that a Jewish nation is now arising to take its place among the nations of the world. But, nationalism in itself remains a temporary, accidental phenomenon. The classical Reformers were wrong in speaking of Jewry as "a religious community," as the Zionists are wrong in their inability to think in terms other than those of a Jewish nation. Actually, Jewry is a *people,* or more specifically, a "religious people." "Eternity for Israel lies only in the quality and consciousness of peoplehood, in being a people of destiny, in being a religious people." [30] While nationhood is a political concept, peoplehood is taken to be a cultural-religious idea, vague enough to afford a comforting refuge to those who seek to avoid the two horns of the dilemma—religion or nationhood.

The preponderance of power within the movement shifted steadily during the thirties from the proponents of "ethical monotheism" as the vital core of Judaism to the aggressive preachers of an Ahad Ha'amist "spiritual Zionism," with the result that the concept of "peoplehood," for all its ambiguity, appeared to be the only means of saving the unity of the

29 *"As a Mighty Stream,"* pp. 424-460.
30 *Ibid.*

movement. A universal concept places things in certain categories, saying in effect, "this object belongs in the following class of objects." The term "peoplehood" left the door open as to whether Jewry belonged in the class of "peoples" like the Poles and the Germans or the class of "peoples" like the Catholics and the Protestants. But, on the other hand, it conveyed a renewed appreciation of the historical quality of the Jewish faith, of the folk-elements abounding in it, of the varied interests into which religion branches out, and finally of the "uniqueness" of the Jewish destiny. Thus, the impact of the "positive-historical" emphasis in Conservatism was felt in the new formulation of "Guiding Principles" that was adopted at Columbus in 1935.

H. The Columbus Platform.

The Columbus Platform of Guiding Principles is notable more for its diplomatic adroitness in avoiding a catastrophic clash on the issue of nationalism than for its lucidity, logic, or forthrightness. Its central emphasis consisted in its reformulation of the character of Jewry, so as to embrace some elements of Zionism. The American Jew was not to consider Palestine a place for personal settlement and self-fulfillment as a Jew, but as a hallowed country, affording the "promise of renewed life for many of our brethren." Unequivocally, it asserted, "We affirm the obligation of all Jewry to aid in its upbuilding as a Jewish homeland by endeavoring to make it not only a haven of refuge for the oppressed but also a center of Jewish culture and spiritual life." [31]

The other clear emphasis in this platform is on the need of respecting the threads of historical continuity in the practice of the Jewish faith. Thus, it speaks of the obligation of each generation to "adapt the teachings of the Torah to its

[31] *"Yearbook,"* Vol. **XLVII.**

basic needs in consonance with the genius of Judaism."
While the character of this "genius" is not explained, the
meaning of this phrase seems to imply a recognition of the
need of respecting the historical precedents or at least reckon-
ing with them. The recognition of the need of making use
of Hebrew in worship contrasts with the argument between
Geiger and Frankel as to whether the employment of
Hebrew was "objectively necessary." [32] It was that controversy
which led to the secession of the Conservative wing from the
Reform Conference.

On the whole, this platform is significant more for the
direction it indicates than for consistency and cogency. Judaism is defined as "the historical religious experience of the
Jewish people. Though growing out of Jewish life, its message is universal, aiming at the union and perfection of mankind under the sovereignty of God. . . ." Manifestly, this
definition fits the total body of Jewish tradition rather than
Judaism, as creed, way of life and pattern of loyalties. As a
living reality, presenting a universal message and a program
of living, Judaism cannot be a body of historical experience,
but an interpretation of experience; nor can it be identified
with "religious experience," historical or not, as this term
which derives from modern Protestant theology hardly reflects the labors and reflections of a Maimonides or a Rashi.

Also, since the past as such cannot exert any claims upon
the present, the essential question remains unresolved, as to
the nature of the enduring, imperative elements of Judaism.
Are they the "message which is universal" or the "historical
religious experience," which is particular? Certainly, the
Reform movement was not willing to accept this "historical
religious experience" in toto. What then is the soul of
Judaism?

The "guiding principles" which follow the definition are

[32] Frankfort Conference, Protokolle: Phillipson's—The R.M., p. 166.

similarly pragmatic guides for action rather than a systematic affirmation of beliefs. Thus, when Judaism is said to be "the soul of which Israel is the body," we are not given any reason for this organic relationship. The platform does not go so far as to say that the collective thoughts and sentiments of Jewish people at any one time constitutes Judaism, nor does it recognize "the group-loyalty of non-religious Jews as the matrix of the Jewish faith, but only as a residual "bond which still unites them with us." Consistently, the platform takes refuge in the past from the horns of the present dilemma. Thus, it speaks of "Judaism as growing out of Jewish life," but without identifying Judaism with the contemporary culture of Jews, relying on the obvious truth of this relationship in the past. Again, in insisting on religious faith as the "heart of Judaism," and in repudiating any secularist conception, it declares "that it is by religion and for its religion that the Jewish people has lived." As if the past could in itself set norms for the present! The whole point of classical Reform was precisely this conscious recognition of the possibility of resisting the blind impetus of the past in the interest of a clearly envisaged ideology and hierarchy of values. The presumed unbreakable bond between the particularistic roots of Judaism and its universalistic fruits remains unexplained.

In regard to the concept of Torah, it is asserted that the people of Israel achieved "unique insight in the realm of religious truth" without indicating the character of this uniqueness. The Torah, "both written and oral, enshrines Israel's growing consciousness of God and the moral law." Again, the question is evaded as to what makes this literature normative—the fact of its being Israel's or the clarity of "the consciousness of God," contained in it. The platform fails to indicate wherein the center of gravity lies, in the people or in the idea. And this fundamental ambiguity was due to the

imperative need of a viable synthesis between the philosophies of classical Reform and "Spiritual Zionism."

An attempt was made at the Conference to spell out the
practical implications of the new platform. Dr. Felix Levy,
then president of the Conference, called for a return to
Halachah—that is, the ordering of Jewish life in accord with
the ancient system of Jewish law. "Paulinianism is a real
danger. . . . It cannot be entirely met by a return to tradition
unless we re-enthrone the Halachah as central to Jewish
life." [33] Yet, this call was sounded strictly on the homiletical
level, without any attempt being made to translate its meaning into detailed recommendations. The distance between
Halachah and the actual practice of the Reform rabbinate
was too great to be bridged. In truth, the slogan, "Return to
Halachah," in Reform circles could only have meaning as
the expression of a mood and a trend of thought, not as a
serious call for the acceptance of a regimen of living.

The Conference rejected Dr. Samuel Schulman's alternative draft for a platform which did stress the importance of
Halachah, the doctrine of the selection of Israel "to bear
witness to God and to His Torah," and the principle that
religion is "the substance of Israel's peoplehood." [34]

In 1937, the Reform movement was in no mood to deal
serenely with purely ideological questions. The dominant
issue was Zionism, and, on that score, the movement reversed
its previous direction, clearly and without equivocation.

I. Classical Reform Today

It must not be supposed that classic Reform was van-
quished altogether by the rise of Jewish nationalism. In the
past decade, the American Council for Judaism made its
debut on a strictly anti-nationalist platform.

33 "Yearbook," XLVII, p. 184.
34 Ibid, p. 420.

"Racist theories and nationalistic philosophies, that have become prevalent in recent years, have caused untold suffering to the world and particularly to Jews. Long ago they became obsolete as realities in Jewish history. . . .

"For centuries, Jews have considered themselves nationals of those countries in which they have lived . . . those countries in which Jews have lived have been their homelands. . . .

"We oppose the effort to establish a national Jewish state in Palestine or anywhere else, as a philosophy of defeatism. . . . We dissent from all those related doctrines that stress the racialism, the nationalism and the theoretical homelessness of the Jews. . . ."[35]

In the past decade, the members of the Council staunchly fought against any and all manifestations of Jewish nationalism. While the movement is identified in the public mind largely with the battle against Zionism, it represents a philosophy of Judaism that few of its political opponents would care to challenge. Many who question the application of the doctrines of classical Reform to contemporary Israel and Zionism accept its fundamental premises.

Perhaps, the noblest exponent of an anti-Zionist Judaism was the great philosopher, Hermann Cohen, who regarded Zionism as a revolt against the destiny of Jewish people. For, he believed, it was the historic mission of the Jewish people to demonstrate that a nationality can find expression and fulfillment along cultural-religious, rather than political lines. Mankind consists of nationalities, of which the Jews are one. But, it is the bane of humanity for each nationality to seek the status of a self-governing unit. It was the manifest destiny of the Jewish people to lead in the conquest of the natural-biological concepts of tribes and nations, by the ethical-cultural-religious concepts of citizen, state, humanity. To yield to the blandishments of Zionism is to concede the de-

[35] *"Statement of Principles,"* August 31, 1943.

78

feat of the central ideas of the Enlightenment and to reverse the grand evolution of the convictions of ethical monotheism.[36]

Cohen lived and labored in the years preceding the Balfour Declaration, when Zionism was scarcely more than a dream and a vision. Yet, the impetus of his thought is felt in intellectual circles even today. For he was a brave protagonist of the rationalistic thesis, that progress consists in the conquest of national forces and impulses by the unfolding "culture-consciousness" of mankind. And within the Jewish world, the unresolved tension between universalist ideals and ethnic loyalties exemplifies the age-old struggle between the earthly biological base of the tribal, "closed society" and the dawning vision of the "open society," with mankind redeemed by refinement and saved by enlightenment.

The foremost living exponent of the classical Reform creed is Rabbi Leo S. Baeck, formerly of Berlin, who went through the furnace of the Theresienstadt concentration camp with head unbowed and faith unbroken. To Baeck, the "essence of Judaism is the Divine command to redeem mankind from evil and its effects, through justice and love. He does not seek to discover by research what the leading motives of Jewish loyalty actually were at any one time, for it is not the momentum of the past but the conscience of the present that is ultimately decisive. He defines the "essence" of Jewish faith as the loftiest reaches of Jewish piety and reflection, regardless of the frequency with which they were attained or the constancy with which they were held. Baeck's "essence" is therefore similar to Cohen's "Religion of reason, as found in the Sources of Judaism."

---

[36] *See* the exchange of open letters between Martin Buber and Hermann Cohen on the subject of Zionism, printed in the *Jüdische Schriften"* of the latter and the *"Jüdische Bewegung"* of the former. Also, *"Religion der Vernunft,"* pp. 28, 30, 42, 183.

However, the idea of God is for Baeck not merely a philosophical postulate, but a vital fact of personal experience. In moments of "tension" or "crisis," man finds himself confronted with the Divine imperative—"Thou shalt." While no specific task is set for us by the command of God, we know ourselves called upon to help build His Kingdom on earth. To Rosenzweig, the ineffable moment of Divine-human confrontation was best caught in the word, "chosen"—man, as the individual, or Israel as the people was "chosen" in love for the Kingdom; to Buber, the "I-Thou" relation was the radiant glow of love, devoid of any immediate reference to other people or the world; to Cohen, the dawn of God in human experience meant the call to perfect "truthfulness," in thought, feeling and will; to Baeck, the awareness of God begins with the felt weakness of "creatureliness" and rises to the proud resolve to become "a partner of the Lord in creation."

Religious faith is not a state of serene peacefulness but of inner tension. We know ourselves to be created beings, basking in the momentary sunlight of existence as we move from darkness unto darkness. Yet, we also feel that our Creator lives within us, in our own deepest being. We are not merely His work, but also His Will and, in infinitesimal part, His reality. "To be both created and yet creator is the heart of Jewish religious consciousness."[37]

In contrast to Schleiermacher, who elaborated this experience of "creatureliness" in terms of "feeling," Baeck points out that in Judaism it is articulated in the accents of ethics. As creature, man knows himself to be loved as an individual, and as creator he knows himself to be free, when he responds to the Divine call in deeds of moral dedication. And these two phases of piety are one in essence.

"In themselves faith and humility are not yet pious. They

[37] Baeck, "*The Essence of Judaism,*" N. Y., 1948, p. 119.

are only the feeling of what God means to us, and therefore are without content insofar as the active personality of man is concerned. Only in the deed does man's personality gain its content."[38]

The transition from the passivity of the creature to the active career of the creator is achieved in response to the Divine challenge, "Where art thou?" or "thou shalt."

"Judaism first experienced that great unconditional 'thou shalt' which the one God speaks. This 'thou shalt' arises from the very foundations of reality, and it presents reality to man, the full and fundamental reality. . . . And because the great 'thou shalt' contains the reality, it also contains the great hope; thus hope itself becomes a commandment, hope too becomes an unconditional, categorical postulation. Thou shalt hope! Revelation, ethical task and promise are here one. This is the revelation, the 'logos' of God, the totality of commandment, the Torah, which, according to ancient simile, was 'before the creation of the world.' "[39]

Unlike Kant's Categorical Imperative which is apprehended as a formal law of being, the "thou shalt" of Judaism is felt as a call to positive action leading toward a goal which is definite, even if it be realizeable only in the "end of days." Thus, the essence of Judaism is an "ethical dynamism," which has already endowed the Western world with its unique flavor. Baeck holds with Geiger that the Jewish people were peculiarly gifted in the possession of "ethical dynamism," the impulse and aspiration toward the building of the Kingdom. St. Paul's break with Judaism resulted from his impatience with the infinity of the task posed by the Divine, "thou shalt." Disillusioned with man's puny efforts, he taught that salvation could only come by the miracle of Divine grace. "The words, 'with all thine heart, with all thy

[38] *Ibid,* p. 134.
[39] *"Why the Jew in the World,"* Commentary, June, 1947.

soul, with all thy might,' were to mean no more the way of the deed but the way of faith." Judaism, however, did not shrink from the infinity of the task, insisting that justice and love were the highways leading to the Kingdom. In justice, the ideal community is achieved, and in love, each individual is appreciated for the uniqueness of his soul. Without Jews or Judaism "the world would be without the great vision and the great will to the way. And it is by these two that the world lives."

For Baeck, the Messianic dream and the laws of Judaism were the instruments needed for the preservation of the Jewish people, that its "ethical dynamism" might not be dissipated. The so-called "rituals" of Judaism were intended to preserve the Jewish ethnic group, so that it might fulfill its "mission" unto mankind. A "fence" had to be built around the dedicated community, and the height of the "fence" varied in direct ratio to the intensity of persecution. But, the observance of "mitzvoth" is not itself a religious deed.

"These (ritual observances) serve not the religious idea itself but mainly the protection it needs—a security for its existence through the existence of the religious community. This and only this is the primary measure of their value."[40]

Since the "mission" of Israel is directed to the world at large, the fact that Jews are dispersed throughout the Western world is not a tragedy, but a God-given opportunity for the fulfillment of our vocation.[41]

J. Current Reform Practice.

The attempt to rebuild the bridges with the past by linking up modern Reform practices with the medieval literature of Halachah has received marked encouragement from the Columbus Platform. Dr. Solomon Freehof's little volume,

[40] "The Essence of Judaism," p. 263.
[41] Ibid, p. 78.

"Reform Jewish Practice and Its Rabbinic Background," describes the prevailing observances of Reform Jews from a distinctly traditional viewpoint, omitting altogether from consideration such negative enactments as the abolition of the dietary laws, the disregard of the ceremonies of "tallith" and "t'fillin," the virtually total neglect of Sabbath observance, etc. These and similar developments are deplored and attributed to the resistless current of popular sentiment. The author conveniently overlooks the conscious defiance of the Law in such practices as lighting Sabbath candles after dark in the Temple as part of the Sabbath service.

The following practices are described against the backdrop of evolving tradition: the institution of one-day observance for all festivals, including Rosh Hashono; the establishment of formal Sunday services, which fall into a semi-Sabbath category because the weekday service is no longer observed; the substitution of the Confirmation ceremony for the traditional observance of Bar Mitzvah, though some temples "permit" the celebration of the traditional observance in a slightly modified form; the elimination of the custom of calling people up to the reading of the Torah ("aliyoth"), though the honors of lifting up the Scroll of the Law and covering it are retained; the institution of reading a portion of the Law at the Friday evening service in the temples where the attendance at the Sabbath morning service is very poor; the reading of the prophetic portion in English (Haftorah); the employment of an organ, a mixed choir (frequently with Gentile singers); worshipping with heads uncovered and in family pews; elimination of the requirements of baptism and circumcision from the conversion ceremony for Gentiles, but circumcision is described as the universal practice for those born in the faith, with non-Jewish doctors being permitted to take the place of the traditional "mohel"; elimination of the "huppa" and the "k'tubah" at weddings and the recognition of a civil divorce as being fully sufficient for remarriage; the recognition of the practice of cremation and the substitution of formal dress for the traditional shrouds ("tachrichim").

The marriage of a Jewish person to an unconverted Gentile is frowned upon by many Reform rabbis; nevertheless, the majority will officiate at such marriages, with or without the participation of a representative of the other faith. This practice, however, remains an open issue at meetings of the Conference. Affiliation with the Christian Science movement has been declared to be incompatible with loyalty to the Jewish Faith.[42] Nevertheless, this principle is not rigidly enforced, and a Christian Scientist of Jewish birth is accorded the right of burial in the Reform cemetery.[43]

---

[42] *"Yearbook,"* vol. XXII, p. 229.
[43] *"Reform Jewish Practice,"* Freehof, p. 144.

4

The Conservative Movement

A. Emergence of the Movement.

In point of organization and the official crystallization of ideology, the Conservative group is the most recent alignment on the American scene. While the Jewish Theological Seminary, the focal point of the movement, was first organized in 1887, largely as a protest against the adoption of the Pittsburgh Platform, the institution virtually ceased to function following the death of its founder and first president, Sabato Morais. Later, as the massive tide of immigration from Central and Eastern Europe brought into being a large, inchoate Jewish population that was not yet integrated into the pattern of American culture, the social gulf between the Reform and Orthodox communities became wide and all but impassable. In order to assist the East-European Jews to achieve their own synthesis of tradition and modernism, a group of public-spirited citizens, headed by Jacob H. Schiff, invited in the year 1902 Prof. Solomon Schechter from England to reorganize the Seminary and to build around it an association of traditional synagogues. In fifty years, the movement has come to embrace some 450 rabbis and 500 synagogues, as well as an impressive number of central institutions.

In Western Europe, the Conservative or moderately Reform interpretation of Judaism had achieved predominance by the end of the nineteenth century. Outside of England, the leading congregations and communities of Germany, Austria and France were Conservative, with the Leipsig and

Augsburg synods of 1869 and 1870, respectively, striving consciously for the attainment of "the golden mean."[1] The Seminary in Breslau, under the leadership of Zechariah Frankel, provided the greatest number of rabbis for the synagogues of the German "culture-sphere," which included the cities of Hungary and the Scandinavian countries.

However, the graduates of this Conservative school did not band together, upon their arrival in the United States, to foster their philosophy and program on a national scale. For many years modern traditionalist rabbis like Jastrow, Szold and Kohut attempted to find a common working basis with the determined leaders of American Reform. Only slowly and reluctantly were the ways of the Conservative and Reform wings of American Jewry parted, with the consequent emergence of the United Synagogue and the Rabbinical Assembly as the organs of a new party. Motivated by a deep attachment to the total community of Israel, the Conservative group was therefore projected upon the American scene as a distinct movement virtually against the will of its founders and leaders, who sought to heal the wounds of sectarianism and to serve the entire body of Israel. It was the hope and conviction of Prof. Schechter that the United Synagogue would become the central rallying point of American Jewry, lending to the Orthodox masses the polish of "culture" and bringing the errant Reformers back to the community, in "unison and peace." At the founding convention of the United Synagogue, he declared:

"Indeed, what we intend to accomplish is not to create a new party, but to consolidate an old one, which has always existed in this country, but was never conscious of its own strength, nor perhaps realized the need of organization. I refer to the large number of Jews who, thoroughly American in habits of life and modes of thinking and, in many cases,

[1] Phillipson, "The Reform Movement," p. 305.

imbued with the best culture of the day, have always maintained conservative principles and remained aloof from the Reform movement which swept over the country. They are sometimes stigmatized as the Neo-Orthodox. This is not correct. Their Orthodoxy is not new. . . . A better knowledge of Jewish history would have taught them that culture combined with religion was the rule with the Jew. . . . The 'new' Orthodoxy represents therefore very little that is new. It was the normal state of the Jew in Spain. . . ."[2]

In his loving estimate of Jewish tradition, Dr. Schechter assumed that the momentum of the fundamentalist trend was in his day completely spent and that a liberal interpretation of Judaism could confidently expect to inherit the mantle of Orthodoxy. All that the Orthodox masses lacked was "culture," and, in their progressive adoption of American ways and patterns of thought, they could be expected to retain "reverence for the Bible as the word of God" and "love for the institutions and memories of the past." Conscious that he represented the healthy mainstream of tradition, Dr. Schecter rejected even the designation "neo-Orthodoxy" as being too suggestive of innovations.

However, the logic of events brought the Conservative movement into being as an identifiable group consciously formulating its own standards of piety, and rendered hollow and meaningless any residual endeavor to pretend otherwise. Today, Conservative synagogues are easily recognized by one or more of the following practices:

With rare exceptions, the women's gallery is abolished and families worship together. Worshippers wear the "tallith" at their morning prayers and "t'fillin" at the daily weekday services. The congregations sponsor an intensive program of Hebrew education and employ either the Orthodox prayerbook or the one of the United Synagogue. The main changes

[2] *"American Jewish Yearbook,"* 1916, p. 62.

in the United Synagogue Prayer-Book consist in the elimination of a petition for the renewal of the sacrificial system. The prayers of the Mussaph services are retained but the tense is changed so that it becomes a recitation of what our ancestors did in the past. The translation of "m'hayeh hamaisim," is so phrased as to suggest God's creative power, not to teach the dogma of the resuscitation of the dead.

Prayers in English are included in the services. Many synagogues employ the organ to aid the cantor and choir, but the cantillation is in the musical tradition of the synagogue. Worshippers sit with covered heads. With the exception of one synagogue, two days of every festival are observed, and all synagogues celebrate the two days of Rosh Hashono. All boys are prepared for the Bar Mitzvah ceremony; the Bas Mitzvah ceremony for girls is rapidly becoming a standard procedure, while the ceremony of Confirmation is also included in the total educational program. The dietary laws are observed in all public functions of the synagogue. The approved pattern of Sabbath observance for Conservative laymen includes permission to ride to the synagogue on the Sabbath, emphasizes the practices making for the hallowing of the day and distinguishes clearly between avoidable and unavoidable types of work. As of the present, Conservative rabbis do not perform marriages for divorcees without a Jewish bill of divorcement ('get") ; by a decision of the Committee on Jewish Laws and Standards a descendant of a priestly family (Cohen) is permitted to marry a divorcee or a convert.

B.   Trends Within the Movement.

In the past decade, thoughtful observers were frequently more impressed with the divisions inside the Conservative movement than with the overall character and ideology of the United Synagogue. It was commonly assumed that the

"right wing" of Conservatism shaded off into liberal Orthodoxy, that the "left wing" represented a blend of Reform
with nationalism, and that the "center" consisted of the
steadily diminishing company of the hesitating and the un-
convinced. Actually, the past generation has witnessed the
steady rise of the "center" group within the movement,
leading to the evolution of a vigorous and scholarly interpretation of Judaism that bids fair to set the dominant
pattern for the future.

Occupying the middle position between Orthodoxy and
Reform, Conservatism may be understood either as a critique
of the former or as a protest against the latter trend. Historically, the Conservative movement has arisen both in America
and in Europe by way of secession from the camp of radical
Reform. But, the congregations which constitute at present
the United Synagogue had come into the Conservative camp
from the ranks of Orthodoxy. The full implications of the
movement have not yet been revealed. However, it is already
clear that it contains vital ideas which lend it coherence,
relate it to the noblest trends of thought in the past and open
it to the influence of the best minds of the present. While
these ideas are not stressed in equal degree by all Conservative rabbis, they do constitute a consensus of basic convictions
that is more significant than the variety of emphases among
the marginal adherents of the movement.

C. Repudiation of the Literalistic Conception of Revelation.

Along with Reform, the Conservative movement does not
teach that every word in the Torah and every statement of
the Oral Law were literally pronounced by the Deity. The
naive picture of revelation as consisting of the "Lord dic-
tating and Moses transcribing" is taken to be no more than
a symbolic representation of the process of Divine inspiration, that is itself beyond the power of human comprehension. "The Torah speaks in the language of men," as the

rabbis put it, and, as our understanding deepens, we must learn to disentangle the human, the conditioned and the temporary elements from the Divine, the absolute and eternal truths. We cannot ever draw the line with either certainty or finality, but we must envisage this line as best we can, in our endeavors to meet the challenge of changing circumstances. To the Conservatives, then, the Torah *contains* the Word of God, especially when it is understood by way of a total self-identification with the historic experience of Israel, but the detailed precepts, phrases and words of the Holy Scriptures are not all, in their bare literalness, the word of God.

On the other hand, the Conservative view differs from the Reform position, as stated in the Pittsburgh Platform, which considered only the moral law as "binding." Jewish tradition, in its entirety, including the Halachah, or the system of precepts and laws, is a steadily unfolding body of revelation which is never wholly free from the manifold limitations of the human mind nor at any time entirely bare of the Divine spark of inspiration. The legalism of the rabbis was not a corruption of prophetic idealism but an inspired, collective endeavor to translate it into the realities of life.

The source of Divine teaching is our sacred tradition in its *entirety,* including the ideas of our philosophical literature and even those of deviationist trends. The greatness of Jewish tradition consists precisely in its richness, variety and hospitality to differing views, permitting various doctrines and practices to recede into the background, as other principles and laws move into the center of attention. Reverence for tradition in its totality, precludes both the revolutionary mood and the piety of naive literalism and legalism, encouraging both the process of continuous reevaluation of the past in the light of the present and the judgment of the present in the light of the past.

There is, of course, ample precedent for this insistence that the word of God is not simply the written letter of the Torah, but that it consists in the synthesis of the letter with the living spirit of interpretation, which issues out of the best scientific and philosophic knowledge of every age. Masters of the "Mishnah," like Rabbi Joshua ben Hananyah, derived this principle from the verse, "it is not in heaven," and, in the Middle Ages, philosophical Judaism took this principle for granted all through its triumphant advance. Yet, the implications of a non-literal doctrine of revelation are more significant in our day because of the development of the scientific method in the study of history, especially the rise of biblical criticism.

For several decades, the Conservative movement shied away from the scientific study of the Holy Scriptures, principally because the science of "higher criticism," as it was developed in Germany by scholars who were keenly conscious of their "Aryan" supremacy, was largely vitiated by a kind of "higher antisemitism," as Schechter aptly phrased it. Nevertheless, it was Profesor Schechter's first ambition, upon his arrival in the United States, to promote the scientific study of Scriptures by Jewish scholars, utilizing the rich treasures of our own commentaries as well as the discoveries and views of modern research and archeology.[3] Rooted deeply in the soil of tradition, Conservative scholars have brought to the study of Scriptures a kind of sympathetic understanding of the genius of the Bible that was sadly lacking in previous years. The massive labors of Y'heskel Kaufman, which served to demonstrate the fundamental errors of radical criticism and the essential monotheism of the Jewish faith, in its earliest beginnings are appreciated and taken up in the Conservative outlook. Thus, for example, Rabbi Solomon Goldman, in his introduction to the Bible,

3 American Jewish Yearbook, 1916, p. 58.

takes account of the massive achievements of modern research; reviews the general field of biblical criticism and the particular question of the authorship of the Book of Genesis; arrives at the conclusion that "the critics have overreached themselves," that "the religion of the Patriarchs was monotheistic," and that Moses was probably the author, editor and compiler of the documents that constitute the first book of the Bible.[4]

The authority of Holy Scriptures for our day is twofold in origin—the truth of its central philosophy of monotheism and the interpretation that it enshrines of the enduring bent of mind of the Jewish people. Monotheism is not so much a series of intellectual propositions, as the nineteenth-century Reformers thought, but a fundamental attitude of the soul, which is validated by human experience generally. For us as Jews, monotheism is, in addition, the soul of our historic heritage and the substance of our collective experience. It is through our complete identification with the life of our people, in the tragic travail of the past as in the living aspirations of the present, that we come to experience the vibrant reality of the monotheistic way of life. Judaism is not only philosophy; it is also a complex of psychic attitudes, a structure of loyalties and sentiments and a pattern of living.

In the Conservative view, the historic unity of God (metaphysical ideas), Torah (the detailed precepts governing the life of the individual), and Israel (the consciousness of ethnic unity and oneness of destiny), has been disturbed by the Reformers in their overemphasis on philosophical abstractions and by the Orthodox in their exclusive concentration on the precepts of the Torah. The impetus of Conservative thought is definitely in the direction of the re-creation of the original tri-partite unity, recognizing in the living people of Israel the synthesizing agent between the testimony of re-

[4] S. Goldman, *"In the Beginning,"* p. 101.

vealed tradition and the growing light of contemporary thought.

In its refusal to cut Judaism to a preconceived pattern of what a "religion" should be like and in its determination not to regard Judaism as a "finished," unchanging set of dogmas and deeds, Conservatism sees "the word of God" as a living stream of tradition and aspiration, rather than as a fixed pattern, or formula, or book, or collection of books.

Conservative scholarship finds ample support for this view in the historical analysis of the evolution of Judaism. As a foremost historian of our time put it:

"Neo-Orthodoxy, equally with Reform, is a deviation from historical Judaism. No less than Reform, it abandoned Judaism's self-rejuvenating historical dynamism. . . . It is Conservative Judaism which seems to show the greatest similarities with the method and substance of teaching of the popular leaders during the declining Second Commonwealth, inasmuch as clinging to the traditional mode of life, it nevertheless allows for the adaptation of basic theological concepts to the changing social and environmental needs."[5]

D. The "Positive-Historical" Viewpoint.

It was in the name of the "positive-historical" approach to the problems of Jewish theology that Zechariah Frankel, founder of the Conservative movement, seceded from the Frankfort Conference of Reform rabbis in the year 1845. The issue in question was whether the use of Hebrew in the service was only "advisable," as the Conference contended, or whether it was absolutely essential.[6] Trivial as this issue might appear to us today, it reflected the fundamental divergence that was to eventuate into the Conservative protest against the unhistorical rationalism of Reform. On any

[5] Prof. Salo Baron as quoted by Robert Gordis in "Conservative Judaism."
[6] Phillipson, "The Reform Movement," p. 190.

rational basis, worshippers should pray in the language they know best, and the law of the Mishnah concurs in this proposition. But, in prayer, the individual must learn to merge his identity with that of the collective body of Israel, and the Hebrew language is the effective medium whereby the individual Jew is made to feel the unity, continuity and distinctiveness of Israel as the people of revelation. Insistence upon Hebrew as "essential" for Jewish worship was, therefore, in effect tantamount to the negation of the basic Reform principle, that religion was strictly a relationship between the individual and God.

Essentially, the awkward phrase, "positive-historical," implies, in the first place, an attitude of humility toward the great achievements of the past. In every age, it is well for man to remember that his ideals and judgments, self-evident as they may appear to him, might only be partial facets of the infinite mystery of reality, the inadequacy of which will be as obvious to future generations as are the certainties and absolutes of past generations to us. It is good to embrace "the spirit of the age" in wholehearted devotion, but our enthusiasm must be tempered by the realization that the "weltanschauung" of our generation, as of all preceding epochs, is after all only a limited and partial view of that which can never wholly be known. Indeed, this fundamental humility is one of the essential functions of religion, in that it provides a perpetual counterbalance to the pride of reason and the inevitable acquisition of blind spots that accompanies the reception of every new vista.

In the nineteenth century, the feeling was widespread that humanity was standing on the final plateau of history, so that all the relative insights of the past were ready to be gathered up in the blaze of the final self-revelation of the Absolute Mind. We have seen how this conviction operated within the Reform movement in the uncritical adoration of "the spirit of the age." Frankel's insistence on "the positive-historical" approach was in effect a call to see the present in the light of the past and to recognize the limitations of our most cherished convictions. In the same spirit, Schechter declared that Judaism would never have survived if Jewish people had been ready to accept any apparent contemporary fad or trend as the final "verdict of history," as Geiger did when he wrote:

"History has given her judgment (against the Hebrew language) even though this judgment is not yet carried out, and all lamentations against this condition of things are useless. No protest is justified against the forces of history."[7]

In the second place, the term "positive-historical" implies an attitude of reverence toward the *processes* whereby changes are affected in the religious life of a people. Frankel, Zunz and Schechter were fundamentally historians. They were not averse to any change in the pattern of worship or the regimen of prescribed rituals, provided that change was brought about organically, naturally, smoothly, as a development of cumulative historical forces, not as an artificial fiat of a few men. As a living tradition, Judaism can and must continue to grow in accord with its inner genius, but it must not be tailored to suit abstract geometric patterns, which may be theoretically more systematic and rational.

Continuing this line of reasoning, the Conservatives generally favor that interpretation of the Law which allows the living authorities of each age ample scope to enact such amendments as are needed for the "strengthening of the faith" ("hizuk hadath"). The chief target of their criticism of Orthodoxy is its tendency to reduce the authority of contemporary rabbis and courts to the vanishing point, so that the domain of law and life are hopelessly separated. As Prof.

[7] *See* Schecter's essay on "Abraham Geiger" and Geiger in "Jüdische Zeitschrift," vol. 7, p. 7.

Schechter first phrased this criticism in a review of Weiss' study of the evolution of the Jewish tradition:

"What Weiss really objects to is a *weak* authority—I mean that phonograph-like authority which is always busy in re-producing the voice of others without an opinion of its own, without originality, without initiative and discretion. The real authorities are those who, drawing their inspiration from the past, also understand how to reconcile us with the present and to prepare us for the future."[8]

In brief, then, the Conservatives favored the vitalization of tradition by strengthening the authority of contemporary rabbis rather than the abandonment of tradition in favor of a rationally reconstructed faith.

In part at least, this debate reflected the issue between the European liberals and conservatives in the general field of public law. Are laws made in accordance with an abstract system of ethics, or must they be allowed to develop in keeping with their own inherent impetus? The liberals of European politics argued in behalf of systematic legislation based upon the implications of "the rights of man," while the Conservatives maintained that freedom must be allowed to broaden slowly, "from precedent to precedent." Applying the Conservative argument to the problems of Judaism, Frankel and later Schechter maintained that the law must issue out of the life of the people, reflecting their sentiments and channeling their aspirations. While the Reformers con-ceived of religion largely as a set of abstract truths and con-sequently assigned to the religious leaders of every age the task of formulating and crystallizing the ideology and pro-gram of Judaism, the Conservatives regarded faith as a complex structure of sentiments, loyalties and ideals, shared by all the people and therefore to be molded by the people.[9]

---

8 Schecter, *"Studies in Judaism,"* Vol. I, p. 212.
9 *See* debate on Frankel's resignation in *"Protokolle,"* Frankfort Conference.

In this "positive-historical" view, Judaism is continuously being modified by the changing habits of the people and by the process of interpretation of Jewish law, which, too, is not meant to be abstract and self-contained, but pragmatic and life-centered. Conservative scholars like Prof. Louis Ginsburg, Louis Finkelstein, Hayim Chernowitz and Saul Lieberman demonstrated in a massive series of researches how the Law reflected the changing needs and aspirations of the people in the varying strata of its gradual formation. Thus, the Conservatives accept the entire structure of Jewish Law as valid for our time, save insofar as it was modified by the practice of the people, insisting, however, that the Law arose as a human response to a Divine call and that it continue to be developed in such a manner as to respond to the deepest spiritual needs of our time.

As to the application of this principle, the Conservative movement has been slow and fumbling. Only in recent years has the attempt been made to systematize, clarify and apply in practice the implications of the Conservative interpretation of Jewish Law. These attempts will be described in a later chapter.

E. The Nationalistic Motif.

Even before the rise of modern Zionism, the Conservative movement was motivated by a deep love for the living people of Israel, in all its peculiarities, foibles and loyalties. While the Reformers sought to eliminate all traces of nationalism from the prayer-book, the Conservatives insisted on the indispensability of Hebrew and on the need of retaining the ideal of rebuilding the historic homeland. As Mannheimer, the leader of Austrian Conservatism, put it: "I am one of those who do not rationalize the Messianic belief; I believe in and defend the national interpretation of this dogma and hope for a national restoration. . . ."[10]

10 Phillipson, *"The Reform Movement,"* p. 87.

In the Conservative view, the very existence and life of the Jewish people was a supreme religious ideal, for they could not envisage the Jewish faith as being separated even in theory from the people that projected it upon the stage of history. Bitterly repudiating the anti-nationalism of the Reformers, Schechter wrote that they (especially Geiger) "saw in Israel a religious corporation, a sort of non-celibate monks, whose *raison d'être* was not in themselves, but outside of them. . . ."

"We would have been spared all the terrible persecutions if we could ever have agreed to eliminate from it the national features and become a mere religious sect."

"It was just those things which distinguished us from our surroundings and separated us from the nations, such as devotion to the Pentateuch, the keeping of the Sabbath, the observance of the covenant of Abraham, and the loyalty to the dietary laws, to which we clung for thousands of years with all our life and for which we brought numberless sacrifices. Is this now the time, when the thought of nationalism is universally accepted, to destroy it as far as Israel is concerned?"[12]

If the inspiration of Reform was the bold rationalism of a Maimonides, the guiding light of Conservatism was Halevi, who taught that Judaism was the living tradition of a Divinely chosen and uniquely endowed people. Taken collectively, Jewry was a people of prophets, and anything that redounded to the benefit of the physical wellbeing of the people strengthened the foundation of the true faith. This organic unity of the particular people with the universal faith was articulated in the accents of contemporary thought by men like Samuel David Luzzato, who saw the Jewish spirit as being arrayed against the secular spirit of Hellenism or

11 *"Studies in Judaism,"* Vol. III, p. 69.
12 *Ibid,* p. 78.

"Atticism," as he put it, in all epochs and in every phase of culture, and Nahman Krochmal, who interpreted the entire sweep of Jewish history in terms of the unbreakable bond between the people Israel and the Absolute Idea of God.

Of particular importance in later years were the ideas of Ahad Ha'am, who saw the genesis of every ideal in the "will to live" of the people and in the progressive unfolding of its national soul. It was the unique bent of the Jewish mind to seek to order all phases of life in accord with "absolute justice." This "Torah of the heart" is the genuine dynamic and enduring impetus of Judaism; all else is temporary, peripheral and expendable. Thus, it is possible to identify oneself with Jewish life for the sake of spiritual self-fulfillment, even if one does not accept the idea of God and does not observe any phase of the ceremonial pattern of the Jewish faith. In an age when intellectuals hesitated to express belief in God, Ahad Ha'am's ideas functioned as powerful centripetal forces for the Jewish community, directing attention to the cultural and spiritual content of the Jewish faith and stimulating a broad loyalty to the total complex of Jewish values. And it was within the hospitable compass of the Conservative movement that the seeds of Ahad Ha'amism found their most fertile soil.

F. The Motif of Anti-Sectarianism.

Allied to the national ideal is the resolve to build bridges of understanding between the varied and contradictory interpretations of the Jewish faith, so as to retain the vision of the all-embracing unity of a common tradition. Thus, secular Zionism was so enthusiastically welcomed by Conservative Jews as to erase the lines of demarcation between them, though, of course, it represented only one phase of the tradition. To the believer in the motto, "nothing that is Jewish is alien to me," every creative expression of Jewish life, one-sided and unbalanced as it may be, is still part of the total organic complex that is Judaism. In particular, the Conservative group was cast in the role of the mediator and interpreter between the Orthodox and Reform conceptions of Judaism. Rabbi Moshe Sofer and Rabbi Malbim were the implacable opponents of Geiger, Holdheim and Zunz, but to the Conservatives, both sets of leaders belonged to the one tradition that they sought to make meaningful for their day and age. While the Reformers concentrated their loving attention upon the *essence* of Judaism, the Conservatives sought to take account of the *totality* of the tradition, with the understanding that varying phases of the tradition might leap into the focus of significance at different times, while other phases temporarily move into the background. Thus Prof. Schechter wrote:

"In other words, is it not time that the new theology should consist in the best that all the men of Israel, including Geiger, gave us, but should modify and qualify his views, dating from a rationalistic age, by the loyalty to the law of Rabbi Akiba Eger and Rabbi Mordecai Baneth, by the deep insight into Jewish history of a Zunz and a Krochmal, by the mysticism of a Baal Shem and some of his best followers, and by the love of Israel's nationality and its perpetuation of Herzl or Ahad Ha'am?"[13]

In this quotation, the argument is pointed against the Reformers, but it was directed with equal logic against the Orthodox, who reduced all of Jewish life to Torah, condensed all of Torah into the "four ells of Halachah," and all of the historically varying trends within Halachah into the rigid molds of the Shulhan Aruch. In opposition to the steadily narrowing spiral of the "faithful" by Orthodox standards, the Conservatives stress the fullness of the historic tradition, which included reverence for all that is

[13] Essay on "Abraham Geiger" in "Studies in Judaism," Vol. III.

genuinely Jewish and all that the cumulative knowledge of the age acknowledges to be true. The precepts of the Halachah were not to be viewed in isolation, but against the historic background from which they emerged and in the light of the total tradition which they expressed. A century of Jewish scholarship has demonstrated the responsiveness of the law and its official interpretation to the exigencies of life and the requirements of the contemporary spiritual climate. Thus, the validity of Halachah is reaffirmed, but only as one of the factors of the rich and varied tradition of Israel.

And within the tradition, the source of authority is shifted from the written word to the living people, in all its confusion, variety and uncertainty. What is lost in definition and clearness is gained in vitality, relevance and comprehensiveness.

"Since then the interpretation of Scripture or the Secondary Meaning is mainly a product of changing historical influences, it follows that the center of authority is actually removed from the Bible and placed in some *living body* which, by reason of its being in touch with the ideal aspirations and the religious needs of the age, is best able to determine the nature of the Secondary Meaning. This living body, however, is not represented by any section of the nation, or any corporate priesthood, or Rabbihood, but by the collective conscience of Catholic Israel as embodied in the Universal Synagogue."[14]

G. The "High Synagogue" Motif.

An enduring emphasis in Conservatism is the high estimate of the importance of rituals and time-honored symbols in religious life. While Geiger maintained that, with the advance of culture, symbols become unnecessary, the Conservative movement in Europe and America insisted that religion

[14] Introduction to *"Studies in Judaism,"* Vol. 1.

was a total involvement of the soul and that its symbols and rites are directed to the vast reaches of the unconscious and the irrational. The massive researches into the psychology of religious consciousness that were conducted under the inspiration of William James, McDougall and the Freudians confirmed the truth of the ancient insights, that symbols of action are of incalculable value in the economy of spiritual life. After a century and a half of unidirectional rationalism, the modern world was reminded that the human personality was rational on the surface only and that symbols of word and deed frequently reached the depths that concepts could only point to. This realization was included in the ideology of American Conservatism, which was taking shape even as students of religion turned their attention from logic and metaphysics to depth-psychology and social anthropology.[15]

Thus, in Conservatism, the prevailing tendency is not to abolish ceremonial practices, but as far as possible, to revitalize them and even to create new ritualistic channels for the articulation of religious feeling. Worship with covered heads and in "tallith" and "t'fillin," the Dietary laws and the distinctive rites of each festival are cherished. The Consecration ceremony for children entering the Hebrew School and the Bas Mitzvah observance, as well as the practice of blessing children on the Sabbath nearest their birthdays, are instances of the search for new vehicles of religious expression. The emphasis on the principle of creativity is particulary strong in the Reconstructionist version of the Conservative philosophy, which will be discussed presently.

H. *The Factor of Neo-Mysticism.*

A renewed appreciation of the mystical element in religious experience is a potent factor in the formation of the Conservative ideology. While in the early days of Reform,

[15] *See* Eric Fromm, *"The Forgotten Language."*

the doctrines of Kabbalah and the institution of Hassidism were derided as monstrous aberrations, the twentieth century saw the rise of a neo-Hassidic movement which glorified the romantic and mystical trends in Jewish tradition. The works of Martin Buber, I. L. Peretz and Sh. Horodetzky exhibited the genuine beauty of mystical piety and its deep roots in the indigenous culture of the East-European Jews.

Thus, Prof. Schechter pleaded for the infusion of the mystical piety of the Baal Shem Tov into the life of the modern Jew.[16] Repeatedly he exposed the dry and narrow approach of the rationalistic Reformers.

"Rationalism could well appreciate all the virtues of manliness, but it could never value properly those qualities of obedience, submissiveness, meekness and self-denial which constitute a holy life."[17]

The impact of mysticism is partially antinomian, since attention is directed away from legalistic correctness and toward the travail of the spirit. To mystics the observance of any law is not as important as the spirit in which it is observed. For this reason, the Lithuanian "mithnagdim," in their zealous passion for the Law, feared and fought the mass-movement of Hassidism. But, the enduring pressure of mysticism is in the direction of a progressive intensification of loyalty to ancient practices and even in behalf of the proliferation of new customs and practices. It is in conformity to the established rituals and ceremonies that the mystical personality finds refuge from the blinding radiance of ecstatic piety, a powerful bond with the religion of the masses, and a persistent protest against the pride of reason. While both rationalism and mysticism seek the spirit behind the Law, the former expects the ceremony to speak to the worshipper whereas the latter expects the worshipper to speak through

[16] Schecter, Introduction, Vol. I, "Studies in Judaism."
[17] Schecter, Vol. I, "Studies in Judaism," p. 72.

the ceremony. Thus, at the various Reform conferences, the rituals which are not connected "directly and naturally" with some worthy spiritual purpose were declared to be no longer valid. In contrast, the Conservative movement follows the guiding principle of Franz Rosenzweig, who, in a famous letter to a group of disciples, declared that it is not the objective character of the ceremony that is decisive, but the question whether or not we today can still bring ourselves to say through the rite or symbol, "Praised art Thou, O Lord, our God."[18]

"Practice precedes theory for us," he wrote, "whereas, with the Reform movement, the contrary was true."[19] In the beginning is the act of commitment to the Jewish faith and destiny —an act which is more volitional than rational, and for which virtually any rite may serve if it is part of the divinely designed synthesis of Torah and Israel. "Your Hassid too did not begin with Kavanah (intention). That will come one day, of course. But, to desire to begin with it, as people tell us we must, is entirely un-Jewish."

To Rosenzweig, God is the creative principle of love, subsisting behind the universe. Flashes of His love interpenetrate the cosmic process from time to time, setting into motion the current of redemption which will one day sweep mankind up to the blessed peaks of the Kingdom of God. It is of the nature of love to be selective. Hence, the recipients of the Divine ray of love inevitably feel themselves to be "chosen." The Jewish people was thus "chosen" by God, in a concrete and historical fashion, insofar as its collective consciousness is illuminated by this central religious experience of its prophets and saints. The individual Jew shares in this transforming experience if he surrenders his individual identity to the collective consciousness of his people, willing, feeling

18 Franz Rosenzweig, *"Briefe,"* p. 543.
19 *Ibid,* p. 356.

and thinking of himself only as a cell in the organism of the nation. Since Israel is fashioned as a community by the Torah, especially the Divine Law, obedience to the Law is an automatic articulation of the sense of belonging to the Jewish community. Only those who belong can enjoy the feeling of being the object of Divine love and of being part of the "chosen" people.

Thus, while Rosenzweig placed the living people in the focus of attention, rather than the letter of the Law, he insisted that the worshipper must make every effort to address God through the approved channels of Halachah, discarding only the rites which have lost altogether the power to stir the religious consciousness. "I should not dare to declare any law as human, because it has not yet been permitted to me to say through it in proper fashion, 'praised art Thou.' " At the same time, he declared, "Judaism is not Law. It creates Law, but is not it. It is to be a Jew."[20]

It is through the symbols of action that the worshipper comes to feel, not as a disembodied "man in general," but as an integral part of the living body of Israel, that was made eternal by the Word of God. "People understand differently when they understand in doing. Every day in the year, Bileam's speaking ass may be a legend to me; on the Sabbath Balaak, when it speaks to me out of the uplifted Torah, it is not."[21]

While Martin Buber is wary of all organized forms of religious expression, especially of all rituals, the impact of his philosophy is felt in a growing reverence for the mystical trends in Jewish thought, especially Hassidism. The early writings of Buber dealt with the nature of the inherent genius of Jewish thought. As the leading exponent of "spiritual Zionism" in Western Europe, Buber sought to define

[20] Agus, *"Modern Philosophies of Judaism,"* pp. 206, 207.
[21] *Ibid.*

the character of the Jewish elan, which he envisaged as a subterranean stream of consciousness, finding expression at various epochs in the emergence of mighty cultural and religious movements. The creative impulse of the Jewish people, he maintained, was not to be sought in the ideas and norms of Judaism, that are assembled in the Talmud, but in the unconscious drives that come to the surface in folk-piety, on the one hand, and in the prophetic-mystical experience of saints, on the other hand. The national "soul" of Israel is like a restless, surging stream, and the dogmas and rituals of official Judaism are the rocks and boulders thrown off by the raging waters.

Buber agreed with Ahad Ha'am in maintaining the thesis that the underlying genius of the Jewish national soul, the "Torah of the heart," must be distinguished from the dogmatic structure of the Jewish faith. But, while "Ahad Ha'am" regarded the pure doctrines of absolutist ethics as constituting the enduring substance of the Jewish way of life, . Buber insisted that the "inner Torah" was no rational ideology of any kind, but an intuitive grasp of the nature of man's relation to the Supreme Being. The Jew of history, especially as he appears in the Holy Scriptures, interpreted the travail of human destiny in terms which derived from this intuitive vision. However, the vision itself cannot ever be fully concretized in man-made schemes. Hence, the successive rise and fall of mystical movements in Jewish life, each endeavoring to renew and recapture the dynamic substance of faith, which consists in a direct confrontation of the human soul with the Living God.

Buber's contribution to the contemporary ferment of ideas consists of three fundamental ideas, which he has elaborated in a great number of books:

(a) The national soul of Israel is the fundamental reality in the spiritual life of all Jews. The artist and the writer become creative, only when they permit the unconscious spirit within them to operate freely. And the unconscious spirit of the individual is at bottom merely an expression of the Great Unconscious spirit of the nation. Hence, it is as a son of one's people, and only as such, that any individual can address himself meaningfully to humanity.

"Now, the folk is to him (the individual) a community of people who were, are and will be a community of dead, living and those yet unborn, who together constitute a unity; and this is his "I" which is but a necessary link eternally determined to occupy a definite place in this great chain. What all the people in this great chain have created and will create, that he feels to be the work of his own inner life; what they have experienced and will experience, that he perceives to be his own inner fate."[22]

The individual Jew is so constituted that he is inevitably sensitive to all contradictions and imperfections of society. Hence, he is always in search of the "Kingdom of God." But, the meaning of his restless striving cannot become clear for him unless he learns to understand himself as a Jew, "for only the one truly bound to his people can answer with his whole being."[23]

To discover his own true being, the Jew must learn to embrace in mind and heart the entire history of his people.

"All religious creation, all genuine personal religion is a discovery and a taking up of an ancient treasure, a development and a liberation of the grown subterranean religion."[24]

(b) In the Hassidic movement of eighteenth century Poland, Buber finds a modern expression of this "subterranean" religion. While Buber does not accept the dog-

---

[22] *"Reden über das Judentum,"* First Lecture.
[23] *"Heruth,"* p. 8.
[24] *Ibid,* p. 10.

matic substructure of Hassidic piety, he calls attention to the pattern of living which arose spontaneously among the untutored, poverty-stricken masses of southern Poland, reflecting the Jewish yearning of God's sovereignty.

In his numerous works on the subject of Hassidism, he stresses especially the following points:

(1) The hassid is perpetually ready for the appearance of God's redemptive power. Hence, his childlike naivete and his eagerness to believe the miracles of the saints. Hence, too, the awakening of the myth-building faculty among the masses. As Plato discovered long ago, it is only through myths that the paradoxical nature of reality may be grasped.

(2) The hassid is taught to worship God in rapture and ardor, and the "tzaddik" attains high levels of ecstasy in his worship. Thus, God is found by the dark and mysterious paths of feeling, not on the prosaic highway of reason.

(3) The hassid achieves unity in his own personality. He is not engaged in an endless struggle against his own lower nature. But, body and soul are joined together in joyous adoration of God.

(4) The hassid is not other-worldly. He is taught to concentrate his efforts upon the achievement of the good life here on earth, especially by way of "deeds of loving kindness." Nor is he expected to confine himself to the well-trodden pathways of ritual piety. The hassid was bidden to discover fresh ways of expressing his religious feeling.

(5) The hassidic community, in which the "tzaddik" forms the living center, is an illustration of the warm fellow-feeling of a society based upon a common religious experience. It is through the confrontation by his soul of the Supreme Being that man attains a gen-

erosity of spirit which makes possible his wholehearted entrance into the intimacies of a genuine, organic community.

(c) Man confronts God as a "person" and enters into a dialogue with Him. In saying "Thou" to God, man discovers his own "I," as a responsible self, a partner of the Lord in the creation of the good society. Buber has described the "I-Thou" dialogue-relationship in so thorough and brilliant a manner that no student of modern thought can afford to ignore it.

Following are the essential points in his presentation:

(1) The "I-Thou" relation is basically different from the attitude that we assume toward things, which he designates as the "I-it" relation. In dealing with things, we live in a world where we ourselves constitute the center. But, in facing a person, we enter a new dimension of existence, where the relation subsisting between the persons involved becomes itself the fiery core of reality.

"If I face a human being as my *Thou,* and say the primary word *I-Thou* to him, he is not a thing among things, and does not consist of things. . . . But, with no neighbor, and whole in himself, he is *Thou* and fills the heavens. This does not mean that nothing exists except himself. But, all else lives in his light."[25]

(2) Though we address human persons as "Thou," we feel that our perception of their personality extends beyond the appearance that confronts us. There is the radiance of infinity about the "Thou" relation, so that we glimpse the Supreme Personality looming behind those who evoke the word "Thou" from us, in all its depth and pathos. "In each *Thou,* we address the eternal Thou."[26]

[25] *"I and Thou,"* p. 8.
[26] *Ibid,* p. 6.

(3) The "I-Thou" relation is wholly quality, not quantity, entirely in the present, not in the space-time world. Thus, it comes as an augury of a domain of existence that is different from the space-time world which we are inclined to regard as the whole of being. It is the key to reality.

(4) Love is the apex of the "I-Thou" relation.

"Love is the responsibility of an 'I' for a 'Thou.' In this lies the likeness—impossible in any feeling whatsoever—of all who love, from the smallest to the greatest and from the blessedly protected man, whose life is rounded in that of a loved being, to him who is all his life nailed to the cross of the world, and who ventures to bring himself to the dreadful point—to love *all men*."[27]

(5) It is through our readiness to love all men and all things and to address them in word and deed as "Thou," that we find God in the world. For God is the eternal Thou. "Men do not find God if they stay in the world. They do not find Him if they leave the world. He who goes out with his whole being to meet his *Thou* and carries it to all being that is in the world, finds Him who cannot be sought."

"If you explore the life of things and of conditioned being you come to the unfathomable, if you deny the life of things and of conditioned being you stand before nothingness, if you hallow this life you meet the living God."[28]

(6) Buber repudiates the goals of so many mystics—that of union with the Divine Being or that of absorption into the Divine Abyss. To him, the ecstatic apex of the "Thou" relation is still a relation between two beings,

[27] "*I and Thou*," p. 15.
[28] "*I and Thou*," p. 79.

and there is no loss of personality. At this point, Buber parts company—and very distinctly—with the vast majority of mystics in Christianity and in the Hindu world.

(7) The dialogue-relation implies a mutual need on the part of both man and God.

"You know always in your heart that you need God more than everything; but do you not know too that God needs you—in the fullness of His eternity, needs you?"[29]

(8) The "I-Thou" relation is double faceted—addressed to man, it points to God; addressed to God, it points to man.

"Meeting with God does not come to man in order that he may concern himself with God, but in order that he may confirm that there is meaning in the world."[30]

In sum, Buber's philosophy is a lengthy homily on the meaning of human and Divine love. The full import of his message is only now beginning to be felt in America.

Prof. Abraham J. Heschel is the exponent of neo-mysticism on the American scene. A member of the faculty of the Jewish Theological Seminary, he is a scholarly and brilliant defender of a non-dogmatic type of Hassidism. Holiness is, to him, a dimension of existence, of which all men are aware, in gradations varying from the sense of wonder and bafflement of the average person to the overwhelming, lightning-like tremors of the saint in the blessed moments of ecstasy. Hence, piety is not a subjective attitude, but a "response" to the Divine call.

"What gives rise to faith is not a sentiment, a state of mind, an aspiration, but an everlasting fact in the universe,

29 *Ibid,* p. 82.
30 *Ibid,* p. 115.

something which is prior to and independent of human knowledge—*the holy dimension* of all existence."[31]

God needs man even as man needs God, and in obedience to the Divine Law, man joins in the fulfillment of the Divine Will. "The pagan gods had selfish needs, while the God of Israel is only in need of man's integrity.[32]

But, "man's integrity" includes his endless yearnings for the good life, yearnings which interpenetrate every aspect of life. Hence, the Law, guiding our life must be regarded as an organic unity, not as a collection of precepts.

"What constitutes the Jewish form of living is not so much the performance of single good deeds, the taking of a step now and then, as the pursuit of a way, being on the way; not so much the acts of fulfilling as the state of being committed to the task, of belonging to an order in which single deeds, aggregates of religious feeling, sporadic sentiments, moral episodes become parts of a complete pattern."[33]

In illustration of this central purpose of building the dimension of holiness into life, Prof. Heschel describes the institution of the Sabbath as "a palace in time with a Kingdom for all."[34] Glancing away from any considerations regarding the origin of the Sabbath or the need of modifying some of its laws, the author devotes himself to the task of explicating the mood of the Sabbath as being the focus of time touched by eternity, spent in mystical wonder and contemplation in contrast to the space-oriented mood of work and civilization. As the approach of the mystic stands in polar opposition to the scientific and pragmatic attitude, so does the spirit of the Sabbath when time is lived with intimations of eternity, differ from the secular and mundane spirit.

[31] *"Man Is Not Alone,"* p. 237.
[32] *Ibid,* p. 245.
[33] *Ibid,* p. 270.
[34] A. J. Heschel, *"The Sabbath."*

It follows that one may not enter the Holy of Holies of Judaism with the boots and tools that are generated by the "spirit of the age." Only from within is reform possible, issuing out of the organic growth of the spirit in the domain of holiness.

Thus, mysticism as a living experience, a communicable mood and a popular attitude functions as a potent brake upon the process of ritualistic reformation and modernization.

I. The Contribution of Rationalism.

The predominant position of Halachah or law in the Jewish pattern of piety was cited by Christian theologians in both ancient and modern times as proof of the "inferiority" of Judaism. Is not the "inwardness" of feeling far superior to the concern of the Pharisee with the exactitude of ritual performance and the casuistries of the Law? By the same token, Jewish scholars are wont to point to the rationality and sober balance of a faith that is firmly raftered by the pillars and joints of a God-given law. Doubtless, the most closely reasoned exposition of the virtue of reverence for law is contained in the massive volumes of Hermann Cohen, the greatest philosopher that German Jewry has produced.

Continuing along Kant's pathway of "critical idealism," Cohen declared the quality of lawfulness to be the ultimate goal of all "pure" directions of the spirit. In the labors of pure reason for the comprehension of the nature of Being, we must not expect to stop at any point and say, "that much is given to us from without as our ineluctable starting-point." As we probe deeper and deeper into the nature of the universe, we find that every material substance inevitably dissolves into a mathematical formula, and the elements of this formula may in turn be analyzed and further resolved into more ultimate elements. Hasn't this process been revealed in the evolution of modern science during the past century, as molecules gave way to atoms, atoms to electrons and protons, while these in turn are even now steadily being decomposed into mesons, waves, curvatures of space, foci of electromagnetic waves, and what not? This process is necessarily endless for the human mind can rest only in the stable groove of a formula describing the laws of change.

Even so, in the domains of ethics and esthetics, the productions of the human spirit take on more and more the quality of lawfulness as they attain progressive refinement through the ages. "Pure" ethics is not a matter of "feeling" kind or charitable, but of acting in accord with an inwardly acknowledged law of action. Cohen envisaged the course of history as leading to a progressive unfolding and expansion of "culture-consciousness," which consists in its turn of the three basic quests of the human personality for truth, for rightness and for beauty. Each one of these quests is fulfilled in the discovery of immutable laws governing the fundamental areas of being.

In Cohen's system, religion constitutes at once the source, the apex and the unifying factor of the unfolding "culture-consciousness." The culture of our age is not the creation of saints, scientists and artists, but their collective discovery. All true discoverers share in common the capacity to overcome selfish concerns and private prejudices so as to apprehend reality as a whole and see it truly. Thus, it is the self-transcending impulse of religion that impels the builders of culture in all domains, though, in their pursuit of a partial goal, they sometimes forget to take account of the fundamental craving for truth which is the stirring of God within their soul.

The God-idea rises out of the hunger for purity, which takes these forms—the assurance of the thinker that reason corresponds to reality and is not merely a human delusion, the faith of the ethical personality that its laws of human action are true to the fundamental nature of things, and the intuition of the artist that beauty of all types is a reflection of the inner harmony of the universe. Inner truthfulness is the ultimate premise and validation of our emergent "culture-consciousness," and this quality of truthfulness is the source of the quest for beauty, righteousness, and truth. Thus, religion, like the God-idea, is twofold in nature. It is a quest for the laws of true being and faith in their validity.

It follows that the virtue of reverence for law should be fundamental in our religious consciousness. Indeed, in Judaism, the believer is trained to be law-abiding, and hence perpetually hungry for the "purity" of conscience and the "purity" of the understanding. Cohen did not believe in a sudden, one-time revelation of the Law at Sinai, but he regarded the central insight of Judaism that piety must be molded through the forms of law as being of decisive importance. It is through mind and conscience that God is revealed in our "culture-consciousness," while the Law of Judaism is intended to fortify our reverence for the basic laws of being. The pious man does not seek to attain mystical oneness with God, but he aspires to make his personal existence count for the attainment of the Divine goals of perfection. To be concerned with the fate of one's soul in this life or in the hereafter is to succumb to the spell of the pagan mentality. Judaism, or the "religion of reason," trains its devotees to labor, not for personal salvation, but for the building of the ideal society. The Jew asks, not "how do I find salvation for my soul?" but "what is my vocation?" or better still, "how can I best serve the goals implied in the eternal laws of thought, ethics and esthetics?" Piety, then, consists in the inner acceptance of the laws of being as the basis of a code of personal behavior.

Manifestly, Cohen's elaborately developed philosophy

served to fortify the Conservative position, especially its insistence on the need of retaining the legal molds of Jewish piety and legislating new standards whenever necessary, in order to cultivate the sense of reverence for the Law.

J.   The Emergence of Existentialism.

The genius of Franz Rosenzweig is felt as a living influence in the intellectual circles that incline toward the impassioned decisiveness of existentialism. Starting out with the insistence that man cannot relate himself to God by the sheer process of objective thought, Rosenzweig declared that the human individual, in his inward being, continuously rebels against the abstractions of philosophy that deny the worth of individual existence. At the same time, our soul is unhappy when left alone in isolation from the universe. It finds the meaning of its life and destiny in the message of love that is directed to it from Him who dwells behind the veil of existence. Thereafter, the soul seeks to unfold the infinite implications of the assurance of Divine love that has come to it. True philosophy, then, begins with an act which is prior to thought, an act which transpires in the space-time world, between two ultimate beings, the individual and God, who endure in the realm of eternity.

In Rosenzweig's view, the Jewish people as a whole owes its unique character and destiny to such an act of Divine Love—an act of revelation, which the collective consciousness of the Jewish people has translated into a host of sacred books and a Law. It is through the Law that the Jewish people have been lifted out of the stream of history and removed from the ceaseless battle of nations for the goods of this world. The Law became for Israel a substitute for land, language, culture and government. Yet, Judaism is more than Law, consisting in that deposit of Divine energy that had been placed by God in the historic memory of the Jewish people.

The bold sweep of Rosenzweig's thought may be captured in a few sentences, but the full import can only be gained from a close study of his writings. Behind the veil of phenomena in the visible universe, Rosenzweig recognizes three ultimate elements—the world as it is in itself, subsisting behind all appearances; the human soul in its deepest reality, apart from the ideas, notions and sentiments floating on the surface of consciousness; God, as He is in Himself, apart from all ideas and arguments concerning Him. Each one of these elements can only be pointed to, but not grasped in thought. Yet, there are contacts between these ultimate elements. The contact between God and men is revelation, the contact between God and the world is creation, the contact between man and the world is redemption.

How do we know that such contacts do indeed take place? The emergence of ever higher forms of life in the cosmic surge of evolution is one answer, demonstrating the continuance of Divine creation. And this argument has been elaborated in such philosophies as those of Henri Bergson and S. H. Alexander. Rosenzweig is interested more in the testimony of the human soul and in the evidence provided by the history of mankind. Out of the travail of his own soul, he had learned that currents of Divine love come to us in blessed moments, like healing rays from the sun, transforming our nature and stamping it with the seal of eternity. These sudden bursts of love from above he describes as acts of revelation, and the experience of Divine revelation he accounts to be the source of piety, and the final foundation of true philosophy.

"Whoever has not yet been reached by the voice of revelation has no right to accept the thought of creation as if it were a scientific hypothesis."

All philosophers, who derived their inspiration from Aristotle, shied away from attributing love to God. Does not love imply needing someone else for self-fulfillment, whereas God is self-sufficient and perfect? Rosenzweig finds in love the one key to the ultimate processes of being. "Love is like language itself, sensual-suprasensual." Love, he points out, comes in two phases—the love of the lover and the beloved. God's love or revelation is the love of the lover, a "momentary self-transformation," shifting from eternity into time, from the absolute stillness of His Being into contact with a particular person or people.

Love is essentially a give and take proposition. Hence, it is experienced in the flow of speech and the rapture of song, while it eludes forever the static mesh of mathematical logic. God's healing Grace, and the receptive humble human soul meet on the fleeting borderline of time and eternity, in an event so utterly unique as to be indescribable. A dialogue between two people in love, who find in each other the fulfillment of their life, furnishes the closest analogy to the event of revelation.

"Does God take the first step, or does man? Is it possible for man to take it? This is a real question. . . . The whole matter continues in the form of an unending dialogue. . . ." [35]

While the love of the lover is arbitrary and momentary, the awakened love of the human soul is as that of the beloved, expressed in a yearning to disseminate love to one's fellowmen and in a humble waiting or solitary prayer for the repetition of the miracle of revelation and the final consummation of its promise. As the wordless glow of the blessed moment yields to the coolness and clarity of speech, God's parting message is phrased as a command to live in love. "Thou shalt love the Lord, Thy God," and "thou shalt love thy neighbor as thyself." Also, the human soul touched by

[35] *"Franz Rosenzweig,"* by Nahum Glatzer, p. 286.

the Divine ray of revelation knows itself to be "chosen" as an instrument of redemption—"I have called thee by thy name; you are mine."

The Holy Scriptures and the sacred literature of Judaism are divinely revealed in the sense that the creative elan which projected them into existence was the genuine reflection of Divine love. This fact may be seen in the congruence of the Bible with this philosophy of love and in the historical effect of the Bible. For human history is the actual record of the process of redemption.

"The Bible is not the most beautiful book in the world, not the deepest, the truest, the wisest, the most fascinating and whatever other superlatives there may be—at least no one can be convinced of these advantages who is not already prejudiced in its favor. But the Bible is the most important book. This one can prove, and even the most enraged Bible-hater has to admit this at least for the past, and through his inveterate hatred, he admits it also for the present. For here there is no question of personal taste or of disposition of the soul or of spiritual direction, but only a question of the hitherto transpired events of world history."[36]

Naturally, Rosenzweig does not accept the doctrine of literal revelation, since the content of revelation is simply the Divine mystery of love. Thus, he wrote to an exponent of neo-orthodoxy:

"Our difference from Orthodoxy consists in the circumstance that we cannot draw any conclusions concerning the literary process of the composition of the Bible and the philological value of the traditional text out of our belief in the sacredness and the peculiar value of Torah. If Wellhausen and all his theories were indeed right, and if the Samaritans really possessed a better text, that would not touch our belief in the slightest."[37]

[36] *"Kleine Schriften,"* p. 178.
[37] *"Briefe,"* p. 581.

Rosenzweig's reverence for history led him to esteem every facet of Jewish life and to stigmatize as "little Jews" the Zionists who reduced Judaism to ethnicism and the Orthodox who froze it into the neat package of what they called Torah. He saw the focal center of Jewish loyalty in the inner acknowledgement of being part of the Jewish people. The sense of blood-unity cannot but lead to the feeling of oneness with the fateful destiny of the Jewish people, and the living community in turn is but the expression in history of the "chosenness" of the Jewish people, by an act of Divine love. Dramatized in the Holy Scriptures in the majestic imagery of the Covenant at Sinai, the "chosenness" of Israel makes of its ethnic base and its spiritual message an unbreakable entity, so that any identification with Jewish life, be it ever so tenuous in the beginning, cannot but lead to the full acceptance of Judaism in the richness of its totality—unless this process is artifically blocked by false concepts of the nature of Jewish life.

The richly suggestive quality of Rosenzweig's thought can hardly be conveyed in any summary. Hegelian to the core, he was empirical in approach, thoroughly undogmatic and self-critical, gentle and saintly—a *homo religiosus* in every fiber of his being. In the past decade, the vogue of Rosenzweig has been growing steadily among American intellectuals. Yet, the German idiom of his thought sets a definite limit to his influence.

Recently Will Herberg assayed to expound the philosophy of existentialism in the dramatic and popular manner of an American journalist. The unhappy dependence of philosophy upon temperament is demonstrated in the transformation of the gentle piety of the Frankfurt saint into the ebullient bouyancy of the "leap of faith" by the impulsive and impetuous Herberg.

In "Judaism and the Modern Man," Will Herberg asserts

first the utter meaninglessness and frustration of life when a man takes himself to be the "measure of all things." The individual cannot find meaning in his own existence, and, in his despair, he looks to a collective entity for the sustenance of his spirit. Thus, the proletariat, the nation or the racial blood-stream becomes the false surrogate for God.

Since then man cannot live without faith in something, the only true alternative before us is the idolatry of our self, individual or collective, or the worship of God. A "leap of faith" is called for, whereby the self emerges out of the imaginary shell which encloses it and finds itself to be suspended from a Divine thread. But, so paradoxical is the nature of faith, that, when once acquired, it appears to have been inescapable.

"We must dare the leap if the gulf is ever to be crossed; but once the decision of faith has been made, it is seen that the leap was possible only because the gulf had already been bridged for us from the other side." [38]

In other words, faith is at once a human, subjective act and a Divine objective fact. Thus, God is not the passive and hidden Ground of Being, but an active Spirit that is somehow akin to our deepest self.

"The ascription of personality to God is thus an affirmation of the fact that in the encounter of faith God meets us as person to person."[39]

It is the Grace of God that makes human rightness possible, not only in the act of faith but in all the spheres of human life.

"The weakness and evil in man operate out of the freedom of his own nature; his capacity for good, though grounded in his nature, needs the Grace of God for its realization."[40]

In this sense, Herberg accepts the reality of "original sin,"

[38] Will Herberg, *"Judaism and the Modern Man,"* p. 39.
[39] *Ibid,* p. 60.
[40] *Ibid,* p. 76.

balancing it by the belief in man's "original perfection" that is due to the unfailing availability of Divine Grace. Human life is perpetually in danger of relapsing from God and into the frustration of sin. Hence, the drama of salvation.

"The salvation we crave is salvation from the fears, the futilities, the frustrations of existence. . . .

"Estranged from God, we are torn out of the very texture of being and left a mere fragment, cut off from the only real source of security available to us. Is it any wonder that thus isolated from what is real within and without, our existence loses its foundation and we are compelled to live out our lives in restless frustration, forever trembling at the brink of chaos and dissolution?"[41]

Up to this point, Herberg developed the general ideology of existentialism, which sees the entire panorama of life from the viewpoint of man facing God in the moment of decision. Proceeding to the analysis of Jewish life and destiny, the author insists on the "uniqueness" of the phenomenon of the Jew, resulting from the covenant between God and Israel that had been effected by an enduring "existential" relationship.

Steering a middle course between fundamentalism and modernism, Herberg accepts the Holy Bible as Divine Revelation, insofar as it tells of the perennial encounter between God and man. Yet, more, Scripture tells of "the self-disclosure of God in his dealings with the world." Revelation is an event in history, divine in substance but human in expression. As the medieval, rationalistic expounders of the Bible found the philosophy of Aristotle in the words of Scripture, so Herberg insists that Scripture is true, but only as interpreted in existential fashion.

"The views of Abraham on the nature of things and even on the 'nature' of the divine were presumably far more

[41] Will Herberg, *"Judaism and the Modern Man,"* pp. 116, 117.

'primitive' than those of Isaiah so many centuries later, but their faith was the same, for they stood in the same crisis of confrontation with God, shared the same ultimate covenantal commitment, and recognized the same Lord and His absolute claim."[42]

Are all works reflecting the same faith equally revealed? Herberg hedges away from this conclusion, declaring that "revelation" at Sinai was for Jews "einmalig," once and for all, " not in the sense of course that God thereafter no longer reveals Himself in his contact with men but in the sense that all other 'visitations' of God, both before and after, yield their meaning only when seen with the eyes of faith from the perspective of this central event."[43]

The circularity of this argument is manifest. Scriptures are read with "the eyes of faith," as faith is contemporaneously understood, and then it becomes the standard of judgment of all other revelation. From a modernist viewpoint, there is no harm in this continuous interaction, Scripture being accepted by collective consent and convention as the text and context of organized religion. But, Herberg takes pains to deny "general" revelation as being a "possibility in fact." He insists that "though God is everywhere to be discerned in his person, activity and works, the mind of sinful man is incapable of finding him through his own unaided powers."[44] If then we cannot trust our modern world-view to be the adequate basis for the separation of the true core of "revelation" from the human and relative myths with which it is encrusted, how can we look to Scripture for guidance? For the Orthodox, the word of God is clearly spelled out in literal truth, and for the liberals, who trust the insight and values of humanity, there is a solid enough base for the

42 *Ibid*, p. 248.
43 Will Herberg, *"Judaism and the Modern Man,"* p. 251.
44 *Ibid*, p. 255.

interpretation of "revelation," distinguishing between the life-giving, eternal grain and the tasteless chaff. But, to accept Scriptures in "essence" only while denying the validity of our human power to discriminate between the shadow and the substance of faith is to maintain a logically indefensible position. "Existentially," of course, the solid basis is the psychological experience of faith, as a felt, immediate awareness of Divine love, containing its own illumination and validation.

The same paradoxical notion is entertained by the author in regard to the concept of Israel. While he does not accept the fundamentalist interpretation of the doctrine of the "chosen people," he insists that "the history of Israel" constitutes a mode of self-revelation of God. It is through the life of Israel, in all its particularity, that God reveals His message to mankind.

"If God is a Living God, operative in and through the particularities of history, then it no longer seems so strange that he should effect His purposes through particular groups of people or even that he should 'create' particular groups for his special purposes."[45]

Herberg maintains, then, that "salvation is of the Jews," in conscious defiance of the entire sweep of modernity and the broad tolerance of liberalism. The very being of Israel is a mysterious anomaly, which can not be understood in the mundane terms of sociology. We are a "unique" people, unclassifiable with other groups and incomprehensible by ordinary human standards.

"It is a *supernatural* community, called into being by God to serve his eternal purposes in history. It is a community created by God's special act of covenant, first with Abraham, whom he 'called' out of the heathen world, and then supremely, with Israel corporately at Sinai."[46]

[45] Herberg, *"Judaism and the Modern Man,"* p. 264.
[46] *Ibid,* p. 271.

This "super-historical" community is charged with the mission of bringing "salvation" to the world. The Jew lives his life "authentically" when he responds affirmatively to the demands and duties that are implied in "Jewish covenant-existence." It is through the laws of the Torah that the Jew takes his "authentic" place in the cosmic scheme of things. But, Torah for the existentialist does not mean simply the rigid precepts of the "Schulchan Aruch." Since it is upon the personal experience of faith that his piety is founded, the author insists on the need of taking account of the human and historical elements in the ritual of Judaism. As a blend of the historical and the "super-historical," the Torah must not be frozen into a rigid set of unvarying laws. "It is the historical belief and practice of the community of Israel— Kelal Yisroel—that provides us with the contents of 'halakah.' "[47]

In sum, Jewish existentialism begins with that double phased experience, which is an act of Grace on the part of God and a "leap of faith" on the part of man at one and the same time. In the light of this total commitment of the soul, the biblical-rabbinic faith emerges as a satisfying exposition of the meaning of human life and the Divine Imperative. The people of Israel emerged through a similar collective "existential" experience, and its entire being is forever caught in the tension between the historical and the "super-historical." The "authentic" response of the individual to the Divine call is to live the life of holiness, and for the Jew, this authentic response implies the wholehearted acceptance of the Law, insofar as it is a living reality to the conscience of "Catholic Israel."

K. *The "Reconstructionist" Movement.*

The "left" wing of the Conservative movement consists of

[47] Herberg, *"Judaism and the Modern Man,"* p. 299.

the disciples and followers of Prof. Mordecai M. Kaplan, for many years the leading member of the faculty of the Jewish Theological Seminary. For seventeen years now, this intra-Conservative group has been loosely organized in a Reconstructionist fellowship, which has its headquarters in the Society for the Advancement of Judaism. "The Reconstructionist," a brilliantly edited and exceedingly stimulating bi-weekly, is the official organ of this group. In addition, a number of pamphlets and books have been published by The Reconstructionist Society in furtherance of its views.

In some of its projects, The Reconstructionist Fellowship transcends the lines of denominational differences, especially in its advocacy of varied programs for the Jewish community as a whole. Also, some Reform rabbis have joined the fellowship, which remains however predominantly Conservative in orientation and practice.

In general, the Reconstructionist trend might be described as pragmatic in philosophy, liberal in theology and national-istic in emphasis. The awkward name chosen by the group reflects the central plank of its platform—to reconstruct the chaotic conglomeration that is contemporaneous American Jewry after the pattern of the "organic community." In place of the crazy-quilt jumble of organizations, the Reconstruc-tionalists contend, there should be formed in each city an all-inclusive communal organization that would provide for every legitimate need and ideal of its members. The rise of the Welfare Funds and Community Councils is a welcome development in this direction, but, even if this process is con-summated in every city, the result will still fall short of the goal of an "organic community." For, while these communal agencies undertake to provide for the philanthropic and rec-reational needs of the people, they rarely assume full respon-sibility for the task of Jewish education and they do not ever undertake to minister to the religious needs of the community. In the "organic community," the synagogue and school should occupy the "nuclear" position, since religion constitutes the main expression of Jewish group life.

In effect, then, the Reconstructionists advocate that American Jewry give up the congregational form of organization, which is indigenous on the American scene, and return instead to the "Kehillah" pattern of Central and Eastern Europe. As to the difficulty of reconciling conflicting interpretations of Judaism, Dr. Kaplan maintains that the Jewish community might well follow the example of any modern nation, which fosters the principle of "unity in diversity." The "organic community" should not find it an insuperable task to work out an equitable arrangement whereby all interpretations of Judaism would be treated with equal consideration and its constituent members would attend the synagogues of their choice.

In addition, to its religious and educational functions, the community-organization would provide through designated committees for Zionist work, public-relations, philanthropic and recreational activities, so that there would be no need for any independent or supplementary organization. Also, those activities which are now neglected, such as new creations in art and music, would be assiduously cultivated by the "organic community," which would envision Jewish life as a whole and lovingly care for its every phase and expression. The separate "organic communities" would be organized into a national community and ultimately into a world-community that would take its place beside the great national states of the world.

"World Jewry should unite as a people, and apply to the United Nations for recognition of its claim to peoplehood."[48]

This plan for the reorganization of American Jewish life is not suggested simply on the ground of neatness of structure

[48] *"The Future of the American Jew,"* p. 80.

or efficiency in operation. For Dr. Kaplan, the "organic community" is an expression in organizational terms of the essential character of the Jewish people. If the pattern of organization does not correspond to the dynamic forces that are operative in any group, then the group disintegrates in frustration and despair. For organizational structure is to the living ideology of a group, as the body is to the soul. In every phase of its organized life, American Jewry should express its character as an ethnic-cultural group, its enduring "peoplehood," so as to articulate and keep alive the "we" feeling of the individual Jew. By his membership in the "organic community," the individual expresses his sense of belonging to the Jewish people, and it is this sense of sharing in the life and destiny of a people that is the matrix of all its cultural creations and values.

In the Reconstructionist ideology, the Conservative emphasis on the living people in the triad of people, God and Torah is carried to its outermost limit. Judaism is defined as the evolving religious civilization of the Jewish people. In his magnum opus, "Judaism as a Civilization," Dr. Kaplan omitted the adjective, "religious," which the Reconstructionist fellowship now uses invariably. Even so, the factor of faith is conceived as only one of the elements of Jewish civilization, though historically the dominant one. It is conceivable that religion in the future might be expressed through forms of cooperative living that have nothing in common with the rites and even the ideas of traditional Judaism. Also, it is quite possible that the creative genius of the people will be unfolded in cultural directions other than those of faith and ethics—such as art, for example. The high esteem for creative expression, among the Reconstructionists, leads them to accord to the domain of art a supreme rank among the shining constellations of the Jewish spirit. Writes Dr. Kaplan in his latest major work, "We can be sure of a Jewish future only when Jewish art is so developed as to reconcile the Jew to his lot in life."[49] As if the art of the ancient Greeks, superb as it undoubtedly was, availed to maintain the Greek people, once they exchanged the gods of Olympus for the Savior from Nazareth!

The Reconstructionists do not minimize the role of religion in the "religious civilization" that is Judaism, especially for Diaspora Jewry, but they maintain that religion itself derives its vital power from the "we"-feeling of the people. The Jewish religion lost its hold upon the masses of our people, when the sense of ethnic loyalty was weakened by outside attractions and inner disorganization. The substitution in America of fragmentary congregational and denominational loyalties for the massive loyalty to the Jewish community as a whole served to weaken the purely religious sentiments of our people.

"It is significant that in past ages, when Jews led an autonomous communal life, this particular complaint that the individual could not experience God in the worship of the synagogue was unheard of."[50]

This assertion is manifestly belied by the sad decline of the Jewish faith in the communities of Poland and Germany that were organized on a Kehillah-basis. Yet, it derives necessarily from the Reconstructionist conception of religion as the sublimation of group-feeling.

On this view, religion springs out of the life of the people, its social function being to hallow and to fortify the institutions, things, events and memories that the people require for their collective existence. Hence, a religion is woefully weakened when it is abstracted into a system of salvation and separated from the ethnic aspirations and concerns of the people among whom it has arisen. Dr. Kaplan asserts this

[49] *"The Future of the American Jew,"* p. 118.
[50] *"Meaning of God in Modern Jewish Religion,"* p. 246.

claim in spite of the magnificent historical triumph of the Christian faith, maintaining that "national creeds" will in time replace the unitary Christian faith, which has arisen through the impetus of "religious imperialism."[51] Like the titans of mythology, a religion is powerful only when it retains contact with the soil of national life, in all its varied and earthy ambitions.

"The Jewish people has demonstrated the validity of the principle, which has been repeatedly verified by the experience of mankind, that a folk religion retains its relevance and vitality so long as it confines itself to those who have evolved it."[52]

It follows that the Jewish religion can only be regenerated if it is put back into the total complex of Jewish life, the individual congregation yielding to the all-inclusive community as the basic unit of identification, and the rites of religion surrendering their claim to the exclusive loyalty of the Jew in favor of all other forms of cultural expression.

"Paradoxical as it may sound, the spiritual regeneration of the Jewish people demands that religion cease to be its sole preoccupation."[53]

The will to live as a Jew is the fundamental source and motivation of Jewish existence, but, to be deserving of our highest loyalty, the life we seek must be conceived in the loftiest spiritual terms. Hence, the emphasis on the creation of new values and the construction of social instruments to serve the high ends of prophetic idealism. "All this effort at reconstruction and reinterpretation must come entirely from the urge of an inward creative life."[54]

The supernaturalist motivations of the traditional Jewish

---

[51] *"Judaism as a Civilization,"* p. 340.
[52] *Ibid,* p. 343.
[53] *Ibid,* p. 345.
[54] *"The Meaning of Reconstructionism,"* p. 25.

faith should be replaced by a this-worldly interpretation of salvation—i.e., the individual fulfills his highest potentialities through the disciplines of the spirit in general and the Jewish way of life in particular. In turn, the Jewish people justifies its existence and survival, by transforming itself into an instrument for the elicitation of the greatest spiritual potential from the Jewish individual.

As to the idea of God, the Reconstructionists are hopelessly pragmatic. The conception of God as the ideal Personality they reject, preferring to think of Him as a "process that makes for salvation."

"It is paradoxical," they maintain, "for a person not to be associated with a physical body," thus dismissing out of hand the long philosophical tradition dating from Plato and Philo and represented in modern philosophy by Lotze in Germany and Bowne in America. The term, "process," reflects the view of modern physics that all existents are not static things, but events in time, or processes. As to how this particular process operates either in nature or in human nature, they are unwilling to speculate provided this "belief in God" results in a commitment to live life on a high spiritual plane. In the words of Kaplan, "when we believe in God, we believe that reality—the world of inner and outer being, the world of society and of nature—is so constituted as to enable man to achieve salvation."[55] Or in still simpler, pragmatic terms, "God is what the world means to the man who believes in the possibility of maximum life and strives for it."[56]

Defined thus generally as an implication of man's striving for the life abundant, the choice between religious faith and atheism is seen to depend more on the glandular makeup of a person than on intellectual arguments. Atheism, on this view, is either a semantic error or a complex of the sickly and

[55] *"Meaning of God in Jewish Religion,"* p. 26.
[56] *Ibid,* p. 328.

131

the frustrated. The intellectual assent to abstract truths that is implied in faith is reduced to the barest minimum. After the fashion of the behaviorists, who did not believe that mental processes were truly causative factors in the determination of human conduct, Dr. Kaplan writes, "The belief in God is not logically inferred from the will to live. It is the psychic manifestation of the will to live." [57] By the same token, the practice of worship is described as an implication of the same "will to live."

"The need for communing with that Power is part of our very will to live as human beings." [58]

With this concept of God and religion, it follows that rituals and ceremonies cannot be accepted as literally revealed precepts, nor as expressions of fundamental truths, but as socially evolved aids to the good life, or, more technically as "religious folkways." We cannot speak of "law" in Jewish religion, the Reconstructionists declare, since we have no sanctions for the enforcement of legal directives. Also, the Jewish community as a whole could legislate only in regard to those elements that are common to all the interpretations and trends that are current in Jewish life. Thus, it can formulate the rules that are to govern the relationship of committees and societies to the central community organization, and it can also deal with the domain of "public law," such as marriage and divorce. In the sphere of rituals, each denominational trend may formulate its own guiding principles and standards, imputing no guilt to those who prefer other "folk-ways" for self-expression.

"The vocabulary of 'law,' 'sin,' 'pardon' is ideologically and pragmatically unjustified as applied to ritual."

Rites and ceremonies are forms of collective art, which spring ideally from the life of the people.

[57] *"Future of the Modern Jew,"* p. 172.
[58] *Ibid,* p. 184.

"But, the moment we get away from the legalistic approach, we treat Jewish observances as religious folkways designed to ensure the enhancement of the value of Jewish life, the affirmative injunctions assume the more important role."[59]

In keeping with this emphasis on the enrichment of Jewish practice through creative expression, the Reconstructionists published a Passover Haggadah, which added hymns and readings concerning the ideal of freedom and the personality of Moses, while deleting passages which they considered unworthy, such as the enumeration of the plagues, the prayer for the punishment of Israel's enemies and the references to Israel as the "chosen people." In their view, the doctrine of the "chosen people" is an unworthy indulgence in self-glorification, no matter how fancifully it is reinterpreted. In this spirit, they edited and published a Prayer-Book, which was accepted for use, however, only in two synagogues.

L. Issues and Practice in the Conservative Movement.

The ideology of Reconstructionism functions as one of the trends within the Conservative movement—fairly influential in some directions, but falling short of predominance. The movement, for the most part, insists on a personal conception of the Deity, the unique historical position of Israel as the people of revelation, the recognition of the totality of the tradition as the source of authority rather than the folkways or practices of the people and the belief in the continued validity of Jewish Law or Halachah, when it is interpreted as part of a dynamic, life-oriented tradition.

For many years, the Law Committee of the Rabbinical Assembly functioned in strict compliance with the letter and spirit of the "Shulhan Aruch." Even the practice of mixed seating in the synagogue was not approved but only con-

59 *"Future of the American Jew," p. 424.*

doned in the spirit of the historian Zunz, who remarked that the spirit of peace and harmony in a community is more important than the harmony or disharmony of organ-music. Thus, in practice, Conservative congregations deviated from Orthodoxy while, in theory, the Law was declared to be unchanged. At the Convention held in Chicago in 1948, a resolution to the effect of binding the movement to strict compliance with the Shulhan Aruch was proposed and defeated. The Law Committee was then reorganized so as to reflect all trends within the movement. At its first meeting, it assumed the designation, Committee on Jewish Law and Standards, in order to indicate that its scope is the application of the totality of the tradition to Jewish life, not merely the interpretation of the letter of the Law. Nor was the Committee to be confined to the task of writing responses to specific inquiries. Wherever new standards were to be set up, the Committee was to propose and to formulate resolutions for the movement.

To the majority of its members, the process of legislating standards of ritual observance is a direct implication of the character of Jewish piety. In Judaism, man's response to the Divine challenge takes the form of a self-imposed "law" of action. While all men might concede the value of prayer and study, the religious Jew imposes upon himself the regular disciplines of prayer three times daily and the mitzvoth of Torah-study at fixed times. This response of the individual is guided and molded by the collective "laws" of the people, so that the resolve of each Jew is reinforced and conditioned by the acceptance and the observance of the entire group.

The fruitfulness of this approach was demonstrated in the analysis of the problem of Sabbath observance. The Committee did not substitute for the Sabbath-halachah a general principle, such as the obligation to hallow the day by positive actions only, nor did it proceed to interpret the Law in blithe disregard of existing conditions. Firstly, it set the problem in a positive setting by launching a campaign for the Revitalization of the Sabbath, calling upon all congregants to pledge the acceptance of certain minimal standards of Sabbath-observance—to refrain from doing work on the Sabbath which is avoidable and which is not in keeping with the spirit of the day, and to hallow the Sabbath-day by positive practices, such as Kiddush and candle lighting, attendance at services, etc. These general rules were spelled out in detail in the course of the campaign, which is even now in progress.

Secondly, the Committee affirmed the applicability of the principle of "takkanah"-legislation to our time and place. Jewish Law can be made and modified today in the same manner as it was made and modified in the past. Accordingly, the Committee called upon the Rabbinical Assembly to permit the practice of riding to the synagogue on the Sabbath, as a new "takkanah" designed to "strengthen the faith," a "takkanah" made necessary by the peculiar circumstances of American life. When it is difficult or impossible to walk, the Committee declared it to be a "mitzvah" to make use of motor transportation for the sake of attending public worship. This decision was approved by the majority-report of the Committee and accepted by the Rabbinical Assembly. The minority-report arrived at virtually the same conclusion.

Whether one "mitzvah" or another is to take precedence in the event of a conflict between their requirements is the kind of question that can only be weighed in the balance of contemporary needs and consequences. Which decision is likely to result in a more vital and meaningful faith for American Jews? In the light of this question only one answer was possible. Nor was it difficult for the Committee to cite specific precedents for the rule that a "great mitzvah" (mitzvah g'dolah) may set aside normal prohibitions. (espe-

135

cially as an "horaath sha-ah," a decision limited to a specific time and place). And regular attendance at Sabbath services is in the circumstances of American life today, a "great mitz-vah," essential for the vitality of our faith.

Thirdly, the Committee declared the use of electrical gad-gets on the Sabbath to be permitted, if the use to which they are put is in consonance with the holiness of the day. Mani-festly, electricity could not have been prohibited by Tal-mudic legislation, even as it could not have been specifically permitted. Therefore, the Committee proceeded to evaluate its use from the standpoint of its relation to contemporary needs, making use in its Responsum of technical distinctions in the Talmud for the purpose of overcoming technical difficulties.

At times, the Committee is stricter in the maintenance of religious standards than the bare letter of the Law. Thus, it makes use of its influence to dissuade Jewish organizations from holding business-meetings on the Sabbath, though tra-ditionally Jewish problems were discussed on holy days in medieval times, care being taken in those days to avoid infringement of the ritualistic laws. It is recognized that in modern circumstances not a shred would be left of the tradi-tional pattern of holiness if Jewish organizations were al-lowed to hold business meetings on the Sabbath. Also, the Committee is even now combatting the suggestion to permit Gentile players on the Sabbath to play dance music for the entertainment of dinner-guests at a Bar Mitzvah celebration in the vestry-hall of the synagogue. Ample precedent for this practice could be cited, from a strictly legalistic viewpoint, especially since the movement sanctions the employment of the organ at the services. Also, the Hassidim would dance on the Sabbath. But, in the opinion of the Committee, the con-sequences of this practice in the circumstances of American life would be deleterious to the dignity of the synagogue and the holiness of the Sabbath. Accordingly, the Committee called upon all Conservative synagogues to discountenance any such practice.

In the domain of Jewish Law, the main issue confronting the movement at this writing is the so-called "Agunah" question, which really includes a number of problems relating to marriage and divorce. Suppose the husband refuses to give a "get" or "halitzah," what recourse is left to the woman? What if a Kohen desires to marry a divorcee or a converted woman? What to do in the event of desertion when the woman obtains a divorce from the civil court and the whereabouts of the husband is unknown? What to do with the many cases that are classified by the government first as "missing in action" and later declared to be dead, without the testimony of living witness that is required by Jewish Law?

Already, in 1937, the late Rabbi J. L. Epstein proposed an elaborate plan involving the principle of conditioned marriage and making it possible for the woman to write her own "get," under the direction of a rabbinic court, in certain cases. Owing to the frantic protests of the Orthodox rabbis, this plan was never put into effect. The present plan of the Committee is all-embracing in scope and radical in approach. The principle of "takkanah"-legislation would be so employed as to solve the above-mentioned problem without removing the rabbi, and the Jewish faith he symbolizes, from the realm of divorce and remarriage. The details of this plan are even now under discussion, but there is virtual agreement within the movement, that Jewish law must be preserved through a dynamic process of interpretation and continuous legislation, reflecting the realities of our day.

5

Summation

Having surveyed the varied theological currents in American Judaism, we may be permitted a speculative prognosis of the future. Are the three major trends drawing closer together, so that we may expect the emergence of a unitary, American pattern, or are they stiffening their respective backs against one another? Both tendencies are in evidence for the present, and are likely to be operative in the foreseeable future. Organizationally, each trend is becoming steadily more effective, self-sufficient and self-conscious. Thus, in the past three years, the three Seminaries in New York launched three schools for the cantorate, each movement insisting on training their own functionaries even in the field of Jewish music. The Jewish Theological Seminary even maintains a Jewish Museum of its own, insisting that its philosophy of Jewish life is expressed in this project, as well as in its national radio and television program and in its Institute for Religious and Social Studies, which is planned for Christian theological students.

On the other hand, the laity of the three groups is largely indifferent to the interdenominational boundary lines. In the pragmatic atmosphere of America, Orthodoxy may fight against mixed pews in New York, while in Texas it may not only accept this and other modifications but point to these concessions as evidences that "change" is not incompatible with its dogmas. The prominent congregation in the Southwest which asked for a "rabbi who would act Conservative but claim to be Orthodox" reflected an attitude that is not rare among Orthodox laymen. The temptation to create hybrid syntheses is particularly strong in the new congregations in Long Island, N. Y., and Los Angeles, Cal., where "anything goes." Synagogues which conduct services with hats and "talaisim" using an Orthodox Prayer-Book may "go Reform" because they like the rabbi, need the subsidy or feel reflected social glory in belonging to the alignment that controls the country clubs. But, the study of these aberrations and combinations belongs to folklore rather than the philosophy of Judaism. Certain it is that not one of the three trends is rigidly fixed and completely isolated. The history of American Judaism is just beginning.

•

Part Two

THE JEWISH COMMUNITY

1

Goals of Jewish Living

NOTE: *This article was written before the establishment of the State of Israel, on May 14, 1948. Its argument today may well be read as a reply to the continuous insistence of Ben Gurion that Zionist loyalty implies the undertaking to settle in the land of Israel.*

1.   From Heaven to Earth

Zion, so long a flaming focus of Jewish feelings and loyalties, is now by the decision of the United Nations Assembly brought down from the blue heaven of dream and fantasy to the grey reality of earthly existence.

The new State can scarcely be expected to do justice to the utopian dimensions which the dream of Zion assumed in the consciousness of our people. Paradoxical as it may sound, the very realization of the dream will probably give rise to a wave of frustration and futility. In part, this melancholy pospect is due to the fact that the Zionist goal will, at last, be reached in but a fraction of the country originally envisaged in the Basle Program and the Balfour Declaration. Even in minds drugged for years by feverish propaganda, the present extent of the homeland cannot possibly loom so large so to hold forth the promise of greatness, leastwise "the solution of the Jewish problem." If, indeed, most of our displaced persons in Europe and a remnant of harassed Jewry in the

Arab lands are successfully transported to Palestine, the limits of its present capacity will have been reached.

Political Zionism, which set out to "normalize" the Jewish people through a State of their own, is now compelled to accept a situation in which their Diaspora existence must be reinterpreted as "normal" after all!

To be sure, in more recent times the Zionist program did not entertain the ambition of bringing all Jews to Palestine. But, in its commonly accepted form, Zionism looked forward to the eventual liquidation of the Diaspora, partly through emigration to the homeland and partly through assimilation. Emigration being out of the question for American Zionists even if they desired it, they now find that the theory of "redemption," which had been preached to them day in and day out, holds up only the unpalatable alternative of total assimilation. Having usurped the place of Judaism in their hearts, Zionism now leaves many of them directionless and confused, facing a spiritual void.

The awakening of the so-called *"Galuth*-affirmers" in the past year is an indication that this problem is moving rapidly to the center of the stage. Unfortunately, most of the Zionist *"Galuth*-affirmers" are hesitant and apologetic, almost shame-faced. Thus, one of them pleads with Zionist extremists to relent somewhat from their rigid position and admit "the right of American Jews to exist" because a powerful Diaspora is good for Palestinian Jews. It will be easier, he points out, for Palestinian merchants and artists to dispose of their products if there are prosperous Jewish communities in other lands, particularly in America. Other writers, arguing similarly against entrenched *"Galuth*-negators" point to the diplomatic and military advantages that will accrue to the new State from its "colonies" in other lands. These arguments amount to a *reductio ad absurdum* of the intrinsic values of Jewish life, in the name of a new kind of imperialism.

Is it morally right to base the welfare and dignity of American Jewry upon the supposed good of the new State? Can it be soberly argued that the prospect of helping the new State financially and politically offers American Jews the only worthy goal for living on as Jews? Or is it that the continued existence of American Jewry requires no goals, being compulsory and automatic?

To the consideration of these and other questions concerning the goals for Jewish living in America, this essay is directed. Upon the answers may well depend the survival or extinction of American Jewry.

For the future of American Jewry is still undecided in spite of its enormous clangor of activity on the surface. It is true that the history of Jewish settlement in this country goes back over three hundred years. But the present community consists for the most part of first- and second-generation immigrants. From their earliest steps upon this soil they have been concerned with aid for their brethren overseas. Their collective consciousness as Jews is still dominated by the philanthropic attitude. Conditioned to think of themselves as the "rich uncles" of honest-to-goodness Jews in Europe and Palestine, they have hardly yet turned their gaze inward to discover the nature of their own American Jewishness.

But the time for earnest soul-searching can no longer be postponed. If the American Jew can find no worthy transcendent purpose to his life as a Jew, he is morally entitled to shake off the appeals so mountainously heaped upon him and seek the quickest road to assimilation. If, on the other hand, he does find a Jewish purpose that is harmonious with his personal convictions, his dignity and his highest ideals, *he should see to it that this purpose is embodied in the theory and practice of the Jewish community.*

For purpose is to the social group as the soul is to the body.

143

2. Towards the Nirvana of Assimilation

Actually it is not only possible but relatively easy for individuals to leave the Jewish group. The entire body of American Israel, to be sure, could not disintegrate in one generation; for many individuals, however, the gateway out of the Jewish fold and destiny is now wide open. They are at liberty to make such decisions—in choosing interests, friends, neighbors, and a mate—as will remove them from the Jewish camp. The label of Jewishness may still stick to them during their own lifetime; but their children and grandchildren will be absorbed into the mainstream of American life. Even Hitler could not reach the descendants of the hundreds of thousands of Jewish converts to Christianity in the post-Mendelssohnian era.

From all reports in the last few years it appears that the pathways out of the Jewish community are being followed by increasing numbers of young people in America. Through indifference, change of names, intermarriage, conversion and semi-conversion, our ranks are being steadily depleted. Who does not know the Jewish character of many of the Christian Science and Community Churches? The children of Jewish members may be expected to continue along the path of assimilation from the point where their parents left off. Why fool ourselves with the false notion that assimilation is impossible because it cannot be completely achieved in one generation? The numbers who left the ranks of Israel in Europe in the nineteenth and twentieth centuries may well run into the millions. On this continent many of the earliest and proudest Jewish families are now no longer identified with their ancestral people.

At present the social factor is the strongest cohesive force in the Jewish group, outside of religion. For most of our people, especially the vast majority who live in the big cities, being a Jew is not so much a matter of religious conviction as simply the line of least resistance, due to the social remnant of ghetto existence, the possession of "Jewish tastes" in food and in habits of enjoyment, and the general tendency to follow the beaten path. In addition, there is always the hovering specter of antisemitism to haunt the thin borderline where the groups meet. All these factors, however, are being progressively weakened.

Thus we can no longer dismiss the persistent question, "Why be a Jew?" in the good old Jewish way, by inverting the question to "Why not?" It is inept to retort that Jewry, being a national entity "even like unto all the nations of the earth," need not perennially look for justification of its existence. Nor is it brighter to insinuate that since no healthy organism questions its right to live, the very act of questioning the purpose of Jewish existence manifests an unhealthy approach to Jewish life. For the ineluctable fact is that the *natural* tendency for all national groups is to dissolve and disappear within the American melting-pot.

If here and there colonies of European nationalities still continue in the isolation of self-imposed ghettos, they are exceptional in the mighty expanse of America's mainstream of life. The bland assumption that Jewry is a national entity does not protect American Israel against the absorptive effects of the melting-pot.

3. The Myth of a "National Will-to-Live"

In the romantic literature of European nationalism one encounters frequently the notion of a "national will-to-live." It is assumed that every nation behaves very much like an individual living organism. This "national will-to-live," it is maintained, operates largely in the subconscious recesses of the mind, producing such ideas, values and movements as are designed to assure the continuance of the nation.

Ahad Ha'am did most to introduce this dark dogma of biological nationalism into the thinking of the modern Jew. He went to the extent of suggesting that the whole Jewish religion was inwardly motivated by this impulse of national group survival. This, rather than our religion itself, produced the numerous "fences" of Jewish law, erecting impassable barriers between Jew and Gentile, creating a ghetto where the Jew could survive. In other words, it was not because the Jew believed in Torah and Talmud that he braved all "the slings and arrows of outrageous fortune"; on the contrary, he developed the beliefs and customs of Judaism in order to erect a Chinese wall of segregation about the tiniest Jewish community, enabling it thus to endure through the ages—a timeless, deathless entity. To Ahad Ha'am, then, the "national will-to-live" was the basic factor in Judaism: the Jew believed because he wanted to believe, and he wanted to believe because he willed to live as a Jew.

From this vantage point, Ahad Ha'am undertook to expose the hollowness and sham of all assimilationist theories. He dubbed the Jews of the West "slaves in freedom." Though they lived under the then relatively unclouded skies of emancipation and freedom, still they were slaves in spirit, for they dared not assert their national character and national aspirations. As Ahad Ha'am would have it, the "national will-to-live" continued to throb within the subconscious souls of the self-effacing Western Jews as mightily as ever; but they refused it a normal expression for fear of offending the national sensitiveness of their neighbors. Therefore, they lived under the stress and strain of a perpetual tug-of-war between their unconscious "national will-to-live" and their conscious assimilationist doctrines. The unhappy mentality of the emancipated Jew was, to Ahad Ha'am, proof of the invincibility of the "national will-to-live." It is a powerful biological force; throw it out of the door, back it comes through the window. You cannot win against nature.

Were this diagnosis correct, there would be no problem of Jewish survival. The "national will-to-live" could be relied upon to stimulate this national impulse by various cultural and political devices such as the upbuilding of a homeland in Palestine and the re-creation there of a new Hebraic culture. Whatever the stratagems required, fundamentally Jewish survival in all lands of the Diaspora was assured by the biological force of national self-preservation.

But the science of sociology has taught us that there is no such social-physiological impulse as the "national will-to-live." The mighty movements of biological nationalism which arose in the nineteenth century and produced their foulest fruits in our day drew their inspiration from popular mythology and vulgar prejudices, not from science or common sense. The monstrous madness of biological nationalism is sufficiently evident from Nazi Germany, Fascist Italy and pre-war Poland. It does, however, still possess a seductive appeal to some otherwise sensible people when applied to their own group. One is reminded of the young physicist who was trying to explain to his romantic girl friend that all flesh and blood was merely a concatenation of identical electrons and protons whirling about in space. Undaunted by the majesty of science, the young lady countered: "But mine are the *most beautiful* electrons!"

It simply is not true that national groups constitute biological entities, like the species of the animal kingdom. In point of fact, modern nations are largely language groups, brought into being through fortuitous historical circumstances which could not possibly have affected the biological character of their members. Numerous instances from all parts of the globe can be adduced to prove that Hitler's conception of the nation as an enlarged family was unhistorical.

The nation-state of the modern period is, in the light of the past and the clearly visible lines of the future, a temporary phenomenon. As the family gave way to the clan, the clan to the tribe, the tribe to the multi-tribal nation, so the nation will give way in time to the multi-national territorial federation. Each step in this long tortuous process involves a diminution of the biological element and proportionate intensification of the political and cultural bonds of cohesion. The "blood-and-soil" type of nationalism may be revived by demagogues from time to time; its menacing shadow still looms large over the horizon; but it belongs to the infantile stage of humanity, in the realms of devils and dragons and the fierce Teutonic gods of forest and thunder.

4. The Fallacy of Mission Theories

Just as it is senseless to demand sacrifices for the sake of an empty and purposeless survivalism, so it is unjustified to assert that our people must live for the sake of its *mission* to mankind.

According to the several mission theories, the Jew is duty-bound to retain his identity in order to bring a unique teaching to mankind. In a sober view most Jews might seem to have little enough to teach anybody; but then it is maintained that insofar as the individual forms part of the living body of Israel, he shares in its sacred undertaking. For he helps to sustain the social organism necessary for the perpetuation of the light of Torah, however conceived and interpreted. Thus every Jewish individual is a member of the missionary society of Israel.

Though the various missions theories lend themselves beautifully to forensic adornments and the kind of oratorical chest-thumping that average audiences acclaim as "brilliant," there is still a residual reluctance on the part of hard-headed Jews to swallow the bait of any missionary dogma. No matter how grandiloquently and passionately avowed at mass meetings, it somehow rings hollow, abstract and even hypocritical in the light of day. The average Jew realizes that Jewish organizational life is hardly oriented in keeping with any kind of missionary doctrine. We do everything but organize missions to the Gentiles. Furthermore, our normal feeling rebels against the implication that, while all other groups exist intrinsically in and for themselves, the Jewish people exist only by virtue of their supposed usefulness to the outside world. But it is only when we proceed to scrutinize at close range the various mission doctrines proposed from time to time that we cannot fail to see their utter inadequacy.

5. Of Reform Judaism

In the psychology of the traditional Jew the consciousness of being the bearer of a special message to the world was seldom predominant. The Prophets, who did speak of Israel as being a witness unto the truth, did not, however, call upon their people to go out into the world and shatter the idols of the nations by their preaching and practice. Certain as the Prophets were of the ultimate triumph of the truths bequeathed to the keeping of Israel, they believed this would be achieved through the providence of God and the normal diffusion of knowledge rather than through any organized preaching efforts on the part of the "sons of the living God." The New Testament does indeed speak of the Pharisees encompassing heaven and earth to make converts to Judaism; but in authentic Jewish sources there is very little evidence for such efforts. While it was undoubtedly a meritorious deed to bring strangers "under the wings of the *Skekinah*," this *mitzvah* was not the primary task of the Congregation of Israel, much less the purpose or goal of Jewish existence.

The mission concept of Reform Judaism was an attempt to reverse the scale of values in the traditional pattern of piety. No longer was it to be taught that the world existed for the sake of Israel, the Torah-people; on the contrary, it was now maintained that Israel existed for the sake of the world. To halt the headlong stampede of German Jewry into the Nirvana of assimilation, Abraham Geiger and his associates enunciated the thesis that it was the duty of Jews to live as Jews in order to help achieve a more perfect world.

In the halcyon days of emancipation, Jews were lured away from the fold by the ideals of abstract cosmopolitanism. Heine's song of the tribe which "dies when it loves" doubtless echoed the dilemma of his generation, which considered Jewish loyalty unworthy of cosmopolites and humanists. To meet this challenge, the Reform thesis, on the contrary, sought to make it appear that the true cosmopolitan ideal required the Jew to remain loyal to his identity. For was not the Jewish people the custodian of the truths of "ethical monotheism," which no other nation possessed in their genuine purity? This was the major premise. The minor premise was that the salvation of mankind depended upon the universal acceptance of "ethical monotheism." The dispersion of Jewry to the ends of the globe was expressly designed by Providence, that these divine principles might be diffused throughout the world.

It was largely because of this idealized conception of Diaspora existence that the *Protest-Rabbiner,* the anti-Zionist rabbis of Herzl's day, protested against the plan to reassemble the scattered segments of Israel in the Holy Land. From their viewpoint, Zionism was not so much a utopian dream as an act of rebellion against God, a disloyal defection from the "Jewish Mission" ordained by Him.

But "ethical monotheism" is no longer a Jewish monopoly. As an abstract idea and even as an article of belief, it is

150

the property—or rather the profession—of the educated Western world. In point of fact, the philosophies of all the
Reformist thinkers were eclectic syntheses of the ideas of
Kant, Fichte and Hegel, rather than expositions of the insights of Akiba and Maimondies. This was quite natural,
since intellectually and spiritually they could not but write
and think as children of their own place and time, battering
at the gates of the unknown with the same instruments as
their neighbors.

The masses of the Jewish people easily sensed the absurdity inherent in the Reformist procedure of first reducing
Judaism to a set of abstract principles, current in nineteenth-
century European philosophy, and then presuming to be the
sole custodians of those principles.

6.   Of Ahad-Ha'am Nationalism

The general impression that only Reformist anti-national-
ists subscribed to a mission philosophy of Jewish existence is
quite erroneous.

Ahad Ha'am strove throughout his life to discover the
exact character of the Jewish "genius" and its "mission." He
believed that the ethics of Judaism reflected the "soul" of
Israel, and marked out its special function in the concert of
nations. Only in his later years did he begin to recognize
that Jewish ethical ideas belong to the domain of Western
civilization in the same sense as the philosophical ideas of
the ancient Greeks. It was necessary, then, to evolve a new
national ideal that would give specific meaning and purpose
to Jewish life in the Diaspora. Such an ideal, he was certain,
would emerge out of the reborn Hebraic culture in Palestine. He could not precisely envisage the character of that
ideal; but he believed that history would be repeated and,
out of the mystic springs of the Jewish soul, there would
somehow emerge a new leap of the spirit into the dark, that

151

would endow the Jewish communities in the Dispersion with a great mission to mankind.

Ahad Ha'am's mystical yearning for a mission is indicative of the dilemma of Jewish secular nationalism. On the one hand, it seeks to win for Israel a "normal" status in a State of its own. On the other hand, it seeks to perpetuate Jewish community life in the Diaspora, even though that is, on its own insistence, "abnormal."

A new version of the Ahad-Ha'am nationalist mission theory, with a more detailed blueprint, was offered by Professor Mordecai M. Kaplan, in his *Judaism as a Civilization*. The Jewish communities in the Diaspora should be reorganized, on an all-inclusive national basis, as minority colonies within the host-nations. These national-colonial communities in all countries of the world would be linked to the central home of the nation in Palestine, by bonds cultural and religious. The mission of the Jewish communities will then be to demonstrate that the ideal of nationalism can be diverted into cultural and religious channels, not needing to find expression in political and military rivalries. This mission is of crucial importance to the progress of mankind, since the naked national impulse, if not directed into useful channels, is capable of bringing ruin to humanity. Having been for generations the favorite target of nationalist virulence, Israel now has the special privilege of demonstrating to the world how the explosive force of nationalism may be transmuted into a creative and healthy impulsive—that is, by being channeled away from the field of politics into the domain of culture and religion.

The utter unreality of this latest conception of the Jewish mission—"Reconstructionism," as it is called by its advocates—appears clearly enough as soon as it is lifted out of the book and placed within the actual context of American life. In the first place, we must note that Jewish nationalism is

152

far from being non-political. Its natural goal is a Jewish State. The State must lean on the political as well as financial support of World Jewry, especially American Jewry. It is not true, therefore, that Jewish nationalism is peculiarly and distinctively non-political.

As to the second phase of the Reconstructionist mission—to demonstrate the potential cultural and religious fruits of nationalism—it should be noted that the reactionary brand of European nationalism was always cultural and religious. The upsurge of modern antisemitism in nineteenth-century Germany and France was due precisely to this extension of the nationalist drive into the fields of culture and religion. The so-called "German-Christians" of more recent days, who sought to free Christianity from the inherent Jewish influence and to evolve a purely German form of religion, were impelled by the selfsame doctrine. A mere cursory survey of the tragic story of European nationalism will convince anyone that the practical fruits of the romantic brand of nationalism are by no means good or pretty—certainly not for Jews. If, then, it be our mission to stimulate attempts on the part of our host-nations to develop their culture on strictly national-racial lines, where are we likely to find ourselves?

Imagine for a moment the Jewish mission to be successful here, in our own country. The Americans of German, Polish, Irish and Anglo-Saxon ancestry have at last "seen the light." They have become organized into tight social groupings, dedicated to the cultivation of their respective "pure" national cultures. The ethnic pride and prejudice of each group would then be carefully nurtured and raised to a high pitch of intensity. Can anyone deny that, in that event, all the romantic poisons of Europe would be speedily transplanted here, in most vicious forms?

Why, then, close our eyes to reality, and dream of nationalist "missions"?

7. The World's Hope

From the standpoint of humanity and morality and good sense, the world is desperately in need rather of more universalist binding forces, through which nationalism may be curbed.

It is the unique glory of Judaism that its Prophets were able to rise above the cramping confines of narrow national loyalties, to recognize the wrongdoings of their own people, to exalt the sway of justice above the claims of tribalism, and to dream of a united world, unmarred by tribal jealousies and wars. It was the glory of nineteenth-century Europe that men, while regarding themselves politically as citizens of their own countries, were also able to regard themselves at the same time as spiritually citizens of Europe. If there is any hope for the future of mankind, it lies in this universalist direction, foreshadowed by the Prophets and furthered by Western liberalism which looked toward the progressive curbing of the nationalist impulse. If there is any mission for any group in the field of nationalism, it is to join the forces that are "agin' it," to labor for the achievement of one world, and prepare the ground for that consummation by stressing the universal common elements of all cultures, and emphasizing the relative unimportance of nationalist traits.

America is the hope of the world precisely because it effected the miracle of *e pluribus unum,* welding the many nations which came to its shores into one great nation. America's example is living proof of the principle that human beings are not fated to be forever divided by the biological factors of race and nation, that the national element can be toned down and the human element toned up, that "a man'a a man for a' that."

8. *Jewish State and Diaspora Survival*

Zionism as consummated in a Jewish State can provide neither the material nor moral grounds for the survival of Israel in the Diaspora.

In the past, the overtones of philanthropy preponderated in the Zionist movement over the political tones. But the moment the Jewish State is set up, Zionism will not be distinguishable from the labors of other citizens in one State on behalf of another State. Such labors may continue to bear the aspect of philanthropy for a short time, as the refugees of this war are helped to get a start in their new home. But, on any permanent basis, such an organization as a World Zionist body is anomalous at best and dangerous on occasion, for it is the business of the State Department to represent the citizens of America in their relations with foreign powers. And loyalty to a foreign state is not consistent with loyalty to the American state and nation.

The thousands of bewildered souls who publicly proclaimed that Zionism had taken the place of Judaism in their hearts are now called upon to reexamine their pattern of loyalties to see whether assimilation is not the logical corollary of their philosophy, if they do not choose to emigrate to Palestine.

The logic of Zionism as understood by Herzl calls for the dissolution of Diaspora Jewry, once the homeland has been established and the Jewish people have become "like unto all the nations." True, the homeland in its present boundaries is far too small for all Jewry; but then, the same thing is true of the Irish and other nationalities. The basic factor is a moral issue, which can only be evaded at our own peril.

Naturally, the pressure for the continuance of the old

forms of allegiance in the Jewish world will be tremendous. It is so much easier to coast along on the momentum of the past than to steer for a safe haven against the turbulent eddies of the present. But the very physical existence of American Jews depends on our ability to understand the nature of the changed relationship between American Israel and the Yishuv which must follow the establishment of a Jewish State.

Whatever relationships the future may hold, this much is axiomatic: the loyalty of American Jews to their country is one and indivisible. Such residual sentiments as they will retain for the Jewish State must be secondary and temporary—most certainly incapable of justifying the arduous efforts needed to assure Jewish survival on this continent.

9. Judaism as Function

We have contended, on the one hand, that American Jewry cannot live without a central purpose and, on the other hand, that the various mission theories which have been evolved to give purpose to Jewish life cannot stand up in the light of common sense. Is there an intermediate position between purposelessness and mission?

The answer will appear only after we clearly recognize the basic fallacy in the two antithetical lines of thought described in the previous sections. Both the champions of automatic survival and the preachers of a mission generally overlooked the fact that they deal with living men and women. While preaching eloquently of the forest they fail to see the trees. If the destiny of the group is not related to personal needs of the individual, the theorists are not only just talking to themselves but sowing confusion at every turn.

To avoid current confusions we must begin with the Jewish individual. Like all men, he is in search of happiness;

and, again like all men, he is subject to demands of the life of the spirit. These two motivations are complementary to each other. True happiness is not a ceaseless roving for pleasures; it is a solid anchorage in this ambivalent world of matter and spirit, of selfish enjoyment and selfless duty.

This living individual American Jew is at once our point of departure and ultimate point of reference, the beginning and the end of our thought. It follows that Judaism must be made to serve the individual—not the other way around, that the individual must serve the cause of Judaism or, *lehavdil*, "Jewishness."

Now if the American Jew is to be served by Judaism, it must fulfil a *function* in his life which is not filled by other aspects of American life. Hence the guiding word in our analysis of Jewish life is "function," in contrast to the fallacious slogans of "mission" and "survival" for "function" is life-centered, while "mission" is "other" centered and "survival" is past-centered.

Judaism must not be viewed as a burden, something imposed from the outside on the back of the American Jew. It must represent an enrichment of his life, directed towards his needs as a human being and as an American.

10. The Religious Function

Let us begin, therefore, by inverting the customary way of approaching this Jewish problem. We do not ask: What does Judaism require of the Jew? And we do not ask: What does the existing Jewish group want?

The first way of putting the question leads to such replies as: (1) Judaism is ethnic loyalty requiring the support of Zionism, anti-defamation efforts, and the like; (2) Judaism is religious loyalty requiring the support of and participation in the religious program and institutions of Judaism; (3) Judaism is cultural loyalty requiring the sponsorship and patronizing of "Jewish activities and expressions." The second way of putting the question looks neither to the past nor to the future, but is intent only upon catering to current popular needs and tastes. While the first approach subjects the living Jews of today to the mores of the past, the second approach is a frank acceptance of the caprices and confusions of the momentary present, "the idols of the market-place."

Our own approach is to orient Jewish life in terms of the future—the state of affairs we should like to bring about. Accordingly, our basic question is: What can Judaism do for the individual Jew of the future? Or, what function can it fulfil in his life?

We assume, to begin with, (1) that the powerful processes of Americanization will continue to integrate the American Jew more and more closely within the general community and culture, and (2) that there will not arise a quasi-Hitlerist movement to push him back into the ghetto. As an American, the Jew will share in the travail and glory of American civilization and American destiny. What will the fact of his Jewishness add to his life? Assuredly not a supplementary national allegiance, as we have already pointed out.

An additional national allegiance simply lacks function in the psychical makeup of an American. Since it cannot be rooted in the indigenous needs and interests of the American Jew, it can only be an unhealthy parasitical growth causing inner conflict and external misrepresentation.

Can Judaism, then, contribute an added "culture" to the life of the American Jew? Here again, the confusion and equivocation clustering around the honorific expression "culture" is cleared away by the sharp scalpel of function. Insofar as an American Jew craves for culture, he is likely to get it within the general American culture: therein he will find artistic energy and expression in all forms, a striving for the application of ideals of justice to contemporary situations, and a secular way of life with a set of folkways that are all-pervasive.

The Survey Commission of the National Jewish Welfare Board—while it rejects the conception of Judaism as a "civilization," realizing that American Jews will live wholly in American civilization—nevertheless sets up the notion of "cultural supplementation." As if the lingering shreds of foreign cultures in first- and second-generation communities could be regarded as the norm and ideal for the future. It has not been shown that "cultural supplementation" is an organic growth springing from the soil of America, rather than a temporary transitional phenomenon. In the case of the Jewish group, the Survey Commission fails to realize that the real question involved is not one of conflict between American and Jewish "civilizations," but rather the lack of any specific *function* for "Jewish civilization."

The simple question is: Does the American find in his heart a craving for "cultural supplementation"? If not, then "Jewish culture," so conceived, does not fulfil an organic permanent need of the American Jew. It won't do to draw a rough parallel and say: As an American the Jewish individual will participate in American culture but also as a Jew he needs "Jewish culture." These two situations are actually not at all parallel. He is an American by being a native or naturalized citizen of this country, subject to all its pervading tangible and intangible influences. The function which American culture fulfils in his life is normal and indispensable; it is an organic part of his being, growing out of his physical and spiritual needs. Insofar as secular "Jewish culture" attempts to supply the same values as American culture, it is superfluous. Psychologically, the craving for "cultural supplementation," insofar as it does exist, is a temporary phenomenon in immigrant populations, a nostalgic longing for the past, not a creative effort for the future. Hence, to saddle a secular "Jewish culture" upon the American Jew is just as gratuitous as to lumber him with an additional national allegiance.

In criticism of this analysis it may be said: But the Jew cannot ever become *just* an American; there is the sting of antisemitism which wounds his pride, makes him feel homeless and alien. Jewish culture, on the one hand, and Jewish national allegiance, on the other, serve to heal the wounds of antisemitism in the Jewish soul; they endow him with the sense of belonging; they serve the function of spiritual armor.

We presume to doubt the therapeutic or armorial value of a secular "Jewish culture" against the slings and wounds of antisemitism.

The actual battle against antisemitism, the methods it calls for, are not in question here. What concerns us at the moment is the psychical wound—the wound of "not belonging"—inflicted by the poisoned arrows of the antisemites. How can anybody fail to see that this wound is not to be cured by the establishment of a quasi-ghetto, a segregated center of "Jewishness?" For that only further aggravates the consciousness of being different. It is clearer still that a spiritual identification with Palestine cannot by the widest stretch of imagination deepen the feeling of "belonging" to the soil and soul of America.

If it is our deep sense of belonging completely to America that is hurt by antisemitism, then the sensible policy is twofold: (1) to strike our roots even deeper in this soil; and (2) to labor hand in hand with all Americans for the extirpation of religious bigotry, social exclusiveness and racial arrogance, out of which lushly spring the poisonous weeds of antisemitism. You cannot combat the taunt of "not-belonging" by first consenting to it in thought and then building a wall against the outside world. You will not find relief from an itchy rash by persistently and systematically scratching it.

The concept of function rescues us from the turbid maze of passions and prejudices encumbering this problem. When the true Jewish quality in the American Jew fulfils its proper function, he will not retreat in thought to a world of his own and yield tacitly to the basic premise of the antisemite that Jew and Gentile cannot live together. On the contrary, he will stand his American ground and fight for his American rights. He will thereby strengthen the ranks of all Americans who fight for equality and humanity.

The soul of the American Jew is so strained and torn today because our dominant leadership has refused to think in terms of spiritual health and growth. Like the prophet Jonah, our secular leaders have sought to "run away from God." The great anathema in their eyes has been the conception of the Jewish people as a religious community. Fleeing from God, for many different reasons, they are like men on a flying trapeze leaping from one pseudo-conception to another, inventing rationales for every perch they alight on through the accident of history. Essentially escapist, they cannot but end up at last in intellectual frustration and despair.

The only healthy function of the Jewish heritage in the American Jew is to supply the element of religion. American life is culturally monolithic but religiously pluralistic. While the civilization of America is essentially religious, the concrete forms and ceremonies of religion are supplied by the diverse religious groups of which this nation is constituted. The ceremonies and symbols of one religion cannot serve as the vessels of piety for another group, differently brought up and conditioned.

As a religious discipline, Judaism performs—or can perform—a healthy, indeed indispensable, function in the life of the American Jew. It does not undercut his feeling of belonging here completely and permanently. It directs his Jewish consciousness into the channels of personal happiness and selfless dedication to the things of God. It interprets Jewish destiny for him in terms to evoke unceasing efforts towards the upbuilding of the universal Kingdom of God. It strengthens his faith in his own worth as a Jew and, at the same time, in the humanity of his neighbors. It lifts the struggle of his people through the ages from the low realm of sordid wretchedness to the height of tragic heroism in the workings of God's cosmic plan. In fine, it transmutes the mental image of the Jew from that of a "non-Aryan" to that of a "son of the living God."

The various expressions of this image in learning and literature, in music and art, constitute our true Jewish culture, our distinctive religious culture, as distinguished from the phony secular "Jewish culture." The latter is but an imitation or reflection of the general American or Western culture, as superfluous as it is generally inferior. And it is preposterous to speak of the works of every writer, painter and musician who happens to have been born a Jew, but is devoid of Judaism, as constituting "Jewish culture."

11. *A Glance at the Historical Background*

Insistence on the religious status of American Israel is quite naturally confused these days with various assimilationist tendencies. To clarify our conception it may be well to examine what the assertion of a religious status for Israel had meant in the past.

For our present purpose we need not enter into a long investigation of the status of the Jewish people in ancient times or medieval, when a self-inclosed system of ideas, laws and institutions prevailed in virtual uniformity throughout

Christian Europe. The modern problem of Jewish adjustment came into being through the emergence of the nation-states.

The relationship of the medieval monarch or prince to his Jewish subjects was based on a contractual arrangement, written or oral, whereby the potentate received a set remuneration for the privileges he granted. It was strictly a business affair, valuable only as it proved useful to the two contracting parties, or at least the more powerful one. Upon the breakdown of the medieval order, the demographic unity of a territory came to be regarded as the natural and proper base for its government as a state. One after another, through the eighteenth, nineteenth and twentieth centuries, the nation-states of Europe came into being, in England, in France, spreading thence eastward, till in our own times the spirit of nationalism shattered the monarchies of Austro-Hungary and tsarist Russia during the First World War.

It was in revolutionary France, towards the close of the eighteenth century, that the need of adjustment to the new situation suddenly faced the Jews. Since the new political order was based upon the bonds of fraternity within the French people, the question as to whether or not the Jews were part of the French family was brought to the fore with startling immediacy. Were the Jews of France a "nation within a nation," or were they Frenchmen of the Jewish faith? Would the French people insist on consanguinity as the only basis for citizenship, or would they be content with a spiritual identification of interest and a sense of common destiny?

12. The Price of Emancipation

Actually, the nations of Europe were not entirely clear in their demands upon the Jews in their midst. The requirement of consanguinity loomed large in the mind of Napoleon, who ordered the Paris Sanhedrin not to oppose intermarriage, even insisting at one time that every third Jewish marriage must be an intermarriage. The romantic-reactionary circles in Europe tended generally to demand the ultimate disappearance of the Jewish group as the condition for emancipation. Doubtless, too, they echoed in this the unexpressed feelings of the masses who, for the most part, were able to think of brotherhood only in biological terms as blood-kinship. So, while opinions varied as to the proper duties of the individual Jew, the people turned sovereign were united in demanding the dissolution of the quasi-national bonds of the Jewish community. Among the liberals who championed the cause of Jewish emancipation there was a clear understanding and virtually unanimous agreement that, as Clermont-Tonner put it, "to the Jews as a nation, nothing is to be granted; to the Jews as individuals, everything."

At the time the national character of the Jewish community was expressed in the social isolationism of the ghetto, the "cultural" differences in language, customs and attire between the Jews and their neighbors, the emotional indifference of the Jews to the national concerns and aspirations of their host-nations, and finally in the Jewish hope for the return to Zion. The antisemites fastened upon these differences as the marks of a separate and forever alien Jewish nation. The liberals, on the other side, maintained that Jewry was essentially a religious community, that the "national" qualities of the Jews were the deplorable products of rejection and persecution by the Gentiles, and that the dream of the return to Zion was a religious fantasy or symbol, devoid of any realistic, practical significance.

This liberal thesis was adopted by the Sanhedrin of French Jewry. With few exceptions, it was repeated by the subsequent Jewish assemblies that steadily fought for and finally secured emancipation in all Western and Central Europe. There was no difference in this respect between the Orthodox and Reform groups. From Moses Mendelssohn to Gabriel Riesser, they proclaimed the eagerness of the Jewish people to become part and parcel of the nation-states.

Did the Jewish leaders in the fight for emancipation realize they were sharply breaking with the past when they declared themselves to be thenceforth Frenchmen of the Jewish faith rather than Jews dwelling in France? Not only the proceedings of the Sanhedrin but the memoranda submitted to the Westphalian Parliament leave no doubt: they were fully aware of the revolutionary import of their choice. In Holland a small portion of Jewry did balk at the conditions of emancipation, but the majority accepted the new era with immense enthusiasm. They realized fully that more was asked of them than was implied in Jeremiah's advice to the exiles in Babylonia, "to seek the peace of the city in which they dwell." At the same time, however, most of them were not ready to accept Hamor and Shechem's description of intertribal fellowship as the pattern for their covenant with the nations: "our daughters we shall give them and their daughters we shall take for ourselves and we shall be one people."

Specifically, as the price of emancipation, the Jews agreed to suspend their own civil law, to merge "culturally" with their respective host-nations, and to interpret the hope of Zion as a purely spiritual symbol. Gabriel Riesser, who led the final stages of the battle for emancipation in Western Europe, was scarcely ever able to understand Jewish nationalism save as a slanderous invention "which our enemies seek to fasten upon us."

In the literature of classical Zionism, and in the writings

of non-Zionist secular nationalists like Dubnow, the leaders of West-European Jewry in the early nineteenth century are castigated as traitors, or semi-traitors, to the cause of Jewish nationalism. This charge is, of course, utterly unfair, since in the era of the Emancipation the madness of nationalism was not yet elevated to the rank of a supreme ideal. However, the bitterness reflected in this charge is only partly the product of the new nationalist ideology. In very great measure it was the result of the sad disillusionment of later generations with the incompleteness of emancipation, its unreality, hypocrisy and futility.

In fact, the reactionary emphasis through the nineteenth century on the biological phase of nationalism made it impossible for the Jewish community to become an integral part of any European nation-state. This development could hardly have been foreseen by the members of the Paris Sanhedrin, who pinned their faith on the liberalism and good sense of the French people. They were no more "traitorous" to the "Jewish nation" than any group of would-be immigrants who decide to embark for a new country and become part of its national life. They considered that in the new alignment only the non-essential folk aspects of Judaism would be given up while the core and substance of their heritage, the Jewish religion would be preserved. They did not desert their group; rather they made a covenant with their host-nations on its behalf.

This action was certainly a break with the past; but it maintained Judaism and promised a glorious future in terms of individual happiness and dignity.

13. *The Meaning of Religious Status Today*

If now we project the problem of the Emancipation period into our own time, we recognize one of the fundamental meanings of the assertion of a religious status for

Jewry. It means the decision to become part not only of the state, but of the state-nation, to share fully in the culture of that nation, and to forego any other national claims or aspirations.

This decision must be made by the Jewish community of every country separately. Should it appear that the probable course of development in a given country will be in the direction of biological nationalism, then the Jew must conclude, however sadly, that there will ultimately be no room for him there. His decision to join any nation-state must be based upon his faith that the moral and humanist elements embraced in the word state will ultimately triumph over the "blood-and-soil" elements connoted by the word nation —that the nation-state will evolve into the state-nation. No greater compliment can be paid any nation than the one implied in the Jew's staking his future on his faith in its soul.

Yet Jews are certainly entitled to refuse this choice and to elect instead to become part of the renascent Jewish nation in Palestine. To a very large extent, however, the course of events in the host country determines the status of the Jewish community. Thus, in Russia the Jews are officially recognized as a minority nationality, while in America and the West generally the status of Jewry is that of a religious community.

Neither the Jewishness of the nationalist Jew of eastern Europe nor the Judaism of the developing American Jew is identical with that unique pattern of loyalties which prevailed in the ghettos of the pre-Emancipation period. In this changing world only what is dead remains unchanged. Adjustment is the law of life; and the law of the spirit dictates: Adjust yourself so that the higher values and talents in your personality shall find their best expression.

14. Our Future in America

In America today the organizational pattern of Jewish life is still in a state of flux, capable of developing either into a religious community or into a racist-nationalist minority. At the moment the dominant trend seems to be a kind of spite-racism. This trend, as we have tried to show, is not dictated by the inherent logic of Judaism or of Jewish life. The elements of religion have indeed been so closely intertwined with those of nationalism in Judaism that no complete separation is possible, even ideally. Nevertheless, the one or the other phase must come ultimately to predominate, whether through outside pressure or inner development, or through the interaction of outer causes and inner motivations. Should the coming decades bring a deterioration in the attitude of the Gentile population, then the nationalist spirit is bound to come to the fore.

While the possibility of an intensified antisemitism cannot be altogether ruled out in advance, there are very good reasons for the belief that "it can't happen here." The indubitable fact, enshrined in the memory of the American nation, of its having arisen out of a mixture of races and nationalities, interposes a supreme obstacle to the emergence here of a romantic blood-based brand of nationalism, with its corollary of racist antisemitism. America is the one great state where the emergence of the nation did not precede the formation of the state. The American nation came into being, in fact, as a massive protest against the voice of blood by the voice of reason and morality.

The revolutionary faith of America, established by the Founding Fathers, is humanist in character, stressing the rights and liberties of the individual. This spirit and tradition of America has been reinforced by the mass-immigrations, making it very unlikely that the European brands of blood-nationalism can flourish on this soil. Though antisemitism may continue to pollute the social life of America for years to come, it cannot derive reinforcement from the kind of nationalism that provided the diabolical driving force to the European movements of hate in the past quarter-century.

In this age of consummate scientific techniques combined with political confusion, none but fools will dare to prophesy. But, being forced in planning for the future to assay the balance of probabilities, one finds, upon sober contemplation, sufficient assurance in the soul of America to forge the structure and destiny of American Jewry on the foundations of that faith.

Yes, the choice between digging in here or preparing for eventual flight must be decided by an act of faith. The failure of emancipation in a large part of Europe was of a piece with the temporary eclipse of the ideals of enlightenment generally. If we still believe in human reason, in the essential goodness of human nature, in the ultimate triumph of the spirit of humanity, then we shall not hesitate to sink our roots deep in this soil and take up the battle against the poisonous weeds in it with the quiet courage and sure strength that derive from confidence in ultimate triumph. If, however, the horrors of Buchenwald and Oswiecim have deadened our faith in human nature and reason, then we must give up in despair the struggle for human rights and concur with our worst enemies in admitting the complete failure of emancipation. In that case, the whole drive of our individual and collective energies should be concentrated upon the sole task of preparation for ultimate flight from the lands of the Diaspora.

This very task was urged upon the delegates to the recent World Hebrew Educational Conference in Jerusalem as the fundamental purpose of Jewish education in America.

169

Indeed, the prevailing opinion at the conference seems to have been that this purpose was to be regarded as the *sole* function of education in the Diaspora. And such is the dialectic of human nature that the counsels of cynicism have a way of "proving" their plausibility through the events they inspire. A leadership that has lost faith in the good-will of our Christian fellow-citizens, and consequently is concerned only with preparations for another exodus, cannot do aught else than evoke and intensify the dark forces it fears.

Happily, the sober sense of the average American Jew is likely to immunize him against the paranoiac counsels of despair and hysteria. The glory of Judaism lies precisely in its emphasis on the essential goodness and potential nobility of men. Perhaps the greatest sentence underlying the democratic way of life is the one singled out by a rabbi in the Talmud as "the most fundamental rule in the Torah —namely, 'This is the book of the generations for man. *In the image of God made He man.'*"

Faith in God is sterile if it is not conceived in terms of faith in man. Religious Jews cannot succumb to a paganism that exalts God in the heavens but conceives man on earth as little better than the beasts of the field. If we failed to build our lives on the cornerstone of faith in our fellow-men, we would deny ourself as both Jews and Americans.

2

Ends and Means of Jewish Life in America

1. The "Managerial Revolution" in Our Midst

Nothing illustrates the confused and sickened mentality of our times so much as the bitter resentment that is aroused by an attempt to analyze critically the goals and instruments of our existence as a community. Thus, several commentators on my "Goals for Jewish Living" maintain that the very act of searching for ultimate goals is malicious and sinister, as it were. One writer declares that the process of questioning is, in itself, destructive of all values, including those of religion, and that, by contrast, an unquestioning acceptance of the totality of Jewish communal life yields, somehow, a feeling of acquiescence and "joy." Another contributor insists angrily that such a discussion is not conducive to Jewish "unity," and that the sacrosanct body of "Jewish leadership" must be trusted implicitly to do what is right. Still another correspondent points to the plethora of Jewish secularist organizations as proof that the assumed unitary "leadership" of Jewish life repudiates the conception of a religious status for American Israel as too "narrow." Finally, an able writer sums it all up by asserting, in effect, that American Jewry must not be deterred by ideals and ideas from pursuing its present course of intellectual *laissez faire,* in which any and all organizations compete freely in the open market for public loyalty and support; if the net result of the contemporary chaos and confusion is the degradation of the Jewish community to the level of a "nationalist-racist" minority, we shall have the satisfaction of knowing that this status was reached through the free and unfettered operation of inherent group impulses, not through any "wilfulness or wrongheadedness."

No greater proof of the urgent need for a critical examination of ends and means in American Jewish life can be cited than this typical composite expression of antagonism to it. Are not ideas and their analysis the proper means by which a healthy community takes its bearing and determines upon its course? The extent to which sober ideological discussion, rather than the momentum of organizational pressure, determines the character and evolution of a community may fairly be taken as an index of its health.

This truth needs to be asserted with even greater force in our day because of the "managerial revolution" which has taken place in our midst, substituting the pressure of organizational dynamics for the free interplay of ideas and loyalties. The weight of an organization today is too often related to the faceless machine-like efficiency it has acquired, rather than to its real value on any rational basis.

2. How "Unique" Are We?

Doubtless, the real opposition of those commentators is directed not at a discussion of goals as such, but at the sharp definition of alternatives in our analysis. We have all become used to—and perhaps spoiled by—the suave and tolerant expositions of those who glibly solve the matter of Jewish status in America by the artful strategy of blurring the concepts of nationality and religion, so that each one may behold in the resultant harmonious formula the image of "whatsoever his heart lusteth after." It has become fashionable in recent years to declare that the categories of nationality and religion are "alien" to the Jewish mind; that the pattern of values in Judaism is a "unique" combination of these two loyalties, which have been supposedly separated in the Christian world through a process of degradation; that, in consequence, Jewish loyalty and Jewish status are neither religious nor national, but partake somehow of both conceptions in something altogether new that is *sui generis*—something that is currently being denominated as "peoplehood."

This strategy is being employed even by writers whose position is really very close to ours, who are nevertheless constrained from holding it explicitly by considerations weightier by far than those of semantics.

Let us examine the strategy.

First, it is naive to declare that the concepts of nationality and religion are borrowed from the "alien" Christian world and that these concepts are incommensurate with the categories of the "Jewish mind." Much else in this modern world would thus be strange to the "Jewish mind," including the extreme solicitude of ultra-modernists for the authentic brand of pre-modern nationalism. In this proposition the term "Jewish mind" is taken to be the mind of the pre-modern Jew of biblical, talmudic or medieval times. But we know that religion and nationality were intimately related also in the ancient pagan world, as well as among the Jews. And in Christian Europe the ties between nationality and religion were severed only by degrees and at the sacrifice of many valiant lives.

To view our own situation in the proper perspective it is well for us to recall the observation of the great historian Ranke: "In most periods of world history nations were held together by religious ties alone." We tend to forget that at the dawn of the modern era the emergent nations of Europe were still closely bound to their established churches, and that it was the separation of church and state, violent or peaceful, that ushered in the era of democracy and made possible the emancipation of the Jew.

If the spirit of modern democracy is rooted in Judaism, how can the very essence of democratic society be "alien" to it?

Furthermore, as modern Jews of Western civilization, we operate necessarily and inescapably with the concepts of the Western world, "alien" as they may or may not have been to the mind of the ancient Jews. Can it be honestly maintained that the modern Jew is incapable of recognizing the difference between national and religious values? Is not our problem due precisely to the acute awareness of this distinction, on the part of both Jews and Gentiles?

The claims of "uniqueness" and "difference" for Jewish nationalism must be exploded before the complex situation of American Jewry can be placed in the perspective of history. It is for this reason that we exposed (in "Goals for Jewish Living") the hollowness of the various "mission" theories, which seek to endow ethnic loyalty with the halo of sanctity. If, as one participant in the symposium suggests, the term "mission" is merely a euphonious designation for the culture of a nation or the religion of a group, then it is entirely meaningless. If, however, it is offered as a means of raising national loyalty out of its proper sphere and elevating it to a supreme end in life, then we may adduce ample evidence from history to prove its inherent menace. For the history of modern times shows nothing so clearly as the beguiling hypnotic lure of romantic messianic nationalism claiming the quality of "uniqueness" and "difference," and the inevitable moral ruin of all such movements.

3. What Do We Mean by Judaism?

Ever since the opening of the modern era there have been among us those who favored the expurgation from the

Jewish religion of all national elements, as well as those who championed the contrary thesis of a Jewish nationalism completely independent of religion. By their very existence the movements of both classical Reform and secular nationalism demonstrated the theoretic possibility of abstracting the religion of Israel from the nationalist aspirations of Jewish people. But neither of these extremes is capable of serving today as the vital nucleus of a philosophy of Jewish life—the one austere and abstract, the other unable to offer a livable alternative to the seemingly inevitable choice it propounds between evacuation from the West and assimilation into it.

For the majority of American Jews the real choice is not between those two extreme interpretations of Jewish loyalty, as they were formulated in the nineteenth century. It is rather between a conception of Judaism that includes the healthy earth-bound and fructifying elements of loyalty to the people of Israel, and a conception of nationalism that includes religious life and expression within its pattern of values. This issue between the two sets of hierarchical values, though they contain for the most part the same elements, is of extreme urgency and pith in molding the mentality of the American Jew. While it may seem to be only a matter of relative emphasis, and therefore of interest only to professional theologians and pedantic theorists, in actual fact it indicates the inner struggle for the soul of the Jew that is even now taking place on the American scene.

To understand why we feel bound to repudiate the philosophies which interpret nationalist loyalty as being the heart of Judaism, even though they condescend to employ religious symbols and practices, we shall do well to remove the cloak of "uniqueness" from this combination and see it as it actually functioned in other nations. For, as a matter of fact, modern nationalism, especially in its romantic reactionary phases, did not all scruple to employ, and thereby subvert for its own purposes, the sentiments and principles of religion.

Thus Fichte, the prophet of modern German nationalism, urged the adoption of a modified Lutheranism as a new national religion, an ambition which attained its climax in Bismarck's *"Kultur-Kampf."* The most popular slogan in the German War of Liberation in the first decade of the nineteenth century was "German freedom, a German God, German faith without a scoff." Nor was Italian nationalism essentially different in its professions. As formulated by Mazzini, nations are "prophets of the Lord," the "social instruments through which a divine mission is fulfilled." "We cannot have Rome," he declared, "without initiating a new religious epoch." He loked forward to the time when "religion would be the soul, the thought of the new state." And in this respect the Russian spokesmen of black reaction spoke the same language as the quasi-socialist Mazzini. Dostoevsky, probing the mysteries of the so-called "Slavic soul," was led to preach reaction and Orthodox Christianity. The arch-reactionary and arch-antisemite Pobiedonostzev regarded Orthodoxy as Russia's national religion, inasmuch as it had been completely suffused with "our Russian soul." "A Russian feels chilled in a Protestant Church," he declared. Hence he felt justified in persecuting all sectarians and in seeking to coalesce pan-Slavism with Russian Orthodoxy as the expression of Slavonic mysticism. That curious and, let it not be forgotten, dangerous conjunction of ideas is clearly if inconsistently expressed in this passage quoted by Professor Salo W. Baron (*Modern Nationalism and Religion,* page 195) : ". . . sacred idea of Slavdom, which is based not upon the quest of power, but on the idea of the equality of all humanity. We fight for freedom, the Orthodox cross and civilization. Behind us is Russia."

These examples of nationalist religious thought should suffice to arouse our suspicion that Hitler's pseudo-religious brand of nationalism was not the product of just a personal aberration but, in large part, the final fruition of the evil seeds planted by those who thought of God as the junior partner of the nation.

Ahad Ha'am, who frankly construed the Jewish religion as the "exilic garments" which the national soul in the past created for itself in order to ward off the inroads of assimilation, was honest and spiritually sensitive enough to repudiate such a servile role for religion in the spiritual makeup of his own generation and the future. For he came to recognize that religion, as the highest expression of the human spirit, can function only as the supreme end in life; hence religion must not be subverted into an instrument for national purposes. In any synthesis of national sentiments with religious values it is the latter that must be raised to the supreme level of importance; the former may be allowed but a subsidiary role, and encouraged only so long as they remain in accord with the standards and ideals of ethics and religion.

Accordingly, in our conception of Judaism the ethical-spiritual values of personal piety constitute the luminous core and substance; while around it, shading off into a penumbra, there cluster the instruments and methods of collective expression, the national sentiments and values in all their variety, concern with the fate of Jews the world over, intimate spiritual identification with the life of the people in the Land of Israel, the love of Hebrew and of all the creative achievements of the Hebraic renaissance. Whatever is creative in Jewish life is dear to us, but not all expressions equally, for they are subject to evaluation and continuous remolding in terms of universal spiritual standards. We regard all activities as falling into a hierarchial pattern of relative value, a ladder of Jacob standing on the ground and reaching up the heavens.

4. *Nationalism as a Creative Force*

We have before indicated the reasons for the hard fact that nationalism, whether frankly secular or dressed up in dubious religious garb, cannot serve as a goal for Jewish life in America. As an independent motive, sheer nationalism—especially as "normalized" since the establishment of the State of Israel—can only lead either in the direction of of headlong assimilation or toward the status of a racist minority.

The enhancement of Jewish pride through the military victories of the Israelis does not at all serve to counter the assimilationist trend. On the contrary, assimilation works most effectively when the minority group is not obsessed by inferiority complexes. History provides abundant illustrations for the thesis that a minority is difficult to assimilate if it is oppressed and humiliated. Thus the emotional boost to Jewish pride, administered by the nascent State of Israel, merely underscores the important truth that the national impulse, as such, is not capable of functioning in America as a goal for Jewish living.

But when subordinated to higher considerations Jewish nationalism may continue to be a powerful creative force, serving the ends of Jewish religion, as it did in the past, by bringing to the aid of piety additional motivation, and by supplying foci of sentimental loyalty within the Jewish community.

For, as we have learned from the study of Judaism and other faiths, religion is not merely an abstract set of dogmas but an organic pattern of values, sentiments and practices, in which a variety of social impulses are utilized, guided and interpreted so as to form a dynamic whole. This, truth, which was not realized by the builders of classical Reform, calls for the establishment of a set of values in the spiritual realm and a pattern of organization in the social realm within which national feelings and aspirations may play a healthy productive role.

When, however, the nationalist ideal is elevated to the status of a supreme goal, it begins by leading our people into an emotional *cul-de-sac*, since it cannot offer a worthy *raison d'être* for American Jewish life; and it ends, through the surge of its blind momentum, by relegating Jewry to the status of a self-segregating racist minority, since it deliberately rejects the goal of assimilation which is the natural end of other immigrant nationalists in America.

5.   *Towards the Clarification of Jewish Being*

The need for clarifying the status and pattern of loyalties of American Jewry is made imperative by factors which, though once overstressed, are now utterly ignored. As we have maintained, the Jewish situation in America is not essentially unique. But it has been overlaid—in the old European pattern—with a cloud of misrepresentations and hazy notions, which cannot now be overlooked. The barrier—compounded of theological devilries, romantic delusions and reactionary guile—for ages interposed between Jews and Gentiles, was rendered the more formidable by Hitlerite propaganda and strategy. The whole point of our analysis is that this barrier, representing Jewry as invincibly "unique," is an accumulated medley of old notions which are without foundation in present realities. They can be dissipated by clear vision and ruthless logic.

Current discussion of the evolving Jewish status in this country still continues to formulate the question in the Napoleonic manner: Are the Jews a nation or a religion? The several arguments, smoothed out into bland *clichés*, have been bandied about backwards and forwards so many times that the underlying volcanic force which first propelled this question to the surface is forgotten.

After the triumph of Zionism in our day is it any longer necessary to belabor the point that neither the category of nationalism nor the category of religion is capable of containing and expressing the full measure of Jewish loyalty? But it is not yet realized that these two much-overworked categories, even when taken jointly, do not adequately reflect the character of Jewish being. It is the elusive quality which escapes both categories that is precisely the essence of the problem.

For in addition to his religious convictions and his sense of kinship with the scattered remnants of his people, the Jew in the past felt himself set apart from other nations in yet a deeper sense. He did not simply belong to another nation, nor did he simply hold on to another faith; he belonged to a group that was "set apart" and that "dwells alone"—an *am segullah.* So that between his people and the other peoples of the world there yawned a gulf deeper by far than the other boundary lines which divide humanity. As the Midrash put it, Abraham was called the "Hebrew" (literally "from across") "for the whole world is ranged on one side and Abraham and his children on the other side."

Echoes of this awareness are found in the doctrines of "the holy seed," the "uncleanness" of other lands and other peoples, the kabbalist and pre-kabbalist beliefs in a special Jewish soul, and in the entire complex of sentiments and valuations and aspirations clustering around the concepts of *"Galuth"* and the Messiah. Even in our own day it is easy to cite instances of psychological self-isolation in proof of the fact that the awareness of being Jewish is not exhausted either by religious conviction or national loyalty, nor by both types of allegiance taken together. Do not even non-Zionists and non-religionists regard with dismay the prospect of their children marrying out of the faith?

To facilitate our analysis we are forced to coin a new term—the "meta-myth."

The meta-myth designates that indeterminate but all-too-real *plus* in the consciousness of Jewish difference, as it is reflected in the minds of both Jews and Gentiles.

6. The Meta-Myth among Gentiles

On the part of Gentiles the meta-myth is echoed in the verbal contrast of Gentile and Jew. The Jew is different in some mysterious manner. In the imagination of the untutored he may appear to be now partaking of divine qualities, now bordering on the diabolical, now superhuman in his tenacity, now subhuman in his spiteful determination to survive; but always, in some dim sense, the traditional stereotype of the Jew held by the Gentiles includes the apprehension of deep cosmic distinction from the rest of humanity.

This feeling has been reflected in the mythological substructure of antisemitism from its very origins. In the Roman world the Jews were popularly baited as "misanthropes," who stubbornly insisted on their separation from the rest of humanity, a stereotype which underlay the accusation then made for the first time that in the Holy Temple the blood of a Greek was used for some mysterious ceremonies. In the Christian religion the meta-myth was elaborated into an all-embracing cosmic design, where the Jew figured as the earthly embodiment and symbol of those who reject and are rejected—the son of the Anti-Christ. From earliest childhood the Christian is still inculcated with the image of the Jew as a dark figure, semi-mythological and semi-diabolical in character, living in this world and yet not of this world, arrayed against mankind in some occult fashion—a hateful, embittered, self-isolating Shylock in the mundane realm; a perennial Satanic mystery in the theological realm. This meta-myth constitutes the apperceptive base for the *Protocols of the Elders of Zion,* the bizarre reasoning of which, we must not forget, is so seductive in its appeal to the Christian mind that so sober and critical a newspaper as the *London Times* at one time printed it as a possibly authentic document.

It remained, however, for the neo-pagans Chamberlain, Rosenberg and Hitler to seize and develop the floating meta-myth into a systematic and all-embracing "Myth of the Twentieth Century," and to use it as the cornerstone for their entire superstructure of propaganda. In the course of time they were driven by the very logic of their mythology to murder the six million Jews in "proof" of the viciousness of the mythological figure of the "non-Aryan."

The meta-myth has not been a cause of antisemitism in the conventional understanding of causality, as it never functioned alone and in the full light of day in the minds of either Jews or Gentiles. But, from its roots in the subconscious, it has lent plausibility and force to any and all causes. It constitutes even today the mystical and emotional miasma which, like tar, clings to the image of the Jew in the public mind, making it possible for the vile feathers of malice, thrown out by professional antisemites, to stick.

It would take us too far afield to search for all the roots of the meta-myth. Suffice it to say that for the last two thousand years it has formed part of a vicious circle of cause and effect, in which the meta-myth provoked persecution which, in turn, served as "proof" of the meta-myth to the subconscious mind, thereby strengthening it the more and setting the stage for a fresh series of persecutions. The tragic history of the Jew in all lands made it appear that never could the Jew find peace among the nations, and that in some mysterious manner this fate was inescapable and inexorable.

The debates in the Emancipation period concerning the either-national-or-religious character of Jewish loyalty were not motivated by a zeal for semantics or a flair for verbal jugglery. The emergent nations of Europe were, even then, not ethnically "pure" nationalities; so that the fact of deriving from a different national origin need not have stood in the way of Jewish emancipation. Did Englishmen attempt to circumscribe the civil rights of Welshmen or Scotsmen? Did the Prussians impose a special tax on the movement of Slavs or on their rights of residence, as they imposed special taxes upon Jews? Why, then, should the conception of Jewish nationhood have appeared to the Jesuits and reactionaries to be a valid reason for repudiation of the Emancipation? And why did even the liberal statesmen of Germany, Austria and Russia feel that only through secular education would the Jews "improve" morally so far as to deserve equality of rights, at a time when their own nations were still largely illiterate?

The answer is to be sought in the dim recesses of the European mind, where the meta-myth ruled with undiminished sway even when the power of the Church was broken. The category of a separate nation echoed the meta-myth in interposing the barrier of alienism between Jew and Gentile. It called attention not so much to the ethnic origin of the Jew as to his persistent refusal to follow the normal course of assimilation pursued naturally by other scattered groups. It compelled the interpretation of this extraordinary Jewish tenacity as being due, on the one hand, to perverse pride, nurtured by centuries of enforced segregation and voluntary self-isolation, hammered out by an endless series of pogroms; and, on the other hand, to the indoctrination of self-worship as the "Chosen People."

The Napoleonic insistence on the clear formulation of the religious nature of Judaism had as its purpose the allaying of the meta-myth, so that the Jew could become part and parcel of Western society without external limitations or inner reservations. But the hovering specter of the sinister, strangely powerful myth continued to be reflected in all the discussions of the Jewish problem through the nineteenth century and down to our own day. It has received a new lease on life through the rise and growth of romantic-religious nationalism, which saw in the Jew the image at once of its fulfillment and negation—fulfillment in the doctrine of the "Chosen People" and negation in the attempt of assimilationist and liberal Jews to become part of the nations.

7. The Meta-Myth and Zionism

The rise of Zionism was directly occasioned by the growing menace of the meta-myth.

The conception of World Jewry as a national entity need not, in itself, have resulted in the movement to reestablish a homeland and regain independent political status. A scattered ethnic group normally solves its problems by gradual dissolution and assimilation. Actually, it was the ominous thundercloud of the meta-myth that convinced Herzl and the western European Zionists that the greater part of European Jewry would have to be evacuated into a re-established homeland while the remainder would be completely assimilated.

Herzl's whimsical suggestion, in his pre-Zionist days, that all Austrian Jewry be converted *en masse*, was not really abandoned by him after he beheld the prophetic vision of a reborn Land of Israel; for the alternative to evacuation, in his message to the Jews of Europe, was still absolute and total assimilation. In his correspondence with the leaders of German and French Jewish assimilationists he argued, with some plausibility, that the Zionist program would make the path of assimilation that much easier. As Dr. Emanuel Neumann recently put it, in his address to the Zionist Organization of America's Convention on "Reorienting Zionist Education Today": "Many people, thousands and perhaps hundreds of thousands, who till now have felt that they could not desert a beleaguered people, will no longer be constrained, but will feel able to depart without those qualms of conscience which have deterred them in the past." In any case, Dr. Herzl felt that a vital and secure type of Jewish life was impossible in the lands of the Diaspora.

East-European Zionists, however, did not envisage their movement as the means of liquidating the Diaspora. On the contrary, they looked upon it as the only way of exploding the meta-myth, and thereby rendering Jewish group-life possible in the form of a minority nationality, in all the lands of the dispersion. Dr. Leo Pinsker diagnosed the meta-myth as a mass psychosis, resulting from the bodyless "ghostly" character of the Jewish nation. He was certain that this psychosis would be cleared up as soon as the Jewish position in the world was "normalized" by the establishment of a territorial center. World Jewry would then be removed from the category of the mysterious and the unique, and classed along with other ethnic minorities in the various lands of the Diaspora.

8.   What Status Now for American Jews?

The establishment of the State of Israel can affect the meta-myth in both directions at once.

On the one side, it might serve to the American public as proof positive of the meta-myth—if it is presented as the means of "redemption" for World Jewry and the solution of the "Jewish problem" in all countries, including our own. The tremendous fanfare of publicity which attended the formation of the State of Israel might then have cumulatively the effect of evoking the image of American Israel as a people in flight, unable or unwilling to follow the course of the other immigrant nationalities which are even now steadily on the way to becoming part and parcel of the emergent American nation. It would serve as "Exhibit A" of the meta-myth—to wit, that the gulf between Jew and Gentile is absolute and unbridgeable, that there can be no peace for the Jew in the Christian world, that he must remain forever unabsorbed and alien, paying willingly indeed the price of patriotism in blood and treasure, as he pays for all else, but remaining inwardly foreign, bound by the indissoluble ties of a uniquely tempered tribalism.

But, on the other side, the birth of the State of Israel might also serve as the means of shattering the meta-myth once and for all, as Leo Pinsker had hoped, by demonstrating the sameness in quality and aspiration of Jewish and non-Jewish national loyalties. This effect will result if it is made sun-clear that the intention in establishing the homeland was not at all the evacuation of American Jewry either in whole or in part, but the founding of a haven of refuge for the persecuted Jews in other lands, and the creation of a cultural-religious center for World Jewry. In that case the emergence of a new type of "productive" and fighting Jew will help to banish the time-worn Jewish stereotype from the minds of Christians, and at the same time aid the American Jew to accept his Jewish origin with pride and his religious heritage with ease and naturalness, as all other Americans accept their origins and religions. To this end the theses of Herzlian Zionism must be repudiated insofar as American Jewry is concerned.

Thus the choice of permanently validating or dissipating the meta-myth depends today upon the judgment and insight of American Jewish leadership. The organization of Jewish life in America on a nationalist basis, quite apart from the presence or absence of concrete political ties with the State of Israel, would serve as an invitation for the awakening of the meta-myth in the minds of Jews and Gentiles alike. When Herzlian Jewish nationalism is put forward as the cause and purpose of Jewish survival, then the inherent ideology of the movement cannot be aught else but a confession of the inevitable triumph of the meta-myth. The incorporation of this fear-born conviction into the organizational structure of Jewish life is bound to affect powerfully the minds of Jews and Gentiles alike, helping to create a climate of opinion favorable to the malignant growth of the meta-myth.

Though the academic theory of Jewish nationalism is in itself innocuous and neutral, an intense survivalist nationalism—being by its very nature unique on the American scene, where other immigrant nationalists commingle naturally to produce the emergent American nation—will of necessity be fitted into the mold of the meta-myth. Thus, while nationalism in general is spelled out in the psychological terms of alienism, erecting the barrier of "mine" and "thine" in the battle for the world's goods, American Jewish nationalism in particular would suffer from the additional burden of association with the distorting and soul-smothering nightmare of the meta-myth.

We are led irresistibly, then, to emphasize the religious purpose of Jewish group survival in this country. Now let us see some of the implications of this position.

9. Corollaries of the Religious Status

The achievement of a religious status for American Jewry cannot be effected by the mere say-so of spokesmen. It is a great and complex task, requiring a many-sided effort in various directions. For the actual living philosophy of a group is expressed but partly and superficially in verbal pronunciamentos. It is expressed largely and deeply in its organizational structure. The implications of an avowed acceptance of religious status may be outlined under three headings: (1) public education; (2) communal structure; and (3) relationship to the State of Israel.

Our field of public education is far wider than the limited sphere usually denoted by the term "Jewish education." It includes, in addition, the message delivered from pulpit and platform, and the tremendous oratorical marathons that are associated with the fund-raising efforts for the United Jewish Appeal. To all these activities the following corollaries of a religious conception apply:

(a) *The preaching of fear to American Jews must cease.*

If we are to sink our roots into this soil, we cannot do it half-heartedly and without faith. In the long run, whipped-up mass hysteria is bound to set in motion a train of events culminating in the very horrors conjured up by the purveyors of fear. One hears so frequently the argument for Jewish insecurity in America: the ultimate catastrophe happened before in Spain where the Jews for a time enjoyed a Golden Age and then suffered the tortures of the Inquisition and the expulsion; it happened before in Poland, once "the Paradise of the Jews," but where ghetto benches and economic exclusion prevailed even before the Nazi subjugation; it happened before in Germany, where assimilation seemed to have prospered most but whence nevertheless the deluge of devastation burst forth upon the Jews of Europe. Why, then, not expect a similar fate for American Jewry?

This popular cadence of calamities, abstracted from the bimillenial history of Diaspora Jewry, lends itself beautifully to the meretricious art of the orator and is particularly beloved by professional fund-raisers. This type of argumentation, drawing as it does a sharp line of distinction between the fate of Jews and that of the other immigrant nationalities that are steadily coalescing to form the American nation, is in reality an appeal to the psychical neurosis of the meta-myth, as previously described. For it lumps all nations together in the one suspicion-laden, pogrom-reeking, hostile category of "goyim"; and it assumes that the gulf between Jew and Gentile will never permanently be bridged by sympathetic understanding.

The sober fact is, of course, that vast differences obtain between any past situation elsewhere and the position of Jews today in America—differences which need not be enumerated here. But one thing should be underscored. *Those who have no faith in America obviously cannot be trusted with the task of building the future of Jewry in America.*

(b) *Diaspora Jewish existence must not be depicted as unworthy and shameful.*

In the flush of enthusiasm over the establishment of the State of Israel the derogatory references to exilic life, current in neo-Hebraic literature, were seized upon with avidity, as if Jews had no right to be decently proud of their people prior to the passing of the Partition Resolution. Characteristic of this self-induced mood was the frequently heard expression, "I am not a *damned* Jew any longer! I got a country of my own." As if the Jew was deservedly damned before the State of Israel was called into being!

189

In the merited adulation of the pioneering type, the *halutz*, one often hears echoes of the philosophy of Israel Hayim Brenner, prophet of *halutziuth,* whose bitter denunciations of Jewish life in the Diaspora formed part of the ideology of the Zionist Labor movement. Brenner held that the Jews in the Diaspora lived "the life of gypsies who attach themselves to the natives for their pleasure, the life of dogs who flatter and serve their masters." The whole millenial travail of World Israel he envisaged as "a bitter mistake, bloated pride, falsehood and delusion." He described the whole exile as a thing of shame, and the Jews who have chosen it as "non-human people, called Jews—wounded dogs." Such is the Brennerian mentality which is so frequently invoked these days as self-evident truth.

Listen to a sentence in the clarion call to teachers of a prominent Jewish educator in America: "The proud, but true, boast of the *Yishuv* is that within one generation the shame and desolation was removed from our land, and the shame of exile and ghetto from our souls." Exile and the ghetto may indeed be construed as calamities; but what is that "shame on our souls"? Why should the oppressed feel ashamed? According to Judaism it is the oppressor who bears shame on his soul, not his victim, "for the Lord seeks the pursued." Are we, in a moment of triumph, to throw overboard our standards of true spiritual dignity? How much wiser were the Rabbis when they upheld the contrary extreme, knowing that between it and human nature the proper balance would be struck. Thus they said: "Those who are insulted, but do not insult, who bear their humiliation and do not reply in kind, of them the sacred verse speaks when it says, 'And those who love Him are even as the sun in its might.'"

(c) *We must be on our guard against the cultivation of a sense of alienism from the American nation.*

Too many of our young people have been taught to ridicule the formula of being "American by nation and Jewish by religion." Even some of our tribunes committed to a religious status for American Jews continue the traditional pastime of satirizing the designation "Americans of the Jewish faith," though it echoes their avowed conception. In the rush of climbing on the secular nationalist bandwagon they seem to have forgotten the redoubtable fact that the totality of national feelings contains barriers of exclusion as well as bonds of inclusion. If nationalism in all its implications is given free rein in the Jewish schools and public life, it will eventually induce a state of mind most congenial to the meta-myth.

The sense of alienism is not to be confused with the popularly discussed fear of "double loyalty," for it functions in the realm of the spirit, not in the domain of politics and patriotism. It is concerned with the inner sense of self-identification which may or may not find expression in overt acts. When this sense of self-identification is not directed into spiritual channels, thus serving as additional motivation for the good life, but is allowed to develop its inherent logic and acquire its own momentum, it cannot but eventuate into a self-induced mood of alienism.

It should also be noted that the line of division on this issue cuts clear across the ranks of organized Zionists, as was demonstrated at the recent conference on "Reorienting Zionist Education Today." In the years ahead the rift between Zionists and non-Zionists will likely disappear; instead, a deep gulf will be revealed between those who regard American Jewish life as viable and worthy in itself, and those who think of it merely as a temporary financial and spiritual colony of the Israeli mother-country, slated for eventual liquidation.

Since the mentality of the latter group is rarely brought into the open, it may be well for us to remember that it forms part of classic Zionist literature and to observe its operation in the writings of one of its best exponents.

10. The Mentality of Colonials of Israel

The late Dr. Jacob Klatzkin, noted Hebrew philosopher, formulated the logic of secular nationalism in words that capture its full dynamic impetus. They can therefore serve as a clear warning to all of us who wish to raise a generation of Jews who will feel perfectly at home on the American scene.

The following quotations are taken from Dr. Klatzkin's Hebrew book, *T'chumim,* which has been used as a basic text of Zionism in at least one American Hebrew Teachers College.

> Know that so long as the nations of the world battle against us, it is a good sign for us. It indicates that our national form is not yet rubbed out and that our alienism is still felt. The ending of the war, or its weakening, would testify to the erasing of our identity and the softening of our alienism. We shall not attain equality of rights anywhere, save in reward for an implied or expressed confession that we are not a national body in itself, but parts of the body of the people of the land— or at the price of complete assimilation.
>
> Who are our enemies and how do they present the case for the prosecution? They look upon us as a separate national group and complain against Israel: one people it is that does not mingle with the nations. One people it is, though scattered and dispersed; and if Jews

declare themselves to be good Germans, good Frenchmen, good Russians, don't believe them: Jews they are, nonetheless. . . .

Who are our friends and how do they present the case for our defense? They see us as the remnants of a dead people and they advocate our cause by saying: "He is already dead and passed out of this world and only the bare name is left. The Jews of our time become progressively bone of our bone and flesh of our flesh; they speak our language and learn our literature and the sancta of our civilization, love the country of their birth, and admire the great of the land and strive mightily for the welfare of the nation. Already their share in the nation's cultural wealth is very great; and if their assimilation into our midst is still not completed and there is left in them some of their ancient alienism, who is to blame for the postponement of the consummation if not the antisemitism of the nationalist reactionaries, which erects boundaries between us and them, preventing a proper amalgamation? Therefore, it is our duty to accord them complete equality, to act towards them as to children of our nation and to treat them as faithful brothers."

And the defendant himself, the Hebrew people, what do we say? If we desire to live a national life in exile, we should tell our defender: "We desire neither your honey nor your sting! The prosecution is right. An alien people we are and we desire to continue in our alienism. We admit the propriety of your being concerned over your national character and your desire to maintain separation between us and yourselves, but we protest against the vulgar forms of this separation.

Thus, instead of forming societies to defend us against antisemites, who seek to limit our rights, we should es-

193

tablish societies to defend us from our friends who fight on our side, as it were. [Pages 70, 71]

Also many of our nationalist Jews, when they demand civil rights, say to the nations: "Citizens, we are like you; we are patriotic and prepared to offer the supreme sacrifice; and we demand one law for us and for you without any kind of distinction or discrimination." It has already become a common cliché in the mouths of our nationalist spokesmen: We are loyal Jews and loyal Germans, loyal Jews and loyal Frenchmen," and so on . . .

But if the power of our ancestors' endurance and if the qualities of truthfulness and national dignity had prevailed among us above the rush for full equality of rights, we should not have hesitated rather to say to the people of the land: "You are strangers to us and we are strangers to you. Your culture is alien to us, as well as your language, your customs, your holidays and the sancta of your life. Your joy is not our joy. Your mourning is not our mourning. Your aspirations and hopes are not our aspirations and hopes. Strangers we are; and insofar as it lies within our power we shall safeguard our alienism and the barriers between us. We do not at all wish you to behave equally toward us and toward the children of your own nation; and we do not aim to share equally with you in the prerogatives of the nation, for complete equality might injure many of our own national rights and humiliate our national personality." [Page 72]

Even if we should assume that exilic life is viable and that after the bankruptcy of religion in our time, complete assimilation is inevitable, we should still have to insist that exilic Judaism is not worthy of existence. [Page 76]

194

What, then, should be done with the Diaspora? Should it be permitted to degenerate more and more?

It should be regarded as the passageway to the redemption of the people in its own land. For many generations to come the land of Israel will require aid from the Diaspora. Israel will draw elements of strength from the Disapora, exploiting little by little the doomed community and through this very exploitation save it. [Page 81]

We should guard exilic Judaism insofar as we can. We should develop within it a national culture, set up in the teeth of reality and the inevitable lines of development. We should multiply fences and prohibitions calculated to protect our particularity and uniqueness. We should erect barriers upon barriers between us and the nations among whom we are steadily being assimilated . . .

There is a purpose to this temporary survival, because it is only a stage of transition. [Page 82]

Nevertheless, we should save the ruins of our religion —not religion itself or its spiritual essence, but its national wealth, its laws. We should save the laws, fences and prohibitions, which have the effect of erecting a ghetto for us among the nations. [Page 83]

This is the basic principle of our national work in the lands of the Diaspora: *the exile is dough for the land of Israel.* And such is the character of this contemporary work: *impudence toward reality."* [Page 85]

It might be objected that the views of Dr. Klatzkin are not representative, since he was an avowed "negator of the Diaspora." But the negation of any long future for Diaspora Jewry, and the determination meanwhile to exploit (*nitzul*) all its human and financial resources for the *Yishuv,* are of the very essence of the Herzlian Zionist ideal, as originally propounded. The moment a future is allowed for the Jews of any country the message of secular Zionism, insofar as that country is concerned, is no longer Zionism but pro-Palestinian refugeeism. As Dr. Robert Gordis has put it: "A secularist who is a Zionist must, if he is logically consistent, become a *Sholel Hagolah,* a negator of a Jewish future in the Diaspora."

11. But What of the Irreligious?

The most telling objection raised against the conception of a religious status for American Jewry is the indubitable fact of its limited inclusiveness. Where does this conception leave the masses of those who are religiously indifferent?

In a formal way, to be sure, this question is easily answered.

First, we might point out that no worthy conception of Judaism is possible that would confer automatically, in blanket fashion, the status of "Jewishness in good standing" upon all and sundry people called Jews. If any such all-inclusive conceptions were proposed, it would have to confer essential meaning and worth either, internally, upon Jewish blood or, externally, upon anti-Jewish animus, since these are the only common ineluctable factors. But racism, whether biological and mystical or spiteful and puerile, is unacceptable in scientific honesty, in moral conscience, or even in sheer expediency.

Remaining on the formal level, we might point out, in the second place, that a truly nationalist conception of Jewish status, which is the only alternative to a religious status, would require personal participation in life of Israel. Hence, genuinely nationalist Jews in America are as much in the minority as religious Jews are supposed to be. Wendell Willkie and Franklin Roosevelt, though of German and Dutch descent, were in no sense members of the German and Dutch nationalities. If, as Ernest Renan put it, "nationality is a plebiscite repeated daily," then the vote of individuals even belonging to it by birth may be altered from day to day. Indeed, on the basis of a national criterion, the process of linguistic assimilation which American Jewry is at present undergoing is of decisive significance.

However, on both sides, the religious and nationalist, there is a broad swath of marginal loyalties, which are shared by the vast majority of American Jews.

We might then take our cue from the Talmud, which offers two complementary definitions of what it takes to belong to the Congregation of Israel. One would exclude all who knowingly transgress any *mitzvah* (commandment) three times. The other would embrace within the fold all who reject the idolatry of other nations. As these two definitions delimit the boundaries of those who belong to the nuclear and to the protoplasmic sections of the living cell of Israel, so might our conception of religious status offer a similar standard of graded belonging, that is bounded by the inexorable hairline of conversion.

But all these replies, correct as they may be on a formal level, do not really capture the essence of the problem. There are among us many spiritually sensitive people unaffiliated with the Synagogue, yet whose entire being is profoundly stirred by Jewish associations and problems. How can they be termed "marginal" without a perversion of Jewish values? Then, on the other side, we have masses of indifferent materialists, included through one avenue or another in the organizational complex of the Jewish community, but not susceptible to any kind of spiritual message or orientation, left cold and unmoved by any appeal to spiritual values.

We must recognize that for several generations Jewish national loyalties were being steadily substituted for religious loyalties. The change has been so all-pervasive and continuous that few of our "best" Jews are now capable of realizing the extent of inner transmutation that has taken place, let alone retrace their steps. The successive calamities that have befallen our people weakened their faith in both God and man, while strengthening their grim reliance on their own collective powers. This new spirit of militant defiance has been subtly molding the residual Jewish loyalties in its own shape and pattern.

The moral task before us, then, is to transmute deep ethnic consciousness into reawakened dedication to the ideals and values of the Jewish spirit. We must chart a path from the sense of being part of an embattled camp to the sense of being a partner of the Lord in the creation of a world patterned after His Word.

This task of psychic alchemy may appear to present insuperable difficulties. Hasn't the course of development in modern times proceeded in the opposite direction, from ethical humanism and religious liberalism to glorified nationalism and romanticized racism, from Kant to Hitler? What, then, leads us to think that the process may be reversed?

Indeed, much can be said by those who despair of so arduous a task. Yet this transformation was effected by the great of our people, time and again, when they achieved a universal faith out of the tears and tribulations of their sorely harassed brethren. It is precisely this achievement that constitutes the greatest contribution of Israel on the altar of humanity. Do not the historic parallels indicate that our task is not utterly hopeless?

12. *The Creative Genius of Jewish History*

If we schematize the fundamental factors in the rise of Judaism, we note a steady repetition of the three elements: (a) sorrowful circumstances; (b) an ideal interpretation;

and (c) the attainment of a new height of dedication to the life of the spirit.

Enslavement in Egypt was interpreted by Moses and his prophetic school as a purifying cauldron for those selected by God to become "a people of priests and a holy nation"; and it was followed by the dedication of the whole people to the ideals of loving the stranger, respecting the slave, honoring the Sabbath Day as an inviolate rest day for servants and masters alike, and *the prohibition of despising Egyptians, their former oppressors*. Thus the so-called normal or human reaction, in which hate breeds hate and all its ugly brood, was transcended. The intense consciousness of persecution was made to yield the glorious fruits of the spirit.

The same scheme was followed by the great prophets of the Babylonian exile. The bitter national catastrophe of defeat, devastation, and exile was interpreted as divine punishment by the Lord of heaven and earth for ethical and religious backsliding, and as evidence of the uncompromising justice of Providence. As a result of this prophetic interpretation, the Babylonian exile raised the level of the Jewish religion from the particularist stage, denoted by scholars as the religion of Israel, to the universalist faith of Judaism.

The genius of Israel effected a similar leap into the realm of the spirit when the Second Temple was destroyed "for the sin of causeless hatred," as the Rabbis put it. The four ells of *Halakah* (the Law) came to take the place of the altar of the priests as the abode of the *"Sh'kinah"* (God's Presence).

All through the later dark centuries of persecution, calamities became the stepping stones for spiritual progress.

As Edmond Fleg put it:

"The Jew has suffered so much, he has endured so many injustices, experienced so completely the misery of life, that pity for the poor and humiliated has become second nature to him. And in his agonized wanderings he has seen at close range so many men of all races and of all countries, different everywhere and everywhere alike, that he has understood, he has felt in the flesh of his flesh, that Man is one as God is one. Thus was formed a race which, though it have the same vices and the same virtues as other races, is yet without doubt the most *human* of all races."

And thus has been charted for us, by the creative genius of Jewish history, the logical path from the Jewish situation in the lands of the Diaspora to the values of the spiritual life.

13. Challenge to the American Jew

American Jewish experience is richly productive of spiritual enlightenment. It can provide an inspiring way of life to those who identify themselves with it and grow in maturity through it.

Our keen awareness of the perversion of fact through prejudice should lead us to devote ourselves all the more to the love of truth, to the accompanying discipline of objective thinking, and to the esteem of learning as a noble end in itself. The deep gulf that yawns between ideals avowed verbally and their sadly limited application we should interpret as a universal human failing to be remedied through the willingness of ever greater numbers to impose the disciplines of good breeding and noble aims upon themselves. Our awareness of the evils resulting from the atavistic sentiments of tribalism and clannishness should lead us to greater efforts in behalf of all causes that strengthen the cementing bonds of humanity. Our consciousness of the ugliness and drabness of provincialism and Babbittry should quicken us to appreciate the universal standards of ethical and esthetic beauty, so that we may help to create that unitary realm of the spirit essential for the ultimate emergence of the unitary society of man. Above all, our ready observation of the vices of others we should construe as a challenge for the ruthless examination of our own shortcomings, in the spirit of the true prophets, repudiating the easy excuses and self-flattering *clichés* purveyed by our publicly acclaimed pseudo-prophets.

Thus our exposed situation in the Diaspora is fertile soil for the creation of spiritually minded men and women.

Granted that this pathway is difficult enough to follow. There are two human reactions to hostility. One is to escape its brunt by hiding under a protective covering of one kind or another and ultimately joining the hostile camp itself. The other is to close ranks defiantly and reply with hate for hate. Both policies are spiritually poisonous, and it is a tossup as to which one is ultimately the most ruinous. The true Jewish way is to rise above the hatred by recognizing it as a universal evil, found in ourselves as well as in others, and to labor for its cure both within ourselves and in the total society of which we are a part.

By cleaving to the spiritual interpretation of Jewish experience we provide a means for the non-religious among us to progress in the realm of the spirit through their Jewish identification. To be sure, we have not shown how the gulf in many men's minds between adherence to spiritual values and the convictions of religion may be bridged. There is in fact a plus of conviction in religious faith, with regard to the roots in eternity of spiritual values, which cannot be obtained by the cultivation of a humanist attitude alone. Spiritually minded people will still find congregational life the best means of continuing their own spiritual progress, through self-identification with Jewish experience in the religious interpretation, and by promoting its values in the social grouping of which they are a part.

14. What Leadership for American Jewry?

If the spiritually sensitive should fail to take or build their place in the leadership ranks of American Jewry, we may almost be certain that World Jewry will fail to acquit itself honorably in these days of unprecedented challenge. It will rather drift along one or both "human" directions—of militancy à la Ben Hecht and mammonism à la Sammy Glick.

So long, then, as an intellectual does not accept Lenin's dictum that "religion is opium for the people," he must not fail to see in the modern congregational setup, with all its present failings, his best available means of promoting spiritual values in the concrete social situation wherein he finds himself.

I would emphasize that all who are genuinely concerned with the advancement of spiritual values among our people will find the institutions and disciplines of religion most suited for their purpose, even if they do not accept *in toto* the ideological basis of the modern Synagogue.

As to our materialists and mammonists who—whether affiliated with the Synagogue or not—subscribe neither to its convictions nor to its spiritual program and implications, the problem is of universal scope; though among us it is aggravated by the prevalence of so many pseudo-philosophies which shed an aura of respectability over any and all types of Jewish identification. However, the more the status of American Jewry is clarified, the easier it should be to bring the straying and groping marginal groups within the historical influence of the Synagogue; and the more truly representative and spiritual should become the leadership of American Jewry.

(published in The Menorah Journal, Winter, 1949)

3

Building our Future in America

1. The Pivot of the Past Generation

Can it be doubted that, in the past generation, the collective energy of American Jewry was centered in the vision of itself as simply an embattled minority? Our religious and cultural characteristics receded into the background. To be sure, not one of our religious spokesmen would have defined the Jewish group thus baldly, without qualification, as just a minority, like other minorities within the American people, struggling for sheer survival. On the conscious level of ideas, the old ideologies, together with some new ones, provided the shifting official facade for the conflicting doctrines and interpretations of "Jewish life." But none of the ideological trends within Judaism could possibly command the depth of emotion that attached to the character and problems of Jewry as a whole. For the most part the conscious "Jewish community" thought of itself as an encircled and besieged minority, battling for sheer existence against the pervasive and hostile power of the majority population.

Among the masses of immigrants the conception of a minority was modelled chiefly after the pattern of the minority-nationalities of Europe, that staged so remarkable a renaissance in the first two decades of the twentieth century, particularly as a result of the Treaty of Versailles. It was through the insistence of the American Jewish Congress, which was brought into being for the purpose of articulating the opinion of the Jewish masses, that the Jewish representatives to the Versailles Conference—including, be it remembered, the leaders of the American Jewish Committee —pressed for the status of a minority-nationality for the Jews of Central Europe.

Nor was the category of a minority-nationality given up even when it became apparent that, on the American scene, immigrant nationalities slowly merge into the general population, with the residual loyalties fading out of sight in two or three generations. The peculiar and complex character of the Jewish heritage made possible a variety of different and even conflicting comparisons. Thus, we were a minority like the Swedes of Minnesota or the Dutch of Pennsylvania, preserving our quaint customs; or like the Irish, fighting for our homeland against the British from the security of the American base; or like the Catholics, cherishing an all-embracing faith that shaded off by degrees into a variety of cultural areas; or we were like the Negroes, scorned as men of lesser breed. But the adjectival modification was not as important as the substantive concept. The basic, ineluctable fact of our Jewish being was our status as a marked and numerically inferior group. Thus it was generally held. Hence our susceptibility to the bias and hostility of the majority population, the need of our being permanently mobilized to fight against discrimination, and the obvious logic of joining other "minorities" in the battle for fairness and equality.

Two factors combined to produce this collective fixation of the past generation, extending into the present. First, the insidious malice of antisemitism attained overwhelming proportions in our day, threatening the utter annihilation of World Jewry, so that all motives other than sheer survival were rendered mainly academic and relatively unimportant. Second, the force of religious conviction was weakened by a tidal wave of skepticism and indifference to the point where the "eternal verities" of the Jewish faith no longer seemed worth living for. With the inner content of Judaism reduced to the vanishing point, and the need of battling for sheer physical survival becoming paramount, American Jewry settled down to live and work with the vision of itself as a "minority," expecting prejudice as a matter of course, and fighting against it doggedly, in routine fashion, virtually as the "way of life" of our collective existence.

It was not in financial terms alone that the two fundamental motivations of Jewish collective activity were Zionism and Anti-defamation. These two fields provided psychical outlets for the fevered emotions of "Jewish life," serving to compensate for the distressing consciousness of minority existence. In the varied activities of Anti-defamation, Jews articulated their frustration and indignation, erecting and ceaselessly mending the protective walls of the inner ghetto, even as they fended the attacks of bigots and fanatics. Through the far-flung efforts of Zionism, the self-assertive instincts of our people were channeled, the sense of oneness of "Jewish fate" was cultivated, bonds were forged with the glory of the past and the promise of the future. While expression was thus afforded to humanitarian activity within the Jewish community, scope was given as well to feelings of despair and cynicism, of resentment and militancy toward the non-Jewish world in the Diaspora and in Zion itself. The practical activities in both domains may or may not have been justified in all instances. Quite apart, however, from any pragmatic or utilitarian considerations, those activities functioned as mass-media for the release of psychical energy, certainly as expressions of the poignant pathos of "Jewishness," possibility also as quasi religious rites—rites reflecting the attitude of the Jew toward his own destiny in particular and toward human life in general.

For many Jewish men and women, thus, either Zionist work or Anti-defamation work, or both, have constituted the sum and substance of Judaism. The entire burden of their self-awareness as Jews has revolved around the painful focus of a trapped and hapless minority. How unrealistic, then, how superficial it is for those of us who urge the diminution, rationalization, and even partial liquidation of the Zionist Organization and the "defense agencies," not to realize that their activities have become psychical necessities— sacred rites, as it were—for their innumerable votaries and followers.

In the field of Jewish education, too, the dominant motivation in the past generation has been the need of building up the "defense-mechanism" of our young. As a minority— it is still being contended—we must provide our young with the spiritual equivalent of an all-covering coat of mail, for protection against the slings of hate and the arrows of malice that are certain to be hurled at them. A study of the texts in our Hebrew and religious schools, and of the aids provided by the Bureaus of Jewish Education, reveals a conspicuous shyness in religious affirmations and a loud emphasis on the "armor theory," in all its variations. There are plenty of other evidences. That a world assembly of top-level Hebrew educators in Jerusalem should seriously debate whether the purpose of Jewish education was *solely* to prepare the young for emigration to Israel, or whether that purpose was only its *major concern,* is itself proof of the extent to which the keen awareness of minority-status had become the most potent factor in Jewish consciousness.

The echoes of this awareness in the literature of the past two decades are too various and wide-ranging to describe here. It is enough to mention the works of Franz Kafka, for whom the Jewish sense of insecurity has become transmuted into a universal judgment concerning the "existential" tragedy of the human race. Who can read *The Castle,* in which the tragic hero is a man without home and status and the outcasts are those who rejected the love of the Master when it was offered, and fail to see the travail of mankind reflected through the prism of Jewish experience? In Jo Sinclair's portrayal, in *Wasteland,* of the young Jew who is cured of self-hatred by psychoanalysis, religious convictions play no role at all: the "hero" is perplexed by the meaning of Jewish identification, his spirit tossed about in stormy upheaval from the crest of self-acceptance to the trough of self-rejection.

Perhaps the keenest expression of this mood is to be found in Norman Katkov's *Eagle at My Eye,* precisely because it is more a stirring social document than a literary work. Dealing with the question of intermarriage, it ignores religious considerations, makes light of all the positive elements in the Jewish heritage, and reveals the painful reality of Jewish consciousness in all its stark horror when it is reduced to the sheer awareness of belonging to a hunted pack, pursued by implacable and crafty foes, neither expecting nor giving quarter. Even so coarse a work of genius as Jones's *From Here to Eternity* captures the essence of its one Jewish character in a bullying aggressiveness that is intended to cover up the agonizing sense of being "different" and "set apart."

The point to remember about all these floating straws in the stormy intellectual sea is the almost complete disappearance of the voice of faith or idealism from the consciousness of so many Jews, leaving only the dregs of minority-feeling—messy, unsightly, insipid.

When your finger is caught in the door, remarked Bialik, you forget about all your other organs and interests, and your whole life seems to be concentrated in the finger. The Hitlerite challenge to our very existence made us all overly and painfully conscious of our numerical weakness and our helplessness—to the sad detriment of the healthy, positive factors in our spiritual makeup. Now that the finger is released from the door—at any rate in Western countries—we must not permit the impetus of the immediate past to prevent us from taking a fresh look at ourselves, so that we may see our life whole and see it truly.

2. The Unique Character of "Jewish Minority-Existence"

Does the term "minority," then, do justice to the character of our Jewish being in America?

The other minorities with which we automatically classify ourselves are either ethnic groups or religious alignments. But we are both these *plus*—plus an indeterminate factor that makes our situation quite unique. Alike in the consciousness of most Jews and in the lingering tradition of most of the Christian population there is an undeniable feeling that the gulf between Jew and Gentile is somehow deeper and more significant than the national dividing lines in the European family or the denominational differences within the same nation. This felt difference is not a matter of race, as is still sometimes supposed, erroneously; for, as has been demonstrated times without number, the Jewish people of Europe and America are biologically of much the same racial strain as the rest of the population. Rather, it is in the dichotomy of *religious traditions* that this profound sense of difference lingers—a dichotomy which persists even when the dogmatic substructures of the two traditions crumble and merge into the general background of Western culture.

In fact, we are a special kind of minority, not to be classified with either the Catholics or the Negroes. While our existence is dependent mostly on our conscious and collective "will to live," there is also a large measure of compulsion in our being. This union of the "must" and the "will," the fate and the faith, seems as ultimate in the long run as the mystery of Providence in the chaotic confusion of human affairs. One thing is certain. If we continue to operate on the basis of an ordinary "minority concept," we undermine the "will to live," the positive spiritual force, of our people. The natural course of a merely physical minority is progressive disappearance. At the same time, however, the compulsive factors in our Jewish being render "the will to die" illusory and self-defeating.

Only the intellectual and moral underworld, and those among us who have lost the last traces of faith, can subscribe to a designation that reflects merely the sheer compulsiveness of our existence. Yet the conception of a religious community, for all its aptness, still fails to capture the full truth of the situation of the Jewish group within the American nation as a whole. We cannot escape the fact that we constitute a minority set off by something deeper than the grooves of purely denominational differences.

What, then, shall we make of our awareness of minority-existence?

Upon the answer to this question may well depend the continued allegiance of our young intellectuals. For to most of the enlightened, to most liberals, the ceremonies and rites of different faiths constitute just so many varied expressions of the one basic truth (if they believe in religious truth at all). What is to prevent a light-hearted change of the language of piety, in the interest of convenience and integration, even as we normally exchange an inherited tongue for the language of the majority? Only the realization that the Jewish tradition, which characterizes our being, possesses unique and non-expendable values, not only for ourselves but for the American nation as a whole. Ours is more than a creed, more than a so-called "way of life," more even than the ethnic-cultural ties of a people. *We are the living bearers of a tradition that both supplements and corrects the onesidedness of the Christian tradition.*

By the attractions of the merely psychical virtues of piety

we can lose as many of our searching souls as we might gain, unless the specific quality of Jewish piety is understood and appreciated.

3. *Two Conceptions of "Jewish Mission"*

In our tradition it is as a consecrated people that we emerged upon the stage of history—"a people of priests and a holy nation." We were to be, unto all the nations of the world, prophets and priests, perhaps also "the suffering servants" in behalf of God and man. This stirring conception was a prophetic development and interpretation of the earlier doctrine of the "Chosen People": that doctrine insisted that our ancestors were selected for their own sake, not as instruments for the salvation of mankind. "The Lord did not set His love upon you, nor choose you, because you were more in number than any people; for ye were the fewest of all people. But because the Lord loved you, and because He would keep the oath which He had sworn unto your fathers. . ." (*Deuteronomy* VII: 7, 8.) Love is selective, arbitrary, evoked only by the sheer being of the beloved, not by any act of hers. But the prophets transmuted this doctrine of an inscrutable divine fiat into a magnificent dedication to the enlightenment and salvation of all the nations of the earth.

Through all the long tribulent centuries of the pre-modern era the Jewish people thought of themselves as the custodians of truth and salvation, their own tragedy serving only to accentuate the arduousness and supreme importance of their divinely appointed task. We are even as the seed rotting in the ground, said Jehudah Halevi; the proud branches waving in the sun are the powerful domains of Christianity and Islam; but when the fruit on those branches ripen in the end of time, it is we who shall reappear as the seed in the core of the ripe fruit. The Biblical designation of Israel as "my eldest son," and the Talmudic reference to "the sons of kings," correspond to the mass-feeling of our people, even in periods of darkest persecution. Said the Chief Rabbi of Vienna in the seventeenth century, Yom-Tov Lipman Heller, when the threat of expulsion was held over the hapless community he headed: "A king had two brothers. The beloved elder brother and true heir was banished from his father's good graces for his sins. Now the younger brother sits proudly at the table, while the elder one gathers the crumbs. If the younger brother in his arrogance take the crumbs away from the elder, would not the father resent this effrontery and punish the younger brother still more severely than ever the elder was chastised? We, the people of Israel, are the older brothers. Beware, lest you take even the crumbs from us." (*Megilath Aivoh*) Thus, proudly, did the rabbis of old carry on the work of "Anti-defamation," conscious as they were of being "the elder brother," to whom belonged the Promise and through whom was to come the Redemption.

With the advent of the Age of Reason and the revolutionary upheaval of Emancipation, only the dwindling remnant of naive Orthodoxy was able to hold on to the belief that, as a people, we had been chosen and consecrated and charged with the task of treasuring *"Torah* and *Mitzvoth."* Yet, after a brief period of hesitation and confusion, the ancient doctrine reappeared in modern garb, with its vital and sustaining power hardly impaired. In the proud ideology of Classical Reform, the Jews were declared to be a Specially Endowed People, gifted with the genius for the religion. As the ancient Greeks had a genius for beauty and systematic reasoning, and the ancient Romans a native bent for law and organization, so the Jews—according to the faith of Classical Reform—were historically the people of pure ethical monotheism. Today the Classical Reformers continue to stand for a healthy and rational, humanist and liberal, life-centered and life-affirming type of piety, in conscious opposition to the various popular distortions of the meaning of faith.

Though the Reform doctrine of a "Jewish mission" to the nations was the favorite target of contemptuous sarcasm on the part of Zionists, the ideology of Cultural Zionism retained the principle of the Jewish people as a Specially Endowed Nation. To Ahad Ha'Am the unique genius of Israel consisted not in its religious faith but rather in its profoundly ethical bent. The ideas of Judaism, he held, are not of decisive importance, since ideas quickly become the property of the entire educated world. To survive, or at all events to live worthily, the Jewish people must find the way of reestablishing itself as a healthy nation, on its own land, where it might evolve new ideals and original forms of living. It is the recreation of the national base in the ancient homeland that will make possible the rebirth of the native "genius" of Israel. So ran the argument. As for Jewish life in the Diaspora, we may hope to become again a Specially Endowed Minority—through our very labors for the reconstitution of the Jewish homeland and through the spiritual productions of a renascent Israel entering into the stream of universal civilization.

These two conceptions still linger in the varying ideological trends within American Judaism today. But if we now seek to activate the community as a whole we cannot take, as its philosophical cornerstone, either the claim of a divine act of consecration in the dawn of history or the equally dogmatic assertion of a unique "genius" in the domain of the spirit. Today these conceptions belong to what might be termed the vertical dimension of spiritual "over-belief," out of which particular groups in the community draw the material for their own specific ideologies. No dogma either of a literalistic belief or of an ethnic pride can serve as foundation for the program of the all-embracing community.

4. The Concept of a "Creative Minority"

Does it follow, then, that the Jewish community as a whole, as an interdenominational structure, is inevitably condemned to deal only with the negative phases of Jewish existence, and thus exalt negativism—or the defense-psychology—to the rank of a predominant philosophy?

By no means. It is possible for the community as a whole to think and act in terms of a *creative minority*. This the community can do without identifying itself with any particular interpretation of Jewish life. It need repudiate only such groups as negate the value of our continued existence in the Diaspora—whether in the name of a totalitarian Zionism or in the name of totalitarian Americanism. And, as a *creative minority,* the Jewish community must be neither "past-centered," devoting itself to the preservation of a sacred tradition for its own sake, nor "Zion-centered," seeking its inspiration in the culture that might one day spring up in Israel. For thus to place the vital focus of its being outward is lethal—as devastating for the spirit of a community as it is debilitating for an individual to live only in the past or hang on the approval of others. The emphasis rather on autonomy, on creativeness, will cherish and foster whatever cultural and spiritual values are generated by every individual interpretation, every aspiration, within the community.

In his massive work, *The Study of History,* Toynbee points to the fact that new cultural creations are virtually always the achievement of minorities that, through a variety of historical events, get set off from the general population. To be sure, Toynbee regards contemporary Jewry as hardly more than "a fossil of Syriac civilization," unaware as he is of the evolution of ideas and institutions within Judaism, unaware of the continuous interplay of challenge and response in the making of the modern Jew. Furthermore, as a Christian theologian, Toynbee can hardly extol the function of the Christian as the perennial savior of civilization, through fresh acts of surrender to God, without writing *finis* to the Jew's history.

Actually, it is the ideal Jew who lives both in the world and above the world at the same time, never so fully enmeshed in the web and coils of immediate narrow loyalties as not to sense the challenge and charm of the more universal values. Thus, even in the Middle Ages, in defiance of the Ghetto walls, it was out of the Jewish community that the pattern of municipal democracy arose; and the challenge was issued for a return to the original springs of faith in the Hebrew Scriptures; and even the idea was fostered of nonconformity in matters of creed; and the liberal doctrines of human goodness and divine rationality were treasured. Later, in Germany and Austria before the Nazi flood, Jews were among the foremost creators and patrons of literature and art; for, aloof as they felt in Central-European society, they clung all the more tenaciously to their roots in the universal homeland of the spirit.

Now what are the characteristics of a "creative minority"?

A "creative minority" is, first, a minority that senses its underlying and essential unity with the general population, even as it is conscious of its own distinguishing attributes. We are not as a lonely island, battered by the endless waves of the encircling ocean, but one of a chain of islands which form a solid continuous range beneath the raging, restless surface. Distinctive as our history and tradition are, they yet constitute a vital part of the realm of ideas and experience upon which American civilization is based. Thus we are part of Christian culture, though apart from it; and, even as we cherish and cultivate our own specific heritage, we must not ignore the massive historical reality, the "Judeo-Christian tradition," which forms the spiritual substratum of Western civilization.

Secondly, a "creative minority" evolves new values for the general community, of which it is a part, out of the peculiar circumstances which set it apart. While not officiously seeking to lead or teach or preach, it expands the cultural horizons of the whole community by developing the implications of its unique position. In this sense the Jewish community, by faithfully tracing out the inner logic of its traditions and developing the implicit truths of its peculiar status, might unfold fresh insights for the guidance of the entire American nation.

Thirdly, a "creative minority" is value-centered and oriented to the future. Neither exhausted by the elemental struggle for bare survival nor overcome by the great glory of the past, its face is turned toward the sunlight of spiritual growth. It refuses either to chafe vainly against the boundaries that enclose it or to look above them with Olympian detachment as if they did not exist.

The unique features of our status within the all-embracing American community are thus fashioned through the impetus of our specific religio-cultural tradition in continuous interaction with the Christian tradition. It is also this dichotomy of traditions that sets the stage for the role we must play as a "creative minority" in the achievement of higher rungs on the ladder of progress. However, before we can profitably study the relationship of the Jewish to the Christian tradition, we must envisage clearly the nature of the challenge that religion in general is now facing.

5. Needed: a Fresh Synthesis of Faith and Reason

For long now the unifying function of a religious tradition in the total complex of culture has been a truth forgotten, so that our century has witnessed a crescendo of disasters, resulting largely from the inability of modern man to achieve inner unity and harmony. In the Western world the classic ideal of a well-rounded culture, embracing all the interests and values of man, was given up stage by stage through the course of the nineteenth century. Principally, the "split" in the soul of modern man was occasioned by the failure of philosophy to relate successfully the values and aspirations of human nature with the hard facts and iron necessities of the physical universe. At his most human levels, man became a stranger in the universe, while increasingly able to handle its physical forces. It was significantly, a German, Immanuel Kant, who first delineated this bifurcation of the human personality, in his meticulously elaborated distinction between the "pure reason" and the "practical reason," the one formulating the laws of comprehension, the other setting forth the laws of action.

The amazing proliferation of genius that is known as the German Romantic Movement took the Kantian analysis for granted, widened the breach between faith and reason to catastrophic proportions, and exhibited the seeds of all the follies that were to become the popular fads of the next century. If the comprehensible and the spiritual are essentially unrelated, the flood-gates are thrown open for the cynical exaltation of cleverness above wisdom, for the deprecation of the higher reaches of the human spirit, for the reduction of all ideals to impulses and needs, for the downgrading of all that is human and divine and for the upgrading of the necessitous, the beastly, and the unconscious.

The romantic flight from reason led to Fichte's thesis of unconscious genius in chosen individuals and in chosen peoples, thereby launching the wave of auto-intoxicated nationalist "crusades." The yawning gulf between reason and faith made possible both the Hegelian adoration of the all-encompassing Prussian State and the Marxist worship of the inevitable and cataclysmic emergence of the Proletarian Revolution. That gulf made possible the Nietzschean vision of the "superman" rising "beyond good and evil" to the apex of a laughing ruthless "blonde beast," and induced the conviction of Sorel that violence is the dynamic expression of the subconscious current of life, hence the source of all progress. That gulf brought about the willingness of modern man to subordinate his soul and conscience to a totalitarian State or Movement, thus driving out religion from the spheres of cultural orchestration and social idealism in the Western democracies. The cult of the irrational in literature and art as well as in politics; the substitution of training in technical skills for the classic goals of education in our big universities; the demise of the "gentleman and scholar" and the rise of the "common man" in all his natural ruggedness and utilitarian standards and vulgar tastes—these things too have resulted from the fission between the "pure" and the "practical" reason.

All these distressing developments of the past century flowed inevitably from the ineluctable fact that the classic synthesis of the age of faith had broken down. Now it is idle to attempt to turn the clock back, to pretend that the failure of all the substitutes for the old religion proves the truth of the old religion. Idle to exhort our contemporaries to repudiate modernism so as to regain the pristine purity and healing balm of the pre-modern world-view, securely founded as it was on authority and mightily raftered by firm dogmas. A healthy synthesis today cannot be achieved by flight from one extreme to the other. It is not faith against reason, nor reason against faith, that we must pursue. We must rather seek to develop a fresh comprehensive philosophy in which all the expressions of human nobility are harmonized, set free, invigorated.

6. This New "Wisdom" of Our Quest

This central quest of our age is now moving toward the orbit of our grasp. The mighty achievements of the physical and social sciences are combining to make possible once again the ancient classical ideal of all-inclusive wisdom. Strange as it may seem, the very advance of science has brought it into the realm of the incomprehensible, and that is where the spiritual nature of man has long resided.

Ponder the impact of the following summation by a leading physicist, Professor Percy Bridgman of Harvard University: "The physicist finds himself in a world from which the bottom has dropped clean out; as he penetrates deeper and deeper, it eludes him by the highly unsportsmanlike device of just becoming meaningless. No refinement of measurement will avail to carry him beyond the portals of this shadowy domain which we cannot even mention without logical inconsistency. A bound is thus forever set to the curiosity of the physicist. What is more, the mere existence of this bound means that he must give up his most cherished faith and convictions. The world is not a world of reason, understandable by the intellect of man, but, as we penetrate ever deeper, the very law of cause and effect, which he had thought to be a formula to which we could force God Himself to subscribe, ceases to have any meaning." (From "The New Version of Science," in *Harper's Magazine* for March, 1929.)

As the disastrous split in the human personality was engendered by the dichotomy between the brightly comprehensible physical universe and the hidden non-rational springs of man's nature, so now the way back to the harmony of wisdom is opened up by the growing realization that the physical universe about us is equally incomprehensible. We now realize that both faith and reason derive from the same fundamental mystery. While only a short while ago the ultimate source of knowledge appeared to be split clean down the middle, we now see it as one, dynamic and all-embracing, a challenge for the construction of a magnificent new synthesis of ideas and ideals, deserving the old function and title of "Wisdom."

7. The Two Religious Traditions of Western Civilization

It is in the light of this central goal of our time that we may obtain a fresh appreciation of the relative merits and functions of the two traditions that constitute the spiritual sub-structure of Western civilization.

In our society a religious tradition constitutes the social instrument whereby the meaning of life, in all its scope and depth, is interpreted and mediated. Now a philosophical synthesis of reason and faith, however consistent in theory, is powerless if it is not embraced in a living tradition and channelized into the religious experience of a social group. While philosophy provides the principles of construction and the engineering blueprints, so to speak, the religious tradition furnishes the bricks and mortar for the ideal structure of wisdom in every generation. For wisdom, we must remember, is a social as well as an individual reality; and it is rooted in personal experience and the cultural momentum of history as well as in the realm of abstract ideas and convictions.

Religious experience is generated at the outer boundary of human capacity—the plane where our physical power ends, reason fails, and the will for self-aggrandizement changes direction and turns into the vertical growth of the spirit. At this hair-line juncture of the temporal and the eternal, the human and the more than human phases merge into the experience of holiness, though in varying proportions. At this apex of the spirit all the fragmentary values of life are led back to their source. Wisdom rises to piety.

In the Christian tradition and its resulting pattern of piety, it is the super-human, or divine, quality of religious experience that is emphasized and fostered. Reason is defied in the awareness of the totally "other," and in the dogmas of the trinity and the incarnation "that are a stumbling-block to the Jews and folly to the Greeks"; the objective rule of conscience is negated in the dogmas of "original sin," of pre-destination and justification by faith, and of a salvation coming as a free and unearned act of Grace from the Deity; the multiple feelings of self-assertion, echoing the natural "love of the world," are turned into the pale frost of asceticism, the inverted pleasure of total surrender, the "creaturely" feeling of unreserved submission.

In the Jewish tradition, on the other hand, what predominates is the human phase of experience of the ultimate. It is the advancing might of reason that carries us to the brink of what is humanly knowable, so that the Oneness of God is our fundamental conviction, as the one all-encompassing formula is the ultimate goal of reason; the principles of conscience, as we know them, are extended to the Infinite and applied to Him, in their double connotation of Justice and Mercy; the feeling of piety is that of active participation in the up-building of the Kingdom of God. Hence it is through the perception of law in the universe, order in history, unvarying norms in the life of the individual and firm standards of decency and dignity in group life, that Jewish tradition leads the worshiper to "the mountain of the Lord." Hence, also, in the cultivation of these virtues Jewish piety is concretized, as it descends from the ecstatic heights of Sinai to the varying levels of mundane reality.

For the Christian, religion enters into life as a continual

protest against the "pride" of the self expanding in the direction of either reason or will or feeling. The negating, meta-human phase of the experience of holiness is propelled into every situation—as in rejecting the aspiration to solve social problems through the humanist insights of intelligence and conscience; or in repudiating the "pharisaic" faith in laws, norms and deeds. Here is the negation of the varied "feelings of this world" in favor of the "feeling of the other."

It would take volumes to show in detail how the two phases of the same fundamental experience are developed differently in the two traditions, each unfolding according to its historical impetus. The important point to remember is that the initial difference of emphasis is magnified into an all-inclusive tradition that touches upon every aspect of life —from the music and mysticism of Wagner to the sociology of Toynbee and the penitent philosophy of the ex-communist Whittaker Chambers. Even when the central focus of the Christian faith is negated, the characteristic emphasis deriving from its tradition continues to be felt. Similarly in Judaism, the impetus of this-worldly idealism may continue to function, at least for a while, even when the central experience of faith is neglected or disavowed. In each case the experience of transcendence is the vital center of an organic and wide-ranging pattern of life that is founded upon a living tradition.

Which tradition, Jewish or Christian, is truer to the nature of things, yielding a more adequate philosophy of life? Let us hope that we have by now outgrown the impulse to indulge in such idle questions. Be it admitted that both the Jewish and Christian traditions are liable to abuse, if uncorrected by their reciprocal influences upon one another. The Jewish tradition, it is true, tends to develop among the orthodox into a one-sided emphasis on the sheer legalism of piety; and among the non-orthodox it tends to pass into a naive and uninspired kind of humanism. On the other hand, the Christian tradition is perennially in danger, on the orthodox level, of separating faith from morals and the intellect; and of degenerating among the neo-orthodox into a sterile anti-intellectualism, unrestrained romanticism and social reaction. The Unitarians and the Universalists, for their part, lean so far over into the domain of Jewish rationalism as to lose the support and impetus of their own historic traditions. With varying effectiveness these liberal groups mediate between the Jewish and Christian faiths, keeping the two streams in continuous contact and interaction. However, they can no more replace the historic faiths than philosophy can take the place of religion.

In continual mutual criticism, even as they challenge and stimulate each other, the two traditions, Jewish and Christian, develop each its own genius best.

8. The Creative Orchestration of Jewish and Christian Traditions

But—and here is the rub—how are the two traditions to stimulate each other without allowing their essential opposition to degenerate into mutual contempt and recrimination? The Christian emphasis can hardly be developed without coming perilously close to a wholesale condemnation, or at least a systematic deprecation, of the Jewish tradition. This emphasis enters indeed into every phase of culture, permeating the study of history, philosophy and literature, and affecting the general climate of opinion. It was thus that modern antisemitism maintained its momentum in the last century, though its source in Christian Orthodoxy weakened and waned—attesting to the power and pervasiveness of the Christian tradition. Franz Rosenzweig, in his mystical view of history, declared that antisemitism was foreordained and inevitable, since it flowed necessarily from the basic dichotomy of the Jewish and Christian traditions. The perpetual likelihood of this opposition turning into hate and contempt loomed to him as inescapable doom, living as he did under the ominously rising shadow of Nazism.

In fact, this danger can be averted only if the mutual interaction of the two traditions is maintained on the highest levels of thought and scholarship. Suffice it to recall the association of "Higher Criticism" of the Bible with "Higher Antisemitism," and the faith of the Pharisees with a mean and narrow-minded legalism, so long as authentic Jewish scholarship in this field was in its early stages, unrecognized by the outside world.

It is the relationship of the Christian and Jewish traditions that sets the stage for the spiritual challenge which the thoughtful Jew senses in the American environment. At the same time it is the mutually supplementary roles of the two traditions within the context of Western civilization that offers to the modern Jew a vision of the unique significance of his faith and culture. Thus the healthy orientation, inner peace and spiritual productiveness of the American Jew depend upon the continuous unfolding of the values implicit in his own tradition. Through this creative process the modern Jew will be enabled to integrate into his life the spiritual values of the Jewish faith, and provide a counter-balance to the Christian emphasis in Western civilization.

Thus we can help to achieve a new all-embracing wisdom, adequate for our time. And thus we can aid Christian students and scholars to recognize the place of Judaism in the over-all pattern of human culture.

9. The Challenge to American Judaism

We have been rather shy about our "mission" to teach other people, and sensitive about the age-old claim to the possession of the "eternal verities" in their purity. There is indeed no justification for any people to lay claim to the possession of unique faculties, or to the exclusive possession of a set of true ideas. Still, we are no worse than our Christian neighbors, even if we are no better. Does the disavowal of any pretensions to superiority involve the concession of inferiority? We do have a cultural heritage and a religious tradition, a pattern of piety shading into a secular philosophy of wisdom, which is as essential for the balance of Western thought as is the piety and wisdom of the Christian. It is the primary function of our cultural tradition to help achieve the classical synthesis of wisdom in our lives. The function of a cultural tradition consists not so much in the ideas it propounds as in the total impact it directs upon the personalities of its sons. To build spiritually healthy, well-balanced Jewish individuals, who will in their turn contribute to the spiritual health of the whole American community—that is our basic concern.

Our young people are inevitably exposed to the impact of the Christian tradition in literature and philosophy, living as we do in a predominantly Christian civilization. Without the counterbalancing influence of the Jewish tradition, they cannot but move step by step to the point of sensing Judaism as a strange and incongruous phenomenon, ultimately even as an anachronistic "fossil" that has somehow cheated the Angel of Death. In such yielding to the dominance of the Christian tradition they not only plant the seeds of self-hatred within their own souls; they deprive the Judeo-Christian cultural pattern of the balancing and healing effects of the Jewish contribution.

The Zionist "negators of the Diaspora" may almost be forgiven their contention that only in Israel can the Jew acquire a solid cultural base for the development of the insights in his rich tradition. Yet, though we can understand and even excuse this widespread mood of retreat and defeat, if we concur in its pessimistic estimate of the potency and charm of Jewish tradition we in effect submit an abject application for spiritual bankruptcy. For if Judaism is of universal value and significance, it need not be sheltered by the walls of a national sovereignty from the free interplay of ideas and sentiments in the Western world. It is here in the Western world that Judaism faces its greatest challenge and here that its right to function as a basic cultural factor must be tested and proven true.

Furthermore, five million Jews in America can no more find spiritual sustenance as "Israeli colonials" than they can afford to assume this status in social or political terms. Israeli culture, whatever forms it may take in the future, will necessarily develop the values of our tradition along nationalist lines. Hence, as time goes on, its reflected influence on the American scene will differ less and less from that of the other national sub-cultures in this country.

As American Jews, we are called upon to rise to a far greater challenge—that of unfolding the values of our tradition in the free and open spaces of a non-parochial universal culture. Thus we may render our contribution to the achievement of that synthesis of wisdom which our age is trying so desperately to attain.

10. Our Duty on the Highest Level

From all the foregoing considerations it follows that we should seek to foster the development of the Jewish tradition on all levels—but especially on the highest academic level, in the colleges and universities. The prime importance of concentrating on the collegiate level is obvious, if we are to win and hold the allegiance of our rising intelligentsia. Having lost one generation of intellectuals, we must assign top priority to the task of infusing the hundreds of thousands of Jewish students on the campuses with the light of Jewish knowledge and the fire of Jewish idealism. Is this task being effectively done today?

There is a huge network across the country of Hillel Foundations, carrying on "Jewish activities" at over two hundred colleges and universities. Do they still reflect the negativist mentality of the past generation, setting up campus-ghettoes, or are they geared for the task of projecting the ideals of Judaism onto the American scene? The university campus is potentially the place where a renaissance of Judaism might begin. Certainly the impact of Judaism on the cultural life of America should be felt primarily on the campus and in the university faculties. Is it then the purpose and function of the Hillel Foundations to expound the Jewish heritage on the campus? Are their directors so chosen as to qualify for high academic posts? Do the students esteem their scholarship and wisdom as of equal standing with that of their profesors? Or is the whole context of the Hillel Foundation social in character, segregationist at worst, "armor-building" at best, reverberating with the negativist undertones of the Anti-defamation mentality? Are the budgets and limited framework of the Foundations adequate for the tasks they are meant to perform?

In any case, we need Departments of Judaism in the great American universities, or at least a series of Chairs of Jewish Literature and Philosophy, together with a system of liberal Fellowships in this field. It is not enough to offer courses in the Hebrew language or ancient Hebrew texts in the Oriental Deparments, for Judaism is no longer an Oriental factor but a vital ingredient in Western culture. Nor should we permit the transformation of an existing Hebrew course into a Department of Israeli Culture, on the pattern of other language courses. The Jewish tradition must be presented as a cultural factor vitally relevant to our own time and place, not merely as a relic from the past or as a foreign national development.

High time indeed for us to envisage the challenge and true function of Judaism on the American scene, and not allow ourselves to be deflected from our purpose by "defense" hysteria, or by the tinsel-substitute of a resurgent nationalism, or by the "fossil mentality" of seeking refuge in the Orient and the Past.

Those who do not believe in the creative potentialities of American Jewish life are willing enough to spend millions in behalf of a halutziut *program of emigration to Israel. Are those of us who envision of Golden Age of Judaism in America equally willing to provide the necessary means for such a glorious consummation?*

(published in "The Menorah Journal," Spring, 1953)

4

The Idea of God

There is nothing that we do or think which does not in some way impinge upon the idea of God. For this idea is the most fundamental and all-embracing of concepts in the range of thought. How then shall we begin to explore the nature of God and arrive at any understanding of His essence? It is commonly believed that every argument must begin with definitions. Indeed, classical Greek philosophy followed this pattern. But in the case of God, we cannot define without begging the question. Was it not pointed out long ago that every definition constitutes a delimitation in some way or other, while God is the Infinite and the Undeterminable? Thus, if we should launch our search for God with a definition we should be compelled to follow Spinoza in assuming as our first axiom that which is the ultimate goal of our investigation.

We might begin by tracing the conceptions of God evolved by the great philosophers of history, and evaluating their adequacy in the light of modern knowledge and research. But if we begin in this fashion, would we ever end? Consider how multifarious are the ways in which God has appeared to man and how profitless the task of demolishing the images and concepts man has fashioned of Him! Such an undertaking appears imperative only if we accept Hegel's dogma that philosophy is nothing but the history of West European thought, being the record of the progressive unfolding of the universal mind through the social and literary molds of the most advanced nations of the world. In recent years, we have grown too humble to pose as the final incarnations of Absolute Reason. Furthermore, we do not go far in our study of the histories of philosophy before we realize that it is one's basic world-view which determines the manner in which he construes the intellectual evolution of mankind. In the beginning is the word of conviction; the whole world is then fashioned accordingly. If we probe deep enough, we find at the base of every metaphysical system either an intuition or a generalization.

We propose therefore to take as our starting point the most fundamental principles of thought, as these have been formulated in our time. Our conception will admittedly be dated, but for this very reason perhaps most meaningful in terms of our contemporary culture.

I

The highway to the heavenly heights of metaphysics is bifurcated at the very beginning into the short road of intuition and the long road of reasoned analysis. This crossroads is never left behind; it looms ahead so long as we persist in the quest of truth, for the short direct road of intuition continues to be ever available, as we proceed along the endless path of reason. Blessed moments of inspiration intersperse our lives, yielding glimpses of the holy and the ineffable. Such moments, however, are arrows shot into space, penetrating the infinite but not encompassing it. Overwhelming in their blinding intensity, they remain ambiguous in significance. They stimulate our imagination and enhance our vision, but in their fleeting vagueness they cannot serve as substitutes for logical thought. The temptation to construct the world of faith upon these evanescent flashes of insight, opposing an independent realm of the holy and the mysterious to the grey reality of mundane thought, is well-nigh irresistible to the religious thinker. Yet those who aim to "speak truth in their heart" dare not yield entirely. Glimpses of intuition have their place in the spiritual economy of life, but they cannot serve as substitutes for sustained reflection. The logic of life requires that we live before we know, that we treasure the flashes of faith before we complete the adventure of reasoned reflection, but this adventure remains our irrevocable task.

Predominantly, modern religious philosophy shies away from the rigid canons of logic. Perhaps it was Kant who set this pattern, when he declared that "pure reason" cannot pronounce judgment regarding metaphysical questions. In any case, the prevailing mood in the past two centuries has tended to relegate religion to the domain of feeling on the ground that the fields of reason and experience had been preempted by the triumphant, all-pervading spirit of science. Religion can only begin where reason ends, and many religious thinkers only too eagerly seek aid and comfort from the occasional perplexities of scientists and their confessions of failure.

This dichotomy of the human spirit may be helpful in allaying friction at college faculty meetings, but it is basically unhealthy and, at bottom, even dishonest. World culture can afford a "split personality" as little as the living individual, for it is emptied of all meaning if it does not seek perpetually to harmonize all fields of knowledge and to synthesize the insights deriving from every discipline of the human mind. By the same token, a faith which is founded on an esoteric experience of mystical unity or a romantic exaggeration of the normal feeling of wonder, bewilderment, and mystery belongs to the poetry of life, not to its substance.

Modern "existential" philosophies of religion are now available in a rich variety of shapes and forms, catering to many tastes; yet, they all have in common an overly elaborated and meticulously nurtured bill of protestations against the objective world and its canons of judgment, as if the best attitudes of our sober mentality constituted somehow a falling away from God. Those who center their faith on the presumed "sudden" incursion of the divine into the souls of men become inevitably, though unwittingly, prophets of doom and despair, since they insist upon the non-divine and even sinful character of man's rational aspirations for the good life, foreboding a monotonous succession of "crises" and catastrophes. Since the continuous application of reason to experience is the only highway of progress open to man, religion in modern times forfeited the sceptre of leadership when, in its most illustrious exponents, it hesitated to tread this highway and retired fearfully into the comforting shadows of subjective intuitions.

By its very nature, faith is an outgrowth of the inner life of man, but if it is not integrated with the total picture painted by science and experience, it cannot be aught else but ethereal poetry, clothed in the coarse garb of theological dark speech. Religion is at once insight and synthesis, the beginning of all wisdom and its final culmination. Hence we must not be content simply with the *feeling* of the Eternally Present, as He appears to the pious and the saintly. If we are to overcome the sense of inner desperation and unbalance which afflicts the consciousnes of modern man, we must learn to recapture the ancient, classical synthesis between the personal God, apprehended in our religious experience, and the God of nature, envisaged as the ultimate goal of reasoned reflection. For, as the Kabbalists put it, God is One in the twin categories of dialectical "remoteness" and intuitive "closeness." In the words of the prophet Isaiah, "I am first and I am last."

Two mighty obstacles block the path of reason, in its quest for God, obstacles thrown up by two opposing schools of thought. On the one hand, proponents of what is generally called "scientism" tell us that the presently charted path of science is all in all, and that any attempt to go beyond the catalogued and classified body of proven knowledge is futile. The world is just as science paints it—a maddening whirl of atoms and electrons, particles and waves. True, the total body of all known facts is as a tiny, brightly lit boat floating upon the dark ocean of the unknown, but then science operates with the only possible method of expanding this luminous area of knowledge. Any attempt to venture beyond the sphere of scientific data is to commit the unpardonable sin of being unscientific.

On the other hand, we are told that reason and experience are inherently incapable of dealing with the quest of metaphysics. Our experience is of the finite, how dare we generalize from it concerning the infinite? And reason? Have not theologians delighted for centuries in dwelling lovingly upon its failures, in order that an inviolate limbo of unknowability might be secured for the varying dogmas of their respective faiths? As to the limitations of both reason and experience, it is not at all difficult to show the woeful inadequacy of our authenticated knowledge for the quest of metaphysics. Have not the most important facts concerning the soul of man been brought to light only in recent years? It is only a generation since the tractability of human nature to mechanical conditioning was discovered, and two generations since we learned of the vast, slumbering depths of the human psyche, dwelling in the recesses of the unconscious.

Let us, then, state at the outset, in answer to both of these objections, that our quest is not for the type of clear and certain knowledge that we have in mathematics or physics. We seek to obtain proximate knowledge of the realm that supervenes knowledge, grounds for faith, the direction of the curves leading from the known to the unknown. Our purpose is to batter down the high wall between religious faith and scientific knowledge, exploring the intervening cross-currents and charting the paths between them.

Accordingly, we reply to those who erect science into a self-sufficient philosophy of life that they err in two directions. In the first place, they fail to realize that we cannot and dare not leave the "unknown" alone, for it comprises the essence of our being, the very ground of our existence, and the meaning of all our strivings. The quest for God and for our own innermost self is one and the same, for if the riddle of selfhood is solved, all is given. The self which thinks and wills, yearns and despairs—what is it? No category of knowledge yet devised embraces it, much less explains it. Depth-psychology may explore its limitations, abnormal psychology may trace its occasional deviations, but in its essence, it remains as mysterious as ever it was in the days of Plato and Aristotle. And this mystery, wrapped in an enigma, is our own being. What sort of wisdom is it then that would ignore the most important object of our quest—to wit, our own selves?

As to the outside physical universe, only the naive can imagine that the atoms and electrons of present-day science constitute the ultimate stuff of existence. Have we not learned in our own day that matter is nothing but "congealed" energy? Einstein's formula for the conversion of matter into energy has become common knowledge in our atomic age. But, is its impact understood? One of the inferences to be drawn from it is certainly to the effect that the world is not simply an aggregation of so many whirling particles, traveling at various speeds. If we define energy as the force that moves matter and matter as congealed energy, what is it that we end up with, but a vicious circle? We will return to this problem in a moment.

At present, we merely wish to indicate the limitations of scientism. They may be listed as follows: first, the failure to recognize the tragic earnestness of the metaphysical quest; secondly, the failure to realize the logical insufficiency of the concepts of physics for the understanding of the essential "stuff" of the universe, since what metaphysics seeks to do is to explain the fundamental concepts of physics, as physics does to chemistry, chemistry to biology and biology to psychology; thirdly, the inability to see that the very nature of the metaphysical quest implies a different method than that employed by science, its objective being the double "unknown" of science—that of the self and that of the whole of the universe.

Now, of course, neither the self nor the whole of the universe can be an object of knowledge in the strict sense of the term, for we cannot stand outside them. Yet we are aware of the self as a unity and we know that the whole is not simply a verbal generalization, since science indicates that the universe is governed by identical laws of cause and effect. The chains of necessity which rule the helium and hydrogen atoms on earth hold in thrall the same atoms as they generate the terrific heat of the sun. Here, on earth, we get messages from elements identical with ours in remote universes, millions of light-years from us. The whole, then, is one.

The method of science is to proceed from the study of the parts to that of the whole. It is a good method, and it works. Suppose, however, it were possible to go from the whole of the universe to the parts as the self does in fact operate in our own being, and in the process, obtaining guidance for life? Such a procedure would be non-scientific, but not unscientific, since it would supplement the data obtained by the usual methods of science.

So much for scientism. As to the protagonists of the ineluctableness of the "unknown," we can only reply that there must be a point by point correspondence between ultimate reality and the concepts to which the path of reason ultimately leads. We are told that knowledge is a function of two factors—of our own mental powers and of the influences that impinge upon our mind and senses from the great "unknown." Accepting this analysis, we see that if the elements of our mental powers are kept constant, by the rigor of logic, then the data in our minds must be related to the "unknown," in a point-by-point correspondence. This argument of the modern "realists" appears incontrovertible, insofar as it refutes the lovers of the Dark Unknown, but the manner in which it is to be applied remains in question.

The path of reason, then, consists in the formulation of the most fundamental laws of existence, as they derive from our total knowledge, and in extending these laws to the whole of the universe. At this point, however, we must confront the titanic figure of Kant and all the schools of philosophy which follow from his basic premise. Is reason to be identified with the ordered summation of our knowledge, or is it to be considered in its "purity," as a self-governing, independently existing entity, becoming ever "purer" as all the data of the senses are abstracted from it? Kant's insistence on the absolute "purity" of logic presented philosophy with an artificial dichotomy, which plagued it for more than a century and a half. First, the world of experience was artificially divided into the mind and the "given" data; then, of course, the twain could never meet again. Without entering into a detailed analysis of the Kantian root-principle and its modern offshoots, we take as our starting point the realistic principle that reason is what reason does—that is, reason is the manner whereby knowledge is ordered in our minds. We refuse to break up the irreducible and to draw a line between "pure" logic and sense-data, for the two are inextricably intertwined and any such line is bound to be arbitrary. Content as we are to obtain proximate knowledge of that which corresponds to ultimate reality, the Kantian critique of reason, drawing an impassable line between the sensible and the realm of metaphysics, does not arise to invalidate our effort.

Let us, then, proceed to discover the most fundamental principles of "reason in operation," reason as it is applied to the understanding of reality, and then note how they may be applied to the twin "unknowns" of our quest—the self and the whole.

II

A study of the logic implied in the methods of science yields two basic generalizations—the principle of causality and the principle of polarity. The first principle has been employed explicitly in philosophy since the days of Aristotle, while the nature of the second principle has been either completely misunderstood, or else variously misinterpreted. Yet this second principle of reason is just as important a clue to the iner structure of reality as the first. The principle of polarity has been variously anticipated and formulated in the history of thought. In our own day, it was best expounded by Morris R. Cohen in his monumental work, *Reason and Nature,* and in a number of smaller works on the logic of science.

This principle, as formulated by Cohen, states that "opposites, such as immediacy and mediation, unity and plurality, the fixed and the flux, substance and function, ideal and real, actual and possible . . ." all enter into the pattern of our understanding (p. 165). Knowledge is so constituted that concepts which are in polar opposition to each other enter into every concrete situation. If only one polar concept is insisted upon as the one true principle, knowledge is reduced to absurdity. "Like the north (positive) and south (negative) poles of a magnet, all [polar concepts] involve each other when applied to a significant entity." (*ibid.*)

Only a student of the history of philosophy is able to appreciate the manifold applications of this principle for the understanding of the ancient controversies between the nominalists and the realists, the mechanists and the vitalists, the idealists and the empiricists. Note, for instance, its application to the question whether reason is only a generalization of sense-data or whether these data are themselves ordered and categorized by reason? Manifestly, both alternatives are absurd, when taken singly. "The principle of polarity warns us that while the rational and sensory elements of our intellect are inseparable, they are distinct. We may grant that in every case of actual, analytic reasoning, some sensory element, no matter how faint, is present, and yet we must insist on the relative independence of the rational element" (p. 196). "The efforts of the human intellect may be viewed as a tension between two poles—one to do justice to the fulness of the concrete case before us, the other to grasp an underlying abstract universal principle that controls much more than the case before us. . . . None of our works shows forces in perfectly stable equilibrium . . . But, in pure science as in personal religion and poetry, intense concentration on one phase rather than justice to many is the dominant trait" (p. 368).

Thus, scientists generally are prone to rule out the possibility of an integrating, purposive principle, operating within a living organism, such a principle being the polar opposite of the mechanistic principle which proceeds from the part to the whole. In this attitude, mechanistic scientists are guilty of ignoring the principle of polarity. "The vice of mechanism in practice is at bottom similar to that of vitalism—it will not open its imagination to the possibility of physically determining factors, quite other than those already known" (p. 282).

The principle of polarity is not an axiom but a generalization, describing the fundamental character of man's sustained attempt to understand himself and the universe. It is the most fundamental generalization available to us, in that it indicates not only the process of understanding but its goal as well. The goal of our intellectual efforts is polar in character—namely, to see every event as a particularization of a system of universal principles. This polarity is reflected in the principle of sufficient reason, which is the fundamental principle of all scientific research. In Cohen's formulation, this principle reads as follows: "Everything is connected in definite ways with definite things, so that its full nature is not revealed except by its position and relations within a system" (p. 150).

The "system" which embraces all events is manifestly the totality of all existence. But this totality is the great "unknown." All events derive from it, all data of knowledge lead to it; yet, the whole remains "unknown."

Can the whole, in its infinite mystery, be understood in terms of the principle of polarity which prevails within it? Cohen refused to draw this inference, on the ground of the "whole" not being "an object of knowledge." However, once we grant that it is not knowledge in the technical sense, that we seek but grounds for faith, such an application becomes logically incontrovertible. And who would be so bold as to scorn the converging rays of knowledge, leading from the finite to the infinite, in the idle quest for full and clear comprehension, for the total embracing of the Deity within the canons of our understanding? Furthermore, the "whole," in a qualitative sense, is given to us in our consciousness of our own personality, as will be made clear in the sequel. The human personality is a chunk of reality and it is understandable only in terms of the polar concepts of purposiveness and mechanism. May it not be then that God and the mechanical universe imply each other, even as the one and the many, space and time, the point and the field? But we are anticipating our argument. Let us return to the task of discovering the fundamental operating concepts in the universe.

When we envisage the whole of existence, in all its mysterious immensity and grandeur, what are the alternative concepts before us? What is the real difference between the naturalists and the theists? Manifestly, the former maintain that the whole is merely a numerical summation of all that exists, with the laws that regulate the finite parts of the visible universe prevailing throughout its invisible and non-reachable positions. The other alternative consists in the attribution to the whole of the qualities of selfhood, consciousness, and purposiveness.

For our present purpose, we may leave out of consideration all transcendental conceptions of the Deity, since they do not assume that creation points to the Creator in any sense save that of logical contradiction or of historical failure. In the transcendental view, the examination of the world about us cannot possibly of itself lead to the idea of God. It is when we realize our "nothingness" and humbly admit our failure, that the Wholly Other is revealed to us. Transcendentalism, by its very definition, cannot favor the endeavor to understand the ultimate nature of being through the instrumentality of reason. Hence the choice before us is the whole as a mechanical summation of parts *versus* the whole as being a self in which particulars may be related

239

to the totality of being in the categories of purposiveness and consciousness.

The naturalist alternative is simply an extension into the infinite of our experience with the physical universe. The theistic position regards our experience with living selves as providing the clue for the understanding of the whole. In living organisms, events occur in accord with the mechanistic laws of physics and chemistry; yet the organism as a whole affects somehow the operation of its tiniest parts, directing all changes toward the goal of preserving the self.

Naturalists may well grant the presence of a vital principle in living organisms and yet insist that there is no reason to generalize from that principle and to regard it as the clue for the understanding of the whole. The very complexity of physical conditions needed for the operation of this principle would militate against its ubiquity—unless it be considered a numinous principle, inhering in a realm that is outside our space-time world. Such a conception, we must point out again, belongs to the philosophy of transcendentalism, which cannot possibly be inferred from the events of the sensible universe. Thus, the very attempt of the vitalists to draw a fundamental line of demarcation between physical and biological phenomena is in fundamental opposition to the theistic endeavor to conceive of the physical universe as an organism, endowed with mind and purpose.

If, on the other hand, life, mind and purpose are seen to be the polar correlatives of space-time and the mechanical laws of motion, then we should be enabled to infer on the strength of the principle of polarity that the whole is mind as well as matter; purposiveness, orderliness and will, as well as mechanism, chaos and law; life as well as death; God as well as nature. The search for God by way of logical analysis implies the inner coherence of all our experience, with the meanest and lowest data of knowledge forming part of a process that transpires between two infinitely remote poles—that of mechanism and matter, on the one hand, and that of spirit and God, on the other hand. The growth of our knowledge is likely to fill in the many lacunae in this process, extending it ever farther into the receding limbo of the two infinites. But we may well ask whether the outlines of this process are not already visible. Faith in the fundamental reality of our moral and spiritual values is still needed to fill in the picture of the whole. The bare outlines, however, emerge out of our present knowledge of the universe. We can hardly begin to understand the world in which we live or our own selves without postulating the divine pole of reality.

III

The universe in which we live is hopelessly mysterious, in its outer reaches as in the unimaginable complexity of its minutest particles. Of the vastness of the infinite void we cannot ever expect to receive more than occasional glimpses. But the world that is open to our senses, how do we understand it? The merest acquaintance with the facts of science awakens us to the realization that the qualities which are apprehended by our senses are not really present in the world as it truly is. In the real world, there are no tastes, colors and sounds, only a hectic chaos of whirling particles and trembling waves. At one time, it was believed that atoms and molecules constituted the irreducible bricks of the universe. The world was a vast assemblage of these tiny particles, travelling through space like myriads of billiard balls, and all the complexities of its phenomena were nothing but reflections of the motions and gyrations of these simple particles.

At present, even the general public is aware that matters are not quite so simple. In the first place, there does not seem to be any limit to the divisibility of matter, with the most recently discovered particles being possibly subject to further breakdowns. We confront now the possibility that empty space may merely be an abstraction, representing a pole of existence, which is only reached asymptotically. In the second place, we now know that matter and energy are at bottom somehow one. In modern physics, it was realized long ago that electrons sometimes behaved as if they were not particles of matter, but multi-dimensional waves of energy. The emergence of the quantum theory, insisting that energy comes in spurts, like particles, and the Einstein relativity theory, erasing the absolute line of distinction between space and matter, made the old vision of the universe as a mass of moving particles completely out of date. Finally, the rapid progress of atomic science in the last decade demonstrated in world-shaking experiments the possibility of converting matter into energy. We know now that matter in all its forms is but a coagulation, as it were, of energy, which is the basic reality in the world about us— the energy of radiation, gravitation, nuclear attraction, electromagnetism, and heat. But with the exception of heat, none of these forms of energy can be understood in the mechanistic terms of whirling particles.

What then is energy? The term has meaning for us in that it is derived from a number of situations in which it is always associated with matter. In physics, energy is defined and measured in terms of the capacity to set matter into motion. But if matter is itself a form of energy, how shall we think of energy?

For a long time, science clung to the notion that the waves of light and electromagnetism were undulations in a quasi-material substance called ether, for motion could be understood only as the motion of something, and the conception of light as waves could be taken to make sense only if there were really something in which the waves could take place. Then the theory of an ether was given up, and the waves of energy were left waving while yet there was nothing to wave. Finally, the relativity theory gave the *coup de grace* to the conception of space as the vast inert container of moving particles, proving that there was no absolute boundary between space and matter, since space was itself quasi-material, "bending" and "contracting" round masses of matter. Thus, the mechanistic theory of the universe is now as dead as a door-nail.

More and more, we are driven to the realization that the physical universe must be viewed in terms of the "field" and "point" polar relationship. The "field" is the pattern of infinite relations to which every "point" in space is subject. As in every polar relationship, each pole represents a direction of being, rather than a definite state or quality. Neither the "point" nor the "field" exist as such, but every existent is a combination of both in varying degrees. The final, irreducible element of existence is as the trembling of a chord, withdrawing into a definite point in space, yet issuing out of itself, in response to the "field" in which it is found. Things are not spatial entities alone, but "events," in Whitehead's terminology, units of space-time, reflecting the tension and the rhythm of the polar relationship.

How profoundly revolutionary is this point-field polar concept! We are accustomed to think of true reality as motionless, massive stability, but now the realization dawns upon us that in reality things are tensions and rhythms. Nothing exists that is wholly self-enclosed, but things are real insofar as they partake of the two opposites—particularity reaching down to a point in space, and responsiveness to the total field of relations. Behold this paradox: if it were possible to take a still shot of the universe at any one point in time, eliminating all incipient relations, the universe would be absolute nothingness! For it is in the tension between the two poles of existence that events endure.

Yet difficult as is the point-field polar concept for the layman, modern mathematics long ago constructed the logical framework for its understanding. It was through the logic inherent in mathematical formulae that Einstein's theories were developed. The groundwork was laid in the seventeenth century by Descartes' theory of analytic geometry, which solved complicated problems of curvature by translating them unto a field of relations, based on two coordinates. The essential congruence of this theory with fundamental reality is demonstrated in the circumstance that by means of it the actual curves of motion in the physical universe could be calculated. Related to the field-concept is the theory of the differential, dy/dx, which expresses in mathematical language the asymptotic character of incipient motion or change. A differential is defined as the ratio of two rates of change when the amount of change approximates zero. With this paradoxical method of "approaching zero," modern mathematics was able to unlock and plot all forms of change, opening up new vast fields of calculation, while the earlier concepts of pre-modern algebra and geometry could only describe an abstract, static world. The differential, as contrasted with the conception of a static point, and the integral, as contrasted with the elementary notion of a class of objects or group of points, reflect together the polar concepts of this dynamic universe, the restless quality of its being, matter and energy "approaching" the two poles of being in itself and in relation respectively, without quite reaching either pole. In the mechanistic view of the universe, the process of explanation consists in the equating of each effect as the arithmetical summation of the forces that impinge upon it, as in Newton's laws of motion. But the question remains unanswered as to the manner in which influence proceeds from part to part—the influence of gravitation, for instance, or the force of nuclear attraction. In the organismic view, each part is explained by the whole, but the differentiation into parts remains unexplained. The principle of polarity offers us a synthesis of both mechanism and organism.

The essence of the polar relationship is seen in the circumstance that when the attempt is made to apprehend either pole as an existent, the result is incomprehensible absurdity. Thus, the attempt to envisage matter is led, through the channels of analysis, to energy, while the corresponding attempt to conceive of energy leads to the description of it as a quality of matter. This paradox is carried over into the ultimate units of the universe whatever they may be. As we have noted, reality in its ultimate shape cannot but bear a point-to-point correspondence with the fundamental character of the phenomena that science describes to us.

We thus arrive at the conception of a universe, in which all parts exist in a state of tension—tension between the tendency to particularization and responsiveness to the total system of which it is a part. If human terms could be used to express this two-way quality of every existent, we could speak of the tension between the poles of self-assertion and self-surrender. In the history of thought, quasi-human expressions were indeed employed to characterize that which must remain inexpressible, since all forms of expression derive from the phenomenal world while fundamental reality reposes behind the veil of phenomena. Suffice it for us at this stage to note the polar character of existence, the tension between point and field which constitutes the ineluctable mold of reality.

IV

We have said that the fundamental character of all existents is given in the tension between "point" and "field."
The meaning of the polar quality of "point" is clear enough,
but what do we mean by the term "field"? Is not the limit
of the field of force in which every existent is found rather
vague and indefinite? To be sure, in the inanimate universe,
there is no definite limit to the field of relations of each
point. Fields of force are superimposed upon each other in
concentric circles, declining in relevance and shading off
into the infinite. While we can envision the end result of
the tendency toward absolute rest in an absolute point, we
do not see the "field," as a terminal goal, but as the first
link in a chain. If the second law of thermodynamics, which
foresees the ultimate running down of the energy in the universe and the achievement of a perfectly stable equilibrium,
were to be fully realized, we should require only a "general
theory of space" to describe the unvarying stillness of sameness and death.

However, there appears to be a contrary tendency in the
universe, running counter to the law of entropy—a tendency for "fields" to assert themselves as particularizations
or "points" over against their environment. A field of force
is a way of reacting to change at any one moment of time.
But when the field is itself individualized to the point of
maintaining a unitary pattern of action, in spite of continuous change, we have in fact an achievement of individuality
—that is, the establishment of a permanent pattern of energy
relations. Thus, when radiation suffusing space condenses
into an atom, establishing a powerful and complex field of
force in a tiny area of space, we recognize in the process the
emergence of an individuated field. The emergence of a
living cell, constituting a unitary pattern of action, in spite
of continuous change, is another great milestone on the

ladder of the individuation of fields of force. Jan Smuts' emphasis on "wholes" in nature, imposing their patterns upon their constituent parts, so that these parts function in a manner that is measurably different from the way they function when they are separated, is of interest in demonstrating additional links in this chain of individuation. Every step consists in the achievement of a pattern representing a measure of freedom from the sway of the outside environment. Atoms, cells, multicellular plants, animal cells, animals, mankind: all these stages of creation represent a continuous ascent upon the infinite ladder of individuation and freedom.

The manner whereby energy condenses into matter or atoms coalesce into cells, as well as all the other steps in the vertical ascent of creation, is properly the subject for scientific research and investigation. Suffice it to note that the universe can only be understood in terms of a polar relationship, between point and field—a relationship which is steadily compounded, the "fields" becoming "points" as against other "fields," the whole picture presenting a continuous state of tension, not only along the horizontal plane of space-time, but also on the vertical plane of individuation and freedom.

In this scale of being, the human personality presents the highest, observable field of individuation. Speaking objectively, the human personality represents the greatest measure of freedom attained in the scale of creation: the capacity to reflect on the experiences stored in memory, to envision alternative procedures, to reason and to evaluate, to imagine and to create are but so many expressions of the field-building capacity or the power of freedom that is stored in the human personality. In turn, freedom must be understood not as a break in the chain of cause and effect, or as the injection of a "non-materialistic" factor in the economy of nature, but as the causation and self-maintenance of a "field" or an individualized pattern of action as against the rest of existence.

If now we have learned to recognize an infinite tendency in the rising scale of being, proceeding from the electro-magnetic field of force that is space to the human personality, we must next inquire whether we can logically escape the assumption of an Infinite Personality, representing the ulti-mate pole of being, on the vertical coordinate of freedom. We have seen that the understanding of the universe re-quires the application of two polar principles that are set over against each other, and we have learned that the same polarity of field and point, whole and part, freedom and mechanism, pervades the whole range of creation. In the human personality, freedom attains its highest manifestation, but it is still far from perfect. Applying the principle of polarity, we conclude that an Absolute Personality represent-ing the highest measure of the field-building capacity, con-stitutes a pole of being, standing in continual opposition to and tension with the mechanistic universe. God and the physical universe are the two polar concepts of thought, and since logical thought is in correspondence with reality, we are justified in concluding that the space-time continuum, as it exists in itself, and the Deity, as the projection into the infinite of the field-making capacity, are the two poles of being.

We have spoken of freedom in the human personality as the power of field-building and field-maintaining. This equa-tion is not apparent at first glance. However, bearing in mind the point-field relationship as the most fundamental generalization of reality, we recall that the emergence of life was a leap unto a higher level of the relationship that obtains throughout existence. In a living cell, each part is manifestly in a functioning relation to the whole, with the result that the field or pattern of force is maintained, while the parts continue to change. In the emergence of consciousness, we see another level of this field-building capacity, the data of the senses being set in relation to each other, with the sensations of the present moment viewed against the experience of the past. So immediate is the field of consciousness, in the simplest experience, as for example, in the apprehension of color or sound, that we are not aware of the operation by which the mind relates the new experience to the accumulated data in it, identifying the new sensation as a definite color or a meaningful sound. Yet we know that colors and sounds are meaningful to us only because they are so related to the ever-growing field of memory. The process of relating each datum to the apperceptive mass of consciousness is incomprehensible on any mechanical basis. Several decades ago, in the heyday of materialism, much was made of Pavlov's conditioned reflex experiments on a dog whose brain had been severed from the spine. The extreme care that had to be taken in order to establish a selective reaction of the dog's saliva to the sound of the bell amounted in fact to the establishment of an artificial field of relations in the dog's nervous system by the experimenter. In a similar manner, it is possible for the hypnotist to affect and distort the consciousness of the person subjected to his influence. But in consciousness, many sensations are automatically related to the field of experience, each falling into its own groove. And precisely this selective capacity is the distinctive quality of consciousness. While in nature, fields of force operate in only one pattern, in the field of consciousness, many different possibilities are viewed in relation to each sensation, until an identity is established. Treating of the different manner in which events are arranged in nature and in consciousness, William James wrote of the "hard" order that prevails in nature as contrasted with the "soft" order of arrangements that is characteristic of consciousness. He was right in calling attention to the flexibility of consciousness, but wrong in his choice of terms. For the distinction is not one of "hardness" and "softness," but of the unitary field of force versus the capacity in consciousness of setting many events in relation to each other and thereby establishing new fields. As life implies the power of the self-maintenance of a field, consciousness implies the capacity of setting data into relation with each other, thereby setting up new fields. Neither life nor mind is explained by these powers, but the progressive advance in terms of the point-field polar relationship is nevertheless apparent.

This polarity is manifested especially in the operation of logical thought. Aristotle it was who first reflected on the nature of logic and formulated the principles of what came to be known as deductive logic. There is the major premise affirming a proposition concerning a class of objects, as when it is said, "All men are two-legged." There is the minor premise, declaring of one individual that he belongs to the above class, such as the statement, "Socrates is a man." Inevitably, the conclusion follows, "Socrates is two-legged." In this syllogistic process, we have first the vision of a class or a field, followed by the recognition of an individual, leading to the inclusion of that individual within the class. In other words, the proces of logical reasoning consists in the setting up of a field of relations between an infinite group of objects, or a class, and an individual object.

Francis Bacon is generally credited with the popularization of the inductive process of reasoning, which advances from a series of particulars to the formulation of a general law, instead of proceeding in the reverse way from the general to the particular. In inductive logic, too, a number of particular facts are classed together and used for the formulation of a law, which describes a field-point relationship.

This type of reasoning first lifts a number of particular events out of one field of relations, then recognizes them as forming a new field, in which each event is related to a class or field of consequences. Bacon was interested not so much in the formulation of known facts as in the discovery of new truths. Hence, not logic, but the creative thinking process was his main concern. Now in the process of thinking, observations of particular events form the starting point, but when the universal law leaps out of the multitude of particulars, the achievement is again made possible only by the setting up of a field or class which embraces all the particulars. Thus, whether you begin at the one end or the other, reasoning consists in the setting up of fields of relations and in studying the identities thus discovered.

Hermann Cohen, who founded the new-Kantian school of "critical" philosophy, sought to discover the manner in which "pure" thought operates—that is, thought which is abstracted from any data that are provided by the senses. The net result of his investigation was the suggestion already referred to that the differential, dy/dx, and the corresponding mathematical process of integration, constitute the twin poles of thought. Here, too, we see the projection of point-field relationships, or the capacity to build fields of relationship, as the essential distinction of the thinking process.

V

Logical thinking is the most perfect form of the field-building capacity that is available to us. Exemplified in the building up of the hypothetical constructs of mathematics, human logic is manifestly not a body of knowledge and procedures, complete in itself, but a continuously expanding circle, certain to transcend all its presently visible boundaries in both scope and refinement. Did Euclid in all his brilliance foresee the possibility of a non-Euclidean geometry of space? Did Newton, in all the exactitude of his calculations, sense the possibility of a "curvature" of space? Even so, we may be certain that the "general field-theory" of Einstein will one day be further refined through the emergence of new concepts—that is, new vistas of fields. Mathematical thought, which is logic in action, is an endless quest for the comprehension of the possibilities of the field-building capacity, and its end is not in sight. It is an advance toward the Deity, the Eternally Present, the Field-Builder of the universe in which we live.

We know that logical thinking is not the only form of activity of the human mind. There is the vast extent of "prelogical" thought, characteristic of the mind of primitive man, to which Lévy-Bruhl pointed, and there are also the profound depths of the unconscious that Freud and his associates have begun to plumb. While we cannot at this point enter into an analysis of these insights, we invite the reader to examine for himself whether all these forms of thinking are not due to the formation in the mind of incomplete fields. In the unconscious, as well as in primitive thought, we have associations formed on the basis of similarities that we, in our clearest moments of reflection, consider "irrelevant" because they do not take the whole of the relevant fields into consideration. By the same token, it will appear upon analysis, that the cures effected by psychiatry are achieved by opening up the vista of a larger field. The impulse that was side-tracked and allowed to fester in a blind-alley is brought into the total pattern of values and ideals of the human personality, so that a rational "adjustment" is achieved. In Otto Rank's writings, particularly, it is made clear that it is the self, as a field-making entity, that is cured through its own assertion and through the encouragement of the analyst.

The process of achieving logical clarity is endless in both extent and subtlety, and if humility succeeds in dissuading us from stopping at any one point, the rational process leads on to the Pole of Being that is God. But the way of reason is not the only road to Deity. Is not our experience of beauty the recognition of the rightness of a pattern of events that enters into our ken? As reason differs from imagination in that the fields built up by the latter are arbitrary while those of the former are "right" and "true," so the beautiful differs from the ugly in that its fields are automatically "approved" by us. There is an element of universality and personal distinterestedness in the awareness of beauty. Things *are* beautiful; they are not made thus by the vagaries of our taste. The fields of relationship, in color or in sound, that constitute beauty and harmony are manifestations of God's fields. In cognizing them, we join in approving His handiwork, even as it said: "And the Lord saw all that He had made, and behold, it was very good."

If the aesthetic appearance is the silent symbol of the relationships projected by Deity, our moral faculties bring home to us the imperative quality of the Divine Field. For the essence of morality is expressed in the double command: to integrate our own self to the fullest, so as to accord every element of our being its rightful place within our personality, and to place our own self within the larger wholes of the family, the state, and the emergent society of mankind. The nature of the first command has been frequently neglected in European thought, owing partly to the formalistic methods of philosophy and partly to the pervasiveness of the neo-platonic contempt for the flesh that has entered into the mainstream of our thinking. Yet it is basic, a modern depth-psychology has demonstrated. The social implications of the progressive awareness of ever larger wholes in society are obvious.

Thus, God as the field-building pole of being is approached through the highways of reason, aesthetics and ethics. We think of Him as the Self of the Universe, related to our self, in its field-building capacity, as our self is related to the material world. Yet these ways of cognizing are only formal, belonging more to philosophy than to religion. Basic as these avenues are, they constitute only the substructure of religion. For it is in attachment to God and His will that religion is born, and once this attachment is discovered, a new level of aspirations and feelings is opened up for the human personality.

It is in prayer that religion is born. In the beginning is the self's immediate reverence before the Master of the universe, its abasement before the Majesty of its source. It is not the believer in God who prays, but it is the worshipper who believes. The polarity of being has its correspondence and reflection in the life of the soul, which moves rhythmically from aggressive self-assertion in the world of reality to passive self-surrender to the Maker of this world.

5

The Meaning of God in our Experience

1. Holiness

Our analysis of the idea of God was conducted in the preceding chapter on the level of thought. We have demonstrated that our mind cannot but apply the two polar concepts of mechanism and spirit to the comprehension of the domain of existence. In turn, mechanistic explanation consists in the reduction of fluid events to stationary points in space-time, while the conception of spirit consists in the fields of relation and field of fields within which all points are contained. The pole of spirit, we have pointed out, is a chain of fields or wholes supervening above wholes. We may think of God as the spiritual Pole of Being, descending into the structure of the lowliest particle of matter and ascending to inscrutable heights of field-building that are related to our minds, as our minds are related to the manifold forms of unconscious life and as unconscious life is related to the silent energies of dead matter.

A conception of God derived from the analysis of thought is unavoidably abstract. What else can we encounter than the subtlest of abstractions if we proceed toward Him on the highway of reason? But, in all our thinking, we cannot help but assume a correspondence between thought and reality. The world, as it is in itself, is by definition, beyond our grasp, since all our knowledge is a product of two factors—the operation of our minds and the raw data of experience. This insight of Kant's is irrefutable, as far as it goes. Yet, we know that the conclusions achieved by logical reasoning correspond somehow to the nature of reality. Else, all our scientific progress would have been impossible. This position of philosophical realism may be expressed in language that borders on the mathematical—since knowledge is a synthesis of mind and reality, and the factor of mind is kept constant by analysis, there must be a point by point agreement between knowledge and reality. Let us, therefore, proceed to see how this conception of God actually figures in our experience. As thinking beings we can point toward God by abstractions, but, as living creatures we should find the marks of His power in our very being.

What is it then within the structure of our personality that we can identify as the factors which correspond to the Divine Pole of being? Manifestly, everything in our nature which integrates our self and makes it part of even greater wholes and subtler unities leads toward God.

Among psychologists there is a growing recognition of the "field" character of the human personality. Our self is not only a magnificent hierarchy of fields, superimposed upon each other, but, it is also fashioned very largely by the social and cultural fields in which it is embraced. And supervening above these fields is the realm of ideal values, for the sake of which the individual may feel himself called upon to negate both the desires of his own self and the dictates of society. These ideal fields appear in our lives as compulsions in which our own individuality is caught up. We are only points in the ideal fields that are unities of a higher nature and we feel their spell in diverse ways—in the attraction of the holy, the good, the true and the beautiful.

Common to these aspirations is firstly the feeling of disinterestedness. Our self is not in the center of the universe, but the ideal *summum bonum,* and we are only the privileged participants. Secondly, the particular object of our appreciation, the good deed, the true proposition, the thing of beauty appear to our minds as belonging to a closed system or a domain of relations of its own peculiar kind. There is no truth that does not point to other truths, no beauty without the richness of suggestion, no goodness that is self-contained. Thirdly, there is in each of these manifestations of spiritual life the feeling of reality. This awareness is extremely difficult to isolate in thought, though it is certainly an aspect of our experience. The contrast between the eternal and the temporal is not only known, but actually felt by us. We are never entirely free of the melancholy awareness of mortality, though we may manage to go on for years, with this haunting specter hovering only on the fringe of consciousness. We know ourselves to be basking in the sunlight of existence, for but a brief moment, and all the events of life impinge upon our minds with the hollow ring of timeliness. Yet, not all events have quite the same ring. When we are face to face with a striking truth, an act of triumphant goodness or an event of surpassing beauty, we recognize the quality of time-transcending reality, as an immediate, direct experience. And we thrill to it as a fact, not merely a reasoned argument.

These three qualities that are common to the three directions of spiritual life are just what we would expect to find in a soul that feels itself to be part of a supra-human ideal field. We participate in the domains of spirit, but spirit itself is a supervening reality, deriving from the Divine Pole of being. This is why each direction of the spirit leads to the awareness of God, though only in a partial way, inconclusively, haltingly, tangentially. It is only when the three directions of spirit are mutually reenforced and complemented that the awareness of reality and transcendence becomes overwhelming in certainty.

It is possible indeed to follow any of the three avenues of the spirit separately, but if we guard the openness and integrity of our personality, we cannot but be aware of their essential unity. And it is when we face the universe as a whole, conscious of our being a separate identity, lonely, ephemeral, dependent, that we surprise our soul in the act of throwing a bridge across the chasm of chaos unto the shore of eternity. This mysterious action of our soul is just what we would expect in a universe, dominated by the spiritual Pole of Being. It provides the motive power for the advance of our mind along the three great avenues of reason, will and feeling, and it constitutes the ultimate source of our spiritual life in all its forms. No better term has ever been devised for this fundamental response of our being to the nature of reality than the designation, the experience of holiness. Many and varied have been the attempts to describe the phases of this experience, in all its variation among people of different cultures and traditions. In Judaism, this fundamental experience of religion is best caught in the words of Isaiah, which are repeated several times daily in our liturgy—"Holy, holy, holy is the Lord of Hosts, the whole earth is full of His Glory.[2]

In the feeling of holiness, there predominates firstly the sense of elevation unto a domain of being, that is far above and beyond anything we can grasp. As the soul feels itself taken up into a different mode of existence, it acknowledges, firstly the *difference* between the Divine Being and all that is humanly conceivable. Holy, that is, removed from and exalted beyond, is the Lord of Hosts—holy, beyond the grasp of rationality, holy, beyond will and its goal, the *summum bonum*, holy, beyond feeling and its focus, the beautiful. But, this sense of difference is only one phase of the experience of holiness. The momentary intimation of transcendence is succeeded by the realization of God's Glory filling the universe. It is precisely through the avenues of activity open to it that the soul may reach out to become part of the Divine

Pole of Being. In holiness, we are raised for a brief moment above this mundane universe, but in the perception of His Glory we are led back to behold His presence in the world all about us and to recognize the tasks He sets before us.

The experience of holiness is thus twofold in character. On the one hand, it proclaims "not yet" to all our human insights; on the other hand, it enhances all our strivings for spiritual growth, saying "yes" to the outreachings of our soul for certainty, goodness and beauty. This dual nature of holiness is inescapable, since it is of the nature of a boundary-awareness to be two-sided, or, to phrase it in the dynamic terms of life, ambivalent. In the history of religious experience, one or the other phase of holiness is turned to the spotlight of consciousness. Thus, either the negative implications of holiness or its positive aspects may be regarded as primary or normative.

In modern theology, existentialists concentrate attention upon the negative phase of holiness. The divine is perceived chiefly on the analogy of a High Court, unconstrained by a written constitution or a set of precedents. Whatever we do is not good enough in the inscrutable judgment of the Court; we strive for the good and yet know ourselves to be sinners; try as we will, we cannot but fail, for sin is inherently part of our existence. The essence of piety is to plead guilty and to throw oneself on the mercy of the Court, and the essence of wisdom is the certainty of human folly and failure. It is precisely through the recognition of failure, or to put it theologically, through the awareness of sin, that men are prepared for the authentic response of the soul that is faith.

There is no question that the existentialist conception of faith corresponds to important phases of the experience of holiness. Yet, from our viewpoint, it appears to reflect only the negative and passive phase of an experience that is substantially positive and active. The word of God is that we identify ourselves with His work, that we share in His Holiness. And we thus identify ourselves both by the active assertion of our spiritual nature as well as by our passive surrender to the charm of the higher "fields," deriving from His Being. From our viewpoint, the primary analogy for the apprehension of the Divine derives not from His judgment, but from His "blessedness"—i.e. His being the Source of an upwelling and triumphant current of blessings. Thus, the basic response for us to make is to accept the challenge God gave to Abraham, at the begining of his mission—"and be thou a blessing." We apprehend the Divine, not in the "defiance" of human standards of truth and rightness, but in the quality of transcendence attaching to all the outgoing actions of the human spirit. The concept of "field-building" awakens the response of active participation, though every self, in the achievement of its own wholeness, is called upon to submit in humility and obedience to the demands of the higher "whole," in the divine Pole of Being.

2. Growth and the Conflict of Loyalties

It follows that there are many ways to God. Since our soul is the focus of influences deriving from many social fields and domains of ideal spirituality, we can respond to His call in several different ways. We are embraced by the fields of family, ethnic group, national entity, political state and humanity in general, and we are also caught up in the elevating fields of universal values and ideals. It would be idle to pretend that all loyalties reenforce each other and that Royce's counsel, "loyalty to loyalties" is a sufficient guide for all occasions. Loyalties are mutually contradictory, more often than not. In fact, all history is a tragic commentary on the inability of most men to resolve successfully their contemporary conflict of loyalties.

For Jewish people, this tension between different conflicting loyalties is a perennial and inescapable problem. Shall the loyalties of Jewish people to their ethnic group or to the nations among whom they live be considered primary and decisive? Shall Jewish loyalty be regarded as a summons to the life of the spirit, or as a bond of blood-brotherhood with the world community of Israel.? When are dual or multiple loyalties entirely legitimate, from the ethical standpoint, and when are they self-stultifying and hence frustrating?

To pose the last question is to provide a partial answer. Manifestly, there can be no general rule, applicable to all circumstances. Our starting point must be this very realization, that naive goodness or general good-will is not a sufficient guide for the resolution of the conflicts of loyalties that are real, all too real. No loyalty is as natural and compelling as a man's love for his parents, and this same loyalty, if held in excessive measure, may prevent him from adjusting happily to the demands of married life.

Our analysis thus far provides only one rule for dealing with the conflict of loyalties—the rule of aiding in the spiritual *growth* of poeple. We regard the Divine phase of being as the vertical dimension, in which every self, upon its emergence, becomes absorbed in a large or more ideal whole. In the achievement of inner unity, the self is active, but in submitting to a higher whole, it must cultivate the qualities of passivity and silent waiting for the mystery of growth to be achieved. Superimposed upon the various wholes of society, we behold the ideal realms of value, in which humanity itself is both embraced and transcended. We may state it then as our general rule that the growth of this Divine enterprise is the ultimate goal, by reference to which our actions should be judged. And this general rule is to be supplemented by the cumulative principles and precepts of Divine revelation.

3. *"The Achievement of an Integrated Personality"*

If our analysis of the universe about us corresponds in some measure to the nature of reality, we should expect to find two fundamental aspirations within the human personality—the yearning for the completion of self-hood and the impulse to integrate the self within the all-embracing whole of the universe. Moreover, both these aspirations would appear concurrently since in the vertical dimension of being, the selves of one level become the constituents of the Self of selves on the higher levels. The achievement of unity within the self makes possible the apprehension of the Universal Self, not merely as an abstract idea, but as a felt reality. For, after all, the mystery of being, in all its polar tension, is actually alive within our own self. On the plane of thought, we envisage the chain of ever more complex fields, but since our personality is itself caught up in this vertical dimension of being, it must contain the awareness of this cosmic pattern of integration, though this awareness is not always brought into the focus of consciousness.

Indeed, it is not difficult to find in the science of psychology ample confirmation of the existence of drives for wholeness and for integration of the self within the greater whole.

The hindrances within the human personality to the attainment of perfect selfhood are many and various. The domain of memory enshrines a good portion of personality, but no man's memory is perfect. In the light of consciousness, the vast areas of experience are held together in one field, but there are depths upon depths in the unconscious, of which we are only now becoming aware. And shimmering upon the restless waves of consciousness are ideas, impulses and drives that are frequently in conflict. Every person is aware in moments at least of the charm and spell of the wholes of life—of the claims of the family, the clan, the tribe, the society of mankind generally. And these claims are sometimes in conflict with the more limited drives and ambitions of his own person.

As Eric Fromm points out, the dilemma of man consists in the need of striking a balance between the claims of his own individuality and the social realities of which he is part. In the entire kingdom of nature, man is the only being capable of becoming an individual. And man's individuality is itself a synthesis of the assertion of freedom and the acceptance of "relatedness" to society and its ideals.

The achievement of unity of personality is thus a gradational endeavor, that is attained progressively on ever higher levels. The physical being of a person may be taken in its isolation from wider social and spiritual fields and regarded as a thing apart. The goal of unity would then call for the pattern of life that is most likely to allow every impulse its due measure of satisfaction. Selfishness in all its forms, from the unreasoned brutishness of the vulgar to the subtle sensualism of the Epicurean sophisticates consists essentially in this delimitation of the field of human personality to the physical body. The business of living is then seen to be a matter of balancing the honey against the sting in various undertakings, so as to achieve as big a preponderance of the totality of pleasures over pains as is possible.

Hedonistic or materialistic philosophies cannot be refuted. But their limitations are obvious, applying as they do only to the lowest levels of consciousness. We have seen that man is capable of envisioning many fields in relation to which his physical body is only a point. These larger wholes comprise the social units of which we are part, the universal domain of ideals, the spell of the great traditions of the past and the lure of the unfolding future. It may be doubted whether any human being was ever completely insensitive to the call of these larger wholes. Failure to respond to these impulses of the spirit results in a feeling of being pushed into the void, belonging within the field in question and yet being barred from it. Thus, pangs of conscience mark the self-imposed isolation of the individual in relation to society. Failure to become part of the cultural stream of society may be felt as the anguish of "not belonging," which is a fairly common experience. The refusal to take account of the "wholes" of tradition and of the call of the future result in a feeling of the emptiness of life, its vacuity and meaninglessness. For meaning is the reflection upon our stream of consciousness of the open horizons of great wholes. We employ the term meaning in general usage, where it indicates a relation between two points, but if our self as a whole is to have meaning, it must be seen as part of an all-embracing "whole." Only the Aristotelian God could be content in His perfection, thinking perpetually of Himself.

Actually, brute selfishness is possible only for brutes. In human society, selfishness becomes a social problem when it is dignified by association with some partial "whole." A person may set the welfare of his family, his clan, his nation, his economic class or his artistic interest above the needs of society generally. The cultured bohemian sees himself as the practitioner of an Art. Nothing is easier for men and women than the elevation of their particular field of interest to the rank of a supreme idol. When the gentle Keats wrote the memorable lines, "Beauty is truth, truth beauty. That is all ye know on earth, and all ye need to know," he could hardly have been aware of the manifold ways in which this principle could be abused. To perceive beauty is indeed to sense the relation of the part to the whole, to become aware of the *harmony* and congruence of many parts, to feel an inner approval of the *rightness* of a shape or a pattern in relation to a field that is felt subconsciously. In this sense, the feeling for beauty is one with the search for truth, which consists likewise in the countinuous building up of fields and in the perception of the relations between them. But, beauty is partial and conditioned by many factors which are not revealed to the light of consciousness. Hence, the pursuit of the beautiful is the ideal essence of idolatry, as the aspiration for the "kingdom of heaven," the ideal society, perfect in all its many facets, is the essence of true religion.

The besetting sin of mankind is idolatry, for, in our human situation, we can only be cognizant of partial wholes. How to submit to the spell of a national tradition and yet to sense the glories of other cultures, how to feel the holiness of the symbols of your own faith while recognizing the relative character of all symbols and rituals, how to appreciate the glories of the moment while seeing all things under the aspect of eternity—these are indeed the paradoxes that each one of us is called upon to resolve in his life.

There are only two aids which we are granted, in order to help us grow upward in spirit, as the tide of time carries us relentlessly forward—the sword of self-scrutiny and the shield of prayer. By means of the former, we subject our loyalties to constant analysis and criticism; by means of the latter we strain to render ourselves receptive to the inflow of the Divine spirit.

d. The Meaning of Prayer

We must begin our analysis of the meaning of prayer with the recognition that it is a mysterious phenomenon. People pray before they are able to give themselves an account of the why and wherefore of worship. Whenever the easy complacency of surface existence is shattered and we are thrown back upon the resources of our own deeper selves, we find ourselves praying. Nor is it blind fear alone that evokes this virtually instinctive reaction from us. The grandeur of beauty, the majesty of some natural phenomenon, the tenderness of love, the charm of infants, whatever it is in our experience that points beyond itself to the unfathomable mystery of existence evokes the wonder of worship from us.

The spontanous outburst of prayer does not necessarily take the form of words. If the verbal channels happen to be blocked by psychological obstacles of one sort or another, our soul will discover other avenues of expression—such as painting, music or social action. Any activity by which our keen appreciation of the universe outside our own being is articulated is a form of prayer. The artist expresses wonderment at the majesty of beauty and his humble homage to the Divine mystery by means of the materials of his art, even, as in the stricter domain of religion, the worshipper exclaims, "it is good to give thanks unto the Lord and to sing unto thy name, O Most High."

But, the artist who is able to transmute faithfully the feeling of prayer into works of beauty is rare indeed. Most generally, the impulses of worship are dissipated into vague sentimentality and a general, all-pervasive uneasiness, if the person has been conditioned against prayer. The momentary smile on the face of the universe vanishes, though the parted lips remain, and every failure to respond to its charm darkens the vision of its successive appearances.

It is out of the depths of our being that the impulse for worship arises, as the psalmist put it, "out of the depths, I called unto Thee, O Lord." Though the act of worship normally takes the form of speech, it issues from psychical levels that are themselves below the surface of conscious speech. The meaning of prayer cannot be discovered therefore by analyzing and clarifying the ideas to be found in the prayer-books of mankind. The logic of prayer does not consist in any particular sequence of ideas, but in the psychological roots and associations of the words that are employed in worship. Phrases that appear tautologous and even meaningless under the scalpel of analysis, may correspond to profound foci of feeling in the dynamic depths of the worshipper's consciousness, while a logical discourse may roll off his tongue, without burrowing into his soul.

Generally speaking, the language of prayer echoes two fundamental states of the soul—the state of appreciation, and that of yearning for the consummation of fulfillment. If the complexities of human emotion be divided into two categories—those resulting from the retreat of the soul and those reflecting its advance into the outer world, then it is the dominance of the latter category that is articulated in worship. Fear, anxiey, selfish ambition, envy, anger, possessiveness and pride—all the attitudes which reflect the recoil of the soul from contact with other beings in the domain of the spirit are expressed in prayer only as springboards from which the soul leaps into the bright sunlight of their corresponding opposites. Thus, a goodly half of prayer consists of hymms, "praising the Lord," whereby our soul articulates its appreciation of the beauty and nobility of existence, echoing the exclamation of God, when He beheld His creation, "behold, it is good." The other half of prayer consists of petitions for the perfection and completion of personality, as if our soul were straining and stretching to grow into the fullness of its ideal being. In both phases of prayer we see the human self rising gradually from the recognition of its own weakness to the perception of the Divine majesty, and thence to the aspiration for the fulfillment of its being. But there is no prayer without the inner assurance that God dwells within us, even as He is in the universe outside our being. And, then, we yearn to expand the walls of our self as far as they would go, so as to allow the utmost room for the growth of His seeds within our soul.

5. *The Personal God and Revelation*

Conceiving of God as the spiritual Pole of Being, we now inquire as to the manner in which we are to envisage His nature. Shall we think of Him in physical—philosophical terms such as Principle, Power, Absolute, Form or Cause, or shall we employ the personalistic-biblical terms of Father, the Merciful One, the Living God? Manifestly, the only concept which can point toward the Deity is that of the human self, which, in our experience constitutes the polar opposite to the concept of mechanical causation. Yet, God is not the Self or Soul of the universe, but, as the Kabbalists correctly pointed out, He is the Soul of the Soul, etc. of the universe. And we have no way of knowing how many links there be found in the spiritual chain of being.

We need hardly point out that, according to our analysis, God's nature is "unknowable," since the term self can only point toward His Being, which is related to self, as self is related to the unconscious life of an organic cell. The biblical insistence on the "unlikeness" of God to any other being or force was taken by Philo to teach the doctrine of the absolute "unknowability" of the Divine nature. "For my thoughts are not your thoughts, says the Lord." "For as the heavens are high above the earth so are My thoughts high above yours." (Isaiah 55,a) (Wolfsohn—"Philo," vol. II)

In respect of the "personal" nature of the Deity and His "unknowability," we find that the biblical view is validated, as against two millenia of philosophical criticism. As David Neumark has pointed out, the tension between the biblical view of the "Living God" and the philosophical conception of a Principle or Power, however glorious in the purity of its abstraction, is essentially unresolveable. All through the Middle Ages, theologians wrestled with the task of reconciling the two conceptions. But, their labors served only to bring this tension into sharper focus. The two views derive respectively from the contemplation of the physical universe and from the introspection of the sainted personality. The process of explanation leads in the case of the physical universe to principles that are susceptible to mathematical formulation, and, in the case of human nature, to the mystery of personality. Nor did the guardians of normative Judaism ever succumb to the temptation of separating the god of nature from the god of the human conscience, allowing all-mightiness to the one and all-goodness to the other, though such a separation appeared at times to be logically inescapable. In spite of the revival of this mode of thought in modern times, normative Judaism continues to insist on the simple unity and uniquenes of His nature.

By the same token, the controvesy as to God's transcendence versus His immanence is settled in Judaism by the insistence that He is both Far and Near. Furthermore, the rabbis point out in their non-technical language—"wherever you find the greatness of the Holy One, blessed be He, there too you find His humility." In the view herein outlined, there is a phase of God's being, that is transcendent to our understanding and experience. For our conscious understanding is like the spectrum of visible light-waves, a fragment of mentality between that which lies below consciousness and that which rises above it. Yet, God is also immanent in the nisus toward spirituality, observable throughout creation, and in the upward striving of men and women for the consummation of the Messianic dream, the achievement of ethical perfection and triumphant holiness.

Does our conception of God allow for the wonder of revelation? Yes, though not in the Fundamentalist sense of the term. Knowledge, in the sense of specific words, ideas and instructions, is a function of the mind, which is ideally sovereign within it own domain. Howsoever an idea enters the field of mind, it must be dealt with strictly on its own merit within the total sphere of available knowledge. But, revelation in the sense of an incursion of Divine energy into the human soul, opening up a new and higher "field" of relations, is exactly what we behold in the history of mankind generally and in the emergence of the congregation of Israel in particular.

It is not through our senses but through our mind that we acquire the capacity to appreciate new facets of value and to sense ever more deeply the charm of the ideal "fields" of the spirit. Ideas exert their own pull, and the spiritual domain of values, bounded by holiness, is likely to take hold of our being ever more decisively, as our minds and hearts are turned toward God. Occasionally, a high plateau of insight is reached by some genius of the spirit, revealing virtually a new way of looking at things. As a result, life acquires fresh depths of meaning, and new values begin to command the hearts of men. Eventually, new social movements arise and new redeeming ideals are projected unto the stage of history. These sudden ascents of the spirit, whether they are achieved by an individual or a people, constitute the thunder which follows the flash of an act of revelation. It is by a system of values that our inner life is determined and the inner history of mankind is molded. And the perception of ever new values in the complexities of life is the work of Divine Revelation.

6

Torah M'Sinai

1. The Problem

It is commonly said that Judaism has no dogmas save the one belief in Sinaitic revelation. If the Divine origin of every word in the Torah is once assumed, then all else that an Orthodox Jew is bidden to accept may easily be inferred from its hallowed precepts.[1] The existence of God and His beneficent Providence, the creation of the world and the duties of man, the whole complex of ideas and motivations that enters into the daily practice of the faith—all this theoretical groundwork of Judaism is either stated or implied in the Pentateuch and the sacred literature that clusters around it. The faith of the typical Orthodox Jew is like a massive inverted pyramid, resting upon the fulcrum of Torah M'Sinai and disdaining the dubious support of dialectics.

Thus, Halevi began his exposition of Judaism with the Biblical account of the historical experience of the Jewish people. Contemptuous of the inevitable uncertainty and multifarious possibilities of error which beset the boldest flights of speculation, Halevi argued that the only safe policy was to follow unquestioningly the well-worn grooves of authenticated tradition.[2] Why worry over theological

---

[1] "Iggereth Hamudoth"—Why should we imitate the Gentiles in the search for basic principles and roots when the Torah consists altogether of basic principles . . . The most fundamental principle upon which all depends is that everything in the Torah is from the mouth of the Almighty."

[2] "Kusari," I, 13.

"proofs," when the whole truth, or as much of it as is needful for human salvation is already revealed in the unambiguous language of the Torah? Speculation certainly cannot improve upon the Word of God; hence, its only conceivable effect is in the negative direction, to vitiate and to undermine the perfect faith of the non-philosophical believer.[3]

Doubtless, the attitude of Halevi was shared by the vast majority of Jewish pietists. Philosophical speculation, pure and unrestrained, was always felt to be a foreign importation. Genuine Judaism was not unreflective, but it did not concern itself with the purely intellectual feat of "proving" the Existence of God and the reality of His Providence. In the sphere of rational reflection, Jewish piety sought to bring into the focus of consciousness the evidences of God's Power and Glory that are to be found in the whole realm of creation, in order that the ubiquitous majesty of the Lord may be fully appreciated, but it never entertained the ambition of actually basing the faith upon such evidence. Thus, the "mussar" schools of Orthodox Judaism discouraged the study of the first chapter of Bachya's, *"Duties of the Heart,"* which offers proofs for the existence and unity of God. Instead, they concentrated the total fervor of their pious souls upon the task outlined in the second chapter of that classic work, that of observing the marks of the Divine in oneself and in the external universe.[4] As to the theoretical groundwork of faith, they needed none, since the dogma of "Torah M'Sinai" was to be regarded as axiomatic.

In the Middle Ages, this dogma was comparatively easy to uphold. The Jews lived among Christians and Moham-

[3] "He who accepts the Torah implicitly, without rationalistic attempts, is better than the one who accepts it, after analysis and speculation."
[4] See article on "Mussar," in the *Festschrift für Jacob Rosenheim;* also, Sh. Rosenfeld's *Reb Yisroel Salanter.*

medans who conceded that at least for a period, the revelations of the Old Testament were absolutely valid. The burden of proof for the discontinuance of the old dispensation was undeniably upon the proponents of the daughter-religions, in regard to whom the rabbis were therefore able to strike the pose of sober, clear-eyed, reasonable skeptics. Thus, the challenge of the dominant religions of the Medieval era could be met in the manner of Halevi on the safe battleground of Sinaitic revelation. At Sinai, all the people witnessed the Divine spectacle and heard the voice of God. If any subsequent revelation was to supersede the one at Sinai, it should have been offered by the Lord with the same eclat and before as large an audience as the one at Sinai. Such an argument was logical enough, so long as no one doubted the authenticity of Holy Writ.[5]

Nevertheless, the Medieval era saw the emergence of philosophic Judaism which sought to base the faith on inner rational conviction as well as on the authority of revealed tradition. Though the philosophers never went so far as to dispense altogether with the dogma of Torah M'Sinai, they did establish another criterion for the truth of faith—its consonance with the canons of logic and philosophy. Every word of the Law was revealed, but the meaning of that word must be such as to accord with the proven principles of human speculation. Thus, two coordinate criteria were set up—that of tradition governing the actions of the Jew and that of rational thought, guiding the interpretation of the Divine Law and metaphysical speculation generally.[6]

[5] Maimonides, Code, Book One, 1—"The Israelites did not believe Moses, our Master, because of the miracles . . . Why then did they believe him? Because at Mount Sinai, our own eyes saw, not those of strangers, our own ears heard, not those of strangers, the fire, the thunder, the flames . . ." See also, "Ikkarim," I, 20.

[6] "Guide of the Perplexed," II, 22.

Philosophical Judaism, then was based upon the two disciplines of reason and revelation. Naturally, both bodies of doctrine had to be modified and transformed, in the synthesis of philosophical Judaism.[7] In the great system of Maimonides, philosophy had to give up the doctrine of the eternity of the universe and revealed faith had to surrender the right to interpret literally or freely any verse or principle of the Torah.

The alliance between Judaism and philosophy was thoroughly unsatisfactory, from the viewpoint of naive piety. The artificiality of Maimonides' synthesis, was most in evidence in his discussion of the reasons for the various commandments, since at that point both realms of discourse had a common border. After the death of Maimonides, philosophical Judaism declined steadily, both in intellectual stature and in popularity, until the expulsion from Spain, when it virtually disappeared from the Jewish scene. The philosophical approach resulted indisputably in a progressive weakening of loyalty to religion, to the point where martyrdom appeared no longer to be worth the price.[8] The "enlightened" Jews did not bare the neck to the knife of crusading fanatics as readily as the non-philosophical Jews. The melancholy experience of Spanish Jewry proved beyond the shadow of a doubt that the tenacity of the faith is sorely weakened by the virus of philosophy. In the sorry circumstances of Jewish life in exile, Judaism could ill afford the debilitating luxury of unrestrained speculation. As a result, post-Medi-

[7] The pressure of the tradition on the philosophers was constant. See "Hazuth Kosho," by Isaac Erame—"that philosophical speculation should not lift its hand or its foot save insofar as it is permitted by Torah and by prophecy."

[8] See the introduction to "Or Hayim," commentary on the Pentateuch; "Hazuth Kosho," by Isaac Erame; "Saifer HaEmunoth" by Shem Tov. All claim that in the face of martyrdom the philosophically minded were the first to leave the Jewish camp.

eval Judaism came to lean more and more on the sole, bare dogma of "Torah M'Sinai," to the almost complete exclusion of the philosophical method and viewpoint.

However, in the modern period, when the spirit of historical criticism forms part of the very being of intelligent, sensitive Jews, it is no longer possible to disregard the criterion of rational reflection. It does not do to assail, *à la* Samson Raphael Hirsch, the "spirit of the times" and to thunder pontifically that the "times" should adjust themselves to the Torah, and not vice versa. For, as a matter of fact, we are the "times." In our conscience, the Torah and whatever we conceive to be the best in modern thought and culture are equally represented. To place oneself on the side of unrelenting dogma and to assail "modern thought" on general principles is therefore as silly an exercise in verbal dialectics as the idiotic pastime of punching one's own shadow. For a naive Jew, whose mind has not absorbed the genius of modern intellectual travail and aspiration, it is indeed quite natural to assail philosophy and all that smacks of it as "dangerous thoughts." But, for a modernly trained Jew to presume to dispose of the problem by a frontal, all-out assault against "modernism" is utterly dishonest, or, if honest, nothing but dialectical schizophrenics.

There is the story of a Rosh Y'shivah who observed that one of his students was in the habit of reciting his prayers with inordinate rapidity. To the rebuke of his master, the student replied that he hurries thru his prayers in order to escape from the "strange thoughts" that might otherwise distract his attention. "It is as if I were driving a wagon thru a crowd of ruffians," explained the student, "I drive with all speed so that the ruffians might not climb aboard the wagon." "In your case," replied the master, "hurrying does no good since the ruffians are already in the wagon." By the same token, it is but futile self-deception for anyone to argue that we can continue the post-Medieval practice of utterly disregarding and defying "modern thought." Our faith should challenge and combat the ethical and spiritual *failings* of our age, but it cannot possibly oppose, without self-stultification, the *ideals* of the age, which we share with our generation. Religion must ever combat the *"yetzer hora"* (Evil Urge) of the age, but, it must never allow itself to be placed in the position of opposing in advance of critical analysis that which the conscience of the age conceives as the *"yetzer tov."* (Good Urge)

2. *Two Pillars*

Philosophical Judaism seeks to base itself on the two pillars of reason and revelation. Our first task then is to prove the rightness of admitting both pillars to the support of the structure of Judaism. The basic thesis of philosophical Judaism needs to be defended against the narrow partisans of rationalism on the one hand, and spiritual naivete on the other hand, for the proponent of a philosophical faith is perennially under attack from both sides. While the advocates of "pure reason" chide him for his appeasement policy in admitting the reality of revelation, the advocates of naive piety attack him for his introduction of an alien criterion of truth in matters of revelation—a criterion that is other than those of revelation itself. The view of non-philosophical Judaism was most succinctly put by the Gaon of Vilna in the maxim, "both Torah and general wisdom stem from the same Divine source and it is the function of Torah to define what expressions of wisdom are valid and permitted." [9] In other words, there is only one criterion of truth, the Torah.

To take up the second objection first, we maintain the spiritual immaturity of belief in revelation, as a general blanket belief, without analysis and without a comparative

[9] *"Aliyoth Eliyah".*

standard of revelation. To be sure, piety as such need not include the passion of philosophy, but it is one thing to ignore the philosophical approach or to be unaware of it and quite another to deny knowingly the validity of the philosophical viewpoint and method in matters of faith. In the case of Orthodox Judaism, faith means the belief in the historicity of Sinaitic revelation as it is described in the literal account of the Torah. Can such faith be defended against the philosophical approach on the ground that philosophy, or human reason, is powerless to judge in matters that are, by their very nature, removed from the reach of reason?—If so, then, the dogma of Sinaitic revelation could be put on an equal plane with the theory of religious metaphysics generally and there would then be no room for the pillar of philosophy in the structure of our faith. But is it so?

The trite remark of Hamlet, "there are more things in heaven and earth than are dreamt of in your philosophy," has its counterpart in many a philosophy of religion. It is undeniable that there are limits to the sway of human reason. Kant supplied the classic defense of the theory that "pure reason" is, by virtue of its structure, incapable of dealing with the numinal world. Recent scientific theorists, like Jeans and Eddington, further expatiated on the limits of reason, from the viewpoint of experimental science. That there are limits to human reason is by now a commonplace. But, this recognition of the limitation imposed upon man's rational faculties does not afford an overall justification for all kinds of belief. Reason, driven out thru the door, enters thru the window, for reason is but another name for mental clarity and vision and spiritual honesty.

When we speak, then, of the validity of faith as against reason, we cannot and do not mean any kind of faith. In modern philosophy, faith is justified either as an experience, or as an application of the "will to believe" to a situation in

which reason is powerless to decide between two alternatives. In the first instance, faith is part of the whole variegated realm of experience, which is the subject matter of
reason. There is, therefore, no conflict between faith and
reason; but then the content of faith is subject to the critique
of both our intelligence and conscience, even as are all
other data of experience. In the second instance, faith is
regarded as a healthy psychical function, wholly in place in
the many areas of legitimate doubt that one confronts in life.
Thus, here, too, we may speak of faith as a proper function
of the mind, alongside of reason. In both cases, there is no
question of faith being opposed to reason.

Faith as experience is a classic conception in the philosophy of religion. Halevi spoke of the "inner vision of prophets and saints," which penetrates unerringly to the Divine
structure of reality.[10] Kant regarded the intuition of the
moral law as a form of reason.[11] Post-Kantian philosophers
spoke of the experience of freedom, pure will, or of the feeling of creaturely surrender to the power of the Creator, or
of love, or of the experience of holiness.[12] Faith, in this sense,
is a form of cognition, that is, to say the least, entirely probable. Reason and the senses permit us only to glimpse the
mass of phenomena, as they appear in this space-time world.
But, we ourselves, are not only phenomena, but noumena as
well. Clearly, we not only think: we *are* as well. The numinous world does not reside only in the realm transcending our
senses; it obviously dwells within us, as the incomprehensible
ground of our empirical self. It is therefore reasonable to
assume an inner correspondence between insights of our
deepest nature and the numinal world. Clearly, "depth calls
unto depth," even when, on the surface of things, no com-

[10] "Kusari," IV, 13.
[11] "Kritik der Praktischen Vernunft," E. Kant.
[12] Jaccobi, Fichte, Schleiermacher, Otto.

munication takes place. Especially, when we learn, from the modern theory of phenomenalism, that sensory knowledge involves an unconscious activity of the human mind, does it become clear that the activity of religious insight into the ever-present, eternal reality of the universe, is a perfectly legitimate source of knowledge.[13] Faith, in this sense, is not sheer wilful belief, but in a very real way, it is itself proof of the proposition it affirms. Thus, when I find within me the consciousness of the dependency or "creaturely" character of the physical universe and note everywhere the seal and stamp of a transcendent God, whose Will and Purpose permeate the whole range of existence, then this faith, in its multiple formulations, is an incontestable form of evidence. Though this insight comes to us only in moments of great spiritual uplift, its truth-value is still momentous. Its acceptance depends only upon the assumption of an inner connection and harmony between our perceptions and the truth—an assumption, which we make instinctively. *But, the belief in the historicity of a past event has nothing to do with faith in this sense, since there can be no inner correspondence between our present feeling and the events of several thousand years ago.*

As to the second meaning of faith, the right to believe a proposition that is necessary for one's salvation, when there are no compelling proofs to the contrary, the dogma of "Torah M'Sinai" finds in it a measure of support that is distinctly limited. The first duty of a *homo sapiens* is to study a question of history by the methods of historical research. There is room for the exercise of the believing faculty only in the residual areas of doubt. Prof. William James, who defended the "right to believe" with the utmost brilliance pointed out that this form of faith can be applied

[13] Max Scheler brilliantly applies the thesis of phenomenalism to the problem of religion.

only in the case of "live" propositions, that is, propositions which are entirely plausible and consonant with one's background. James' defense of faith is really an excellent apologia for those who are emotionally predisposed to a certain belief, but who hesitate to yield to it, for fear of offending their rational principles. But, the dogma of "Torah M'Sinai," in its fundamentalist interpretation, is no longer a "live" proposition to those who have made their own the spirit of Western culture and the modern methods of research in the history of religions.

Clearly, the dogma of "Torah M'Sinai" cannot possibly be regarded as a self-sufficient axiom; in any modern formulation, it must be presented as a corollary of more basic considerations. It cannot therefore be represented as the sole and sufficient ground of Judaism.

Equally unwarranted is the attempt to dispense altogether with the doctrine of revelation and to found Judaism on the sole support of reason. This attempt was very popular in the nineteenth century when the concept of "natural religion" was in great vogue. Belief in God, the moral law and immortality were conceived to be the content of ethical "monotheism." Judaism was a true faith, only in so far as these ideas were to be found in its literature.[14] Rituals and ceremonies were of value only as so many illustrations of these principles, or as apt symbols of Divine truth, or as the unifying bonds of the Jewish group. On this view, the Law is stripped of every vestige of authority, the whole range of tradition is denied any inherent truth-value, and worship becomes a mere human exercise in mnemonics.

14 An echo of this line of reasoning is found in the title of Hermann Cohen's great work on Judaism, "Religion des Vernunft's aus den Quellen des Judentums." The kernel is the religion of reason; the sources of Judaism are the shell.

The errors implicit in this rationalistic version of Judaism will be shown in the course of the discussion in this paper. Suffice it at this point to indicate that this view utterly ignores the character of the religious consciousness. While the fundamentalists' religion is devoid of reason, the rationalists' religion has nothing in common with the actual, native religious bent of living men and women. To attempt the dissolution of religion in rationalistic and moralistic generalizations is as idle and unreal an exercise as the attempt to reduce the feeling of the beautiful to laws of logical necessity.

Religion transcends the proper sphere of reason in several ways. First, as a domain of valuation. All valuational processes are concerned with the perception of fundamental data and relations. The religious consciousness is a realm of unique values, *sui generis,* even as art and music, so that in it the concepts of ethics and esthetics acquire a special tone and substance. Beauty is transmuted into a feeling of the Divine, duty is viewed as self-orientation to the Divine Will and the measure of right and wrong is construed as the judgment of God. As a fundamental attitude of the soul, creative of new values, piety evolves a specific realm of judgments and ideals that must be judged in their own terms.

Second, as a form of knowledge. In the religious consciousness, all objects are seen as "dependent," "creaturely," functions of a higher power. This is not a reasoned inference, but an immediate intuition of the transcendent, even as all external objects are apprehended as transcending our mental world and all persons are felt to be transcendent in yet a higher sense. "Foxhole religion" is not primitive superstition. It merely brings to a head the feeling of dependence that is part of the core of religion. The intuition of the finiteness and limitation of the whole visible universe is a basic ingredient of the religious consciousness. Religion without the feeling of transcendence is like the shell without the seed. And transcendence is an experience that escapes the net of pure rationalism.

Third, the organic character of religious tradition. Organized religion is more than an attempt to regulate life in accord with certain clearly envisaged truths. Product of a particular kind of religious experience, it tends to perpetuate its own special brand of piety. Its truth-value is greater than the sum total of true principles proclaimed by it, for it is life as well as thought, reality as well as truth. And reality is always particular, not universal. Rationalistic generalizations are incapable of grasping the particular qualities of actual, living faiths. The religious consciousness, in actual fact, is a distinctly particularized phenomenon. Especially is this true in the case of Judaism, which possesses a definite organic character.

Fourth, revelation is an actual phenomenon, not merely a euphemism, and Judaism is a revealed religion. The meaning and proof of these statements will occupy our attention in the succeeding chapters.

3. The Pillar of Philosophy

In the Medieval period, certain basic terms and principles of philosophy were universally accepted. When Maimonides took up the task of effecting a synthesis between Judaism and philosophy, he and his contemporaries knew very clearly what the term philosophy stood for. The authority of "the philosopher" was so great that Averroes' interpretation of the Aristotelian system was looked upon as the last word of human reason. Maimonides was constrained to modify Aristotelianism in respect to the doctrine of creation, but except for this point he accepted the authority of Aristotle virtually without question. Today, when we speak of the pillar of philosophy in the structure of faith, we are conscious of the basic lack of agreement on the most fundamental questions. Idealists and realists, phenomenalists, naturalists and pragmatists—each proclaim their own world-view and employ their own special terminology. How then can we speak of the voice of philosophy as a criterion of truth and a pillar of the faith?

The answer to this question is twofold: First, beneath the variety of philosophical systems, there is the one substratum of thought which is common to all philosophers. Second, we must, in the realm of faith, give up any residual striving for uniformity and recognize the right of each individual to work out his own synthesis of philosophy and faith. We shall therefore first set down the common qualities of modern philosophy and then outline our own conception of the final result of the long travail of human thought.

Firstly, then, philosophy implies the philosophical temper, by which is meant the most exacting self-criticism and self-examination. While the determination to analyze and scrutinize all ideas and opinion is the mark of all educated people, it is the central passion and preoccupation of the philosopher. Modern philosophy is not even content to allow the faculty of reason to function as the final judge and arbiter. Descartes, who launched philosophy on a new path, began by doubting all sources of knowledge, and Kant set the pace for "critical" thinking by submitting the categories of reason to the rigors of thoroughgoing criticism. All modern philosophic systems begin with an examination of the epistemological problem. Doubt and self-criticism, then, are the basic ingredients of the philosophic temper.

Secondly, philosophy connotes the philosophical ideal, which strives for the ordering of all knowledge into a unified system. It is the aim of philosophy to discover the original formula of the universe, in which all mental and physical events may be understood as so many variables in an eternal structure of constants. Thus, Einstein's lifelong search for the basic formula of matter and energy is really the attempt of a scientist to assay a solution to the quest of philosophy. It is assumed, to begin with, that truth is not a private matter, which is automatically corrupted when it is generalized and tested by the reason and conscience of universal humanity. All things must be studied against this background and then related to the whole pattern of accumulated knowledge. Thus, the comparative method of the historical and social sciences is a direct implication of the inevitable trend of the modern spirit.

Thirdly, the philosophical subject-matter, which is the realm of human experience. Modern thought is profoundly conscious of the decisive verdicts of personal and universal experience. "Pure" abstractions, however neatly excogitated and catalogued are regarded with suspicion and even contempt. Speculative thought, like the manifold branches of science, must start with authenticated experience and lead to conclusions which will not wilt and wither in the press of earthly affairs. Thus, we are suspicious of abstract "proofs" for the existence of God, no matter how precisely they are argued. For it is the meaning of God in human experience that we are after, not a dogmatic, verbal formula, that is not relevant to the affairs of the market place.

The ways in which this common core of philosophy conflicts with the fundamentalist mentality are obvious. Orthodox Judaism in Russia and Poland sealed itself with seven seals against the fresh winds of philosophy. It is pertinent to inquire, however, whether the concept of revelation as the foundation of faith is ruled out by the philosophical approach. Do the principles of criticism, universality and empiricism negate the entire conception of Divine revelation in human history?—No. Not, if revelation is defined in a way which reckons sincerely with the demands of philosophy.

The concept of Divine Revelation denotes the belief that truth and creative vision may come to man from God, thru channels other than the physical senses. Obviously, then, this belief conflicts with the naturalistic philosophies which maintain the proposition "that nothing is in the mind which was not previously in the sense." It is, however, fully in harmony with the philosophies which emphasize the creative novel elements in the course of evolution and the history of mankind. There is no question then of harmonizing our faith with all and sundry philosophies, as if religion and reason were mutually neutral, belonging to two separate worlds. It is incumbent upon us to begin our "cheshbon hanefesh" by vindicating our philosophical position thru the methods of philosophy.

We conceive of revelation, as consisting of a twofold activity—the orientation of man to God and the message of God to man. It is possible for man to ignore his relation to God and to guide his life solely by naturalistic and utilitarian ethics, since the human mind is endowed with the power to abstract select phases from the total complex of reality. However, we maintain, such a policy is based upon the wilful overlooking of the demands of the highest states of man's consciousness. The existence of man is, like the periphery of an ellipse, related to both the physical focus in the phenominal world and the spiritual focus in the numinal world. Freedom is the mark of the spiritual life. We are free to disregard utterly the rhythm and measure of the spirit, but once we surrender to its sway, we find ourselves constrained and directed by ideals that are not of our own making.

The moral law, in its various formulations, from Moses to Hillel and from Kant to Hermann Cohen, is the content of this earnest endeavor to heed the call of the spirit. We may designate the intuition of the objective validity of ethical values as the first phase of the phenomenon of revelation. In this phase, revelation may be described as the property of the generality of mankind, though only in a potential sense. It is not true, that all men apprehend at all times the "Categorical Imperative" of Kant, but it is true that all men are endowed with the capacity of recognizing the validity of the moral law and that, at one time or another in their life, they do recognize it. This is the deeper meaning of the belief that man was created in the image of God and that his knowledge of good and evil was later corrupted. Thus, the first stage of revelation is the recognition of Divine law.

We may designate as the second stage of revelation the highest levels of religious feeling, when the awareness of the Divine mystery and majesty is the supreme note in man's consciousness. This is the level of genuine prayer, the realization of standing before the Almighty.

"The feeling of the Holy" overwhelms the worshipper and he is moved to say with the psalmist, "And I, the nearness of the Lord did I seek." Awareness of the holy is compounded of pure feeling and the volitional element of dedication to the Will of God. Thus, the second stage of revelation includes the first one, though in a richer context of feeling. Awareness of objective law is transformed into an acceptance of the Will of God; legalistic conformity is lifted to the point of self-consecration and respect for law is turned into love of the good. In this way, religion functions as the source and mainspring of the ethical consciousness, the moral law being the conceptualized, crystallized expression of the fluid content of revelation. In this, its second stage, revelation may still be considered as the property of all men, since it is ideally possible for virtually all men to experience the electric sensation of genuine religious feeling.

The intuition of the moral law and the experience of religious feeling may be designated as Divine revelation in the broad meaning of the term since, thru them, the phenomenal veil is torn aside for brief moments. In its narrower significance, the term Divine Revelation denotes the third stage of inspiration, when new insight and creative energy are vouchsafed to the soul of man. This stage is, in contrast to the lower levels of the phenomenon, no longer common to the experience of all men. Creative genius and prophetic insight are unfortunately restricted to the chosen few, so that we must perforce depart from the common ground of universal experience when we deal with these rare phenomena. Nevertheless, we do not part company with human experience at this point, for the marks of Divine Revelation in history are themselves part of the authenticated record of the experience of the human race. The history of progress is not a straight arithmetical progression, in which every succeeding generation adds its digit of culture to the total heap; it is rather an irregular curve, in which the inspiration of genius furnishes the drive and direction for every upward surge of the human spirit. The truth of this observation may be illustrated in the diverse fields of human endeavor.

An analysis of evolution and progress is outside the scope of this essay. We have already referred the reader to the writers, whose philosophy of history is here assumed. Suffice it merely to point out that, in the specific field of religion, the appearance of Judaism as a powerful force in the midst of the pagan world is an objective illustration of the effect of the phenomenon of revelation, in its third and highest sense.

An exhaustive psychological study of this phase of revelation would have to be based upon the records of the inner life of the great men, who gave fresh impetus and renewed inspiration to the spiritual life of their generation. In the case of Judaism, such a study would be concerned with the spiritual travail of the prophets and the key builders of Judaism thru the ages. From the philosophical viewpoint, it is sufficient to establish the reality of this phenomenon, which is related to the first and second stages of revelation, as these in turn are related to the ordinary consciousness. As religion is the source of the moral law and absolute morality is the source of the common decencies in life, so is Divine Revelation in the specific sense of the term, the source and origin of religion. And as the second phase of revelation includes and fortifies the first, so does the third phase prove its authenticity by the intensification it affords to the first two phases of revelation. The fund of piety that is mankind's most precious asset is the product of the forces set in motion by the incursion of Divine creative energy in the hearts and minds of geniuses of faith. Insofar as religion was able to rise above the quasi-magic of ritual and the shadowy underworld of superstition, it was almost entirely moved by the inspiration and authority of God-intoxicated men. Religion, in the specific or Jewish meaning of the term, is thus seen to be inherently related to the ethical ideal, as the roots of the tree are to its fruits. It is in this sense that Hermann Cohen rightly regarded ethics as the yardstick of religion.

This point needs to be further clarified for it touches directly upon the Conservative conception of the authority of Jewish law. While, in our view, revelation consists of three progressively higher levels—ethical intuition, the feeling of the holy, and the covenant or destiny experience, in which each successive state attains a greater measure of insight, we insist that, in evaluating the genuineness and worth of the highest insights, the middle level must be taken as normative, and that, in judging the value of the emotional complex on the second level, the principles of ethics must be regarded as both touchstone and yardstick. For whereas the higher states of revelation gain in inspiration and in creative power over the lower ones, they decrease correspondingly in the quality of objectivity. Organized religion which attempts to safeguard the insights of the few for the enlightenment of the many cannot afford to ignore the guidance of objectivity. Thus, concerning every form of piety, it is legitimate to inquire whether it conduces to the good life of ethics, and in regard to every claim of Divine inspiration, it is necessary to employ the yardsticks of genuine piety, as we know it. Similarly, in Jewish law, the authenticity of new prophetic revelation is to be tested by its conformity with the principles of Torah.

The character of organized religion introduces a subjective standard in the evaluation of revelation, in addition to the objective norms of ethics and piety. After all, it can scarcely be denied that the psalmist was right when he wrote of the heavens declaring the works of the Lord. In a sense, every blade of grass and clod of earth is an embodiment of God's creative power. But, while God speaks thru all things, we comprehend His Word, only thru the channels of conscience, whole-souled dedication and deepest truthfulness. By the same token, His revealed word may strike a responsive chord and awaken dormant energies in one people or one group, while, in the case of other peoples, it glances off tangentially from the convex mirror of the soul, leaving neither light nor heat to mark its course. God's Word is One, but the hearers are many, and meaning is the function of both speaking and hearing. The comprehension of God's Word requires the kind of listening, which is preceded by a doing—that is, a training of the mind and heart, which narrows even while it refines. The slow climb of mankind from the morass of primitive thinking is proof of the fact that receptivity to the Divine word is not a native quality of the human species. Revelation must not only be true in itself; it must also *become* true to people. This becoming true is a function of the actual social process, in which the values of one generation become the stepping stones of progress for the next generation. Habituation in revealed disciplines may be expected to prepare an individual or a group for the assimilation of ever higher reaches of Divine truth. Upon this basic requirement the justification of particular religious traditions is based. But, these individualized traditions cultivate special forms of piety and operate with certain sancta, which embody a logic of their own. The group demarcates a limited range of the revealed Word, and what it lacks in scope or extent, it seeks to atone for in depth and devotion. Subjective symbolization and objective meaning are intertwined in one historical pattern, which achieve the double result of limiting a field of vision and bringing it into focus. From the universal, philosophic viewpoint, historical religions may well be judged in accordance with the extent to which the one or the other effect is attained. Does it narrow more than it cleanses the windows of the soul? If so, then the religion in question stands condemned. But, if it is justified on this universal ground, all the insights of revelation must be judged not only in terms of general piety, but in the framework of the specific, pattern of piety that is the particular heritage of any one group. Thus, we arrive at the paradoxical conclusion that what may well be true revelation for any one group may also be totally meaningless and valueless to another group. For members of the same group and its sancta, the subjective phase of piety is utterly non-critical. It is a readiness to do and to listen, to understand thru the deed, as Maimonides interprets the meaning of God's reply to Moses in Exodus XXXIII, 23. This principle underlies the basic theory of Halachic Judaism, that the moment one accepts the Torah, one makes himself subject to the whole range of punishments in Jewish law. He is no longer free to pick and choose, according to the caprice of his own will. The freedom of his own mind is now limited by the inescapable subjectivity of the life of piety.

290

Is it possible for a living faith to be free from subjectivity? —Not entirely, for objective truth is never wholly attainable and every faith that is lived necessarily incorporates contemporary elements, which appear to be objective only because they are the "idols of the market place." Also, religious values, in contradistinction to philosophical principles are comprehended thru their being practiced not merely thru being thought. Philosophy, like mathematics, is universal; religion, like speech cannot but be particularized—and it is a form of speech that embraces the whole of life and spans the past with the future.

From the discussion in this chapter, the following principles emerge: revelation is a real phenomenon; objective standards whereby revelation may be gaged are the principles of ethics and the feelings of piety; piety, as a psychic attitude, is conditioned by a historical tradition and therefore subjective in character; hence, subjective standards are valid, within the boundaries of a historic faith.

We are now prepared to recognize the borders of the philosophical realm of revelation. From the objective or philosophical viewpoint, the only content of revelation that is valid is a universal truth or value. This follows from the very nature of our reasoning faculties, which abstract the universal essence from every individual phenomenon. To enter the mood of objectivity means to disregard the accidental and the individual, to separate the particular expression and the accidental association from the permanent and universal essence that underlies all forms of genuine revelation. Since revelation occurs between man and God, it is obviously unscientific and therefore untruthful to assume that the human or particular element is not felt in the content of revelation. Inevitably, the "Torah speaks the language of men," in all its finiteness, limitation and particularity. Thus, objectively, God's speech is not verbal expression; God's command is not a specific precept; God's behest is not the fire, clamor and whirlwind of dogmatic rivalries.

The particular and accidental elements of revelation belong to the subjective phase of revelation. This is not to say that they are valueless or untrue. On the contrary, as we pointed out, it is the subjective element that converts the experience of inspiration into the life of piety, philosophical insight into the "rod and staff" that is religion, high minded reflection and intuition into the flesh and blood of holiness. The subjective attitude is staunchly traditional in character: it seeks to preserve the body along with the soul, the shell along with the seed; oftentimes, indeed, it lays greater stress on the accumulated dust of the ages than on the living kernel of religion. Without it, religion cannot become a social force, nor can it be truly effective in the daily life of the individual. It follows that the subjective phases of revelation must not only be recognized, but fully encouraged and cultivated, provided always that they do not conflict with the above mentioned objective standards of revelation. In the "sh'ma," we speak of "the Lord, *our* God"; so long as we speak of the Lord, in the third person, we are outside the sphere of religion. When "He" is *our* God, He is the God of religion. On the threshold of piety, there is the determination to make a body of ideals and practices, *our* way of listening to the Word of God, our way in all earnestness and completeness, without any reservations.

4. *Judaism as Revealed Faith*

The above concept of revelation permits us to recognize the Divine inspiration of our sacred heritage, without ignoring the proven and probable facts of history. It is undeniable that the religious teaching of Israel was a unique phenomenon in the ancient world and that its essential truth was in strange contrast to he heathen ways of thinking and ways of acting. Religion, in the proper sense of the term, appeared upon the stage of history first in the Holy Land. Historians, may differ as to the exact time when the "religion of Israel" as they are pleased to call it, was metamorphosed into the purely monotheistic faith of Judaism. The German school of "higher criticism" sought to push that date forward, by hook or crook. But, the fact itself that Divine truth manifested itself in the consciousness of the Jewish people and its sacred literature could not possibly be gainsaid. Here was a people, small in numbers and poor in the possessions of this world, but so mighty in spirit that it became "a prophet to the nations," smashing their idols and vindicating its faith, despite the most critical ordeals of history and in the glare of the subtlest methods of modern philosophy! If religion is the central system of values and ideals in society, then the revelation of the Divine in the Torah was the most epoch making process in history. Here is a miracle, if ever there was one!

The splendor of Divine revelation in Israel is not lessened by the attempts of historians and archaelogists to trace the steps of its evolution and fill in the details of the ancient panorama of culture. Judaism grew out of a definite historical milieu. This fact was never denied by traditional Judaism. "In the beginning, our ancestors worshipped heathen gods," and does it really matter how long this "beginning" lasted?—The important fact is that there came a time when the intuitions of Israel confronted the whole non-Jewish world with a set of truths that were radically new and profoundly true.

An excellent discussion of the novel elements in Judaism is found in Y. Kaufman's *Toldoth Ha-Emunah Ha-Yisraelith.* He proves that the basic world-view of Israel was a unique phenomenon from the very earliest stages of its recorded history. Basically, this is also the view of W. F. Albright who dissents however, from Kaufman's conception of a "national soul." The Midrashic interpretation of "Abraham the Hebrew," as meaning that "Abraham was on one side and the entire world on the other side" is illustrated by Kaufman in countless ways. So far was Israel from the pagan mentality that its writers and prophets could not even understand the symbols and concepts of pagan mythology. In the heart of Israel, a new "idea" was born, which set it off as a unique people and determined its destiny. This "idea" was not an explicit logical or metaphysical proposition, but a dynamic focus of intellectual convictions and spiritual energy that could not but transform the whole world-view of humanity. In its non-erotic and non-mythological conception of the Deity, in the conjunction of absolute morality with absolute power, in its ruthless condemnation of magic, in its non-shamanic conception of prophecy; in its recognition of only two foci of world history, the will of God and the will of man; in its exaltation of God above and beyond the forces of nature, Judaism was a unique phenomenon. Therefore, all who share the conviction of its truth, cannot but regard it as a revealed faith, in the highest sense of the term.

Not only does the philosophy of Judaism belong in the category of revealed truth, but the manner in which this philosophy became implemented in the lives of the Jewish people is inseparable from the original intuition. The Jewish grasp of the Divine mystery of existence resulted in an overpowering sense of dedication, which was expressed in the covenant concept. Jewish monotheism implied from the very beginning the belief in a covenant concluded between "the Judge of the whole world" and the seed of Abraham. This is the distinctive quality of the religious, as distinguished from the purely cognitive intuition, that it does not merely perceive objective truth, but that it sees the place of its own self in the total scheme of things. Religious seeing contains the factors of feeling and willing, self-giving and self-purifying. It is not only perception, but dedication and action as well. Thus, the original insight of Judaism was never simply Knowledge of the One God, but a consecration to the service of the One God.

The covenant concept, which runs thru the pages of the Holy Bible from cover to cover and which underlies the whole mentality of halachic Judaism, is a unique form of the religious feeling of dedication. It includes the idea of law. A covenant is a legal concept, in fact, the basic concept of law. Judaism was thus a religion of law, not merely in its historical development, but in its very soul and essence. God was intuited primarily as the Righteous Judge and Ruler, whose Will is seen at once in the laws of nature and in the inner laws of the human conscience. Dedication to God means the free acceptance on the part of man of the law of God, as it operates thruout the universe. "Everything obeys," says Ecclesiastes in his concluding word; therefore, "fear the Lord and keep His Commandments, for this is the whole of man."

The classic founders of Reform perceived the Divine truth in the philosophy of Judaism, which they termed "ethical monotheism," but they failed to recognize that the covenant idea and its eventual elaboration into a legalistic regimen of thought and action was the inevitable consequence of the basic insight of Judaism. They were laboring, for the most part, under the influence of the Protestant Church which stressed the element of "feeling" in religious experience. Consequently, they were impatient of the tremendous burden of "halachah," that had grown up in the course of the centuries. They deplored the dry legalism of the Shulchan Aruch and Talmud, preferring to consider themselves the disciples of the Hebrew prophets. In their hasty disregard

295

of the psychology of religion, they failed to heed the truth that the rituals of a religion could not be divorced from the basic pattern of piety that is characteristic of it. Protestant Christianity is based primarily upon the experience of conversion and religious "feeling" generally. Its strength and its weakness as a spiritual force in the lives of men are both traceable to this inner core of Christian piety. Thru the dynamism of its feeling, Christianity impels men on occasion to the loftiest heights of nobility and self-sacrifice. On the other hand, this very accentuation of the inner life of the spirit encourages at times a bifurcation between the issues of the market place and the domain of religion. Such an unfortunate dichotomy, in essence a reversion to Dyonisiac paganism, was indeed characteristic of German Christianity, in the decades which followed the First World War. Politics and religion were kept so rigidly apart that it was possible for many avowed followers of the "religion of love" to witness without protest the incredible atrocities of Nazidom.

Judaism fosters a pattern of piety that is essentially different from and complementary to that of Christianity. The experience of the "nearness of God" is immediately translated by the Jew into an awareness of the Command of God. If the complex "varieties of religious experience" be divided in accordance with the preponderance in them of either the element of ethical challenge or of the feelings of "surrender," "awe," "sweetness," "peace," "love," etc., then it may fairly be said that Judaism is primarily an "ethical challenge" religion, while Protestant Christianity is a "feeling" religion. These two phases of religious experience are by no means antagonistic. Contrariwise, they are in fact two halves of one whole. So long as mutual respect and understanding obtains between them, their interaction cannot but result in spiritual gain to both faiths and to humanity as a whole. Nothing however, can be gained thru any light-hearted rejection of the legal pattern of Judaism, in blind imitation of the Christian form of piety. Clearly, then, the Divine character of Judaism extends not only to the moral and spiritual teachings of our sacred literature, but to the intuition as well of the legal character of the religious life. The man of piety seeks to crystallize his devotion in the form of self-imposed laws for, as we have seen, religion descends into life, from creativity to feeling and from feeling to law. Thus, the assumption of vows is one of the earliest and most universal forms of religious observance. Since, however, no man lives alone and religion is essentially a social affair, we arrive at the principle of Halachah in Judaism.

Thus far, the objective criteria of religion guided us; the subjective criterion of revelation may now be applied. Since the legalistic pattern of piety is the mold into which our own religious experience has grown, the normal feelings of piety impel us to accept the Halachah subjectively as the particular stream of faith, in which we live, move and have our being. Halachah is for us the way in which God's word is progressively being shaped into ways of life. This view is in perfect harmony with our historical knowledge of the evolution of Halachah. The laws of Halachah were not only consciously ordained for the purpose of fostering the "normative" consciousness; they were also in part subconsciously evolved out of the inner religious drive, to translate "feeling" into "law." In this way, the regimen of Halachah made the observant Jew feel that the whole world was encompassed by the sway of Divine Law. There was scarcely a question of thought and conduct that did not fall within the scope of the law. Inner experience and outer life were fused into one. The danger of impotent subjectivity in religion was averted by the sternly objective attitude of Halachah. The central insistence of Judaism was that the energy of piety be not dissipated in sentimentalities. There was no limit to the reach of justice and the Will of God. Inevitably, then, the "nearness of God," not as a mystical "sweet, comforting Presence," but as an all-pervasive will, became ingrained in the consciousness of the pious Jew. Historically, it cannot possibly be doubted that Jewish piety resulted in the emergence of great and noble saints—above all, that the average, normal type of man produced under its auspices was of the highest calibre in terms of decency, probity and general spirituality. Of course, law without feeling is sterile and dry, as was demonstrated by the upsurge of Hassidism in the eighteenth century. Constant watchfulness is needed to prevent legalistic piety from sinking to the level of sheer rote performance.

Does the recognition of the Divine origin of the principle of law imply necesarily the acceptance of all the minutiae of Jewish law, as they are recorded in the Shulchan Aruch? —This question must be answered thru a double analysis, from the historical and the psychological points of view. First then, we must make it clear from the objective viewpoint that the revealed character of Jewish legislation refers to the general subconscious spiritual drive which underlies the whole body of Halachah, not to the details of the Law. The vital fluid of the Torah-tree derives from the numinous soil of the Divine, but the actual contours of the branches and the leaves are the product of a variety of climatic and accidental causes. It is of the very essence of the reasoning process to recognize that the particular is accidental and contingent. Thus, Maimonides, in his disquisition on the reasons for the "mitzvoh," declares that the details of the Law are not amenable to any rational justification. In honesty and consistency, Maimonides' principle should be pursued to its uttermost conclusion in the distinction between objective and subjective phases of revelation. All that we can and do affirm is the Divine character of the principle of

Halachah. From the viewpoint of history, we know that the Shulchan Aruch did not spring fullblown from the mind of Moses. It is the product of gradual evolution, in which diverse social and economic factors were conjoined with those of a purely religious character. The history of every institution in Judaism should be carefully studied, so as to uncover the spiritual factors, which gave rise to it. When this task of historical research is completed, it will be possible to assay the various phases of Jewish law with greater exactness.

In the meantime, we must not overlook the subjective character of piety. Since the pattern of Jewish piety consists in the awareness of the ubiquitous majesty of Divine Law, it is necessary to beware of the kind of changes that destroy the spell of the Law and bear the obvious stamp of artificiality. The rabbis of every age have the power to make new laws, especially when gathered in a "Great Assembly." But, the new must be so delicately grafted upon the old that the health of the tree as a whole will not be affected. New legislation must not ever be a confession of weakness and it must derive from the same springs of holiness. Laws come and laws go, but the validity of the Law as such must be reaffirmed thru the process of change itself.

5. Unity of the Two Pillars

Philosophical Judaism appears to the dogmatist to be a house divided against itself. There is a perpetual tug of war in its very heart between the conflicting claims of reason and faith. The religious philosopher either oscillates uncertainly between the two realms of the spirit, or else he treads like an acrobat the thin borderline between them. In contrast, the dogmatist is wholly at peace with himself, certain at every step of what he should do and what he should believe. By the same token, the non-religious rationalist is also free from the tension of inner conflict and the unpleasantness resulting from the claims of two rival sources of authority. In the particular sphere of Judaism, the discomfiture of the Conservative thinker *vis-à-vis* his Orthodox and Reform colleagues is an instance of this dilemma. Those who found their faith on the one pillar of reason or of revelation are always very clear as to their principles and policies. Conservative Judaism, in its attempt to hold on to the two pillars of the spirit, seems to be floundering pitifully in the open sea, without compass or rudder, the helpless plaything of the wind and the tide. But, is it or must it be so? Must the guidance of both faith and reason be construed as the service of two hostile or even different masters?

There is no denying that, on the superficial level, the faith of one who would ground his faith on the two pillars of revelation and reason appears to be inconsistent. However, the more we probe beneath the surface of things, the more we come to realize that the life of the spirit is a ceaseless movement between the two poles of objectivity and subjectivity. He who would keep his soul turned to the rhythm of truth must forever be on the move. He cannot stop at either pole and embrace the whole truth in his bosom; back and forth, he must move between the subjective and objective poles of the spirit, if he is not to petrify in static, sterile self-admiration. For reason and faith imply and fructify each other. When each is taken as sufficient unto belief, it becomes unproductive and even self-stultifying. Let us see how this observation applies to the problems of religion.

On the very first level of intellectual orientation, man is confronted with the choice between two sources of knowledge, faith and reason. If he should make the common mistake of assuming this choice to be exclusive in character, then, spiritual disaster is inevitable. Should he choose the one of reason, he will soon discover that it is founded on a faith or trust in the workings of the human mind and in the objectivity of truth. Different philosophers expressed this fact in different ways, but the circumstance itself of reason being based upon the feelings of "truthfulness," to use the term of Herman Cohen's, is incontestable. Should this trust be rejected, then reliance on reason becomes a snare and delusion, an inevitable descent toward the depths of skepticism and despair. The pole of reason or objectivity must be constantly replenished with subjective insights, if it is to keep from degenerating into a hollow mockery of itself. First, it must assimilate the subjective feeling of trust in reason itself. Second, it must operate with the subjective intuitive valuations of the sanctity of the human person, the validity of the goal of the Good or the validity of the moral law and the perception of beauty and harmony. Third, it renews itself and ascends to a higher level only thru periodic intuitive insights, that is, periodic reversions to the pole of subjectivity.

By the same token, if, on the threshold of thought, one should choose the pole of faith, or subjectivity, then he must couple it with reverence for the claims of reason, or objectivity, if he is to escape the manifold pitfalls of unbridled superstition and unmitigated fanaticism. Is not the history of religion replete with dire object lessons of the danger of relying blindly on faith? In the desperate search of our age for a living faith, we tend to forget the evil excesses to which faith might be carried, if it is not subjected again and again to the scrutiny of reason. Within the very core of faith, there is to be found the light of reason, the attitude of passivity and receptivity toward the outer reality and the rigorous determination to submit to he compulsion of things as they are. But, this core of reason in the heart of faith needs to be constantly renewed by the readiness to submit to intellectual criticism, if it is to render the spiritual life of man fruitful and constructive. The moment men of piety lose the nerve to face the critque of reason their faith is on the way to becoming a satanic burden, dragging them down, instead of a beacon of light urging them upward.

Thus, on the level of practical piety, the ceaseless movement between the two poles of subjectivity and ojectivity, may be observed. Piety, as a psychical attitude, is essentially subjective. It is the attitude of the individual in isolation, as Whitehead put it, or it is "the correlation between man and God," as Herman Cohen phrased it. The human soul stands alone before its Maker, in utter disregard of the world and its values. Worldly approval or disapproval, success or failure, is of no account; the one thing that matters is the felt Presence of God, His Will and His Word. The more the spirit of piety comes into its own, the more it seeks the inwardness of things—the contrite spirit rather than the sacrifice of goats and lambs, the intention rather than the deed itself. At the same time, there is also implicit in the character of piety the drive to objectify its expressions so that they might assume visible and tangible, objective form. The piety of the Hassidim and that of the Mithnagdim, the one emphasizing intention, the other, the conformity of the deed to the prescribed law, are not mutually antagonistic. In the dialectic of piety, both movements are included—from subjectivity to objectivity, and vice versa. Franz Rosenzweig pointed out that love is similarly constituted of subjective intimacy and the desire to have it paraded before the world. To condemn objective piety on the grounds of inwardness is therefore to betray the marks of spiritual astigmatism. The Pharisee's murmured motto, "explain my duty and I shall do it" and the contemporary Jew's satisfaction in having perfunctorily recited the prayers, "*Ob-gedavent*," are not therefore caricatures of religion, but merely one sided phases of it. For the life of the spirit is not a static reflection and crystallization of the Truth, but a dynamic apprehension of it from every changing angle, in the ceaseless change of perspective from subjectivity to objectivity, and back again.

Thus, too, standing on the borderline between the humanistic world and the life of religion, it is not only a legitimate but an inescapable spiritual obligation to comply with the two approaches of the human mind. The objective viewpoint requires us to assay critically all religions; the subjective attitude bids us to make one living faith, our faith, our way of impregnating our life with the beauty and the restlessness of piety. Actually, the subjective choice between religions is made in the process of growing into maturity; between it and the objective approach there should be constant inter-action and mutual accomodation.

Coming down now to the problems of Judaism proper, we maintain that our employment of a two-fold evaluation in the assaying of laws and ceremonies is true to the inward nature of piety. On the one hand, we accept the Halachah subjectively; on the other hand, we subject specific halachic precepts to criticism by means of the objective standards of piety and the good life that derive from the *yetzer tov* of modern thought and civilization. Both approaches are integral to the life of the spirit; we cannot afford to give up either one without forfeiting the soul of our faith.

As a matter of fact, Judaism attained its highest levels, when it was brought into contact with foreign civilizations. If you go thru the Hall of Fame of Judaism and seek out those with whom you feel the greatest spiritual kinship, you will find that your choice will comprise almost exclusively men who combined the wisdom of Shem with the beauty of

303

Japheth. It is only unrealistic romanticism and nationalist astigmatism that combine to glorify the naive, "pure," self-fascinated products of the "national soul." In history, as in nature, productivity springs from the intermingling of cultures and influences. Isolationism in thought is as sterile as it is inane and futile in politics.

How may the two methods be synthesized in practice?— Why has the actual course of Conservative Judaism been a matter of perpetual half-way measures and "muddling thru?" —The two questions are interrelated. When neither the objective nor the subjective viewpoint and method are taken seriously, no constructive progress is possible. The logic of our argument bids us to pursue each movement of the spirit sincerely and unflinchingly and not to permit the two poles to neutralize each other in helpless futility.

First, the implications of the subjective phase of piety must be clarified and embraced in utter earnestness. The Conservative Movement must not be characterized thru its negative phases only, the several respects in which it has broken away from Orthodoxy. It must undertake a campaign for the stimulation of a minimum of religious observances among our people, stressing in particular those precepts which contribute decisively and directly to the cultivation of the spirit of piety, such as the acceptance of regular weekly worship and study periods. *These observances must be taken up as laws, not merely as ideals.*

If the pattern of Jewish piety is to be revived and revitalized, the principle of *Halachah* must become a real factor once again in the life of our people. Enormous efforts will have to be exerted in this direction before we shall be ready for the application of objective standards to the revision of existing Jewish law. In the past, changes in Jewish law were brought about by progressive neglect and indifference toward this or that ceremonial observance. Manifestly, progress by the steady deterioration of Jewish standards can only lead to the disintegration of Jewish piety. We must stand for progress thru the increase of piety, instead of adaptation through growing disrespect for Jewish law. Our first task then is to mobilize our total forces for a subjective intensification of piety and religious observance.

Along with this effort, we must learn to apply objective standards of piety to the further development of Halachah. In accepting the body of Jewish Law, we do not and cannot endorse all the methods whereby the Halachah was brought into being and whereby it developed into its present form. We cannot consider a "g'zerah shavah," for instance, as a valid method for deducing new laws. The goal of cultivating the spirit of piety and the need of preserving the overall pattern of Judaism should be for us the decisive considerations. It must be remembered that while the practices of Halachah may be accepted as a way of life, its methods of reasoning and deductions cannot be taken up by us if they do not accord with our own convictions.

Failure to recognize the distinction between *Halachah,* as a body of laws, and *Halachah* as a body of beliefs and dialectical devices underlying those laws and determining their application and growth, is in large measure responsible for the intellectual frustration prevalent in Conservative circles. Yet, it is obvious that matters of thought cannot be coerced by such principles as *K'lal Yisroel.* While much of the reasoning in the Talmud and Responsa remains valid for us, there is also much that we cannot in honesty accept as valid *in se.* The body of tradition we must take up as the pattern in which our piety was molded, but the soul of our ancestors cannot take the place of our own soul. In the revision of Halachah we must be guided by the principles which are valid in our own mind, not by the frozen letters of the Law which can only lead to the progressive petrification and self-isolation of Judaism.

The concept of revelation herein outlined is in many respects foreshadowed in classical Jewish thought. It leads to definite principles in the interpretation and application of Jewish law.

(published in "Conservative Judaism," February, 1947)

7

Law in Conservative Judaism

Need for a Readjustment of Jewish Law

The conception of revelation, outlined in the first part of this essay, has many points of contact with the opinions and judgments of diverse philosophic luminaries in the past. However, we do not lay claim on its behalf for the designation, orthodox. The subjective acceptance of the Law, as the way of serving God, we maintain to be the fundamental quality in the Jewish pattern of piety. But, we also allow room for the objective analysis and consideration of various aspects of the Law, in terms of the universal values of piety and in the light of the actual results and effects of certain Halachic precepts in the circumstances of the modern world. We regard the two attitudes not as antithetical forces, but as complementary phases of the life of the spirit. Before the organic structure of Jewish life was shattered by the Romans, both attitudes found expression in the teaching and legislation of the Rabbis. Thru the vicissitudes of exilic life, the subjective attitude came to prevail more and more, as the wounded soul of our people sought to strengthen the barricades against the hostile world. It is now our task to demonstrate how the two attitudes may be harmonized in the daily life of the modern observant Jew.

In the daily practice of Judaism, the subjective attitude must prevail very largely. In the routine of life, a faith cannot be lived and doubted at the same time. The essential characteristic of Jewish piety consists in the acceptance of and implicit obedience to the Divine Will, concretized into Divine Law. Objective considerations are normally left to the corps of intellectual leaders—prophets, scribes, Sages and Rabbis. The Synhedrin of the past carried out the function of objectively assaying the operations and achievements of the various phases of Jewish Law, instituting the necessary "takkanot," in accord with their findings.

The problem we face today, making the emergence of a Conservative movement logically inevitable, arises out of the circumstance that the historical instruments of objective self-criticism and adjustment has broken down. The breakdown of a living authority in Jewish religion did not occur all at once, the Synhedrin having been followed successively by the "vineyard of Yavneh," the assembly at Ussha, the school of R. Judah the Prince, the academies of Babylonia, the "Geonim," the occasional assemblies thru the Middle Ages, down to the present when there exists virtually no authority at all. Concomitantly with this breakdown of the social instruments for religious leadership, there took place a similar degenerative process in the inner structure of "Halachah." The guiding principles of "Halachah" have become so constituted, thru the continuous preponderance of the subjective attitude as to lead automatically to an irreversible process in legislation. Whatever may have been desirable at any one time, became fixed for all time thru such legalistic methods as the following: the "derivation" of the principle from the interpretation of a verse, the principle that no court can annul the "takkanot" of a previous court, unless it be greater than the first in wisdom and in numbers, and the concomitant principle—a typical product of subjective piety, that in the succession of generations, scholarship and piety are steadily decaying.

Thus, if Judaism is to become again a living faith, significant in terms of modern ideas and values and relevant to the psychological needs of today, an instrument must be forged whereby both poles of the life of the spirit may be harmonized and concretized in the life of our people.

Why The Law Committee is Insufficient

In our attitude toward "Halachah," three logical positions are possible. We may accept it as one organic body, with all its practical precepts, its legal principles and its structure of authority, as embodied in the orthodox rabbinate. Or, we may accept it, in part, and reject it in part, using as the principle of selection, ideas derived from our basic philosophy of life. Or, we may reject "Halachah" altogether as an unnecessary encumbrance for modern life.

The first position is Orthodox. Let no one fool himself into believing that by juggling the principles of the "Shulchan Aruch" thru the minds of the Law Committee of the Rabbinical Assembly, any other result can be obtained than that which is reflected in the current Responsa literature of the Orthodox rabbis. We need a law making body, not a law interpreting committee. So long as the basic materials for decision are identical, no other results are possible. In our current historiography, it is customary to describe some of the great Halachists as "m'kilim," responsive to the needs of their day, and to tar others with the brush of "machmirim," strict adherents of the letter of the law. Accordingly, it was felt that if the Conservative "Halachah" committee were to assume the consistent attitude of "l'hokail" a vital movement would emerge in the course of time, combining "Halachah" with life. Actually, this conception is based upon an extreme exaggeration of the area of freedom in Jewish law. If one takes up the orthodox position in respect of "Halachah," his sphere of choice is reduced to the very minimum. In spite of the so-called "diffusion of authority" in the Jewish law, an "Halachah"-true Jew has a straight and narrow path to follow. His authorities are the "g'dolai Yisroel" of every age. For him, a "gadol b'yisroel" is defined not only in terms of surpassing Talmudic erudition, but also by reference to the standards of piety, which are themselves defined in terms of "Halachah." We deal here with a closed circle of authority, which may have its own schools of interpretation and emphasis, its own unsolved problems and moot points, but which is nonetheless contained within well-defined borders. One may argue ad infinitum on the relative importance of "minhag" and "Halachah," but one cannot, by any such "pilpul" alter the fact that whatever the proper balance between these two sources of authority be, that circumstance is reflected in the actual practice of the "Halachah"-true world—those who abide by the decisions of the "g'dolai Yisroel." A "minhag" is a valid source of authority only when it is a "minhag Vatikin." (Custom of the proven pious). One hears frequently these days of Reform rabbis describing the practices of their members and the ceremonies of their temples as falling under the category of "minhag America," as if that designation implied automatic halachic endorsement. In reality, "Halacha" is not only a set of principles, precepts and precedents, but a "way" of making decisions, entailing a set of authorities in the past and in the present. If we think of the Talmud, "Shulchan Aruch" and the Responsa literature as the sole collective source material of halachic authority, then we must accord those who mold themselves exclusively in the pattern of these books the prerogative of expressing the voice of "Halachah."

The Way of Takkanot

Manifestly, then, the Conservative movement cannot be described as falling within the limits of "Halachah"-true Judaism. On the other hand, it does not reject "Halachah" in the slightest in theory and it does not accept Halachah very largely in practice. What, then, is our principle of selection?—Obviously, this principle of selection must be justified in terms of our basic philosophy of religion; at the same time, it must be fitted formally into the structure of "Halachah."

Reform Judaism started out by revoking the principle of legislation from Judaism, step by step. It began by chafing under the strain of "chumroth," (severities) imposed by the latter day rabbis; then it proceeded to abolish the enactments of the "Geonim" and "Rishonim," (early authorities) following up this step with the revocation of the authority of the Talmud and then finally negating Biblical law as well. Some conservative thinkers in our day seem to favor the same course of action. They think nothing of opposing the Orthodox authorities of their own day or of the immediate past, but they still presume to invoke the authority of the "Rishonim," failing to see that by restricting steadily the realm of rabbinic legislation to the ever more distant past they launch themselves unto the slippery incline of Karaitic thinking, which is utterly retrogressive and futile. If we follow the principle that the rabbis of our own days are incompetents and that the rabbis of the past were all-knowing, we undermine the very basis for development and growth in religion, even while we presume to speak in the name of religious progress. Obviously, the past cannot of its own momentum effectively progress in the contemporary world. Again, if we deny Divine sanction to the "Rishonim" and grant it to the masters of the Talmud, or if we deny it to the Amoraim and Tannaim, reserving it for the prophets, we should be operating with a mechanical principle of selection, for which there is no basis in our philosophy of Judaism. The Karaites did believe in the literal revelation of the Torah and they further assumed that the rabbis of the Talmud corrupted the Mosaic tradition. We do not hold to

311

either of these views. Furthermore, for us Divine revelation is expressed as much thru the conscience of Israel, the "sons of the prophets," as thru the vision of the prophets themselves. From our viewpoint, then, the present is more determinative than the past, and the immediate past more authoritative than the remote past.

It seems to me that the only proper course for Conservative Judaism consists not in the progressive diminution of the sphere of legislation, but, on the contrary, in its steady expansion. We must learn to utilize the principle of "takkanot" in charting the path of our movement. This principle is fully in accord with our dynamic conception of revelation. It renders Jewish law flexible and timely affording a legal channel of expression for the living "conscience of catholic Israel." In Jewish law, the sphere of "takkanot" is virtually limitless. According to Maimonides, the enactments of the rabbinical courts, which derive their binding power from the principle of "lo Tosur" (Thou shalt not depart from the decision of the Court) have the force of a Torah-itic commandment. While in theory, "takkanot" cannot permanently supersede the laws of the Torah or the rabbinic enactments of the past, they can do so temporarily "l'sha'a," if the enactment is justified by local and contemporary conditions. Here, then, is an instrument, which is capable of doing exactly that which Conservative Judaism maintains needs to be done. Let us see how this instrument may and should function in our movement.

Proposal for a "Jewish Academy"

"Takkanot" can be made in Jewish law, by the elected representatives of the communities together with their rabbinic authorities. Thus, they must have two sanctions—the one deriving from the most sensitive conscience and the most creative scholarship of the age, the other deriving from the democratic principle of "the consent of the governed." Accordingly, we must form an assembly capable of discussing intelligently and thoroughly all aspects of Jewish life, whence concrete suggestions for "takkanot," should emerge from time to time. Also, we must provide for periodic convocations of laymen and rabbis, representative of the entire movement, who shall be empowered to accept or reject the proposed "takkanot." To exercise the first function, we propose the establishment of a Jewish Academy, consisting of selected rabbis, scholars and laymen, who would discuss thoroughly and regularly all phases of Jewish doctrine and practice. The second function must naturally be left to a joint special session of the United Synagogue and the Rabbinical Assembly.

The term "Jewish Academy" is chosen in order to suggest the resemblance to the French Academy and to eschew the notion of claiming the authority of the ancient Synhedrin. Like the French Academy, it should consist of the greatest men in our movement, those who have achieved distinction in the fields of scholarship, rabbinic leadership, Jewish education and social welfare. Like the Academy, too, appointments should be made for life or for long terms—such appointments constituting the highest marks of recognition in our movement. This academy should meet at regular intervals to discuss institutions of Jewish life, principles and dogmas of the faith, the latest developments in various fields of study bearing upon the philosophy of religion and ways and means of dealing with specific problems. Its first task shall be to lead and guide our movement in a nationwide, "tshuvah" effort, calculated to reestablish a minimum of observance among the members of our congregations. Its members should be made available for periodic consultation with congregational groups, so as to stimulate and arouse a deep loyalty to Judaism.

In short, the Academy would become the central guiding agency for Conservative Judaism, the upper house for legislation in our movement.

This suggestion is so obvious and natural that one need not argue in favor of it so much as in refutation of the criticisms that might be directed at it. Let us therefore proceed to analyze the possible objections to this plan.

Firstly, it will be said that the "takkanot" will have to be so far reaching in the beginning that the established structure of "Halachah" will be incapable of withstanding the impact of sudden change. The residual loyalty to Jewish law in the hearts of our people will in consequence not be channeled thru the new "takkanot," but will be totally shattered. The distance between theory and practice in Conservative ranks is presently so vast, that any attempt to bring the law down to life, cannot but begin with a tremendous antimonian effort, that will of its own momentum undermine the respect which Jewish law still evokes among our people. The first acts of the projected Jewish Academy will have to be directed against some sections of "Halachah," it may be said. Therefore, the negative character of the Academy would be fixed in the public mind, thereby accelerating the present stream of defections from Jewish law.

The answer to this objection is that the initial "takkanot" need not at all be negative. The processes of life, of their own impetus, combine to render certain phases of the Law obsolete. Our task is very largely of a positive character—to strengthen and protect those phases of Judaism, which are most significant from our viewpoint. By doing little or nothing to encourage the regular attendance of women in "mikvoth," and by doing all in our power to stimulate attendance in synagogues, we shall be directing the course of Jewish life. There is no need for "takkanot" to sanction non-observance, but there is great need for "takkanot" to raise the level of observance. Certainly, our first endeavors should be directed toward the achievement of a minimum of observance among our people—so that membership in a synagogue shall not be purely a financial transaction. The term "conservative," must be made to stand for a positive commitment to Judaism, not only for minor changes in public worship.

The next series of "takkanot" shall deal with the correction of certain abuses in Jewish life, as in the matter of desertion and the refusal of the husband to grant a divorce.

Whatever changes need be made in the order of the services, cannot be described as negative in character, since their purpose will be the improvement of the spiritual quality of worship and the attraction of greater numbers of people to the synagogue.

Secondly, it will be argued that a group of associated synagogues, such as the United Synagogue, cannot be considered legally a Kahal, for the purpose of making "takkanot." Takkanot involving the Jewish religion cannot be made by different communities or even by the Jewries of entire countries, but they presuppose the ingathering of Israel in the Holy Land and the re-establishment of a Synhedrin in Jerusalem. The "takkanot" that were made by diverse communities in the past were minor in character and cannot be compared with the radical departure that is likely to be represented by a series of "takkanot," expressive of the Conservative ideology. The principle of "catholic Israel" militates against any break with other sections of the Jewish people.

This argument would be irrefutable, if there had existed presently that degree of universality of observance which the "Shulchan Aruch" postulates. The fact is, however, that the masses of our people have already broken away from the ancient moorings of Jewish Law and that the Reform movement which rejected nearly the whole of ritual law is still considered part and parcel of the Jewish community. Accordingly, our task is not one of breaking down fences, but, on the contrary, of erecting dams against the eroding floodwaters of desertion from the standards of the synagogue.

An association of synagogues in our time may be likened to an association of communities in the past, especially in reference to matters affecting congregational life, since uniformity of observance among Jewish people today is out of the question. To wait for the agreement of the entire Jewish people would be tantamount in practice to the utter bankruptcy of our religious leadership—a shamefaced confession to the taunt of Longfellow that the Jew walks backwards with his eyes glued to the dead letters of the book held in his hands. Nor would such a course of action be justified in theory, since now there is neither an identity of basic convictions between us, the Reformed, the indifferent and the Orthodox, nor an institution like the Synhedrin of old, thru which differences of opinion can be reconciled and adjudicated.

As to the actual scope of community "takkanot," we know that from the objective psychological viewpoint, as distinguished from the subjective one of strict legalism, there is ample precedent for virtually all that needs to be done. The "takkanot" of Rabbenu Gershom were certainly most far reaching in sociological terms, though they were meant for and were accepted by only the Ashkenazic Jews. But, even if it be granted that there is not enough precedent for what might have to be thus legislated, is not our time and circumstances so strikingly new as to justify the creation of new precedents?

Another possible objection to the plan herein outlined is

that there exists presently no agreement in Conservative ranks, concerning basic and vital issues; that, in consequence, any attempt to legislate thru "takkanot" would lead to the widening of existing splits; that the group which would rally round the plan would be too small to command any respect and achieve any permanent results.

As a matter of practical judgment, this objection must certainly be weighed with great care. Doubtless, we dare not attempt to make up with one fell blow for a century of arrested progress. Caution and extreme deliberation will be needed, but it is impossible to evade the inherent logic of the situation. Whatever the relative strength of the various groups in Conservative Judaism may happen to be at this moment, the following considerations remain true: that the basic division in Judaism are in respect of Halachah; that the middle position between the full acceptance of the Orthodox and the complete repudiation of Reform can be theoretically grounded either on the Karaitic principle, repudiating the authority of the rabbis, or on the "lo tossur" principle, the magna charta of rabbinic legislation. Since the Karaitic principle, in spite of its initial coincidence with the trend of popular feeling, and the apathy of our leadership is intellectually sterile and practically a weak-kneed Reform movement, lacking boldness and consistency, it follows that the Conservative movement can only follow the pathway of "takkanot," or else disappear from the scene, as a movement.

The question raised by this objection, therefore, is a very fundamental one—to wit, is there room on the American scene for a Conservative movement, as distinguished from a Conservative way-station? To phrase the question is to answer it. There is not only room, but crying need, for a Conservative movement. If there were no such steadily emerging movement, it would have had to be created. For our time calls for a bold constructive approach, which neither Reform nor Orthodoxy can give—the former thriving on the growing decay of tradition, the latter reduced to a desperate holding action.

Actually, I am convinced that, if the pathway of "takkanot" is chosen by the Conservative movement, its following will grow from year to year, thru the accession of the liberal graduates of "yeshivoth" and the younger Reform rabbis, who are even now dimly groping toward the Conservative position. There is no firmness either to the right of us or to the left of us. Voices clamoring for a living authority and a "new Halachah" can be heard on all sides. Yet, only the Conservative movement is strategically so situated as to be capable of forging a firm instrument of leadership.

What if our "takkanoth" are repudiated by the Orthodox and spurned by the Reform elements? Shall we not then be contributing to a widening of the existing splits in American Jewish life?—In answer, let us reflect that the present course of inaction is not at all conducive to unity or uniformity, save that of the cemetery. A bold course of action would serve to galvanize our own movement and imbue it with enthusiasm and conviction. It would enable our own men to preach, to teach and to guide with utter sincerity, feeling themselves part of a movement, that really knows whither it is going. It would help to overcome the mood of frustration and cynicism, which vitiates the effectiveness of so many of our men, releasing thereby untapped springs of creative energy. If it be true that our movement today lacks enough men of outstanding spiritual calibre, is not that lack itself to be attributed to the lassitude and confusion of our leadership? Why, not having lacked genius and character in the past, should we assume that we shall lack it in the future? If, then, many of the earnest souls in the Orthodox and Reform camps should choose to join our group, well and good. If their reaction will be largely one of repudiation, they cannot fail to emulate our example of courageous action and to proceed to mend their own fences in their own way. The net result in either case cannot but be beneficial.

(published in "Conservative Judaism, February, 1948)

8

Laws as Standards

Laws as Standards

What does Jewish Law, or more accurately, Halachah, mean to us? We can scarcely deal with any issue in religious life today, without first wrestling with this question with all the earnestness of which we are capable. To be sure, life is prior to thought and often enough we may be called upon to act before our thought has been fully crystallized. But, in the realm of the spirit, nothing is ultimately significant and enduring, that is not basically and essentially truthful, deriving from the fundamental convictions and dynamic motivations that constitute the permament core of religion, and that remain eternally valid in the midst of a changing world. From a tactical viewpoint, peripheral considerations are frequently decisive, but we cannot build securely on a solid foundation if we do not envisage clearly the eternal validity and perennially fresh vital essence of Jewish law. What then is this vital essence?

The Orthodox fundamentalist and the classical Reformist are at one in regarding this question as meaningless. The latter disdains *à la* St. Paul, any "religion of laws," and the former is likely to stare aghast at the audacity of investigating what is obviously so simple. The Halachah, in all its ramifications is God-given. Both the Written and the Oral Laws were dictated to Moses at Sinai, and the laws that were subsequently instituted by the properly constituted auhorities were also inspired by the "Ruah HaKodesh." While areas of indetermination may remain here and there as a task for future generations, the "Shulchan Aruch" in its entirety, including the commentaries of Shach and Taz, was generally believed to "have been written with the aid of 'Ruach Ha-Kodesh,'" so that the source of Jewish law was always the Divine Being. Even when a "minhag" (custom) attained the force of law it was not because of a high estimate of the will of the demos, but simply because Israel as a whole was conceived to be holy and quasi-prophetic, sensing Divine truth, in its innermost being.

To the literalist, then, Jewish Law, in all its life encompassing scope, was law, in the exact meaning of the term, since it was dictated by the King of the Universe and promulgated thru His official channels. The Lord had concluded a covenant with His people, requiring them, as their part of the bargain, to observe His multiple commandments, in order that they might be prosperous in this life and blessed in the hereafter. In this mental world, God is envisioned as the austere King of Kings, promulgating laws for His subjects; as the King Father in heaven teaching His children the proper rules of conduct; as the Judge at the end of days, sitting on His Throne of Judgment, with the Torah in His lap; and as a diligent student of the same laws and principles which He has bequeathed to His people. Thus, the Law is either the expression of God's inscrutable Will or the result of His kindness and solicitude for the best interests of His children, or the reflection of cosmic principles that inhere irrevocably in creation itself. In any event, the Law is superior to all human judgments and must be regarded as absolute in its validity and inexorable in its application.

The full stream of Judaism, thru the ages, contained many trends, in addition to the massive current of naive piety. For the sake of clarity in analysis, however, the literalist mentality must be envisaged in all its naivete and inner consistency, in order that the full consequences of its rejection may be realized. Unfortunately, the debates concerning Halachah are all too frequently confounded by ambiguous phrases, which half-conceal and half-reveal mental attitudes that are themselves ambivalent, being compounded of both belief and unbelief.

Let us begin our analysis then with a frank and clear rejection of the literalist Orthodox position. We do not believe that God dictated the Torah to Moses, as a scribe to a pupil, and that He had transmitted to Moses all the comments, interpretations and inferences relating to it that were later recorded in the Oral Law. Having taken this step, we find ourselves still profoundly convinced of the importance of the Law and its supreme significance. But if these vague sentiments of reverence are to serve as the enduring foundations for Judaism of the future, they must be envisaged in all clarity as proven true in terms of the contemporary situation and as rooted firmly in the eternal scheme of things. How then shall we think of Halachah?

The readers of the "Reconstructionist" are best acquainted with the conception of "folkways" as the alternative to the Orthodox conception of the Divinely instituted "mitzvoth." This conception implies that, in the past, the laws were simply the practices of Jewish people, some being derived from pre-Jewish sources and some growing out of their own experience and aspiration; that, in the present, their claim upon the individual is compounded of filial sentiment, national pride, the gregarious instinct and the need of the individual to seek and find his physical and spiritual salvation thru the channels of community life; that, in the future, these ceremonies might well be replaced by different social organs that will respond more adequately to the then prevailing folk needs. The term "folkway," evokes the romantic admiration for plain people, who are free from the frequently disturbing and always challenging virus of rationality. It echoes the idealized image of the peasant that was so characteristic a feature of mid-nineteenth century nationalistic literature in Germany and Russia. It is idyllic, almost pastoral in its connotations, redolent of fields and forests, of pre-cityfied, even if not pre-civilized existence. But, even while it thus echoes the cravings of romantic nationalism, it seems to speak in the scientific accents of the anthropologist, studying primitive societies, and the modern American sociologist, studying the ghettoes of European immigrants in our large metropolitan centers.

Nevertheless, in spite of its romantic undertones and its scientific resonance the term, "folkways," can hardly be regarded as offering an adequate concept for Jewish law in our life. The amazing brilliance and insight with which it was developed assure for it a place in the history of Jewish thought, but, as a contemporary philosophy it is sadly inadequate. Primarily, it lacks the moral quality, which alone evokes a sense of obligation and a feeling of consecration. Why should we strive with might and main to preserve folkways? Their importance is supposed to reside in their inherent appeal and charm, not in any axiomatic claim to loyalty. Is the nostalgic reverence for parental practice to be glorified as an absolute imperative? Such a consummation would indeed offer a strange climax to the great adventure of Judaism, which began with a revolt against established customs and parental mores, as expressed in the command given to Abraham, "go, thou, from thy land, the place where thou wast born and from the house of thy fathers." Nor, does this state of mind in actual practice achieve more than the treasuring of "tallith" and "t'fillin" in public and private museums, the practice of visiting with the old folks on Yom Kippur and the crowding of synagogues for Yizkor, leading perhaps also to the well-known facetious extreme of eating an extra Kosher dish in celebration of Yahrzeit.

Certainly, if we pursue the implications of this concept backwards into the past and forward into life, we cannot but repudiate it with vehement finality. For, does it not present to us the image of our people, clinging to its ways and customs, in the face of direst consequences, for no reason save that those were indeed their ways and customs? The motivation of Jewish piety was actually neither sheer stubbornness nor primitive clannishness, but the noblest imperative of spiritual integrity. It was derived from a deep conviction in the *truth* of Israel's religious heritage, and the consequent common sense preference of eternal reward for temporary bliss.

In this interpretation, however, the glory of Jewish martyrdom for the sake of Divine truth and the soberness of its mentality would be interpreted as the senseless stubbornness of a clannish people, fanatically isolating itself from the ways of the world, forebearing all mundane goods and spiritual values for the sake of mere tribal customs. Is the ardor of tribalism so beautiful a phenomenon, when we observe it among the backward peoples of this globe, that we should be tempted to reinterpret the Jewish past or reconstruct the Jewish present by means of it?—If today, we should see a people tenaciously clinging to its folkways to the point of sacrificing fortune, well-being and even life itself, in an environment where larger horizons, broader loyalties and a fuller life is possible, we should unhesitatingly condemn them as being both monstrously foolish and bitterly reactionary. If, then, the interpretation of Jewish laws as folkways is painfully inadequate to account for their historic function, it cannot serve as a proper vehicle for the momentum of loyalty to transmit its impetus for a creative life in the future. The ideal of clinging tenaciously to folkways, regardless of their intrinsic charm and worth, could only appeal to a transitional generation, that lost the purpose but retained the sentiment of group survival, remaining, for no good reason that it could give, morbidly sensitive to the specter of the melting pot. In a balanced view, the so called "militant" survivalist, who deems group survival per se to be a supreme end of existence is guilty of idolatry, religiously speaking, of vicious abstraction, logically speaking, and of sheer foolishness, practically speaking. Our ancestors were not guilty, in any one of these respects; why should we expect our children, who are likely to outstrip us in worldly wisdom, to fall victims to these delusions?

Conceived in a totally different realm of discourse, the Ahad Ha'amist conception of Jewish law as the "exilic garments" of Israel's soul is equally erroneous and misleading. In this view, the vast legal structure of the Jewish faith is interpreted as the product of the subterranean functioning of the national will to live. In the case of an individual, the powerful instincts of self-preservation generate ideas, attitudes and actions that are intended to guard his life, even, if on the rational level, they are "dressed up" in all kinds of rationalizations. The "real reason" for the multifarious actions of people is generally the impulse of self-preservation, though often enough people prefer to explain their actions in terms of "good reasons." In the same manner, the "real reason" for the progressive building up of the high fences of Halachah was to assure the survival of the Jewish people, with the entire complex series of religious motivation serving only as the respectable facade for the dynamism of the national instinct. After the Babylonian exile, when the existence of Israel was placed in jeopardy, the national "will to live" began to weave the web of prohibition and interdiction; which had the effect of erecting an impassable barrier between Jew and Gentile and halting the trend of national dissolution. Later, as exile became ever more inexorably the normal state of Jewish existence, this tendency gathered momentum until, even as the turtle, the Jew came to carry his own home with him, wherever he went, permitting but a few chinks in his shell, for outside influences to penetrate.

On this interpretation, Jewish ritual law is indispensable from the standpoint of Jewish survival in the Diaspora. While Ahad Ha'am was too inwardly truthful to maintain that religion should serve the ends of nationalism for the people of his generation, many of his followers agreed with Smolenskin and Lilienblum that the "mitzvoth" should continue to be regarded as the national commandments for Israel in exile.

In the United States, this cluster of motivations was a powerful factor among the Conservative-minded laity and rabbinate. One ventures to assert that in the sermons of all wings of American Judaism, the national motif is by far predominant whenever the so called "Jewish way of life," is preached. Implied in this interpretation is the estimation of group survival, not only as a biological instinct but also as a high spiritual obligation, so that the products of the national soul might be regarded as somehow "religious" as well. Echoes of the Halevian conception of Israel as a holy, prophetic people, that will in time be asked by all other nations "what the morrow will bring," were mingled with the sentiments of the Hebraic renaissance and the widespread hysteria of European nationalism, in order to furnish the composite apologia for Jewish ritual, that was actually in vogue in our own time.

Does this conception offer a valid interpretation of the past, adequate motivation in the present or eternal values for the future?—Obviously, it fails in all three domains. In respect of our historic past, a generation of nationalistic historians, led by Simon Dubnow, has not succeeded in hiding the incontrovertible fact that the fundamental motivations of Jewish life, all thru the centuries, were derived from their religious convictions and that the survival of the Jewish nationality was an effect rather than a cause. In every generation, Jewish people were willing enough to compromise in regard to all nationalistic values, forsaking their land, language, mores, allegiance to an extra-national authority and accepting foreign national obligations, cultures and even irredentist sentiments with alacrity. But, they were adamant as the rock of Gibraltar, when the slighest tittle of the Law was involved, remembering the injunction that when a government is suspected of designs against the Jewish faith, resistance to the death must be offered even in so slight a matter as the proper manner of lacing one's shoes.

Nor, can it be maintained that the survival of every branch of a biological or historical group must be regarded as a supreme end in itself. It is of the very essence of the ethical approach, to view all things objectively, to limit the value of every part by the consideration of the welfare of the whole, to think in terms of the unique value of every individual, not the group, and to view with extreme suspicion the tendency to glorify whatever is associated with the first person possessive pronoun. Certainly, if we judge the tree of romantic, biological nationalism by its fruits, we cannot but regard it as a most vicious and most insidiously corrupting aberration of the human mind. With Nazism as the logical culmination of the illogic of total tribalism, it would be the height of folly to regard the miracle of Israel's survival in the past and the rationale of its life in the present as being due to an inversion of the same dark philosophy of blood and folk.

As to the future, can any one seriously claim today that the nationalistic motive can be usefully employed as the foundation for Jewish law? Since the survival of Israel is presumably assured, thru the resurgence of the state of Israel, the nationalists in our midst can now afford to forego the aid of religious ceremonies. Those who take their national sentiments seriously will either go to Israel, or else be content to warm themselves by the reflected fire of Israel's reborn secular life and culture. Those in whom the fervor of nationalism is of a lesser intensity will be prone to regard the establishment of the state of Lsrael and its gradual fortification as being a sufficient fulfillment of the impulse for group survival. Is not this the attitude of the vast majority of America's immigrant nationalities that are even now commingling to produce the emergent American nation?—To be sure, the sudden resurgence of Israel's strength has moved many people to "accept" their Jewishness, but correspondingly this self-acceptance, being a return to a normalcy of feeling, is lacking in spiritual content and is quite incapable of opposing the assimilatory trend. On the contrary, it is likely to smooth the path of assimilation, by removing the Jewish feelings of inferiority and allaying the disturbing consciousnes of Jewish "difference."

Still a different version of the nationalist conception of Jewish law is offered by the so called "historical school," which was begun by Zechariah Frankel and expanded into impressive proportions by Solomon Schecter. To the historians of this school, history is a form of inverted prophecy and is therefore its own vindication. Jewish law, as it developed thru the ages, is an organic product of slow gestation reflecting the inner genius and the profundities of the Jewish national character. Accordingly, no merely rational considerations can be allowed to outweigh the massive, historical processes, which echo the depths of the national soul by their very irrationalities. The spiritual history of a people, especially the structure of its laws, represents the gradual unfolding of its inner psyche. Hence, these laws, must not be fundamentally disturbed; they should be allowed to change only in line with their own "positive-historical" grooves—for the law is the incarnation of the people's soul.

It is characteristic of romantic positions, founded as they are on the uncertain haze of emotion and the peculiarly conditioned slant of their adherents that they reveal their weakness the moment they are fully expressed in unsentimental and objective terms. Thus, as here formulated, the historical approach is manifestly the outgrowth of an exaggerated emphasis on a half-truth. It is certain that the legal structure of a people, deprived of a governmental authority, is the means whereby its unity is maintained. It is also true that, in its creative period, the noblest ideals of a people are translated into the concrete terms of its legislation. But, considered a priori and in the abstract, what is to prevent historic processes that functioned relatively well in the past to function poorly in the present, or even to cease functioning altogether?—Historic processes in law, language, literature, politics and every other phase of culture are, after all, products of multiple factors and relative circumstances. How can they be regarded as sources of absolute value, sufficient unto themselves?

Actually, the plausibility of the "positive-historical" position is derived not from the intrinsic logic of its argument, but from the combined momentum of an ancient Jewish trend and a resurgent European reactionary movement. In appearance, at least, Jewish law seemed to be an independent domain, self-justifying and self-evaluating, regardless of fluctuations in the intellectual climate. Considerations of philosophy and theology appear to have been irrelevant to the unfolding inner logic of Halachah. This fact is due, of course, firstly to the civil and public character of the major part of Jewish law. In such legislation, cognizance is universally taken of deeds, not opinions. Thus, in Greece and in Rome, as well as in Judea, charges of "atheism" were

329

concerned with deeds, not with thoughts. Secondly, it is of the nature of the legal process for cases to be decided by reference to precedent and accepted maxims, rather then by a reconsideration of first principles. Thirdly, Halachah was hammered out in its present shape, largely by people who were entirely consistent in their religious views, but who were not rationalistic philosophers. Needless to say that it is a far cry from this statement of a historic fact to the value-proposition that philosophy which is systematized common sense, *should* have nothing to do with Halachah. It is a form of self-stultification that Maimonides would not even allow God to impose upon man. How can practice be permanently separate from its justification in theory? The centuries-long tendency to separate Halacha from Aggadah may have served a useful purpose in the Gaonic times, when it was set in motion, but it is not inherently justifiable. Men like Bialik and Kuk, beginning from diametrically opposed starting points, agreed that only thru the realignment of Aggadah with Halachah is progress in Judaism made possible.

In addition to reflecting the traditional independence of the domain of Halachah, the "positive-historical" school expressed in the field of Judaism the nineteenth-century philosophy of German reaction. It was the legal historian Savigny, who first put forward the view that German law must not be radically modified, inasmuch as it reflected the unfolding soul of the German nation, thereby offering a rationale for the maintenance of the semi-feudal *ancien regime* against the challenge of the liberal forces unleashed by the French Revolution. Savigny transferred the Tertullianian reverence for the absurdities of dogma to the sphere of politics and law, maintaining that the seeming irrationalities of German law were the more sacred to the nation because of their evident unreason. His interpretation fitted in beautifully with the then current biological conception of the life of nations, as propounded especially by Herder and the Schlegel brothers. It was further deepened by the influential and profound works of Fichte, who expounded the thesis that the Germanic soul had a special affinity with Vernunft, a form of reason that could not be understood at all by the proponents of superficial rationalism, such as the French and Jewish liberals. Finally, Hegel climaxed the entire movement by his pedantic portrayal of the history of culture as being the invariant forms of the universal mind. The practical import of Hegel's conception was the representation of the Prussian state and its legal structure as the ultimate revelation of the Divine Being. For history is Divine Judgment, as it were, and its processes, as outlined in the past, mark out the grooves of change for the future.

It is in this intellectual atmosphere that it seemed so reasonable to base the validity of Halachah solely on its "positive-historical" character. Stripped of these connotations, it becomes clear that the historical processes of Halachah should be subject to reevaluation in terms of contemporary ideas, canons of criticism and necessities of circumstance.

The common core of the three interpretations analyzed herein is the conception of folk, nation or people as accounting not merely for the external shape and historical character of the Halachah, but as constituting the source of the validity and significance of Jewish Law. Manifestly, this sociological aspect of the law, revealing the massive group momentum inherent in it cannot be gainsaid. No man lives alone, and the bonds of group loyalty into which we fall by birth, constitute for us the natural matrix of our ideals, determining their external shape and slant. Against those who desert their natural groups to seek salvation elsewhere, the sociological argument is effective. But, to those who stay within, this phase is the body of the law, as it were, not its soul, and to attempt to base the value of law solely upon the character of the group is both futile and irrational. Only the absolute values of the spiritual life and the happiness of the individual Jew can be regarded as the axiomatic, irreducible foci of Jewish Law. For these are ultimates, in terms of which all group values must be judged.

To discover what Halachah should mean for us today, we have to bear in mind firstly that the relationship of the Jew to God is its incontrovertible starting point. Secondly, in Judaism the laws were not only conceived as the word of God, but they were so conceived because of their inherent worth as instruments of piety. True, they were God-given, but God is not a tyrant, imposing a yoke of obligations out of selfish need or sheer caprice. What does the Lord require of thee?—To fear Him, to love Him, and to walk in His pathways. The mitzvoth were given in order that men might be purified thru them. Thirdly, the mitzvoth were not simply ordained for Jews by the fiat of the Lord; they became obligatory only when the Jewish people accepted them formally in the classic phrase, "na'aseh v'nishma." Thus, the Torah was offered to the other nations, but it is not for them obligatory since they never accepted it. Fourthly, in addition to the moral-legal basis of Halachah, there was always the consciousness of historic necessity, the ever present momentum of the past of which every generation must take account. The Israelites, at Sinai, were historically committed already, because of the covenant with their ancestors; and the acceptance of all future generations is only in part voluntary and in part compelled by the realities of history. As the legend put it, the souls of all Israelites down to the end of time were gathered together for the Theophany at Sinai. Fifthly, the precepts of Halachah constituted the minimal standards of the community, by no means exhausting the full task and vocation of man. The good man must rise above the general level, "lifnim m'shuras hadin," and Jerusalem was destroyed because its inhabitants insisted on the strict letter of the law.

Combining all these elements into one formula we arrive at the conception of Halachah as the Divinely inspired and self-imposed disciplines of the Jewish people, undertaken for the purpose of elevating the level of individual and group life to the highest rungs of the ideals of Judaism. In this conception, the ideals of Judaism, insofar as they determine the standard images of the perfect individual and the perfect society, are recognized to be the goal and purpose of the entire Halachic structure, while the ritual ceremonies are identified as instruments, of relative value and significance. The source of the validity of Halachah is thus twofold—deriving in part from the consent of the people and in part from the inherent truth of the ideal embodied in it. If one grants supreme validity to any one ideal of Judaism, to the extent of desiring to share in the Jewish faith and destiny, then he cannot but accord a measure of authority to the legislation of the group as a whole. On the other hand, this allegiance to authority cannot be of an absolute character, since other values and ideals of his may conceivably be in conflict with the precepts of his people's legislation. The relative authority of any law is thus determined jointly by the degree to which it represents the common consent of our people and the measure in which it serves the highest ideals of Judaism.

The expression "divinely inspired and self-imposed" is intended to reflect the fact that the law is derived from both the insight of inspired titans of the spirit and the voluntary acceptance of the people generally. Of especial importance is the insistence on the Divine stamp of the central method of Judaism—the determination to translate abstract ideals into concrete ways of life for the people as a whole. Thus, the vague sentiment of loving God was concretized into the precept to pray three times daily; the recognition of our dependence upon Him, into the requirement to precede every new sensation of enjoyment by a "b'rochoh"; the idle contemplation of His Nature into firstly the command to study the Torah day and night and secondly the ethically spelled out aspiration to emulate His ways as the infinitely, perfect Personality. This method must be regarded as the cornerstone of Judaism, the one ideal which makes all other ideals practically meaningful and which transforms Judaism from a philosophy of monotheism into a monotheistic religion. It is compounded of a profound sense of personal consecration and a healthy regard for the conscience and welfare of the community as a whole.

This conception of the Halachah is true to its historical character and development. While it describes the law as being the product of Israel, the two directions of religious love are interpreted as phases of one process. In our view, God is conceived as the Pole of Absolute, Ideal Personality in the back and forth flux of the multiple processes of reality, and the love of Him as the highest peak of the Divine process in the heart of man. For, in the love of God, all moral and esthetic values are fused together into a new and creative unity. If all ideals be conceived as dynamic motivations, deriving from God and leading to Him, then the love of God must be regarded as the parent-ideal, the living focus of the spiritual realm. And the entire Halachah, in its manifold stages of growth and regardless of the diverse origins of some of its practices, may be viewed as being motivated by the one sustained attempt to incorporate the love of God as a living reality in every phase of public and private experience. Thus, a Maimonides may speculate on the ideal possibility of worshipping God in wordless silence and rite-less contemplation and recognize at the same time that for most people, such an ideal is all too frequently a snare and a delusion.

No conception of Jewish Law is worthy of consideration if it does not truly capture some of the motivation, which actually functioned in the historic past of our people. For we do not have either the desire or the will to create a new religion. Accordingly, we must inquire whether the interpretation of Law as legislated spiritual disciplines is indeed justified by the testimony of history.

In form, this conception is identical with the major part of Halachah, the part that is described as "d'rabonon," containing the officially authorized interpretations, "takkanoth" and "g'zeroth." This class of ordinances is thought of as providing an outer area of disciplines intended to safeguard the iner area of Torah-itic "mitzvoth." The exact boundaries of this area are subject to dispute, Maimonides having provided the widest conception current in rabbinic literature of the extent of the area of laws, that derive their authority from the insight of the rabbis and their collective legislation. Obviously, from the standpoint of historical criticism, there is scarcely a shred of "Halachah," that is not dependent in the last analysis on an authoritative rabbinic interpretation that was duly recorded at one time or another. As Maimonides put it in a different connection, "the gates of interpretation are not closed to us." The words of the Torah are sufficiently tractable to be incorporated into almost any system of legislation. But, the words of the living Torah have been frozen into rigid laws by layer after layer of rabbinic legislation. Thus, in the critical view, the distinction between Torah-itic and rabbinic laws vanishes, so that the final source is "de'rabonon."

The realization of this truth need by no means be con-

335

fined to those who repudiate the literal version of "Torah min Ha-shomayim." All who think in historical terms must find it difficult to resist such a conclusion. Hence, the extreme emphasis in halachic literature on the authority of "divre soferim." Consider the implications of utterances such as the following:

"Whoever disputes a word of theirs is as one who opposes God and His Torah, for all their words are of God, and even a Midrash of Moses himself, master of the prophets, could not possibly be set against their words, for their wisdom and pilpul is the word which God commanded unto Moses." (Shaarei Tzedek—Gaonic Responsa)

"For they are assisted by the Shekinah, and it is not possible that their agreed opinions shall be contrary to the intent of the Torah . . ." (Kusari, III, 41)

Now, the authority of the rabbis was not due to the mere fact of their election, but to their reputed saintliness, capped as it was believed to be by the gift of "Ruah haKodesh." The authority of the Shulhan Aruch was in no small measure due to the mystical visions of its author. Thus, the legislation of the rabbis, designated collectively as "d'rabonon" coincides in form at least with the conception of Jewish law, as outlined herein. It was believed to be "divinely inspired"; the disciplines were "self-imposed," for until and unless the people generally accepted a rabbinic ordinance it was considered as being automatically null and void. The purpose of rabbinic legislation was to maintain the "ideals of Judaism," as the rabbis understood them, identifying them on occasion with the ritual of the faith. Our conception of the ideals comprising the essence of Judaism belongs to the tradition of the prophetic-philosophic school of thought, to an analysis of which we shall now turn.

In order to understand the relationship of the substance

of our conception, as distinguished from its form, to the basic currents of historical Jewish piety, we must launch upon an inquiry into the motivations that were supposed to underlie the rites and precepts of Judaism. What were the so called "ta-amai ha-mitzvoth," the motives and purposes which, the Jew felt, supplied sufficient reason for his practice?—The author intends to deal with this question in a special study that will be published elsewhere. Here, it is sufficient to indicate the existence of three categories of explanation, which functioned, sometimes separately, sometimes jointly, as the frames of reference for the reasons of the commandments. There was firstly, the mentality of folk piety, to which God was a quasi-human being, both King and Father. As King, His "mitzvoth" were commands that could not be questioned; as Father, it could be taken for granted, that His Commands were somehow intended for the good of mankind, bringing with them life and blessing. A covenant was concluded between Israel and the Lord, requiring the people of Israel, as their part of the agreement to serve Him in ways agreeable to Him. True, a faithful servant will not pester His Master with demands for immediate reward, but the Lord could be trusted "to pay the reward of your work." Whether or not the intent of any particular "mitzvah" be apparent, the ultimate reason is to serve the Lord and to submit to His inscrutable Will.

In the philosophical current of Judaism, all arbitrariness and caprice is removed from the conception of God and the purpose of the "mitzvoth" is conceived to be unequivocally the spiritual perfection of the individual and the ethical perfection of society. The efficacy of the "mitzvoth" consists not in their favorable effect upon the Divine Will, but in their influence upon the human soul, and their reward is supposed to be the automatic, natural rewards of a life dedicated to truth and goodness. The core of Judaism, in this view, is the cluster of universal intellectual and ethical values, and all rites and ceremonies are merely the instruments of its implementation. Thus, Maimonides, after ridiculing those who revel in the occasional irrationalities of the Commandments, offers the classic formulation of the philosophic approach: "But, the matter is without question as we have mentioned—to wit, that every one of the 613 Commandments is motivated either by the purpose of imparting true ideas, or counteracting wrongful opinions, or the establishment of a just order, or the correction of injustice, or the training in good virtues, or the correction of evil practices. Accordingly, the purposes of all the mitzvoth fall into the three categories of true ideas, good virtues and the just order of society . . . . Thus, these three categories are entirely sufficient to account for every one of the mitzvoth." (Guide, III, 31)

In the philosophy of Maimonides, the highest gift available to man is the attainment of a bond of union with Active Reason and the consequent assurance of immortality. This gift belongs primarily to the faithful devotees of the moral and intellectual life, and only secondarily to the observers of the "mitzvoth," for the "mitzvoth" are instruments of the life of the spirit, and instruments sometimes fail to achieve their purpose.

The very clarity with which Maimonides presented the viewpoint of philosophical Judaism provoked a violent reaction among the naive believers and their defenders, as is amply demonstrated in the commentaries upon the "Guide" and the polemics that followed upon its publication. But, the sophisticated defenders of fundamentalist Orthodoxy cannot ever be satisfied with the mere reiteration of the naive viewpoint. For philosophy compels even its opponents to accept some if not all of its spirit. Thus, the anti-philosophical defense of the "ta-amai ha mitzvoth" produced, in the course of time, a quasi-philosophical super-orthodoxy, which is enshrined in the literature of Kabbalah. As I have shown elsewhere, the logic of Kabbalah consists in a polar blend of the personalistic thinking of naive piety and the mechanistic thinking of rationalistic philosophy.[1]

As a result, the Kabbalistic "ta-amai ha mitzvoth" assume an automatic effect of the commandments upon the soul, but not in universal terms. Also, the commandments are related to cosmic forces, but not to universal values. Every "Mitzvah" is thought of as a chain descending from the spiritual world, bringing down holiness and achieving "unity" and bliss in the world, redeeming it from the power of evil—yes, redeeming even the Divine in the world, so that Israel Baal Shem Tov could even dare to interpret the phrase, "the Lord is your shadow," as meaning that the Deity is affected automatically and made to respond mechanically to our actions and intentions just as a shadow reflects the motion of a body. On the other hand, every "averah" (sin) is compared to a chain linking this world to the manifold worlds of "tum'ah," (uncleanliness) so that the sinner becomes chained and bound by his sin, even as the Hebrew word, "o-ssur," meaning prohibited, also signifies, being "bound" —bound, that is, to the Satanic forces of evil.

The three systems of "reasons for the commandments" were not always kept rigidly apart, for it is a rare thinker who dares to be thoroughly honest and mercilessly self-critical. Jewish pietistic literature is particularly noted for its multifarious eclecticism. Also, the mystical current of piety, motivated by the urge of seeking the "nearness of the Lord," is oftentimes added to all the three fundamental world-views in Judaism, making the process of analysis that much more difficult. Indeed, one of the deeply rooted errors in Jewish historiography is the bland identification of mys-

[1] *"Saifer Hashono,"* 1947.

ticism with Kabbalah and the consequent failure to recognize the distinction between the several types of mysticism corresponding to the three fundamental patterns of Jewish piety. Nevertheless, upon analysis, the three systems of "ta-amai ha-mitzvoth" become easily distinguishable.

With this analysis in mind, it appears clearly that we today cannot accept either the naive type of philosophy of Halachah or the Kabbalistic type. Only the current of philosophical piety, which relates the mitzvoth to the universal ends of the spiritual life, offers an approach adequate to our minds. This current which was by no means confined to the technical literature of Jewish philosophy, always reflected Judaism at its best and at its noblest. The remark attributed to Aristotle that "all Jews are philosophers" does contain a grain of truth, since the impact of Judaism upon the cultural atmosphere of every age was almost always due to the tenacious conviction inherent in it of the supremacy and the ultimate triumph of the values of the spirit—a conviction which is of the essence of the philosophical mood.

To us, then, the laws of Judaism are disciplines and standards accepted for the sake of universal, spiritual ends. To be sure, even the most rarefied expression of philosophical piety was encumbered in the past with dogmatic elements. How else could the gulf between the piety of the masses and the ideas of the philosophers be bridged? Thus, Maimonides exempted Moses from the general category of inspired thinkers, allowing for him a far greater measure of authority than his philosophy permitted. He also maintained that certain dogmatic beliefs, that were not true, were nevertheless to be accepted in order to avoid shocking the masses and disrupting the unity of the community ("emunoth hechrohiy-oth," socially needed beliefs.) While we may readily concur with Maimonides' estimate of the value of dogma and uniform practice for the community of his day, we cannot but assert the obvious truth that in our day insistence on dogma and uniform practice could not possibly serve the cause of unity. In our age, such insistence could serve in fact only as a disruptive force, since only a fraction of our people subscribe to the totality of Jewish law.

If we remove from the philosophical pattern of Jewish piety the dogmatic elements which were never essential to it, we have a conception of Jewish law, which is completely capable of meeting the challenge of our times. The builders of classical Reform sought consciously to build upon the foundations of what they termed "prophetic Judaism," thereby echoing a concept that was derived from the Christian reading of Jewish history. While this concept inspired the magnificent careers of some outstanding personalities, it could not serve as the basis for an enduring faith. The emphasis implicit in it could in fact only contribute to the trend of self-effacement, disintegration and dissolution, thereby making the claim of Christianity to be the rightful heir of prophetic Judaism appear to be incontrovertible. By contrast, philosophical Judaism is not individualistic, sentimental, vague and other-wordly; it is sober, well-balanced, thoroughly grounded in the realm of eternal truth and eminently capable of translating the vital essence of Judaism into the realities of our time.

Viewing Halachah as a set of standards and disciplines, we conceive of it as a vertical series, a ladder of Jacob, consisting of many rungs that lead from the earthly to the heavenly. There is ample precedent in traditional thought for this conception of multiple "madraigoth" (levels) in piety. Indeed, a better view still is to think of a threefold ladder, corresponding to the three pillars of the faith, Torah, Avodah and G'milus Hassadim. Thus, it is possible to climb high on one ladder while remaining on the lower rungs of the other ladders. This conception stands in clear contrast to the rigid uniformity of law, in the orthodox sense, that may be compared to a horizontal bridge, in which any breach is fatal. Thus, in halachah conceived as law, one is classed as a "mumar" (renegade) if he defies any one precept consistently and consciously, even if he scrupulously observes every other commandment. In this view, compromise and adjustment could only be sponsored by the guile of the opportunist or the despair of the pietist.

On the other hand, the conception of "Halachah plus Mussar" (law and ethics) as a series of vertical standards permits us to regard all Jewish groups, seeking sincerely to elevate the level of spiritual life, as falling within the pattern of one common endeavor. No longer need the transgressor of one more commandment look upon himself as living outside Halachah, so that he no longer has any reason to cling to the rest of the commandments. It becomes possible to recognize the unity of the goal and the relative unity of the pathway, even while taking into account realistically the actual diversity in the standards accepted by different groups and individuals within the several groups. At the same time, this recognition is not a sterile formula intended to smooth the path of practical statesmanship; on the contrary, it is the one conception that makes possible a sustained endeavor in behalf of the continuous and steady raising of standards in Jewish life.

Realizing the vast gulf between Halachah and the practices of the people, we may still reject the extremes of desperate Orthodoxy and wholesale repudiation and instead proceed to outline a series of standards, that, given maximum effort, could become the accepted practice of our people. Then, we could look forward to a gradual and progressive lifting of standards and their extension to ever wider sections of our people. This could be done without presuming to change the Law save by the implication that the items not included in the program are regarded as non-essential. It is the irresistible tide of social life that renders one paragraph after another of the Law obsolete. And it is for us to resist this process in the areas that are vital to Jewish spirituality.

Selecting the practices that are of primary importance, we should consider them as the first step on the ladder of Judaism and bend all our efforts for their acceptance by as broad a section of our people as possible. Technically, this policy of setting minimal standards to meet contemporary realities may be expressed in halachic terms as "horaoth sha-a." As our success grows, it may be possible to set a higher rung as the next immediate goal. In this way, we shall be making fruitful in our day the profound insights which underlie the structure of Halachah.

Essentially, the question before us is whether to maintain the steadily disintegrating outer shell of halachah, or to permit its vital seed to produce nourishing fruits for our day. If we think of Halacha as legislated standards and then consider the widening gulf between Halachah and life, we cannot but be moved to undertake to bridge the gulf by setting standards for our people, which they might accept and which truly contain, "ma-or Sheb'yahadut," the light which leads steadily upward.

(published in "Conservative Judaism," May, 1950)

9

Pluralism in Law

We are all prejudiced in favor of simplicity. The exuberant richness of experience frightens us, and we seek solace in the building up of a set of simple categories, in which all the manifold events of life are fitted by hook or by crook. In theory, who will dare deny that there are two sides to every story? But, in practice, how many of us will dare apply this rule to the central convictions of our life? It is not two sides we seek instinctively, but one view, one explanation that will be final and all-embracing. By preference, we are all monists.

In the understanding of the nature of law, monism has had a grand field day. In classical literature and in the Medieval world, law was conceived as deriving from one source, a source as pure and sacred as the one of the mythical four rivers flowing out of the Garden of Eden. Thus, Aristotle defined law as "reason unaffected by desire." And human reason in turn is but the reflection of the Active Reason that derives from the Deity. Cicero, speaking for the Roman Stoics, elaborated this principle still further when he declared, "law is the highest reason implanted in nature, which commands what ought to be and forbids the opposite." This monistic conception was favored in modern times especially in Germany, attaining classic formulation in the work of Herrmann Cohen, who insisted that the relation of law to ethics was precisely as direct and immediate as that of mathematics to logic.

In this respect as in so many others, the nineteenth century brought about a radical revolution. Karl Marx argued that the laws of economic necessity accounted fully for the development of jurisprudence. There is no Divine Justice, but only the demon of class-interest, working its diabolical plan through subterranean chanels. Freud supplied his contribution to the understanding of the laws of penology by a bold look into the dark underworld of human motivation. The utilitarians of England worked out a ledger-book type of legal philosophy on the principle of balancing advantages against disadvantages, so as to serve "the greatest good of the greatest number."

By the opening of the twentieth century, the idealistic conception of law gave way to its polar opposite, the positivistic philosophy. Law was now conceived not as a self-contained logical system, but as a strictly empirical phenomenon. Law was simply the description of the manner in which society works, foretelling how judges are likely to decide in any given situation. Its development in the course of history was not due to the unfolding of an inner logic, but to the varying circumstances and pressures within society. As a description of court-procedure, law was inseparable from the actual process of legal administration and enforcement. Hence, there could be no law, if there were no sanctions to induce compliance. As the leading jurist of America, Oliver Wendell Holmes, summed up the philosophy of the positivitists—"The life of the law is not logic, but experience."

It was only in the second quarter of this century that a synthesis was achieved between both types of monism—the one deriving law altogether from reason, the other basing it all upon experience. In the legal philosophy of men like Morris R. Cohen and Roscoe Pound, a new science of jurisprudence is unfolded, which allows room for both factors. Any system of law, by its very nature, contains an idealistic element which lifts it beyond the realm of custom or force. On the other hand, the testimony of historians and sociologists is virtually unanimous in behalf of the pluralistic origin of the diverse legal principles that constitute our law. As Dean Roscoe Pound summarized this balanced view, designated by him as "sociological jurisprudence"—It is all for putting the human factor in the central place and relegating logic to its true position as an instrument."

But, if the law be derived from many sources, what is it that makes it into a unified system? The answer is that two main factors fashion the system of law which governs our society—an objective factor, the existence of a system of legal administration and interpretation, and a subjective factor, the inner acceptance of the law by the citizenry generally, as being right and proper. Between society as a whole and the individual citizen there is an implied contract, so that compliance with the law is felt in conscience as a moral imperative. When Socrates refused to take advantage of the good-will of the guards and escape from jail, insisting instead on drinking the hemlock, he demonstrated the validity of observing the law as an ethical principle. Similarly, in Jewish law, the son of Shimeon ben Shottah offered his life in support of a legal principle, saying to his father, then the head of the Synhedrin—"make me like a threshold and step across me."

This survey of the philosophy of law helps us to understand the problem of Jewish law. While religious law cannot be equated with the legal system of any secular society, there are nevertheless inevitable parallels in development, insofar as law does form an essential ingredient of Jewish piety. It should therefore occasion no surprise if we encounter an identical situation in the philosophy of Jewish law as we find in the general theory of jurisprudence.

At first glance, idealistic monism seems to be the only legitimate school of interpretation. Indeed, in Judaism, this approach was carried to fantastic lengths. Down to recent years, Orthodoxy insisted that all of Jewish law in its entire millenial sweep, beginning with the Torah and going up to the standard commentaries of the Shulhan Arukh, the Shach and Taz, were the products of "Ruah Hakodesh" (the Spirit of Holiness). In part, this extremist attitude was adopted in opposition to the challange of Karaism (the movement which rejected the validity of the Oral Law, as it is contained in Mishnah and Talmud.) But, once this position was taken, it was never consciously repudiated. Thus, Saadia Gaon declared that the rabbinic policy to require in the Diaspora the observance of two days of every festival was a revealed doctrine, given to Moses at Sinai.

> "There was no doubt from the beginning. But God ordered His servant Moses to tell the Israelites that in the land of Israel they should celebrate the festival one day and outside of Israel two days. And thus it was from the beginning . . ."
>
> ("T'shuvoth Hageonim," 11)

In the same maner, the passages in the Talmud referring to Moses' foreknowledge of future rabbinic enactments were interpreted in a specific, literal sense—i.e. all the later "takkanoth" were actually revealed to Moses. ("M'gillah, 19b; "Shavuoth," 39a)

The Medieval philosopher, Halevi declared that every item of Jewish law, enacted up to his day was sanctioned by Divine inspiration. Concerning the Mishnah, he maintained "that flesh and blood could not have composed a work of like perfection," (Kusari III, 67) thus echoing the well-known Moslem argument regarding the Koran. The

Talmud, too, was composed by men who saw sacred visions and heard divine echoes. (Ibid, 73)

Orthodox monism derived added strength from the exuberant fantasies of the Kabbalah. Interpreting the disputes in the Talmud as being the earthly manifestations of mysterious, heavenly processes, the Talmud and the law ceased to have any relevance to life and came to be regarded as a revealed body of occult knowledge. The laws of Judaism did not arise out of life and for the sake of life, but out of heavenly events and in response to them. "But, the fact is that for every opinion there was a special mystical attachment above." ("Sh'nai Luhoth Habrith," Kieltz, page 19)

Naturally, this belief attributing Divine inspiration in blanket fashion to all the molders of Jewish Law, down the centuries, required that all previous generations be idealized to an extravagant degree. In the Talmud itself, we encounter the beginnings of this exaggerated reverence for the past in such maxims as—"If the early teachers be like angels, we are like human beings, and if they were like human beings we are like donkeys." (Sabbath, 112b) In the dark centuries of the Medieval era, this fantastic product of filial piety was allowed to expand beyond all rhyme and reason, largely through the influence of Kabbalah. Rabbi Hayim of Volozhin defended the bitter opposition of his teacher, the Gaon Elijah of Vilna, to the innovations in liturgy introduced by the Hassidim. Conceding that these innovations did not run counter to any fundamental, legal principle, this protagonist of Lithuanian Judaism insisted on a general "hands off" policy in regard to the Prayer Book, declaring that not a word may be altered in the liturgy. Composed by men who were familiar with the "lights" and "channels" in the upper spheres, that are associated with its every letter, the Prayer Book could be altered only by men who were similarly endowed. The Hassidim, of course, believed that their "Tsaddikim" were aided by the Divine Spirit, "Ruah Hakodesh." ("Nefesh HaHayim," II, 9)

In the collection of Responsa, protesting against the early innovations of the Reform movement, we encounter various formulations of the principle that the dogma of "Torah Min Hashomayim" (Torah from Heaven) implies the belief that the early Sages were spiritual supermen, "for they used to draw down the Spirit of Holiness from above. But we, sunk in sins how dare a sinner be proud or look for beauty of expression." ("Aileh Divrai Ha-B'rith")

Nor is this attitude confined to the early exponents of Orthodoxy. In a book published in 1949, the claim is put forward that the common people of previous generations were as familiar with the occult "lights" and "channels" as we of this depraved modern age are with the effects of electricity. "For their life in the higher worlds was like our life in this world." ("Shaiurai Daath," New York, pp. 97, 106)

In this way, theological monism sought to guard against the slightest break in the dikes of the Law. Everything was divine, nothing was human. The alternative is between all or nothing, for in a legal certificate, "if a part is invalid, the whole is invalid."

*　　*　　*

Luckily, the trend of theological monism was only one of the many streams making up the rich and turbulent river of Judaism. For Judaism was not ever monolithic in thought, save perhaps during the darkest centuries of history at the end of the Middle Ages. As a rule, single-tracked fundamentalism was balanced by a powerful, broad-gauged liberalism,

349

inherent in the tradition. Thus, even the orthodox parties of various epochs did not represent one identical position. The Mizrachi party which campaigns on the platform, "the land of Israel for the people of Israel in accordance with the Torah of Israel," does not really aim to enforce the laws calling for the punishment by death of all who desecrate the Sabbath. The number of laws which would not be applied by the party claiming to stand "for all of the law" would take a thick volume to describe. (See author's "Obsolescence in Jewish Law," in "Conservative Judaism," June, 1951)

The pluralistic character of Jewish law was maintained by some of the leading exponents of Judaism. Rabbi Joshua ben Hannayah defended the principle that human reason and majority opinion had their place in the making of the law. In one of the most beautiful legends in the Talmud, we are told that Rabbi Eliezer cited as proof of correctness of his position a number of miracles, including a voice from heaven. Rabbi Joshua countered all such arguments with the verse, "it is not in heaven—" i. e. the dictates of human judgement are to prevail in the formulation of law, not the presumed voice of Divine inspiration. (Baba Metsia, 59b)

In another picturesque story, we are told that God, too, repeats the disputed opinions of the rabbis on earth, as He studies the Torah in heaven. To the question, "is there doubt before heaven?" He replies, "Both these and these are words of the Living God." (Gittin, 6b)

A Midrash counters the monistic bias by asking if it was humanly possible for Moses to learn the whole Torah in forty days. The answer given is that Moses was taught "K'lalim," (rules), by means of which decisions were to be made in the varying cicumstances of life. (Rabba, Exodus, 41, 6) This solution was elaborated especially by Rabbi Joseph Albo, the great fourteenth century philosopher, who taught that a Divine faith had to be flexible. As the good doctor will vary his prescription to the differing needs of every individual, so did the good Lord ordain that the Law be adjustable to the circumstances of every age. He projects the possibility of some Dietary laws being set aside, but he also cautions that the individual Jew dare not presume to act in such matters on his own initiative.

"It is therefore fitting that the decision regarding all necessary amendments shall be the prerogative only of the scholars, for wisdom is a gift from God. Thus, in every generation they will see to it that the Torah of God shall be perfect, not lacking in anything. . ."   (Ikkarim III, 23; III, 16; III, 13)

Maimonides, the leading authority in Judaism, declared that in regard to detailed specifications of the law, there cannot be any Divine purpose, for details belong to the accidents of history. ("Guide," III, 26) That this position of Maimonides was not upheld by some of the greatest legalists goes without question. Rabbi Moses Isserles, author of the chief emendations of the Shulhan Aruch, set out to reveal the symbolic import of the details of the sacrifices — an enterprise which Maimonides declared to be "rank insanity." ("Torath Ha Olah")

Maimonides allowed that some laws were taken up in Judaism on account of the pervasive influence of the surrounding cultures. Thus the ritual of sacrifices was ordained, because the Israelites in the days of Moses were not prepared for a more spiritual kind of Divine service. ("Guide," III, 32) If the laws regarding ritual purity, especially of women, appear to us to be unduly cumbersome, it is because we do not realize that, in comparison with the then prevailing mores among the pagans, the laws of the Torah represented bold progress toward a sane way of living. Thus, the Torah yielded "to the accepted customs of the time, and the Sabeans

351

(pagans) made a great to do about ritual purity." (Ibid, III, 47)

Maimonides realized that a rational faith could not be rigid and inflexible, in its practices and precepts. For, if the purpose of the ritual is to serve the spiritual needs of men and women, then it is undeniable that the utility of social instruments varies in accord with the changes in the circumstances and mores of social life.

"Knowing that it will be necessary either to add to the laws of the Torah or to set aside some of them, in accord with the needs of different places, times and circumstances, the Lord gave this power to the scholars of every age." ("Guide," III, 41)

Though the knowledge of history was exceedinglgy meager in his generation, Maimonides did not share the naive belief that the Bible and the Talmud agreed in every detail. Thus, in his discussion of the *lex talionis,* the law requiring an eye for an eye, he points out the difference between the attitude of Scripture and the interpretation of the Talmud. ("Guide," III, 41).

A century of historical research has laid bare the actual process of the evolution of Jewish law. The numerous factors that entered into its making cannot always be understood with clarity and certainty. Yet, it is possible for us to distinguish in the formative period of Jewish law some raw material, deriving from the mores of the age, and the operation of the religious ideal, seeking to infuse every area of life with the elevating spirit of holiness. While in form Jewish practices differed on occasion but little from the practices of their neighbors, in spirit Judaism was always an impassioned protest against the debasing tendencies of the day. There is hardly a ritual practice in Judaism that differs essentially from the numerous rites and ceremonies

352

that prevailed in the ancient world. The dynamic essence of Judaism lies in the orientation and impetus of its legislation, not in the details and specifications of the Law.

Thus, comparisons have been made between the laws of the Babylonians, Hittites, Assyrians and the laws of the Torah. One is struck, first of all, with the fact that the ancient codes were far more extensive and detailed than the legal documents included in the Pentateuch. Seen against the background of the contemporary cultures, the verses of the Torah are read as so many protests against the existing legislation of the day, or, as emendations of them, in keeping with the creative religious consciousness of the Jewish people.

In the Torah, for example, the tendency toward the softening of penalties for theft, already evident in the successive layers of the Babylonians code, is boldly carried forward. Originally, the penalty for theft was death, then this penalty was restricted to the theft of temple property, then the penalty was commuted to the payment of thirty times the amount stolen, in the case of theft from the state or the church, or ten times the amount stolen, in the case of theft from a private citizen. Still, if the thief could not pay the fine, he was to be put to death. In the Pentateuch, the penalty for theft is the payment of double the amount stolen, in most cases; four and five times the amount, in the event of resale. In all cases, the thief could be sold into slavery for a limited amount of time, if he could not pay the fine, but he was never to be mutilated or put to death.

(Pritchard—"Ancient Near Eastern Texts," p. 166)

The similarity in general detail and dissimilarity in spirit between Babylonian and biblical law is evident also in the laws governing torts. Ponder the biblical insistence on equality before the law with these two ordinances from the Code of Hammurabi—"If a seignior has knocked out a

353

tooth of a seignior of his own rank, they shall knock out his tooth.

If he has knocked out a commoner's tooth, he shall pay one-third mina of silver." (Ibid, p. 175)

Against the background of this legislation, we realize that the point of the biblical command, "an eye for an eye" was to assert the utter impartiality of the law in dealing with offenses to people of differing social status. There is to be no distinction of ranks before the law.

Along with this insistence on equality, the Pentatench illustrates the legal implications of the belief that man is made in the "image of God." Every individual is thus important in his own right, not only as a member of someone's family. This doctrine precluded a mechanical application of the *lex talionis*—such as, the law requiring the bulder's son to be put to death, if a house put up by him collapsed and children died in the wreckage, or the law calling for the ravishing of the daughter of a rapist, by the victim's father. (Ibid, No. 229; Middle Assyrian Laws, Tablet A, 55)

In the comparative study of the laws governing family relations, the resemblances again are in the domain of external forms, and the contrast is in the spiritual impetus, marking biblical and later Talmudic legislation. To the biblical authors, sexual offenses are sins against God, not merely acts of infidelity toward one or more human beings. Thus, in spite of their general tendency toward leniency, the Bible and Talmud reject the principle of the Hittite Code, which stipulates that a man can forgive his wife for the sin of adultery. (Ibid, Hittite Code, No. 198)

Similarly, it was unthinkable for the biblical authors to permit the wife of a soldier to stay in another man's home, until the return of her husband. (Ibid, Middle Assyian Laws, No. 45)

Doubtless, it was this impassioned concern with the purity

and integrity of the family that led to the disavowal in Jewish law of the practice of child adoption—a practice that was sanctioned and minutely regulated in the ancient codes.

As we pursue the growth of Halachah through the documents of the Mishnah and Talmud, we find again that the rabbis made use of the methods and institutions of their contemporary culture. As Prof. Saul Lieberman has pointed out, the principles whereby the Torah was interpreted were adapted from the prevailing methods of Greek grammarians. ("Hellenism in Jewish Palestine"—Lieberman) But, what the rabbis did with the aid of those methods was to translate the ideal aspirations of the prophets into a concrete regimen of life for a whole people. Naturally, legislation of this type was bound to reflect the social pressures and the economic realities of the early centuries of our era, as well as the differing views of nationalist zealots and their opponents. ("M'komo shel Hahalachah B'chochmath Yisrael" by L. Ginsberg; "Toldoth HaHalacha," vol. IV. 4; See also Kassuto's Hebrew commentary on the Book of Exodus.)

In sum, a consistent analysis of the history of Halacha demonstrates that it was developed in the same manner as secular systems of law, through the operation of an ideal factor upon the manifold pressures of society. In the case of secular law, the ideal factor was the inherent logic of the ethical impulse, the aspiration for justice; in the case of Halachah, it was the inspired yearning of prophets, saints and sages for the sanctification of all phases of life. Thus, Halachah is both human and divine—human in its detailed formulation and divine in its essential drive.

The non-monistic character of Jewish tradition may also be seen in the fact that there is no provision for any absolute authority in matters of belief and action. For those who like to walk to heaven on a bridge of steel, there is small comfort indeed within the multifarious domain of tradition. Whenever we encounter a source of authority we also find qualifying factors, so that every decision emerges out of a balance of multiple considerations.

The earliest authority in Judaism was the prophet, and the Book of Deuteronomy specifically refers to the prophets of every generation as possessing the prerogative of rendering decisions in the name of God. (Deuteronomy XVIII, 14-22) In the Talmud, this authority was considerably restricted, and in actual practice, it disappeared completely from Jewish life. ("Yebamoth," 90b) Jeremiah speaks of the "Torah of the priests, the word of the prophets and the counsel of the wise." (Jeremiah 18, 18) In theory, prophecy disappeared from the purview of the Jewish faith, following the death of Malachi. Yet, the system of Jewish law depends for its consummation upon the renewal of the practice of ordination, the reestablishment of the Synhedrin and the return of the Synhedrin to its proper place in the Holy Temple—all developments which assume the interposition of prophetic authority. A goodly portion of the Talmud deals with matters which cannot be reinstituted save through the advent of a prophet. Within the total context of Jewish law, then, room is left for the exercise of prophetic authority, though only in a limited domain and as a preparation for the Messianic Era.

It is frequently asserted that in Judaism, the dead letter of the book holds sway. Needless to say that the Holy Scriptures as such are not the source of authority, since the Oral Law was to govern the interpretation of every biblical verse. The insistence on restricting the authority of the book by the living process of interpretation was precisely the main tenet of the Pharisaic party. Both rationalistic commentators and mystifying Kabbalists operated on the principle, enunciated best by Maimonides, "the gates of interpretation are not closed to us." Nor is the Talmud in Judaism regarded as an infallible authority, like the Koran in Islam. By its very nature as a record of the disputes and discussions in the academies, it cannot serve by itself either as a code of laws or a catechism of beliefs. Indeed, the opinions of those who were in the minority at the academies were preserved in order to permit future courts to reconsider the question in accord with the needs of their day. ("Aidoyoth," I, 5. See Albeck edition, and the Tosefta quoted by RaBD.) As a sacred book, the authority of the Babylonian Talmud was balanced by the Palestinian Talmud, the Midrashim, the decisions of the Geonim, the prevailing practices of the people, the literature of Kabbalah and of Jewish philosophy.

Monolithic authority may be exerted by a self-perpetuating hierarchy, which arrogates to itself the power of ultimate decision in matters of faith. Here, too, we find the seeds of such an institution in Judaism, so balanced however by opposing motives as to be unworkable. The High Court in Jerusalem, as outlined by Maimonides, was to be just such a self-perpetuating body, exerting supreme sway in regard to almost every aspect of Jewish life. Yet, in actual fact, it is doubtful whether any such institution ever existed for any length of time. During the major part of the Second Commonwealth, the sectarian divisions of Judaism were so profound as to leave hardly any scope for the operation of a unitary authoritative body. Most scholars are of the opinion that there were two Synhedrins in the last one hundred years of the Second Commonwealth. The Academy of Jamnia functioned as a quasi-Synhedrin for a while, and the Palestinian academies attempted to retain a kind of hegemony over the Jews of the Diaspora, by their monopoly over the power of ordination ("s'michah"). Yet, this rearguard action did not succeed in resisting the advance of historical forces, and the Babylonian Talmud came to assume in time preeminence over the Talmud of the Palestinian academies. In the sixteenth century, an attempt was made to renew the power of ordination, but this belated endeavor to turn back the clock died aborning.

The project of renewing the Synhedrin is discussed in a different chapter of this book. The inner contradiction in the idea of the Synhedrin is exposed, in that the Synhedrin can only function as the representative body of the entire Jewish people, even while its very concept belongs in the context of ideas long outgrown by the vast majority of Jewish people.

It follows therefore that the rich texture of Jewish tradition is woven out of many diverse strands, and that the distinction of absolute authority cannot be claimed in behalf of any one strand. The amorphous and many sided character of Jewish tradition keeps opposing elements in a dynamic equilibrium, making possible a fresh and creative response to the challenge of every age.

In sum, if Jewish law is to function today, it can only be conceived in the pluralistic pattern of general law. As we have seen, the elements of unity in law are objectively the interpretive body, and subjectively, the willingness on the part of every individual to abide by its precepts. In the domain of religion, the subjective factor is naturally far more important than in civil life. Yet, without the objective factor, there can be no law, in the strict sense of the word.

The divergencies in religious observances today are too great to warrant any hope for the establishment of any unitary body of intepretation. For us of the Conservative movement, the road ahead is clear—the establishment of a rabbinic and lay body for the interpretation of Jewish law as standards of action for our day and the endeavor to persuade ever greater numbers of our people to make these norms and standards part of their own life. We need not fear disunity within the Jewish community, but rather disunity and contradiction within the soul of the individual Jew.

(The substance of a lecture given at the summer Institute for Graduates of the Jewish Theological Seiminary. July, 1953)

10

Ancient Synhedrin or Synhedrin Academy?

No issue in Jewish life affords so delicate a test of one's philosophy of Judaism as the proposal to reestablish the ancient Synhedrin. Compounded of hazy dream-concepts drawn out of the depths of the folk consciousness, as well as of shrewd calculations of partisan strategy, this issue brings to the arena of politics the vagaries of messianic speculation and dares to cast the pitiless spotlight of mundane reality upon the twilight world of naive faith. For the most part, Jewish thinkers have shied away from any attempt to formulate without precision their vision of the days of the future. But now that the State of Israel has been established, the question is bound to arise: What about the Messiah, the Temple, the sacrifices—and the Synhedrin?

"Return our judges as in the days of old and our advisers as in the beginning. . . ." Over and over again, our people have prayed through the long, dark night of exile for the restoration of the ancient judicial system crowned by the Synhedrin, the *Bet-Din Ha-Gadol.* Jewish life in all its pathos and tragedy was founded upon the single base of the Torah, but the living source of Torah was a legend and a dream. Biblical Judaism had never envisaged the situation which prevailed through the many centuries of exile, when no single person or institution could legislate for the entire Jewish people. In the Bible, a living authority is stipulated either in the form of a true prophet or in the capacity of the judge who sits in the appointed place. In later years, the High

Court of the Synhedrin was presumed to be the "place from which teaching issues for Israel."

Exilic existence was never accepted by the masses of our people as in any sense right or final. Long as was the *Galut,* it remained a temporary trial and a passing phase. Hearts and eyes alike were turned to the restoration. It was to be expected, therefore, that once the State of Israel had become a reality, voices would arise calling for reestablishment of the Synhedrin. Rabbi Judah L. Maimon, Minister of Religions in Israel, emerged as the chief protagonist of a renewed Synhedrin, employing the power and prestige of his office for the propagation of this aim. Instantly, the lines were drawn, for and against the project—the old European-trained rabbis in Israel and America protesting, the neo-Orthodox applauding, the secularists deriding. All groups centered, and apparently continue to center, their discussion on the dead shell of the ancient institution, as if one could seriously discuss a proposal to resuscitate the dead. It would seem to be the first principle of historical wisdom to separate the seed from the shell, to recognize that the stream of life flows from vessel to vessel, while the vessels themselves remain lifeless, albeit not without significance. Is not the living substance of institutions the proper object of our concern, rather than the shadows cast by them at one period of history? An historical approach to the ideal of a reconstituted Synhedrin is not only possible but very essential if the State of Israel is to fulfill its function within the total framework of Judaism.

Before proceeding to outline the implications of this viewpoint, let us first deal with the following questions in their proper order:

1. What is meant by the Synhedrin in Jewish tradition?
2. What was the Synhedrin as an historical institution?
3. Can the Synhedrin be revived?

4. What is the permanent validity of the Synhedrin-ideal?

I. Traditional Conception of the Synhedrin

Long after the Synhedrin in Jerusalem had ceased to function, the ideal image of the institution continued to be refined and exalted in the folk imagination. Reality was forgotten; the bitter struggles, the long, tenacious conflicts, and even bloody battles that had swirled around the institution were gradually lost in the oblivion of folk memory. What remained, the picture of an institution purged and purified from the unholy dross of human affairs, is found in various talmudic passages, which were summarized by Maimonides as follows (*Hilkot Mamerim, I*):

> The High Court in Jerusalem was the bearer of the substance of the Oral Law, the pillar of teaching; from it law and judgment issued to all Israel. It was meant in the promise and positive commandment of the Torah: "In accord with the Torah which they will show you. . . ."
>
> He who believes in Moses our Teacher, and in his Torah, is obligated to rely upon it in all matters of religion. . . .
>
> In matters of tradition, there was never any dispute. Wherever you find a dispute, you know it is not a tradition stemming directly from Moses our Teacher. In regard to deductions inferred from the Law, whatever the High Court, in its majority, decrees, becomes law.
>
> So long as the High Court was in existence in Jerusalem, there was no dispute in Israel. . . . When the High Court was discontinued, dispute multiplied in Israel.

The tannaitic source from which Maimonides quoted was even more disturbed over the confusion and chaos that was presumed to have resulted from the demise of the Synhedrin. After describing in detail the manner in which a legal decision could be taken from a lower to a higher court until it was brought for final adjudication to the High Court, sitting "in the Hall of Hewn Stones," in the Holy Temple, the author, R. Jose, concludes: "But ever since the disciples of Hillel and Shammai multiplied, disputes proliferated in Israel, and the Torah became like two Torahs . . ." (B. Sanh. 88b).

Any scholar who refused to accept the decision of the High Court and publicly taught that which was contrary to its word was declared to be a "rebellious scholar" (*zaken mamre*). "They would bring him up to the High Court in Jerusalem and there keep him in confinement until the pilgrim festival, when he would be taken out and put to death publicly, by strangulation" (Maimonides, *op. cit.*, III, 8.) [1]

Empowered thus to assert its authority, the Synhedrin had exclusive jurisdiction in certain matters, in addition to exercising the functions of the highest court of appeals. Thus, the Synhedrin alone could arrange for the ordeal of the suspected woman, the rebellious son, the idolatrous city, and the case of an entire tribe which deviated from the Law. A false prophet and a high priest were subject to the exclusive jurisdiction of the Sanhedrin. No war of aggression could be declared by the king save with the permission of the Synhedrin (B. Sanh. 2a). No king or high priest could be appointed save with the consent of the Sanhedrin of seventy-one members (Tos. Synh. 3).

From this enumeration of the functions of the Synhedrin, it is obvious that it was envisaged as a legislative as well as

[1] The term "rebellious scholar" refers to a person who contradicts the Sanhedrin, not to a heretic, at least not as a heretic is usually understood: "He who does not accept the validity of the Oral Law is not the rebellious scholar mentioned in the Torah; he belongs to the category of *Epikores,* whom all men may surrender to death" (Maimonides, *op. cit.*, III, 1).

a judicial body, investigating the needs and problems of the community and designing its ordinances accordingly. In a fanciful passage of the Talmud, King David is pictured as being spurred on to a war of conquest by the Synhedrin, which reported to him on the intolerable economic conditions in the country: "Thy people Israel require sustenance" (B. Synh. 16a).

The Synhedrin was conceived as a self-perpetuating body. Its members consisted of ordained rabbis, who had received their ordination from similarly ordained men, the chain of authority through the Holy Spirit extending back to Moses, "who ordained the first set of seventy scholars, and the presence of God rested upon them. Thus, those who were ordained drew their authority, man from man, back to the court of Joshua and the court of Moses our Teacher." This type of ordination passed out of Jewish life with the decay and ultimate disappearance of the Palestinian center, partly because the rabbis taught "that scholars may not be ordained outside the Holy Land" (Maimonides, *Hilchoth Sanhedrin*).

This august body of seventy-one duly ordained scholars would appoint judges in every city, including those in the Diaspora, and gradually promote the deserving among them up the ladder of judicial preference. Ideally, therefore, the Synhedrin represented the principle of government by Torah-scholars. Authority in the Synhedrin flowed from the top down—from master to disciple, by way of ordination; from the High Court to the meanest village judge, by way of the ladder of appointment and promotion.[2]

[2] This traditionally envisaged Sanhedrin is said to have voluntarily abdicated its major functions some forty years before the destruction of the Temple (29 C.E.). Thus we read: "Forty years before the destruction of the Temple, the Sanhedrin moved away from its place and settled in a store" (B. Sanh. 41a). Rashi understands this voluntary exile to have been caused by the "multiplication of murderers." Apparently the Sanhedrin found itself unable

In the view of tradition, the Synhedrin was an aspect of the presence of God in Israel. As the Divine Presence moved step by step away from Israel, so the Synhedrin too moved from place to place, losing progressively in divine power and authority. But wherever it was, the Synhedrin was essentially an academy of scholars, presided over by a Nasi. Gradually, however, the authority of the Babylonian academies increased, until they came to overshadow the Palestinian center of learning. The Babylonian Talmud was accepted as the final source of authority, while the Jerusalem Talmud was virtually ignored, being used only for the purpose of clarifying moot points in its Babylonian counterpart. The Geonim of Sura and Pumbeditha sometimes referred to their respective academies as being "in place of" or "like" the Synhedrin. The academy in Palestine also occasionally referred to itself in similar terms. Thus seen through the gathering mists of time, the Synhedrin grew steadily in stature and authority. In the mind of Judah Halevi, for example, it appeared to be a living instrument of the voice of God. The members of the Synhedrin were supposed to have been endowed with every form of earthly wisdom, possessing each in its consummate degree. In addition, they had enjoyed the "direct aid of the Shekinah" as they sat in judgment close to the holy vessels and the altar, which were especially designed to channelize the flow of divine inspiration. (*Kusari,* III, 39, 41).

As the Synhedrin retreated into the background of the

to cope with the situation and abdicated. Thereafter, the laws of murder ceased to be applied throughout the country, since every court derived its authority from the Sanhedrin, which could only function as such when it was seated in the Holy Temple. It is obvious that this passage cannot be taken at its face value, for surely courts do not abdicate their functions because "murderers multiply." Nor is there reference in this passage to the circumstance that the death penalty was then the prerogative of the Roman procurator.

past, it became part of the vision of the messianic future. In the time to come, Elijah the Prophet would initiate the great act of redemption by appearing before the High Court of the Synhedrin and presenting his credentials, as it were, to this great tribunal (B. Erub. 43b).

So much for the Synhedrin in the mind of tradition.

II. The Synhedrin in the Light of History

What was the Synhedrin actually in the light of history? This problem is one of the most obscure and complex in Jewish historiography. The beginnings of the institution are wrapped in mystery, and so is the manner of its functioning in the last generations of the Second Commonwealth. In all likelihood, the Synhedrin shared political power with the Hasmonean princes in the first decades of their rise to power. Many historians assume the existence in the Roman period of two Synhedrins—one political and the other religious, or one Herodian and the other Pharisaic, or one Sadducean and the other Pharisaic. This much is certain, however. During the period of its official predominance, the Synhedrin did not maintain unity in Jewish life. During the Second Commonwealth, the Pharisees and Sadducees battled for control over it. Johanan Hyrkanos, son of the last of the Hasmonean brothers, threw the weight of his power to the Sadducees, turned the Synhedrin over to their control, and promulgated the cancellation of some previously instituted Pharisaic ordinances. His successor, Alexander Jannai, was engaged in a bloody civil war. When he died, his wife brought the Pharisees back to power. Thereafter, the pendulum swung back and forth. Herod massacred all the members of the Synhedrin save one, and in all likelihood appointed his own High Court. Academies of study, led by Hillel and Shammai, took the place of the one supreme court, and there were occasional gatherings of all the scholars for the purpose of enacting new legislation. One such gathering is particularily important, for on that day the Shammaites outnumbered the Hillelites and passed eighteen severe decrees, which had the effect of raising a high barrier between the Jews and their Gentile neighbors. Though the Shammaite majority was achieved by accident and by the employment of force, the decree could not be revoked for many generations.

In addition to the two major contending parties, there were the Essenes, who developed a mystical ritual and philosophy of their own; the Zealots, adherents of what Josephus called the Fourth Philosophy; the Hellenistic Jews of the Diaspora, who maintained varying degrees of allegiance to the central body; the folk-Pharisaic teachers, out of whom Jesus perhaps emerged; as well as numberless other sects. Moreover, the Jews of Egypt had a temple of their own, in which sacrifices were offered, in violation of biblical law. Clearly, the Synhedrin did not maintain unity in Israel.

In the gaonic period, authority was concentrated in the exilarchic-gaonic hierarchy, which was restricted to a small number of pedigreed families. Bitter disputes divided the Babylonian institutions and alienated the Babylonian community from the Palestinian as long as the latter maintained an organized existence. The revival of a small Palestinian center in the tenth century led to the famous controversy between Ben Meir and Saadia, when the festivals were celebrated on different days by the communities following the Palestinian and Babylonian academies respectively. Saadia won in behalf of the Babylonian academies, while the Palestinian center declined steadily until it disappeared altogether during the period of the Crusades.

Following the expulsion from Spain at the end of the fifteenth century, the Palestinian Jewish community began to grow in numbers and influence. In the middle of the sixteenth century, the Galilean town of Safed was the home of many world-renowned Talmudists and Kabbalists. Messianic dreams and mystical visions of redemption filled the air. The eagerly awaited Messiah had not arrived, but the tremor of his wings was felt by distraught and sensitive souls.

In this atmosphere, charged with expectancy and tense with tales of visions and revelations, was born the movement to renew the long-lapsed institution of ordination essential to membership in a Synhedrin. The remnant in Safed felt that theirs was the duty to prepare the ground for the advent of the fulness of redemption by establishing the central institution of Torah-authority, which alone could rightfully welcome Elijah and the Messiah.

The rabbis of Safed were also deeply concerned with the problem of penance and repentance. Turkish lands were filled with erstwhile Marranoes who were terrified at the threat of *karet* ("cut off," in this world and the next) that hovered over their heads because they had yielded to pressure and accepted conversion, even though they had repudiated it in their hearts. Flagellation could, in the logic of talmudic legalism, remove the awful threat of *karet*, but flagellation could be imposed only by a duly ordained court. To save the repentant Marranoes from *karet*, the reestablishment of the Synhedrin was necessary.

This combination of motives prompted the rabbis of Safed to attempt to renew the ancient ordination and to select R. Jacob Berab for the honor of being the first to be ordained. Had their action met with unanimous endorsement, the Synhedrin might perhaps have been gradually renewed and fortified. But R. Levi b. Chaviv of Jerusalem disputed the wisdom and authority of their bold step, and the attempt at regeneration died aborning.

In restrospect, it can be seen that the arguments of the proponents and opponents of the renewal of ordination hinged on the question of relative priority in the process of redemption. Should ordination be renewed and the Synhedrin be reestablished by the concurrence of the rabbis dwelling in the land of Israel, so that Elijah and the Messiah might report to them when the hour of redemption struck? Or was the order to be reversed, with Elijah, in due time, ordaining the members of the Synhedrin? The rabbis of Safed and Jerusalem even debated the question whether Elijah could ordain the members of a renewed Synhedrin. The entire matter evaporated in such speculations.

It was left to a histrionic non-Jew to bring the issue of the Synhedrin to the forum of public discussion once again. Napoleon, who loved to pose in the spotlight of history, was not satisfied with the degree of authority which the Assembly of Notables possessed. In order to make certain of Jewish acceptance of the conditions of French democracy, he convened a "synhedrin" at Paris to ratify the answers of the lay assemblage. In the Christian mind, the Synhedrin had condemned Jesus and had erected barriers against the Gentile world; therefore it was the Synhedrin that must remove those barriers so as to make "fraternity" possible between Jews and non-Jews. With this fantastic farce, the Synhedrin disappeared as an issue from the stage of Jewish life until it was revived again in our day by Rabbi J. L. Maimon.

III.   Can the Synhedrin Be Revived?

Once we remove the issue of a reconstituted Synhedrin from its context in dogma and Halacha, and proceed to analyze its functions in a modern democratic society, we realize at once how hopelessly archaic and obsolete it really is. The Synhedrin is by its very nature an institution that represents the totality of Israel. It is based on the assumption that the Torah, in its fundamentalist interpretation, is binding upon all Israel. Today, the Orthodox groups that would accept such an interpretation constitute a small minority of the total number of Jews in Israel and in the Diaspora. But the Talmud affirms the principle that a law which is not accepted by all the people is not morally binding upon them. Were the Synhedrin to be restricted to the Orthodox community, the barriers between the Orthodox minority and the non-Orthodox majority would become steadily greater. The inevitable result would be the development in Israel of a form of "Trennungs-Orthodoxie," more fanatical and destructive than the German-Hungarian variety. The Orthdox community would be driven ever more definitely into the direction of naive fundamentalism. Moreover, since the scope of the authority of the Synhedrin includes virtually all that affects the life of Jewish people, the creation of a Synhedrin would inevitably involve the establishment of a government within a government, leading to an endless train of troubles.

For all these reasons and others, the revival of the Synhedrin cannot really be favored by the progressive elements in Orthodoxy, let alone the Conservative and Reform groups. Reviewing the difficulties inherent in the proposition, Rabbi S. K. Mirsky, famed Orthodox scholar and editor of *Talpiot,* asserts categorically: "The truth is that no man in Israel proposes the reinstitution of a Synhedrin possessing the power to impose capital punishment and to deal with all the matters which appertained to the Synhedrin that existed at the time of the Holy Temple. Do we then deal with fools?" (*Talpiot,* Dec. 1950, p. 123).

It seems incredible to Rabbi Mirsky that any one should seriously propose the renewal of the ancient Synhedrin.[30]

8 Rabbi Mirsky proposes that instead of a Sanhedrin, a yeshivah, or institution of learning, be established, comprising the best minds in all existing

Yet this is precisely the proposition of Rabbi Maimon, apparently with the sole exception of the power to impose capital punishment. Rabbi Maimon is motivated not so much by the desire of a pietistic antiquarian for the revival of ancient splendor as by the sober considerations of realistic strategy. It cannot be denied, even by its defenders, that traditional Halacha is antiquated, inflexible, and ill-suited to the needs and ideals of the modern age. Many Orthodox rabbis who violently castigate the endeavors of the Conservative rabbinate to bring the Law into harmony with life, nevertheless sincerely believe that many drastic changes in the Law are long overdue. They do not oppose the specific modifications of the Law so much as the principle of modification. They cannot help but recognize the pressing need for radical changes, but they dispute the right of any existing authority to effect such changes. In their view, only a duly constituted Synhedrin would be entitled to enact such legislation as would permit mixed pews in the synagogues and the employment of an organ in the service; the relaxation of the Sabbath laws so as to allow riding to the synagogue or the use of electric lights; the raising of the status of women insofar as their rights as witnesses and judges are concerned; the modernization of Jewish civil and criminal law so that it could be used in the courts of Israel; the modernization of the laws of divorce, *agunah,* and *halitzah,* so as to remove the glaring injustices in this area; and the like.

These progressive Orthodox circles, then, favor the revival of the Synhedrin as a means of modernizing Orthodox prac-

Torah institutions of Israel and the Diaspora. This institution would grow in prestige and power until, in the unforseeable future, it might possibly evolve into a quasi-Synhedrin. Rabbi Maimon also proposes to begin with a yeshivah of some sort, but he does not pretend to await messianic developments. He aims definitely and distinctly at a Synhedrin, and he believes that "in four or five years," the proposed yeshivah could evolve into a full-fledged Synhedrin (*Yedion Misrad Ha-Datot,* Nov. 1950, p. 26) .

tice. They do not think of the Synhedrin as a precursor to the Messiah but as a means of mitigating the intolerable rigidity of the Law. It can easily be seen, however, that were an Orthodox Synhedrin constituted, it would be speedily torn apart between the truly Orthodox people, who really believe in the existing body of practices and customs, esteeming them to the pinnacle of divine perfection, and those who in practice remain loyal to the forms of Orthodoxy, but who in thought yearn for flexibility and adaptability, having been stirred by the vitalizing breath of modern life and thought.

Leaving aside for the present the practical question as to which group is likely to prevail within a reconstituted Orthodox Synhedrin and the theoretical question as to whether there exists sufficient common ground for them to work together, let us ask ourselves: Did Judaism really freeze its forms into a rigid inflexible pattern as soon as the Synhedrin was discontinued? In other words, is the revival of the Synhedrin indispensable for the modernization of the Jewish Law in all its branches?

An examination of the principles of Jewish religious legislation leaves no room for doubt that the *takkanah*-making power of a Jewish assembly is virtually unlimited. It was not for the lack of an instrument that the ritual law was frozen and rendered out of joint with the times, but because of the somberness of the pietistic mood, the failure of nerve, and the narrowness of vision. To effect the necessary changes, a new spirit and a new approach are needed, not the evoking of an institution, which in its literal sense is utterly and irrevocably obsolete.

That new laws were instituted following the dissolution of the last vestige of the Synhedrin in the land of Israel is abundantly evident. The Babylonian Talmud, in all the vastness of its scope, was accepted as authoritative, superseding the Palestinian Talmud, which had been edited a century and a half earlier by those who were duly ordained.

The Babylonian Talmud instituted a number of modifications of the ancient customs in the direction of leniency, arousing the ire of the fanatical die-hards, whose smoldering resentment flared up many generations later in the rise of the Karaite movement. Nevertheless, the Babylonian Talmud, composed in the Diaspora by an academy of non-ordained scholars, superseded the body of tradition that was authoritatively codified in the Palestinian academies by duly ordained rabbis.

Thus, the Rif writes (end of Tractate Erubim) : "Since the sense of the discussion in our [Babylonian] Talmud favors a lenient decision, we do not heed the prohibitions contained in the Jerusalem Talmud, for we rely on our Talmud, which was made later. The sages who edited it knew the Palestinian Talmud better than we do."

The Babylonian sages did not seem to be hampered by any feeling of lack of authority in imposing the laws of the Talmud upon the communities under their rule. While they did not possess the prerogative of enforcing the penalties of the Torah, they did apply so-called rabbinic flagellation, which was physically quite equal in pain and effectiveness.

The geonim did not hesitate to promulgate new ordinances in accord with the needs of their day. Thus, they would compel a man to divorce his wife if she demanded it, because they feared that otherwise the woman might have recourse to non-Jewish courts. Sensitive to the Karaite criticism of the legends in the Talmud, they declared the entire Aggada of Talmud and Midrash to be devoid of authority.

When the focus of Jewish life shifted to the lands of western Europe, the rabbis knew themselves to be entitled to institute such *takkanot* as were needed in their day and age, abolishing old prohibitions and legislating new ones without waiting for a Synhedrin. Rabbenu Gershom's imposition of monogamy upon Ashkenazi Jewry is the best known of these ordinances. Maimonides writes: "If a court finds it necessary to abolish temporarily a positive commandment, or to violate a negative commandment, in order to bring many people back to the faith or to save many from stumbling in various matters, it is permitted to act in accord with the need of the hour. As a surgeon may see fit to cut off a person's hand or a foot in order to save his life, so a court may at any one time teach the violation of some of the mitzvot, for a time, in order to save them in their totality . . ." (*Hilkot Mamerin*, II, 4).

As a general rule, Sephardic authorities held that the elected representatives of a community had every right to legislate for its members. An oft-quoted decision of R. Solomon Ibn Adret's reads: "Every community is permitted to erect fences and to legislate in their city as the High Court was permitted to establish ordinances for the whole of Israel" (Rashba, *Responsa*, 280).

It follows from all this that the revival of the Synhedrin is not needed for the purpose of aligning the Law with the needs of modern life. An assembly of rabbis from the land of Israel could well legislate such amendments as are now needed in Israel. They might find it advisable to associate with themselves rabbis from other parts of the world so as to increase the range of applicability of their legislation. But it is neither expedient nor proper to invoke the mystic aura of the Synhedrin for the purpose of overcoming the resistance of die-hards to amending the Law. You cannot generate the spirit of self-renewal by trying to turn back the clock of time and pretending to breathe fresh life into an institution that Jewry has outgrown by many centuries. You cannot move forward, by going backward; you cannot capture and direct the spirit of religious rebirth by conjuring up the ghosts of long ago, especially when they have died a natural death.

IV. What Is Permanent in the Synhedrin Ideal?

While the revival of the Synhedrin, in whole or in part, cannot be favored, the attempt can and should be made to translate for our times the creative ideas that were inherent in this ancient institution. It is the seed of the ancient Synhedrin that we must discover and transplant in Israel reborn.

The Synhedrin represents first of all the living vehicle of the spirit of *K'lal Yisrael*. In our day and age, there is profound need of an institution that would represent the unity of life, thought, and inspiration that is Judaism. We cannot have conformity in religious practice since the ceremonial pattern of faith is largely affected by the changing forms of civilization. The Jewish people in our day live in several different civilizations—the Anglo-American, the Continental European, the Sephardic-Mediterranean, and the stagnant Oriental cultures. Within each civilization group, there are people of varying degrees of integration with the most creative phases of their own culture. The patterns of religious practice that may be desirable in Israel are not necessarily suitable for Jewish people in America. Unity in the sense of conformity of religious ritual is utterly unthinkable in the circumstances of our time.

Unity in the political field is equally illusory. The government of Israel cannot pretend to speak for Jews living outside its boundaries, and the World Zionist Organization is vainly struggling to hold on to a semblance of function in this rapidly changing world. It was originally supposed to be a "parliament in transition" of a people about to be settled in a new territory. Today, the settlement is almost completed, and American Jewry, the vital focus of the Diaspora, does not claim to be in transit. Once the momentum of smooth shibboleths and vested interests is spent, the ghost of the World Zionist Organization will be allowed its deserved rest.

Yet the unity of the Jewish people should be expressed in a concrete fashion. In recent decades, when the pressure of Jewish needs compelled collective action on an organized political basis and when Jewish leadership was influenced by the prevailing political fashion in western Europe, it was natural enough for the Jewish craving for unity to find expression in such organizations as the World Zionist Organization and the World Jewish Congress. Now that the needs have changed, we should revert to the kind of institution that best reflects the genius of our tradition.

I would therefore suggest the creation of a Synhedrin-Academy to consist of Jewish scholars and leaders in every field of culture and achievement, chosen from among the world-wide community of Israel. Meeting annually, this convocation of the best representatives of the spirit of Judaism would deal with the moral and spiritual problems of the land of Israel, of the Jewish people, and of humanity. Its discussions and decisions would, of course, not be binding upon the government of Israel, though it would no doubt take up for review and critical appraisal the moral issues involved in the debates and proceedings of the Kenesset.

In addition to its plenary sessions, or in preparation for them, the Synhedrin-Academy could appoint commissions to study the various problems of Israel and humanity, utilizing the facilities of the government of Israel for the dissemination of its findings. Its commissions could also be made available for the settlement of labor disputes in Israel, and for the discovery of a moral basis for the solution of the manifold cultural, religious, and social conflicts that inevitably arise in the birth of a new society.

The discussions of the Synhedrin-Academy, constituting as they would a running commentary upon the varied problems of the Jew in particular and of man in general, would in time perhaps come to form a new Talmud, expressive of the best thought of our time. World Jewry, through its leading representatives, would be given the opportunity to think together, and to unfold the implications of Jewish tradition for the understanding of the crises of our own day and age.

The conception of a Synhedrin-Academy is new only in its application to the modern scene. It actually embodies the best elements in our tradition and reflects the peculiar genius of our faith. We know that in Judaism life and faith are not discrete entities. It has ever been the spirit and tendency of Judaism to invade every phase of life and to impress its seal upon all aspects of existence. Nothing which is human is outside the sphere of Judaism.

It has been said of Judaism that it is a religion of law, in contrast to Christianity, which is held to be predominantly a religion of "feeling." Neither designation is quite correct, but the contrast is justified at least in the difference of orientation and emphasis between the two faiths. In Judaism, inwardness is a virtue, but Torah, in its development along the main highway of Halacha, stresses the implications of righteous living for the individual and the community. Said a sage of an earlier age: "Nothing that a Jew does is just neutral or ethically indifferent; every action constitutes either a *mitzvah* or an *aberah*."

But if Judaism thus strives to bring every aspect of life within its domain, is it not its logic, then, to establish an absolute theocracy? This question goes right to the heart of the project to revive the ancient Synhedrin and reveals the inevitable failure of that idea. The way out of this dilemma is to repudiate the sterile concept of the Synhedrin as a judicial and legislative body, and to replace it with the notion of a Synhedrin-Academy, which would develop the

377

implications of a moral and spiritual approach without imposing its views upon the people as a matter of law.

In Judaism, the principle of absolute freedom of the moral agent acts as a counterbalance to the dogmatic delineation of the last implications of the moral law. This polarity of the moral act would make it possible for the Synhedrin-Academy to search out the ultimate meaning of the spiritual dimension of life, while at the same time remaining merely an advisory agency, appealing to the uncoerced consent of the free and the responsible.

The ideal of a Synhedrin-Academy is applicable to all countries, but it is of special urgency in the land of Israel, where it might serve as the living embodiment of the spiritual-cultural entity that is Israel. We do not want to convert the prophet into the politician; let the two be heard side by side for the enlightenment of mankind.

SUPPLEMENTARY NOTES

I. Rabbi J. L. Maimon's Hiddush Ha-Sanhedrin

Rabbi J. L. Maimon discusses the function of a renewed Sanhedrin in exceedingly vague terms. He draws a parallel with the Great Assembly, which was organized by Ezra and Nehemiah at the beginning of the Second Commonwealth, and which established new forms and patterns for Jewish life. But though he implies that a similar function would fall to the renewed Sanhedrin, he insists that all the decisions of the ancient Sanhedrin were simply expressions and enactments of laws they had received from their masters, going back to the time of Moses (pp. 9, 28). Thus, the contradiction between the spirit of self-renewal and the mood of tenacious clinging to a revealed, all-embracing body of laws and practices, is not transcended in the author's mind.

In general, Rabbi Maimon defines the Sanhedrin as the instrument for uniting the rule of Torah with the state, so that Israel might not be "like unto the other nations." "This longing for a

Jewish state paralleling the governments of other nations is non-Hebraic, non-messianic, and not in accord with the entire course of our history. . . . For a state, as conceived in the actions of both East or West, is by its innermost structure, essence, and purpose, nothing but a danger to the ethnical development of mankind. . . . Some readers will tell me, 'Our state will be different' . . . But, I beg you, let us not deceive ourselves and others. A state, patterned along national lines, will behave no differently than it does among the other nations . . . It must serve as a means to a higher goal and a nobler purpose—that of the cultivation of Torah and the intensification of the influence of Judaism; for 'Zion and Torah' have been inseparable in all generations and at all times; both, Torah and the state, require each other and supplement each other" (pp. 30, 31).

This general statement does not indicate how the Sanhedrin would fit into the structure of a democratic state. Rabbi Maimon writes:

"This task, to point out to the state the path that it must follow, to open up anew the wells and fountains of our original creation, which foreign cultures have clogged up, to show us and our children after us the beauty of our Torah, its laws and commandments—for this noble function, many-branched and laden with responsibility, we require the renewal of the Sanhedrin in our new state . . . With the creation of the government of Israel, new horizons were opened up for religious, traditional Torah-Judaism . . . The day will soon come when answers to the most difficult questions will be asked, questions that have been occasioned by the rise of the state and the numerous inventions of modern life . . ." (pp. 32, 33).

The "inventions of modern life" are with us, here and now, and the questions arising from their use are real and concrete. Yet Rabbi Maimon does not cite one specific example in which the Sanhedrin would act differently from the Chief Rabbinate and the other halachic authorities in Israel. He lists the chief functions of the renewed Sanhedrin as being: " (1) to explain the meaning of Torah; (2) to search out the details of each *mitzvah*, in all its branches; (3) to order new decrees and to legislate new ordinances, when the hour or generation require it" (p. 58). Each one of these functions has been exercised by the rabbis of every age. Rabbi Maimon does not indicate wherein the renewed Sanhedrin would differ from assemblies of rabbis in the past, such as the Council of the Four Lands, for example.

Rabbi Maimon is even willing to forego the conception of the Sanhedrin as the highest judicial body and to think of it as an advisory body. "This Sanhedrin that we hope to see renewed will not have the power to impose the penalty of death, since it will not be seated in the Hall of Hewn Stones. But its functions will be many and highly important—to exalt the Torah and to intensify its influence upon our state, without compulsion or force, but through wisdom and sagacity, understanding and knowledge" (p. 44).

In the last analysis, his appeal is directed to the vague and inchoate hopes of the messianic future: "The renewal of the Sanhedrin must precede the advent of the Messiah" (p. 23); "This attempt to cause the 'shekinah' to rest in the camp of Israel we can achieve only through the renewal of the Sanhedrin in our renewed state" (p. 29).

These pious yearnings, however, coincide emotionally with the shrewd calculation of practical strategy: "It is necessary merely for all of us to *feel* that the star of Torah-Judaism can and ought to rise only through the renewal of the Sanhedrin" (p. 44).

II. On the Sanhedrin as an Instrument of Progress in Jewish Life

The progressive Orthodox rabbis, who hope that a renewed Sanhedrin would abolish the irksome and spiritually obsolete ordinances of the *Shulhan Aruch,* have not yet become articulate in an earnest fashion. However, a great halachic authority of the past generation—whose views were repudiated by his colleagues —stated their case with brilliance and erudition in his book, *Malki Bakodesh* (J. L. Hirshenson, *Malki Bakodesh,* Hoboken, N. J., 1921).

Speaking of the renewal of ordination and the establishment of a Sanhedrin, Rabbi Hirshenson writes (vol. ii, pp. 7-8).

"The decrees and Torah-fences, which our sages established in accord with their obligation to 'maintain the watches of the Lord,' were always made with wisdom, knowledge, and deep understanding in response to the circumstances of the time. Many of these ordinances were designed for the preservation of our people in exile, and are not suited to the life of a free people, aiming to be like unto the other nations.

"When we endured the life of the *galut,* fences and prohibitions were adequate to our spiritual needs . . . But, they are not adapted to the spirit of a free people . . . The fences which rob them of their freedom will not help them but cause them to rebel . . . To guide free men and women, we must strive to awaken the delights of morality and the spirit, to stir the soul that it might glory in noble ideals, not to decree prohibitions upon ourselves . . .

"The function of the Sanhedrin is but one—to offer patterns of spiritual living to a vital people . . . They must see to it that life shall not narrow faith, nor faith narrow the province of life . . . They will have to employ the power of leniency, abolishing the restrictions which serve no useful purpose, for this indeed is one of the functions of Elijah and his court . . .

"But all these amendments must be made in accord with faith and Halacha, not after the fashion of the Reform leaders, who sought to improve the faith by breaking holes in the wall of the Torah of Israel. Actually, it is possible to open a broad door through the wall of the Torah and the halakah . . ."

Rabbi Hirshenson's views were denounced by the majority of his Orthodox colleagues. Rabbi Kuk, who himself cherished hopes for the renewal of the Sanhedrin, agreed with Rabbi Hirshenson only in the view that the renewal of the Sanhedrin should be accomplished before the Holy Temple was built and in advance of the coming of the Messiah. In a letter to Rabbi Hirshenson, he wrote:

"But I agree with you that we may not proceed to renew the practice of bringing sacrifices prior to an open appearance of the Holy Spirit in Israel. But this hope is not too remote or too wondrous to contemplate. It may be well that the Master whom we seek will arrive in his Temple suddenly, along with the angel of the Covenant for whom we long. Then, the Holy Temple will be built . . ."

11

Future of the American Jew—A Review[1]

The author of this book has been preoccupied all his life
with the problems suggested by its title. While the attention
of our generation was almost wholly focused on the tragedy
of European Jewry and the promise of the emergent State of
Israel, Professor Kaplan has not ceased to remind us that
the future of our own community cannot be taken for
granted. His thundering insistence on the need for "recon-
structing" Judaism, in its theoretical structure and in its
communal organization, has served as a clarion call, which
did not go unheeded, even if it was not fully accepted. Ever
since the publication of his classic, work, *Judaism as a Civilization,* his blueprint for the reorganization of American
Jewish society constituted the kind of challenge which could
be either embraced or rejected, but not ignored. In the
fourteen years which have intervened between the appearance of his first major opus and the one presently under
discussion, he drew to the banner of The Reconstructionist
Society some of the most vigorous and fruitful writers in the
ranks of the rabbinate and of Jewish leadership generally.
In a series of essays and minor books published in the last
decade and a half, he continued to offer supplementary expositions of the different phases of his thesis. Though it
includes some previously published portions, the present
volume is, on the whole, a complete and systematic presentation of the author's philosophy and program.

[1] *The Future of the American Jew,* by Mordecai M. Kaplan. New York, The
Macmillan Co., 1948, pp. xx+571.

Naturally, no reviewer can possibly do justice to the immense scope and profundity of this volume, which deals in an earnest and thought-provoking manner with every phase of Jewish life. Accordingly, this reviewer will confine himself to a critical analysis of the central argument of the volume, it being understood that the value of this monumental work, even as that of a precious many-colored tapestry, is far in excess of the strength of the central thread of reasoning, which will be subjected herein to our scrutiny.

The Problem

What, then, is the core of the volume? The future of the American Jew is put under a question mark, but not on account of the widespread fear of an eruption of antisemitic fury paralleling the course of events in Nazi Germany. The author rightly condemns the irresponsible propaganda which insinuates, day in and day out, at mass meetings throughout the country, that the concentration camps in Europe were only an example of what is in store for us in this country. He believes in the soul of America and in the essential invincibility of the spirit of democracy. Far from fearing the physical extinction of the Jewish population in America, he looks forward to the steady growth of the ideals of freedom and democracy which serve to bring the Jew ever closer to his neighbors. Though he does not believe that antisemitism, nourished through myth and malice for centuries, can be fully eradicated in our time, he feels that the gates are not shut tight against those who would flee our camp. There is a certain measure of inevitability in our lives as Jews, but it is not absolute or inexorable. Thus, we may lose the capacity to live Jewishly with joy and zest, even if our Judaism lingers on to a slow and painful extinction. Hence, Jewish survival in America may not be taken for granted.

Already the signs of danger are manifold. There is, in the first place, that much discussed sense of inferiority and insecurity which besets the modern Jew. Generally speaking, he is likely to echo the notorious remark of Heinrich Heine, "Judaism is not a religion, but a misfortune." This note is dominant, of course, in the minds of the peripheral masses of our people, who remain unaffected by all the movements in our midst, but it is undeniably present also in the background of the consciousness even of those who lead our synagogues and direct the Zionist movement. At a recent trades' meeting of the U. J. A. in Chicago, following the announcement of the establishment of the State of Israel, a wealthy owner of a chain of Super-Markets arose and, brandishing a bottle of whiskey, shouted, "Now, people can't call me a 'damn Jew' any more. I got a country of my own." If a so-called "good Jew" could thus imply that the insulting epithet was previously justified, what must be the attitude to his Jewish heritage of the marginal Jew? That the Jewish quality is not an asset, but a liability, seems to be the silent premise of the thinking of more people than we dare admit, though some are determined to make the most of it.

No wonder, then, that symptoms of disintegration are to be seen on all sides,—in the sorry statistics of Jewish education, in the enormous numbers of our people who shun the synagogues and in the increasing mixed marriages. Only recently Nathan Goldberg published a study which indicates that, in some sections of the country, at least, the rate of inter-marriage has increased from one per cent at the turn of the century, to six per cent at the present time. What, then, should be done, in order to stem the tide of disintegration and desertion?

The answer of Dr. Kaplan results directly from his analysis of the situation. The reason for the breakdown of Jewish loyalties in our time is to be sought in the character of the twin challenges that the Jewish community has thus far proved unable to meet. The challenge of democratic nationalism arose as an aftermath of the French Revolution, which shattered the walls of the Ghetto, removed the yoke of civil disabilities and made the Jewish people part of the nations among whom they lived. The Synhedrin at Paris and the subsequent gatherings of Jewish notables in Westphalia and in the German principalities concurred generally in the proposition that the Jewish people was thenceforth to be regarded as a religious community. Thus the politico-socio-economic basis was removed from the previously self-governing Jewish communities and the individual Jew was set free to participate in the general civilization of the outside world. At the same time, the binding power of the Jewish religion was weakened by the agnostic and humanistic bent of the modern spirit, which the author designates as the challenge of naturalism. Our task is, therefore, defined as the problem of dealing with the challenges of democratic nationalism and naturalism.

At this point, Dr. Kaplan observes that both nationalism and naturalism appear in beneficent and malignant forms. Thus, nationalism manifested itself in our own day as the all-consuming fury of Nazism, which derived from the principle that the welfare and growth of the nation were the supreme ends of existence so that even genocide is justified if it serves the interests of the nation. Democratic nationalism, on the other hand, limits the claim of the nationalistic ideal by the considerations of the welfare of humanity and the rights of the individual. In the same way, the spirit of naturalism sometimes appears in the mischievous guise of "scientism," the determination to regard nothing as valid which is not proven true by the experimental methods of science—an attitude which cannot but issue in total nihilism, since no moral or spiritual values are susceptible of experimental verification. A higher naturalism, which is usually denoted by the term, humanism, includes the moral standards and aspirations of man within its scheme of values and allows an area of doubt beyond the borders of proven facts, wherein the "right to believe" is recognized as legitimate. This true form of naturalism recognizes that there is more to life than eating, drinking and making merry. Our true self-fulfilment as human beings is attained only when we are enabled "to add our mite toward rendering this wordly life more livable for generations to come." (p. 32)

It would seem from this analysis that the liberal type of nationalism and the humanistic type of naturalism ought to constitute the response of the Jew to the challenge of the modern spirit. Thus, in alliance with other liberal forces, the Jews would seek to combat the romantic "blood and soil" manifestations of nationalism; to magnify the significance of the concept of statehood, a term which embraces all citizens without any distinctions of race, creed or color; and to deprecate the importance of the biological and ethnic factors in the nationalistic ideal. By the same token, the challenge of naturalism would be met by drawing a clear line of demarcation between the sweet kernel and the hard shell, accepting the one and rejecting the other. Such a solution, however, does not meet with the favor of the author, who feels that the resulting synthesis would not offer the Jew sufficient motivation to remain within the fold. The only kind of motivation remaining on this basis is religious, since liberal nationalism does not favor the idea of minority national groups clinging to their own ways perpetually and forming ghettos of their own. Since it sees no special value in national folkways, liberal nationalism expects both the minority and the majority groups to regard the folkways of the minority with amused tolerance and to smooth the road for the eventual levelling of all barriers between them.

In contrast, romantic nationalism envisages the nation as a quasi-biological entity, in which the elements of culture and religion express the national psyche or genius, and the national folkways are treasured as the authentic expressions of the nation's character. The natural ally of organized religion is romantic nationalism, especially if the religion in question had long been historically associated with the life of the nation. But, romantic nationalism is manifestly a menace to the status of Jewish people everywhere and to the peace of the world, as was demonstrated by German Nazism. Should the Jew, then, ally himself with the liberal types of of nationalism and thereby help undermine the ethnic loyalties in Jewish society, or should he throw in his fortune with romantic nationalism for the sake of the added impetus it might provide for Jewish civilization?

Dr. Kaplan attempts to evade both horns of the dilemma. While paying his respects to democratic nationalism, he seeks to make its romantic phases "safe for Jewish life." Accordingly, he proposes a blend of romantic nationalism and humanist naturalism, in which different facets of the synthetic conception are exposed to face the brunt of the differing attacks against Judaism. When faced with the naturalistic attack against the worthwhileness of the Jewish religion, the author would expound the nationalistic phase of Jewish loyalty, while against the challenge of democratic nationalism, which regards as reactionary the attempt of minority nationalities to defy the natural processes of assimilation, he would argue that Jewish loyalty is essentially religious in character.

Phrased thus baldly, the Reconstructionist conception appears to be evasive in its essence and utterly artificial. It seems to embrace the modern doctrines of democratic nationalism and naturalism; yet, it takes refuge from the challenge of the former in the vague, quasi-religious penumbra of the latter, while it seeks to escape from the full impetus of the latter movement by resorting to the dark limbo of the romantic phases of the former.

Professor Kaplan employs his vast erudition and keen perception to marshall an impressive array of facts in favor of the naturalness and reasonableness of the program that he advocates. He demonstrates that religion is the natural fruition of a people's civilization. In ancient times, prior to the emergence of Zoroastrianism, every people had its own religion, which was the natural expression of its culture. It was then almost unthinkable for a people to accept an alien religion, save as a part of the process of complete amalgamation with another group. Thus the Alexandrines, in their petition to the Roman emperor, Claudius, asked how the Jews, who did not take part in the rites, could be citizens of Alexandria? It follows that religion may not be viewed as an independent sphere of life and thought, offering its own intellectual justification and emotional motivation, capable of being abstracted and set up as a thing apart from the rest of the nation's life. The conditions prevailing in primitive societies must be regarded as the norm, and the entire history of Europe and America, which culminated in the modern principle of the separation of Church and State, must be judged as being no more than a temporary episode. Eventually, the modern nations, too, will develop religions of their own, as the Nazis tried to do for the German people. For, essentially "religion is the product of a people's life, the soul of its civilization." (p. 45)

"The religious element in a people's civilization is objectified in those institutions, places, historic events, popular heroes and all other objects of popular reverence to which superlative importance, or sanctity, is ascribed. These *sancta*, the attitude toward life that they imply and the specific observances that they inspire, together constitute the religion of a people." (p. 46)

388

Since religion and nationalism are thus one in their roots, it is possible for us to consider the legitimacy of their synthesis in Jewish loyalty. Accordingly, the author offers the conception of "Judaism as a religious civilization," as, the theoretical foundation for the "reconstruction" of Jewish life.

Judaism as a Religious Civilization

In his first major work, Professor Kaplan described Judaism as a civilization. For a number of years, however, the term, religious civilization, has been current in Reconstructionist literature. The significance of this new emphasis is explained by the author as follows:

"Since, then, every civilization has religious *sancta*, what do we mean when we speak of Judaism as a religious civilization? We affirm the truth that the Jewish people, under the leadership of its Lawgivers, Prophets and Sages, considered the chief function of its collective life to be the fostering of its *sancta*. It sought *consciously* to make its collective experience yield meaning for the enrichment of the life of the individual Jew." (p. 46)

This explanation, it appears obvious to the reviewer, does not capture the essential plus involved in the transmutation of a civilization into a religion, or a religious civilization, since it is quite possible for a nationalist movement, especially under oppression, to seek consciously the fostering of its *sancta* and to believe that, in so doing, it enriches the life of the individual, without presuming to become a religion. After all, religion is a domain of the spirit containing a series of metaphysical propositions, no matter how dimly or naively conceived, a fundamental orientation of heart and mind toward the mystery of the universe and a regimen of life reflecting these beliefs and attitudes. In the case of the Jewish religion, it was not collective Jewish experience, as such,

389

that became the content and import of the Jewish religion, but the interpretation of that experience in the light of certain ethical and spiritual principles.

Manifestly, neither enslavement in Egypt, nor liberation from it, was, in itself, capable of conditioning people to love the stranger, to respect the slave, to observe the Sabbath as a day of rest for all laborers, and to hold no Egyptian in contempt. History records entirely contrary reactions to similar experiences. The suffering of Israel was not unique in ancient times, but the prophetic insights and ideals, in the light of which the travail of Israel was interpreted, constituted a new and challenging revelation of the Divine Will. Thus, we should fail to grasp the essence of the Jewish religion, if we were to view it as simply the product of Jewish historical experiences. In general, Dr. Kaplan's definition leaves but a minor role for the ideational element in the great religions and is suited more for an anthropologist, studying the ways of primitive society, than for the purpose of capturing the essential forces in modern Jewish society.

But, leaving aside for the moment the question of the historical accuracy of the above quoted statement in reflecting the motivation of pre-modern Jewry, let us endeavor to understand wherein this conception differs from the previously current notions of Judaism. The author contrasts his conception with that of classical Reform, which confirmed the formula of the Paris Synhedrin, on the one hand, and with that of the Versailles Conference, which worked out the principle of minority national autonomy, on the other hand. The Reform conception of Judaism as a religion he describes as reducing Judaism to a collection of "universal and eternal truths to be derived from our sacred writings. These truths are not in the category of Jewish laws and distinctive cultural forms, which are purely national in character and, therefore, obsolete, now that Jews are either willing or expected to renounce their nationhood." (p. 34)

Dismissing Neo-Orthodoxy as dogmatic and Conservative Judaism as lacking "a definite ideology," he does not recognize the need for outlining the difference between his conception and that of the positive-historical group, which, in a general way, represented the dominant opinion in West European Jewry, and which is presently held by a considerable section of the rabbinate, the section, to-wit, which is neither classical Reform, nor secularistic, nor yet Reconstructionist. While the definitive formulations of this group may differ in details of emphasis, it recognizes, on the one hand, that the central motivations of Jewish life in history were religious, and, on the other hand, it maintains that the recognition of this fact does not call for the pruning of the cultural and historical elements from the body of Jewish faith and practice. It must not be forgotten that the Paris Synhedrin, which accepted for Jewry the status of a religious community, did not consist of Reform rabbis, and that the non-Reform communities in Western Europe and America did not challenge this concept until the advent of modern Herzlian Zionism. These facts are cited herein, not for the purpose of suggesting that the author's view has been anticipated, but, on the contrary, to demonstrate the contrast between it and the positive-historical view, which may be designated as Conservative.

In the Conservative view, then, Judaism is defined as the religion of Israel. Anyone who breaks completely with the Jewish faith is no longer to be regarded as part of the congregation of Israel. The basic motivation and purpose of Jewish life is, and must remain, the resolve to mold oneself in the Torah pattern of piety so as to be pure in the sight of God and man. Those who are religiously indifferent and ag-

391

nostic, but who share in some observances, be it only those of circumcision and burial, are still to be considered part of the Jewish community, so long as they do not break with the Jewish religion, through conversion or through an overt act of renunciation. The Jewish community should, accordingly, be regarded as a religious community, with the religious institutions constituting the core of its organizational structure. This unequivocal affirmation of the religious status of Jewry does not, however, imply the rejection of the Hebrew language, of Zion, or of the unity of world Israel. In every religious group historical elements are taken in and molded into an organic pattern of symbols, ceremonies and loyalties—an ideational and valuational structure which may evolve through its own momentum, or change through the responses evoked from it to the various challenges of time, but which endures, nonetheless, as an organic whole. The Jewish pattern of piety places the living Jewish people, with all its memories, aspirations and cultural achievements, in the center of the cosmic drama, so that whatever is genuinely and creatively Jewish is viewed through the perspectives of faith and then adjudged its proper place in the hierarchy of Jewish values. This conception is essentially the traditional one, minus the element of fundamentalist dogma, or it may also be regarded as the Reform conception, minus the Mendelssohnian-Spinozistic distinction between the essential principles of Judaism, which are admitted to be true and eternal, and the "laws," which are supposed to be national in character.

Is this conception identical with the one proposed by the author? In spite of occasional ambiguities, which seem to be in accord with this conception, the whole purport of the argument in this volume militates against this view. He does, indeed, maintain that "we Jews shall strive to achieve a community status which is analogous to that of the Catholic

Church." (p. 99) Thus, he seems to be arguing for the status of a religious community, though the parallel with the Catholic Church is misleading, since the essence of the Catholic organization is uniformity in dogma and hierarchial authoritarianism, whereas the essence of the Jewish situation is utter diversity in belief and democratic equality. He is, on occasion, ready to admit that Protestant Christianity, too, may be regarded as a religious civilization. Hence, the logical conclusion would seem to be that the status of American Jewry should be exactly analogous to those of the Catholic and Protestant churches. But, this impression is negated completely by the suggestion that he describes as being "the first step toward self-emancipation" to wit, that "World Jewry should unite as a people, and apply to the United Nations for recognition of its claim to peoplehood." (p. 80)

What are the boundaries of a civilization? Most historians employ the term civilization in a wider sense than is connoted by the conception of a national culture. Thus, we speak of Western civilization as the common culture of Western Europe and America. Certainly, in this sense, the civilization of America Jewry is identical with that of Western Catholism and Protestantism. By the same token, there is far more of a gulf in civilizational terms between the American and Yemenite Jews, than there is between the Jewish and Protestant Americans. As a civilization is commonly understood to be a composite of certain cultural attitudes, forms of social structure, moral standards and ways of life, there is no reason to assume that the modern Jew differs in any civilizational aspect from his Christian neighbor. Actually, Dr. Kaplan employs the term, civilization, in a strictly national or ethnic sense, when he applies it to Judaism, since he makes no effort to prove that the Jewish attitude to the universe is somehow different from that of Western man.

Fundamentally, his argument implies that the invisible

bonds which unite Jewry and make of it an organic society are national in character. However, in the West, generally, and in America, in particular, national loyalties cannot permanently serve as the basis for Jewish survival, since such loyalties are incompatible with the spirit of democratic nationalism of the dominant majority. Hence, the national group loyalties of Jewry must be clothed in the guise of a religious community so as to parallel in external appearance the Catholic and Protestant churches. This guise is not a disguise, in the author's opinion, since the Jewish community serves the same *function* for the Jew as the church does for the Christian.

"The function of a religion is to enable those who live by it to achieve salvation, or life abundant. If the indivisible peoplehood of the Jews is as indispensable a means to the salvation of the Jew, as the church is to the Christian, it serves a religious function." (p. 100)

To those who may be inclined to refute the logic of indentifying two objects which perform, supposedly, the same function, the author offers the reflection that nationalism and religion are essentially two phases of the same social fact. Both derive from the "we-feeling" of a group, the "awareness of peoplehood." This awareness may be channeled in either of two directions, depending upon the type of leadership which molds its form and directs the course of its development.

"This leadership has been historically of two types: (1) The political type which is expert in dealing with factors of a visible and tangible character, (2) the ecclesiastical type, which is expert in dealing with factors and forces of an invisible and an intangible type." (p. 87) Nationalism, then, is an expression of one phase of "peoplehood," while religion is an expression of the other phases. Normally, that is in primitive societies, religion and nationalism constitute one whole. However, "historical circumstances have thus brought it about that in the Western civilization, the individual is a member of two peoples at the same time, the people he calls his nation and the people he calls his church." (p. 87) Apparently, the author considers this development either anomalous, or unfortunate. At any rate, he finds in the concept of "peoplehood" the original, common ground of both nationalism and religion, and he, therefore, counsels the reconstruction of Jewish community life in keeping with this concept. Accordingly, his basic formula consists of the twofold slogan "Judaism as a religious civilization" and the "Jews as an indivisible people," with the first slogan indicating the external form and pattern of Jewish life and the second supplying the inner motivation for it.

The importance of a definition consists in the success and felicity with which it separates the essential from the accidental and thereby reveals the dynamic soul of things. To define Judaism as a religious civilization, rather than as a civilizational religion, is to set the ethnic and cultural factors in the substantive core of Jewish life, and to relegate the elements of religion to the rank of a phase or a quality of the life of the group. When this definition is expounded in the context of an argument describing religion as the resultant product of a civilizational group, the full import of the suggested definition is revealed. It would transfer the vague and amorphous loyalty associated with the goal of being "a good Jew" from the sphere of religion to that of nationality and culture, in the belief that religious loyalty would ultimately and automatically result from the life of the ethnic group. The initial appeal of Judaism to the Jew must be directed to the sense of ethnic loyalty. But, do we have a right to demand ethnic loyalty from the Jewish group in a country such as ours, which is founded on the expectation of the ultimate commingling of all immigrant nationalities to produce the one great nation of America? Obviously, the natural trend in this country is for all incoming national groups to forget their former cultures and to blend in the civilization of America. So called "intercultural education" is not really opposed to this prevailing trend, as is sometimes erroneously supposed. On the contrary, intercultural activities are favored as a means of hastening the emergence of an American civilization, free from the personality-warping diseases of inferiority and superiority, and synthesizing within it the best elements of all immigrant cultures. Thus, the American dream is squarely opposed to the stubborn nurturing of divisive parochial loyalties among its constituent groups. On the other hand, Professor Baron's description of Jewish loyalty as "religious ethnicism" is not inadequate, insofar as it captures the character of Jewish cohesiveness at the present time.

The author concedes in this volume that ethnic loyalty cannot any longer be regarded as a moral imperative. In contrast to his earlier description of nationhood "as a call of the spirit," he now discloses that ethnic loyalty is justified only insofar as it is productive of spiritual values (p. 91). However, he insists that the hostility of antisemites makes it improper for a Jew to leave his people. Hence, the initial impetus for Jewish loyalty is provided by the sting of antisemitism. This impulse is then developed through the emotional logic of spitefulness into the ambition to survive as a group. In turn, the philosophy of spite-survivalism is spiritualized into loyalty to Judaism as a religious civilization, a consummation which corresponds to the "normal" pattern in primitive societies.

Possibly, questions, such as the following, will occur to the reader at this point:

Granted, that in ancient times religion and nationalism were largely undifferentiated, is not the process of differentiation itself a mark of growth and progress? If so, is it not then a mark of reaction for the Jew to seek to revert to his pre-French Revolution status? If the concept, "peoplehood" was appropriate in ancient society and in contemporary primitive societies, is it not an obsolete concept in our own times, when the terms nationalism and religion clearly refer to different fields of activity and different motivations? Is it not indisputably true that in modern times the movements which seek to align nationalism with religion are, without exception, of the darkest hues of reaction and antisemitic to boot? Finally, if, as the author chooses to phrase it, every American belongs to two peoples, "the people he calls his church and the people he calls his nation," why should not the status of the Jew be entirely similar, so that he might know himself to belong to the American people in the sense of nationality, and the Jewish people in the sense of religion? Why, then, take so much pains to blur the lines between the concepts of nationalism and religion?

Cogent as the arguments implied in these questions may be, we must not lose sight of the main reason which prompted the author to reject the plain conception of a religious status for American Jewry. "It would leave the majority of Jews without status," he declares, "because the majority of Jews today do not identify their Jewishness with any positive religious convictions." The author feels that this "majority of Jews" would not be helped by any conception which describes their loyalties as peripheral in character. Also, he feels that the term religion has never truly been the proper object of Jewish loyalty, since the term religion does not even occur in the original vocabulary of the Hebrew language. Again, he points out that "to the average Gentile, any person who has the least connection with the Jewish people, past or present, is a Jew." Furthermore, the Jew must be cushioned against the effects of antisemitism, which attacks all Jews, irrespective of their opinions on religion. The religionist would admit, of course, the need for organizations, other than the synagogue, to deal with the varied needs of Jewish people, but he would still insist that the Jew, *qua* Jew, is a member of a religious community and that, in terms of inner Jewish valuation, religious loyalty is decisive. This position is disputed by the author, who defines the ideal of being a "good Jew" in this order of preference, "socially, culturally and religiously," so that one "who lives a full Jewish life" is to be preferred to one who is loyal to the "religion, which has differentiated the Jews from the rest of the world." (p. 162) He believes that Judaism has always derived largely from the consciousness of kinship and the sense of oneness, occasioned by a common ancestry and common suffering. It is upon this "we-feeling," accordingly, that a visible and satisfying type of Jewish life must be founded. To this end, Jewish society, as presently constituted, must be reconstructed into an organic entity, so that it might evoke and respond to the group-consciousness of Jewish people.

The Organic Community

The chief plank in the Reconstructionist platform is the one which calls for "the creation of an adequate social structure for democratic Jewish communal life in the Diaspora." (p. 36) Dr. Kaplan regards the organization of the organic community as the one decisive act, which will make possible the needed revitalization of Jewish life and thus cure all the ills with which we are presently afflicted. By the term "organic community," he means the inclusion of all Jewish people in any geographic area in one organization, which will then assume responsibility for all the varied needs of Judaism and the Jewish people. His proposal differs from the two trends which are presently operative on the American scene. It is not identical with the drive, which is nearly consummated in most communities, to organize Jewish Community Councils, on a federative basis, so as to include in their governing boards representatives of all local Jewish organizations. In all these Community Councils, the needs of social welfare and anti-defamation are prominently included in the budget; in nearly all of them, provision is made for so-called "center activities," whether or not a "Y" building is maintained; in a considerable and increasing number, the program of Jewish education is subsidized, in whole, or in part. In recent years, there has also occurred an awakening of the national, regional and metropolitan associations of congregations, on a denominational basis, and there have been sporadic attempts to organize synagogues in local areas in one association, corresponding to the pattern of the Synagogue Council on the national level. Dr. Kaplan's proposal represents an attempt to merge the congregational and communal types of organizations into one united community, in which the religious and educational institutions will enjoy the position of "primacy."

The organic community might be regarded ideally as an extension of the synagogue and its educational institutions, since, in the language of the author, the position of the synagogue is "nuclear." The diversity of religious practice among the various synagogues and temples, however, makes it impossible for the religious bodies to form the organizational core of the community. Also, the inclusion in the communal structure of individuals and groups, avowedly indifferent or even opposed to the fostering of the Jewish religion, inevitably implies the shunting aside of the religious and educational institutions from the central role. In order that the organic community might reflect faithfully the "we-feeling," of an "indivisible people," it must be organized on an all-inclusive basis. Thus, the organic community would be built on the common desire of its members "to continue as Jews," no matter how differently they may construe the meaning of Jewishness.

Even the bare formalism of the survivalist cannot be assumed as a fundamental cohesive bond, since the "organic community" aspires to embrace all Jewish organizations, providing its protective wing to all who are hurt by the sting of antisemitism. Were the community organization to be restricted to the survivalists only, it would be subject to the criticism of limited inclusiveness which the author directs against the conception of a religious status.

Accordingly, gray and neutral Jewishness, not the positive commitments of Judaism, would inevitably be the common denominator of the so-called organic community, and the position of "primacy" for the synagogue in a religiously neutral community cannot be aught else on the American scene but a sham and a pretense. As a matter of fact, he proposes this "nuclear" role, not only for the synagogues and educational institutions, but also for the "communal centers," which are, at best, dedicated to the promotion of that soulless and non-commital entity known as "Jewish content." Actually, the centers catering, for the most part, to the motives of ethnic gregariousness, are more likely to occupy the "nuclear" position in the emergent pattern of the community council than the synagogue.

The author's proposal for an "organic community" should not be regarded as a pure and abstract concept, which must not be sullied by being placed in the actual context of American Jewish life. While it is true that the community councils do not at present include synagogues in their budgetary programs, they do include the representatives of the congregations in their governing boards. They constitute, therefore, a fair reflection of the kind of leadership that the organic community would possess. It is absolutely absurd for one who is acquainted with the mentality of those who guide the destinies of the Jewish community councils to expect a religious revival to originate from that source, even if the term, religion, is interpreted as naturalistically as you please. The author recognizes the shortcomings of the present leadership of the community councils and urges an educational program to improve it. He exposes the fallacy of those who seek to justify their secularist outlook and program by the principle of the separation of church and state. He regards it as the proper function of the council to intensify the group spirit of the Jew" and "to build up his morale." He calls for an overhauling of the entire educational system, for a conscious cultivation of Jewish art and for a determined effort to foster all forms of Jewish culture. All these efforts are certainly laudable, but one remains puzzled as to the manner in which these activities might be expected "to give all Jews a purpose to live for as Jews," (p. 116) or to revive the sadly lagging loyalties to "Judaism as a *religious* civilization." One may be forgiven for a measure of skepticism toward the author's faith in the therapeutic quality of Jewish art, as when he writes, "We can be sure of a Jewish future only when Jewish art is so developed as to reconcile the Jew to his lot in life." (p. 118) The fact is that Hellenic art did not preserve the Hellenes, while the Jewish religion, without the benefit of art during long and trying centuries, did preserve the Jewish people. Also, when the Hellenes turned Christian, their ethnic consciousness and pride ceased, for all their vaunted art. A similar objection, based upon the fate of the immigrant groups in America may be raised to the author's glib assumption that the prospect of helping to build the state of Israel may serve to take the place of the belief in Messiah, as a basic motivation for Jewish life in the Diaspora. Thus, he writes, "If the vision of an ideal social life to be achieved in the days of the Messiah made it worthwhile for our ancestors to carry on, even to the point of martyrdom, the purposeful

401

effort of our people to live a worthy, hence a godly life in Eretz Yisrael, has made it worthwhile for modern Jews to carry on despite the almost universal undercurrent of ill-will and hostility." (p. 126)

The author's faith in the salutary effects of the organic community is not based entirely either upon the performance of the community council to date, or upon the tangible undertakings, in the fields of education and art, that they might sponsor in the future. The real force of his argument is directed at what he conceives to be the source of the Jew's irreligion today.

"In part, the indifference is due to the fact that Jewish religion is identified in the minds of most Jews with a particular traditional doctrine to which they find it intellectually impossible to subscribe, rather than with the whole process by which a living civilization evolves its *sancta*. In part, it is due to that social disorganization to which attention was called when community organization was discussed. Religion is a function of community life; therefore, it thrives or languishes equally with other aspects of Jewish civilization in proportion as that life is vigorous or feeble." (p. 48)

Since "religion" is a function of community life we have but to organize an efficient community and the loyalties of religion will be reborn automatically. The group life of Jewish people will engender foci of attention and affection that will become the new *sancta* of Jewish religion, and will predispose an increasing number of men and women to appreciate some of the sancta of the past, as being products of Jewish experience and genius.

This thesis deserves very careful examination. If it be true, then the practical suggestions of the author cannot be gainsaid. If it be not true, then the rest of the Reconstructionist philosophy turns out to be a group of disjointed suggestions, without inner coherence and relevance. Will the present irreligious Jew become converted to Judaism when he learns to see it as "the whole process by which a living civilization evolves its *sancta*?" One may legitimately doubt this proposition, since the whole intent of the modern secularist's position is that a modern "living civilization" may continue to evolve without availing itself of the methods of religion. Professor Baron's recent study of *Modern Nationalism and Religion* demostrates the continous interaction between the two forces in modern life, but also reveals their essential and complete independence of each other, when both movements are at their best levels. Mature, liberal nationalism is secular and nationalistic. Ahad Ha'am was certainly a Jewish survivalist and a most impassioned advocate of Jewish culture. Yet, he felt that religion was a proper "garment" for the Jewish spirit in the past, but that in the future, Jewish civilization must be liberated from the sway of religion. The analogy between the function of religion in primitive societies and its function today is utterly misleading, since it ignores the entire intellectual tradition of the modern world. The emergence of Judaism and its daughter-religion constituted, in fact, a definite break with the primitive unity of patriotism, civilization and religion. Thus, it was possible for Jewry in the diaspora to assimilate culturally and politically, while remaining loyal in religion. Conversely, it is possible for members of "Kibbutsim" in Palestine, where the sense of community is so powerful as to leave scarcely any room for private life, nevertheless, to live without scarcely a shred of Jewish religion, in the conventional sense of the term. If, on the other hand, Jewish religion is interpreted so unconventionally and arbitrarily as to lend the aura of sanctity to every expression of Jewish group life, then it is merely tautologous and irrelevant to declare that Jewish communal life produces Jewish religion. The author likes to refer to the Jewish religion as the "soul" of Judaism, but it remains

403

ambiguous as to whether the term soul is used by him in the behaviorist sense, as the expression of the body, or in the traditional sense, as a spiritual essence of which the body is a partial expression.

It may also be pointed out that the organic community, if it ever becomes a reality, will not be a radically new phenomenon. The "Kultus-Gemeindes" in Germany, the Consistoires in France and the Kehillahs in modern Poland were all organic communities, organized along democratic lines. The German-Jewish community was even able to set the rate of taxes for its upkeep according to the income of its members and to get the government to act as its tax-collecting agency. Nevertheless, affiliation with the Jewish community was voluntary. One could resign from the Jewish community, by conversion to another faith, or by signing a declaration of being religion-less. The Gemeinde took care of all its religious, educational, recreational and relief needs, even as the organic community is supposed to do. Did the community organization of German Jewry evoke greater religious loyalty from its members than do the corresponding American organizations, in spite of all their faults? No historian can possibly answer this question in the affirmative. The rate of intermarriage in Germany was far greater than it is here and the rate of conversions, perhaps a thousandfold greater. While the mixed marriages in America generally remain within the Jewish fold, the Gentile partner being converted to Judaism, the exact opposite was the rule in Germany and Austria. The American Jew is also immeasurably more loyal to world Jewry and happy with himself as a Jew than was his German counterpart, who frequently suffered from the dread disease of "Judenhass."

The avowed purpose of the author is to bring to Jewish secularists an appreciation of and a willingness to participate in Jewish religion, so that the energies of Jewish life might be, not those of fear, but those of hope. Observing his effort however, as it is unfolded in the volume under discussion, one is left wondering as to whether he is really pulling the proponents of "Jewishness" up to Judaism, or whether he is being pulled down by them. The motives of the author are not in question, of course, but the probable net result of his teaching, which tends to reduce the barriers between the secular and the holy to the vanishing point. This tendency is, naturally, a direct development of his conception of God to an examination of which we must now turn.

The Concepts of God and Religion

The present volume adds very little to the understanding of the author's conception of God, as it was expounded in his previous works. In *The Meaning of God in Modern Jewish Religion*, Professor Kaplan defined belief in God as being not an abstract proposition, but an attitude which "reckons with life's creative forces and potentialities as forming an organic unity, and as giving meaning to life by virtue of that unity." (p. 26) Are the "creative forces" in existence an "organic unity," standing apart from the rest of the forces in the universe or are they simply part of the energy of existence? Is there really a Being, Who thinks, wills and cares for the values man call "creative?" Or, is belief in God merely a euphemistic expression for an affirmative response to life? In all his works, Professor Kaplan manages to avoid facing these questions. He goes so far as to declare that God is "the Power that endorsed what we believe ought to be and that guarantees that it will be," (ibid., p. 324) without feeling the need of setting up standards, whereby we, modern humanists, may properly feel more justified in counting upon the endorsements of the Almighty, than were all the heathens of "this believing world." He declares that "God is what the world means to the man who believes in the possibility of maximum life and strives for it." (ibid., p. 328) But, he offers no criteria whereby our conception of the maximum life might be seen to be more in accord with reality, than that of the hedonists, libertines or Nietzscheans. His conception remains, therefore, ambiguous and relativistic.

In this book he begins his exposition by deprecating the importance of "logical arguments" in arriving at the conception of God and at the proof of His existence. Belief in God precedes historically all proofs of the existence of God and is, itself, not a rational inference, but one phase of that "vital Process" of which the complementary phase is "the will to live." "The belief in God is not logically inferred from the will to live. It is the psychic manifestation of the will to live." (p. 172) Since belief in God originates thus instinctively or intuitively, what grounds do we, as irrational beings, have for believing that there is indeed a "Power predisposing man to his ultimate, human good, salvation or self-fulfillment?" The author does not feel himself to be under any obligation to provide an answer to this question. As the will to live, or the quest of salvation is universal among men, so is or should be, the belief in God, since it is nothing but an implication of the search for salvation. According to the author's reasoning, the inescapable fact of the presence of millions who love life and strive for the life abundant and who yet do not believe in God, can be understood only as a confusion of definitions. If, to believe that the world is so constituted as to make for salvation is to believe in God, then Lucretius, who set out to prove that there was no God, in order that humanity might lead its life without fear of the Divine thunderbolt, really himself believed in God.

The persistence of Dr. Kaplan in regarding the idea of God from the standpoint of its function in primitive societies is to be explained by the inference which he draws from his sociological analysis. "Thus, the laws that any civilizational group regards as its fundamental purpose, as a group, are considered a revelation of God." (p. 174) Applying this to our own day, we lay down the theoretical groundwork for our own religious civilization. We may set up the principles and practices which, in our view, accord with the fundamental purpose of Jewish life, and label them collectively as "the revelation of God." Interested as he is in practical conclusions, the author is profoundly impatient with metaphysical speculations. The chief problem, to him, is not how to lead people "to believe in the cosmic Power that sustains human life, whether we designate it 'God' or any other name," (p. 182) but how to conceive of Him. He concludes that God may not be regarded as a Person, "since it is paradoxical for a person not to be associated with a physical body," but as a process. This argument ignores the long and intricate philosophical tradition associated with the concept of person and substitutes for it a concept so general as to be virtually meaningless in the psychological realm of piety. No one would care to pray to a process, which may be a resultant of any number of unexplained causes.

The philosophically minded reader will revolt at this and many other passages in the author's exposition of the God idea. Suffice it to say that, weak as his metaphysics may be, he does believe in the need of and supreme value of worship, though he agrees "that it is tantamount to praying to oneself." "The need for communing with that Power is part of our very will to live as human beings." (p. 184) Accordingly, he describes the rites and ceremonies of religion as being essential to the attainment of the good life and he insists that humanism must mature into spiritual religion, if it is to acquire the necessary motivation and enthusiasm to attain its purpose.

Having thus made peace between the concept of God and

407

the spirit of naturalism, the author explains the implication of this concept for the "reconstruction" of the Jewish religion. As a general rule, he declares, "We must, therefore, base the Jewish religion of tomorrow not on what our ancestors have told of their experience with God, but on our own experience with God." (p. 210) He advocates, accordingly, an active type of piety, which feels closer to God, in the very process of change and adjustment, than in the passive attitude of compliance. As Abraham's action in breaking the idols of his father was not an irreligious deed, but, on the contrary, an expression of his newly born faith, so Dr. Kaplan's acceptance of the idea of God as a Process leads him to find religious satisfaction in the sheer adventure of creative modification, functional reinterpretation and social reconstruction. Though he still accords formal veneration to the Conservative principle of "continuity," he finds spiritual exhiliration in the process of change itself, reflecting thereby the state of mind of twentieth century America and the dynamic mentality of Faustian man generally.

Thus, he rejects vehemently the concept of the "chosen people" and he refuses to interpret it in acceptable terms, on the ground that its invidiousness is ineradicable. To the charge that in rejecting this concept, which permeates the Bible and the Talmud, we imply an insulting judgment concerning our ancestors, Dr. Kaplan would reply that development is the law of life and that the awareness of progressing beyond the attainments of previous generations is itself a religious value. He lists four possible reinterpretations of the "chosen people" concept, all referring to the past and indicates their shortcomings, but he fails to take account of the unique experiences, status and destiny of our people in our own time, which require to be molded in a religious pattern of thought. Every Jew today is aware of the unique role assigned to our people to be the "suffering servant" of every generation. On the surface, it is a most undesirable role, so much so that the spirit of rebellion against Jewish faith is rife in our midst and the typical Jew is "kicking against the pricks." What better concept than that of the "chosen people" can be found, which is suited for the channeling of Jewish resentment and rancor into spiritual directions? Dr. Kaplan's own conception of "vocation" is a fitting reinterpretation of the traditional concept. Yet, he does not offer his interpretation as a continous development of the old idea, but as a radically new doctrine, experiencing, as as he does, a sense of religious exaltation in purging modern Judaism of the inherited dross of primitive religion and naive superstition.

In much the same spirit, he deals with the problem of Halachah in all its varied aspects. In the first place, he maintains that the very concept of law is inapplicable today, since "no law can function without sanctions." (p. 390) But, inasmuch as no civilization in turn can function without some kind of law, he proposes that the organic community be set up first and that it then arrange for a new Halachah that would "set forth the duties, the authority, the qualifications for office and the conditions of tenure of all Jewish public servants and establish codes of right relations between different Jewish corporate agencies," as well as regulate "the machinery of fund raising" for various causes. In addition to this domain of "rules of order," where the community would presumably be able to invoke its own sanctions, there is the field of marital relations which Jewish society cannot ignore. He does not explain, however, how the problems of marriage and divorce can be dealt with by the organic community, without compromising its neutrality between the Orthodox, Conservative and Reform groups. Yet, if each group continues to legislate for itself in matters of this sort, there will not be a unitary community, in this most important phase of Jewish civilization.

Jewish law, properly so-called, is restricted to these two areas—the strictly religious domain of ritual and ceremonial practice, as well as the standards of personal life being free from the reach of sanctions. "The vocabulary of 'law,' 'sin,' 'pardon,' is ideologically and pragmatically unjustified as applied to ritual." (p. 419) In the spheres of individual observance and congregational practice, the community should apply the principle of unity in diversity, "so that no stigma should attach to those who permit themselves a wide latitude in their departure from traditional norms." Each congregation will be permitted and encouraged to set up its own standards of individual and congregational practice. In addition, he proposes the drawing up of a new code that will offer an evaluation of the different rites and set forth a minimum, as well as a maximum, level of observance. Since the minimum must be small enough to retain within the community the extreme Reform groups and the totally indifferent ones, while the maximum must be large enough to embrace the Orthodox, the area of discretion that will be left to the choice of the individual is manifestly considerable. The different rites of Judaism should be evaluated by means of two criteria—the principle of group survival and the principle of individual salvation. Some rituals may not help the individual to find life more meaningful and worthwhile, but they might have survival value, from the standpoint of the group. How they can have such a value, when the group in question is the community as a whole, which regards no rite as binding, the author does not explain. He does, however, lay great stress on the development of new rituals, that will presumably be observed more widely, because they will have grown out of "the needs and experiences of modern Jews."

Does the author build up a formidable case for his thesis that the concepts of "law," "sin" and "pardon" should be banished from the sphere of religious life? A critical reader will find it impossible to answer the question in the affirmative. We do speak of the moral law and of the laws of the spirit, even if we do not envisage any tangible sanctions, insuring their enforcement. The very essence of the Moral Law is the fact that, in Kantian terminology, it is autonomous, not heteronomous, so that no act is moral, in the true sense of the term, if external sanctions enter into its motivation. In the address of man to God, that is a prayer, it is for man to view the potential good vested by God in his person as a Divine mandate for his realization. Any failure to attain the mark set him by the Creator is sin. On this view, the pardon of God is signalled by the reborn resolve in the heart of man to actualize in the fullest measure his Divine gifts and creative potentialities. The moral law, from the religious viewpoint, is not a purely negative Golden Rule, as in Hillel's formulation, nor a formal maxim, as in Kant's formulation, but an act of facing the Almighty and rendering account to Him of one's life. Rituals are accordingly the "laws" which the religious person imposes upon himself, in order that he might rise higher in the sight of God. Thus, while a philosopher might concede value to the act of prayer, the man of piety imposes upon himself the "law" of praying three times daily. No one will care to dispute the value of studying Torah, but one becomes religious only when one makes it a personal obligation to set aside daily and weekly periods for the study of Torah.

As no one lives in a vacuum, this act of autonomous legislation is normally taken over by the group, so that the noble

411

resolve of each individual is reinforced by the "law" of the group. This principle underlies the reasoning of the Halachah, which derives its authority from the voluntary acceptance of the people. Characteristic from this viewpoint, is the principle of *shavyai anafshai haticha dissura,* which according to some authorities, forms the basis for most of the non-Torahitic Halachah. It indicates that Halachah is essentially the self-legislation of the Jewish group. One may, therefore, recognize the areas of Jewish law which have become obsolete, without condemning the "legalistic approach," and substituting for it the purely descriptive term of religious folkways" (p. 424) —a designation, which leaves the heart cold and unmoved. On the contrary, it is the much abused legalistic approach of Judaism, which holds forth the only hope of lifting progressively the moral and spiritual level of men. The world today is surfeited with beautiful phrases and floating ideals, but it lacks the discipline necessary to translate ideals into life through self-imposed laws of conduct. As the rejection of the law by St. Paul proved to be the final act of severance of the new faith from its matrix in Judaism, so will the rejection of the principle of the Halachah doom any efforts to establish American Judaism on a permanently sound basis.

It cannot be denied, however, that Dr. Kaplan's conception of Jewish law and ritual is of a piece with his conception of God and his view of religion generally. His philosophy is frankly naturalistic, requiring no faith, other than a way of speaking for the love of life, and no spiritual commitment other than the survival of the group. His attention is focused sharply on the religiously indifferent, those who are unhappy with themselves as Jews, the bewildered and bedeviled masses drifting along in confusion on the margins of organized Jewish life. It is to them that he would offer a philosophy of Jewish life. And it is by its appeal to the peripheral, unaffiliated Jew that his philosophy of Judaism will ultimately be tested.

Summation

In sum, Dr. Kaplan, pointing to the masses of people who are presently affected very slightly, or not at all, by the message of the synagogue, declares that the major reason for the breakdown of the Jewish loyalty is twofold—the naturalistic bent of the modern mind and the disintegration of the Jewish community. His solution, accordingly, is to recast the faith of Judaism from its traditional supernaturalistic mold into a modern, naturalistic pattern. This requires a fundamental transformation in the idea of God, so that it shall no longer represent a Person, but a Process, the sum total of all those processes that make for a good life. On this basis, faith in God comes to be identified with the healthy-minded reaction to life, and it becomes unnecessary to be concerned with proofs for His existence. Call Him God, or any other name, the reality would be disputed only by professional pessimists and casuistic metaphysicians. This transformation in the idea of God necessitates a total revaluation of the traditional rites and ceremonies and a resolve to create new rites and symbols that will express the spirit of our time.

Having thus reconstructed Jewish religion, Dr. Kaplan proceeds to supply motivation for it by suggesting the reestablishment of the organic community. Since religion is the final fruition of group life, it may be expected that the "we-feeling" induced by the vitalized community would emerge in religious forms. The organic community would represent in organizational terms the concept of Judaism as a religious civilization. It would draw under its banner all who wish to see Jewish life of any kind perpetuated. It would devote all its energies to the building up of the civilizational elements of Judaism, trusting that Jewish religion, as the soul of Jewish civilization, would be automatically vitalized by the renascent community and civilization.

In the light of our foregoing analysis, many points in the author's thesis remain open to question. However, there can be no doubt that his philosophy echoes, in the main, the vague and groping sentiments of American Jewry, which is becoming increasingly community-minded and naturalistically-minded. Whether or not his program will come to mold the pattern of the presently amorphous loyalties of the Jewish masses, only time will tell.

Undoubtedly, in the last ten years, the ethnic consciousness of American Jews has been inflamed to a feverish intensity, verging at times on the delirious. This whipped up wave of embittered ethnicism must be directed into religious channels, if the Jewish awareness is to become a source of spiritual growth, instead of being, as it frequently is today, a perpetual protestation and an endless lamentation. The problem before us, then, consists in so directing Jewish life, as to lead from ethnicism to Judaism. Dr. Kaplan's solution of this problem compares favorably with similar efforts made by philosophers like Rousseau, Fichte and Mazzini, to produce a religion out of resurgent nationalism. But, what to the French, the Germans and the Italians was sheer speculation, is inescapable necessity to us Jews. Thus, no one who is truly aware of the nature of the Jewish problem will reject Dr. Kaplan's solution *in toto,* much as he may disagree with some of his arguments.

(Published in *The Jewish Quarterly Review,* October, 1948.)

"*A Jewish View of Protestant Theology*"
Tillich's Theology from the Jewish Viewpoint

A review-article based on "The Theology of Paul Tillich"
The Library of Living Theology, volume one, Macmillan,
369 pp., 1953.

(1)

In the worldwide panorama of religious thought, there
is no phenomenon more interesting than Professor Paul Tillich, who has been selected as the subject of the first volume
in the projected series of the Library of Living Theology.
There is scarcely a phase of modern thought or culture that
is not somehow embraced in the world-view of this com-
manding philosopher. Delicate nuances in modern art, new
insights in modern philosophy, new surges of mass enthusiasm in our time, bright new visions hovering uncertainly
on the horizon—whatever throws fresh light on the creative
mystery that is the human personality is taken up by Tillich
and made to yield significance in the life of faith. Nothing
that is human is alien to his theology.

Thus, "The Theology of Paul Tillich" contains essays
dealing with the relation of his thought to secular culture,
his conception of religious socialism, his attitude toward
biblical criticism, his view of the church, his philosophy of
history, etc. Nor are these phases of his thought unrelated
to the central ideas and motivations in his system. German

to the core, in his passion for systematization and his delight in the sheerest of abstractions, he is also American, in his attention to the concerns and experiences of living people. For all I know to the contrary, he may well be the first German theologian of highest rank to have achieved a successful transition from the German universe of discourse to the American.

Born in Germany to a Lutheran pastor, his first interest in religious philosophy consisted in the search for weapons whereby he might batter down the austere authoritarianism of German Protestantism as it was represented for him in the personality of his father. After attaining an amazing mastery of the history of philosophic thought, he became alternately a professor of philosophy and a theologian. For a few years, he was allied with the neo-Orthodox Karl Barth in a furious debate against the "liberals." But, he was repelled by the rock-ribbed dogmatism, the resolute narrowness of the neo-orthodox, which derived from their belief that it is impossible for man to come nigh unto God through the exercise of any of his faculties. To the neo-Orthodox, every achievement of mankind is perverted by sin and doomed to frustration and failure. Salvation can only come from the side of God, by an "unconditioned" act of Divine Grace. On the other hand, the liberals, as Tillich saw them, virtually worshipped themselves, seeing God as the extension unto the canvass of infinity of their own intellectual efforts and social goals. To Tillich, modern liberal culture "both reveals and conceals God"; there is both a "yes" and a "no" in every human endeavor to achieve the good life. All things can lead to God if they are seen against the background of the "Unconditioned Ground," and all things can become demonic, if they are taken to be sufficient unto themselves. This thought is reminiscent of the Baal Shem Tov's counsel —"when you see aught that is beautiful, such as a beautiful woman, ask, whence does this beauty come?—Is it not from God?—Then turn immediately to His Worship."

But, while the Baal Shem Tov would turn immediately from the beauty of the world to its Source, Tillich remains so far enmeshed in the coils of his "dialectical theology," as not to be able to offer clear guidance for the task of discriminating between the demonic and the divine in the historical situation. Rejecting the humanistic norms of goodness and harmony, he finds the ultimate criterion in Christ. But, then, he takes the life of Christ to be normative, not in a literal, but in a symbolic, homiletic sense. The Christian norm must be seen in the light of an "ecstatic" religious experience. What this criterion actually means in any concrete situation remains exceedingly dubious. Emanuel Hirsch, a theological ally and associate of Tillich's in his early Germanic period, encountered no difficulty in turning the weapons of "dialectical theology" against the Weimar republic, hailing the monstrous fury of Hitlerism as a "holy storm," and "a power full of blessing." Hirsch used much the same language as Tillich when he extolled the year 1933 as affording authoritative revelation equally as much as the year 33.

Tillich, it must be admitted, was greater than his concepts. Repudiating Nazism as a modern form of paganism, he early found a secure haven in the United States, whence he attacked the deviations and aberrations of his former colleagues in the school of "dialetical theology." It is interesting that, in his quest for secure moorings against the bewildering tides of confusion, Tillich turned to the teachings of the Hebrew prophets. His former associates, he declared, were misled by the spell of the "priestly" mentality, which can only bless and sanctify whatever the people desire, whereas it is the "prophetic" mentality which subjects the fire and fury of the contemporary situation to the criticism of "the still, small voice," that the world needs most urgently.

Tillich's revolt against the seduction of the "priestly" mentality is of great interest to Jews, since this very criticism lies at the base of the historical Jewish critique of Christianity as a whole. Rabbinic Judaism was a direct continuation of the prophetic movement, seeking to spell out in concrete terms the prophetic vision of the ideal society. While the theory and the practice of sacrifices were continued in normative Judaism, the ideal of "Torah and mitzvoth" came to occupy the luminous center of Jewish consciousness, with the priests and all the rites that depended on them being shunted ever more definitely toward the periphery. In Christianity, on the other hand, Judaism was stood on its head, as it were, with the doctrine of sacrifice crowding all else aside so as to become the one master-key to piety and salvation. The sacrifice of lambs did not avail; thenceforth, the sacrifice of the Lamb would conquer sin. In the sacraments of the church, this reversion to elements in Judaism that were outgrown even then, was nailed down in concrete detail and made out to be the essence of religion. In turning to the Hebrew prophets for support against the perversion of theology, Tillich in effect acknowledged the dependence of a healthful Christian message on the living faith of Judaism.

However, it was not to Judaism that Tillich consciously turned, in the years of profound crisis, but to Catholicism, considering seriously the possibility of conversion to that faith. For a while, it appeared that Protestantism in Germany would succumb completely to the Hitlerite "wave of the future," while the Catholic Church still stood adamant and immovable. Paradoxical as it may sound, it was for the sake of Judaism in Christianity, that this great Protestant theologian contemplated entering the Catholic Church.

418

Happily, the Protestant church discovered hidden resources of strength in the midst of adversity. Tillich remained a Protestant, perhaps the most Protestant of all, for to him "the protestant principle" consists in the perpetual search for ever deeper truths.

(2)

From the standpoint of Judaism, the theology of Tillich is of special interest because it remains so distinctively Christian, in spite of its author's genius for harmonization and his valiant effort to retain the insights of prophetic Judaism as well as of modern humanism. While some of the contributors to this volume question the authentically Christian motifs in his theology, a Jewish reader notes the Christian bent at many crucial points in his thought. Even his fondness for paradoxical expressions is typical of the historical Christian tradition. Thus, he writes of the endeavor to prove the existence of God as atheism, of the need to worship "God beyond God," and of the need of a Messiah to redeem mankind from "the burden of religion." These paradoxes are inherent in the style of thought which discovers salvation in an "ecstatic" experience and delights in its gospel being "a stumbling block to the Jews, folly to the Greeks."

For the Jewish reader, it is important to realize the profound gulf that yawns between the Jewish and Christian traditions, even when the two patterns of thought and feeling are not accepted in a fundamentalist spirit. The differences do not consist merely of so many dogmas, so many practices, so many varying sets of symbols. The two traditions belong to the same historical field of culture and they are equally subject to the challenge of the same modern ideas and forces. Yet, they embody different modes of interpreting the highest insights of human life, its character and its destiny. And these modes predetermine the conclusions of the

419

authentic representatives of the two traditions, when they set out to explore the mystery of existence. In the realm of fundamental convictions and values, we are destined to move within closed circles, since we aim at conclusions which are already assumed in our fundamental premises. As a philosopher, Tillich is willing to grant the relativity of the "Christian circle of ideas," that he nevertheless accepts as a Christian and a theologian. Since the Jewish and Christian "circles" both overlap and diverge, it is highly instructive for the exponents of the one tradition to follow the bold ideological adventures of great minds in the other tradition.

Judaism and Christianity are mutually supplementary traditions, stressing the opposite ends of the same experience. When the human soul, in its yearning for God reaches the mysterious outer limits of its being, transcending in an ineffable moment the boundaries of its conscious existence, we have the living core of religion, the incomprehensible encounter between man and God. This human-divine moment cannot be permanently frozen into "clear and adequate" ideas, remaining, as it necessarily must, on the "boundary" of life. In Judaism, the religious experience is steadily seen from the human side of the "boundary," calling attention to the thoughts, actions and feelings which lead to the "nearness of God." Its guiding motif is the sense of duty, ere, in the ecstasy of religious devotion, it dissolves into the fluidity of feeling—devotion, love, unity, peace. Yet, not duty as a rational concept in itself but duty to God is the vital focus of Judaism—a mediating position between conscience and religious feeling.

Unity with the Divine is not held out as a goal. Even concerning the command to "cleave unto the Lord," the Talmud inquires, "how is it possible to cleave unto the Lord?—Is He not as a consuming flame?—It means therefore to walk in His path." (Kethuboth, 111b) And it is upon the exploring of those "paths," that the mighty genius of our people was concentrated. "Make ye in the wilderness (of this world) a pathway unto the Lord." (Isaiah 40) As to the nature of the Divine, it is futile or even dangerous to speculate. "I wish they would leave me (i.e. God) alone and keep my Torah." It is the way, and the way alone that matters. What are the elements in the human personality that point Godward? Search them out, cultivate them, for they are the seeds of His Kingdom! We can only know the Divine in man, not the Divine in His own numinous being. Hence, to be religious is "to walk in His paths"—to seek justice and to study its applications; to love the fulness of human dignity and discover the conditions for its protection and growth; to widen the horizon of knowledge, but in humility and reverence.

In Christianity, the attempt is made to see and to interpret the core of religious experience from the side of the Supreme Being. The vital core is not the "way" of faith, but the apex of ecstasy, when the twin lights of intelligence and conscience are absorbed and transmuted by the sheer intensity of the blaze of feeling. Hence, its message cannot but be expressed in "paradoxes." The way of religion is from the Divine to the human, not from the human to the Divine. All human endeavors are doomed to frustration and failure, tainted as they are by "original sin." The creature is guilty by its very existence, as a self-conscious being. The way to salvation consists in the shattering of all human pretensions to knowledge, beauty and righteousness, so that man acknowledges at last—"I am nothing; Thou art all." By his very existence, man is in need of being "saved," and when he is saved, he is "reborn." Religion says "No," with lightning and thunder, not only to man's lower nature, but to his best insights as well—to his glimpses of rationality, his cognition of the moral laws, his perception of beauty and his endeavors to build the kingdom of God of earth. Thus, Simone Weil refused to take the final steps of conversion to Christianity, utterly alienated though she was from the faith of Judaism, because she was enamored of "the beauty of this world." And, as man and the world pale into insignificance, the nature of God and His saving Grace come to the fore. Hence, the intense preoccupation with metaphysics, on the one hand, and the ecstasy of the mystics, on the other hand. The nature of God and the fate of man come to be the two central foci of faith, rather than, as in the Jewish philosophy of history, God's challenge to man as it is flung on the stage of the world and man's reluctant response to this challenge. The "works" of man cannot lead to salvation, save insofar as they furnish proof of the operation in him of the quasi-magical current of "faith." "For no one can say Jesus is the Lord, save in Christ." The very affirmation of the absurd is proof of a supra-rational power.[1]

From the Christian viewpoint, Judaism cannot but be regarded as "preparation" for the true faith, since it builds upon the insights leading to religious experience, rather than upon those deriving from the luminous apex of mystical ecstasy. From the Jewish viewpoint, Christianity partakes of the qualities of paganism and mythology, since it operates with the concept of human *fate,* rather than the nature of the human *task,* shifting attention from man's vocation on earth to his concerns with his lot. Both traditions are liable to abuse—but, in different ways, Judaism turning into uninspired humanism or glorified ethnicism, Christianity turning into an other-worldly, unprophetic, sacramental mystery-religion. At their best, the two traditions are mutually cor-

8 In his brilliant article, "Judaism and Christianity: Rivals or Partners," James Parkes discusses the two traditions in terms of their emphasis on the welfare of society and the salvation of the individual respectively. This distinction dovetails into our analysis, but it is not basic or primary in the religious consciousness of either faith.—*"Commentary,"* May, 1946.

rective.[2] If the history of thought is clear on any one point it is this, that no one person can ever succeed in synthesizing the insights of the two faiths, on their deepest levels.

(3)

Paul Tillich is no exception to this rule. He seeks to correct somewhat the one-sided interpretation of Christianity. In his polemics against Karl Barth, he strives to achieve a more equitably balanced view of the divine-human encounter, maintaining that religious truth must be achieved by the twofold process of "detachment" and "involvement." He recognizes that in all branches of secular culture, God is "revealed as well as concealed." He follows Kant in the recognition that the moral law is indeed the voice of God. "The only point at which the prison of finitude is open is the realm of moral experience, because in it something unconditional breaks into the whole of temporal and causal conditions." (Systematic Theology," I, 33-34) Yet, precisely because he is so keenly aware of the one-sidedness of the Orthodox or neo-Orthodox Christian tradition, his writings are remarkable for the persistence in them of the essentially Christian impetus of thought and feeling.

Perhaps, the best key for the understanding of Tillich's philosophy is given to us in the fine collection of sermons and meditations, published under the title, "Shaking of the Foundations." The practical import of his message can be seen in the one-sided, polarized illumination that he casts upon the nature of religion. He appeals to the feeling of fear that lurks just below the surface of the modern consciousness. The nightmarish vision of atomic destruction is invoked. The "foundations are shaking." Man is able to pulverize the foundations upon which he stands, and he is demonic

[2] The implication of this interaction between the two traditions are traced by this reviewer in "The Menorah Journal," Spring, 1953.

enough to attempt it. The prophets were able to face this vision of universal dissolution, because they thought of God as "the shaker of the foundations," providing a more ultimate foundation, below the foundation. Please note that Tillich does not allay man's fear of catastrophe; he builds up the sense of fear first, and then proceeds to counteract it by evoking a vague, all-covering feeling of faith.

The same studied alternation of feeling provides the structure of a sermon called, "We Live in Two Orders." Taking as his text the fortieth chapter of Isaiah, Tillich points out that the prophet was aware of "two orders of being: the human, political, historical order, and the divine, eternal order." Because he knew these two orders, he could speak as he did, moving continually "between the depth of human nothingness and the great height of divine creativity." The point to remember is, that in Tillich's interpretation, the divine order as such does not enter into the mundane, human order, as a comprehensible, continuous factor of amelioration and uplift. The prophet finds "peace of mind" or "peace of soul," by looking away from the misery of mankind to the majesty of God.

Nor is God found only in this glimpse of the blessedness of the Eternal. Sometimes it is in the blackness of demonic fury, when man rebels against God, seeking to "murder Him," that God is somehow found. (Is there aught that is impossible to the strange rhythm of feeling and the even stranger logic of paradoxical thought?) —At this point, Tillich joins hands with Nietzsche, who sought to recreate the myth of man killing God, and then finding Him reborn within one's own being. In mythology this motif is found in superabundance, but, in modern theology, it is but another illustration of Tillich's passion for all-inclusiveness. "We are known in a depth of darkness, through which we ourselves do not even dare look. . . . That infinite tension is the atmosphere in which religion lives." (Ibid, p. 50)

In religion, this tension is generated, but also transcended. Begining with the evocation of fear and anxiety, it leads to the feeling of "peace," the sense of being good. Sin is the feeling of "separation" and grace that of "re-union."

". . . as though a voice were saying: 'You are accepted. *You are accepted,* accepted by that which is greater than you, and the name of which you do not know. Do not ask for the name now; perhaps you will find it later. Do not try to do anything now, perhaps later you will do much. Do not seek for anything; do not perform anything; do not intend anything. Simply accept the fact that you are accepted."

(Ibid, p. 162)

In another connection, he articulates the "answer" of religion to the anxious soul-searching of man in similar terms . . . "suddenly we are grasped by a peace which is above reason, that is above our theoretical seeking for the true, and above our practical striving for the good." (Ibid, p. 100)

From all the above, there emerges the picture of religion as a state of tension between peace and fear, sinking into depths of fear, of sin and horor, then rising unto heights of exaltation, mystical self-reassurance and peace. This oscillation of feeling is certainly a phase of religious experience—but only a phase, showing man as he moves between fear and faith, worrying about his fate and about the standing of his soul with God. In Judaism, man is worried not so much about his *fate*, as about his *duty*. He does not implore God to release him from the burden of guilt or the agony of fear. His fear and love are both directed to God, and his anxiety finds expression in eagerness to fulfill the Will of God on earth. The beginning of wisdom is fear of the Lord, not fear for one's individual destiny, nor that vague torment called "fear in general," or "anxiety."

Contrast the polarity of "anxiety-peace" with the import of the following quotations from our classic, pietistic literature:

"The foundation of piety and the root of the perfect service of God is the progressive endeavor to clarify and verify for man what his *duty* in the world is. . . ." ("M'silath Y'sharim," I)

"Though, in truth, from His side, all of existence is equally filled by His Being, without any distinctions or divisions, as if creation had not taken place at all . . ., *we must not contemplate this fact at all,* but seek to do His mitzvoth in the world that is revealed to our understanding . . ."
("Nefesh HaHayim," III, 6)

And as to those, (not Prof. Tillich), who confuse *feeling* spiritually good with *doing* "that which is good and straight in the sight of the Lord, Thy God," and those glib salesmen of "strength through faith," who identify the sense of peace with the acme of religious experience, we may recall the warning of Jeremiah—

"They healed the woe of my people lightly, saying peace, peace, when there is no peace." (Jeremiah, VI, 14)

(4)

In the Terry Lectures of 1952, published under the title, "The Courage to Be," Prof. Tillich illumines for us an interesting phase of his metaphysics. At the core of existence is "the courage to be"; hence, this courage is also the inmost substance of human character. How shall we understand this paradoxical combination of courage and being? —Being is manifestly the most inclusive of terms, while courage includes the idea of overcoming resistance. Thus, the term, "the courage to be" reveals the polar character of the universe—it is both being and non-being, the Ground out of which all that is intelligible emerges and the Abyss into which it dissolves and sinks.

From the metaphysical viewpoint, this concept comes close to the insistence of the Thomists, that Being is the only fitting concept for the understanding of the nature of reality. When Tillich prefixes the concept of being with the term courage, he introduces a dynamic quality, which becomes paramount in his thinking. To him, the Protestant principle, means that one must never rest content with any ideas or sentiments or ideologies, or dogmas. Whatever is, at any one moment, is to be transcended, for the pulsation of being at the heart of the universe does not permit any ideal or conception or law to stand still in static perfection. As a metaphysical concept, then, the "courage to be" is akin to the fundamental intuition of the philosophies of life—such as, those of Bergson, Euken and Nietzsche.

As an interpretation of the nature of human life and destiny, "the courage to be" is remarkable for the lack in it of the ethical factor. Like Nietzsche's "will to power" it purports to probe beyond the "merely ethical" plane to the dark depths that extend "beyond good and evil." Here, again, we encounter a fundamental divergence from the Hebrew Bible, especially as interpreted Judaism. While the content of piety in Judaism is not exhausted by the imperatives of ethics, the laws of ethics can no more be transcended than the principles of mathematics.[3]

While, in certain situations, the exercise of courage may be a supremely ethical act, there are also situations when courage is exerted in behalf of evil or selfish gains. Certainly, the term the courage to be, is ethically neutral, for it all depends on what follows the verb "to be."

[3] A parallel thought may be found in the "Tanya," by R. Shneur Zalman, where the readiness for martyrdom is taken to be the specific expression of the Divine soul in man. This courage to be part of God is explained in turn as being an unconscious recognition of the relative non-existence of this world, when it is viewed as God beholds it, against the totality of all ranks of being.

Tillich regards this concept as basic because he does not approach the human situation with fixed standards of moral judgement. The problem of society is not to him the contest between good and evil, within the individual or within society, but the task of allaying man's "anxiety" countering his "sense of estrangement" and endowing his career on earth with "meaning." I have put all these terms in parantheses because it may well be doubted whether these key-words of the "existential" theologians refer to the enduring substance of human life or whether they are merely fashionable shibboleths, magnifying all out of proportion the harried feelings of fringe-people in fringe-situations. After an evening spent in conversation with a Russian, Tillich is said to have exclaimed in amazement—"Wunderbar, Sie hat keine Angst." But, is the attainment of freedom from anxiety indeed a rare or inexplicable phenomenon? ("The Th. of P. T.," p. 159)

Religion is presented as the counterpoise to a threefold anxiety-fearfulness regarding death, sin, and the meaninglessness of life. The neurotic seeks to escape the pangs of anxiety by escaping from the tasks of life. In religion, anxiety is overcome by courage, and this courage is not an artificial creation of man, but a flow of reassurance from God.

What, now, if a person is not affected by pangs of anxiety? —Does religion have no message for him?—Or is its message, perchance, "be anxious that you may be reassured." The approach of the psychiatrist robs religion of its moral substance and vitiates the reasoning even of a theologian like Tillich, who, is, in many respects, a great prophetic figure. Anxiety becomes endemic whenever a "system of participation," in which the individual's loyalties were fully absorbed, is broken down. Ours is such an age, says Tillich. But, we are offered no criterion whereby these "systems of participation" may be judged.

428

As we survey the pietistic literature of Judaism in all its vast scope and variety, we find almost no reference to the so-called "anxiety of meaninglessness." Tillich defines anxiety as fear, without a specific object, and he assumes it to be an inevitable phase of the human situation. This assumption may well be questioned. Fear of death, fear of sin, fear of men, and fear of the manifold afflictions of life—all these specific fears we certainly encountered in abundance, but the sick-minded, nameless fear, that existentialists make so much of may be only a secondary phenomenon, that is grossly exaggerated and distorted.[4]

In Tillich's philosophy, anxiety is the human reflection of "separation" from being, and courage to be is the courage "to accept acceptance." What is the net meaning for the life of religion of this metaphysical "dark speech?"—In answer, we find that it is "theism transcended." "The ethical and social character of the Kingdom of God, the personal nature of human faith and divine forgiveness, the historical vision of the universe, the idea of a divine purpose, the infinite distance between creator and creature, the absolute separation between God and the world, the conflict between holy God and sinful man, the person to person character of prayer and practical devotion" —all these elements of theism must be transcended "because they are one-sided." (Ibid, p. 183) They assume that man is separable from God, standing over against him. "This is the God Nietzsche said had to be killed because nobody can tolerate being made into a mere object of absolute knowledge and absolute control." (Ibid, p. 185) We may note parenthetically that Judaism conceived of God in just this manner, and yet did not re-

[4] The Baalshem Tov regarded even the anxiety of guilt as a "wile of Satan," which is harmful to the good life. In the "Tanya," a clear line of distinction is drawn between anxiety in regard to sin, which is to be steadily cultivated, and anxiety regarding sickness or death, which is to be shunned.

duce man into a mere "object." As Rabbi Akiba put it, "all is foreseen and yet freedom is granted," and "beloved is man for he was created in the image of God." ("Aboth")

Theism is transcended in "the experience we have called absolute faith. It is the accepting of the acceptance without somebody or something that accepts." And this type of religion, for all its subtlety and grandeur, requires as its symbolic structure the conception of a "God above God" that only Christianity offers. "It is the church under the Cross, which alone can do this" i.e.—"mediate a courage which takes doubt and meaningless into itself." (Ibid, p. 188) To be sure, Kabbalah too, teaches the conception of the incomprehensible God, above the personalized God of theism. ("Ain Sof," or "Atika Kadisha" and "Z'ir Anpin") Nevertheless, we may readily agree that such speculations are characteristic of the inherent bent of Chritianity, which takes as its starting point the other side of the Divine-human encounter, viewing the entire scheme of things by the "criterion" of the supernatural mystery of "God who has become man." But, the Jew holds back from trespassing upon the realm of the Beyond, posing these sober warnings—Is not theism transcended also theism negated? While theism and morality point beyond themselves to the ultimate mystery of the Divine Being, this "pointing" cannot be normative for us as human beings. For us, there can be nothing that soars "beyond good and evil," the sacred and the profane, the rationally creative and the rationally demonic. The "criterion" cannot be the "paradox" of "God beyond God," but the ethical-rational voice of God in the human heart. As to the bold ventures into the beyond—how can the demonic be distinguished from the Divine? Is not this warning precisely the message of the prophet—"For my thoughts are not your thoughts . . .?" (Isaiah 55.8)

430

(5)

Of special interest to Jewish readers is Tillich's doctrine of the "Kairos," or "the fulness of time." In the complex evolution of human affairs, there are certain critical moments, when, in the midst of agony and travail the old society perishes and a new society comes into being. Such moments constitute repetitions in history of the Messianic advent. Hence, it is the duty of the Christian to embrace the "new being" of the world that is struggling to be born, though on strictly moral grounds, the "new society" may appear to be preponderately evil. Such "turning points in history" are to be recognized by means of an inward, "ecstatic" experience, rather than in the light of clear and static, universal principles.

"The appearance of the new is the concrete crisis of the old, the historical judgement against it. The new creation may be worse than the old one which is brought into crisis by it. But, in the special historical moment it is en Kairo, while the old creation is not." (The Protestant Era," p. 38)

Analyzing this doctrine from the Jewish viewpoint, we note first that Tillich takes the concrete, historical situation seriously. He does not disdain mundane reality as being inevitably sinful and theologically doomed. Giving the doctrine of "original sin" a recondite, metaphysical interpretation, (the separation of "existence" from "essence") he strives to reintroduce into Christian thought the prophetic emphasis on social justice. The unfortunate heritage of Martin Luther's cruel crusade against the poor peasants was courageously opposed by Tillich and his associates in the movement for "religious socialism." Religion was more than the individual's "anxiety" and his personal "salvation." The voice of God speaks to us out of the "lightning and thunder" of every contemporary situation and the infinite task of

431

building His Kingdom on earth has direct implications for every age.

But, here the resemblance ends. As a Christian, Tillich does not regard the new age as growing organically out of the old one, constituting a direct continuation of its values and norms. No, the new age presumes to "judge" the old dispensation, setting forth its own criteria of judgement. Morally and logically, the "wave of the future" may appear to be downright diabolical, but then the new age can only be judged by those who make the spiritual "leap" into its atmosphere, dying to the Law, as it were, and rising again into new "life." Thus, the Christian view of the substitution of the new Gospel for the Old Law is for Tillich the normative stereotype of the appearance of a new age in history.

The implicit dangers of this philosophy are self-evident to men of our generation and Prof. E. Heimann of The new School for Social Research calls attention to these dangers in a brilliant essay which is included in this volume. Tillich himself was better than his philosophy, which appears to bless every "turning point in history" and to oscillate from the Messianic impetuosity of the Kairos to the "sacred void," when the men of religion bow their heads and bide their time. In normative Judaism, the Messianic hope was always present as aspiration and consolation, making for a restrained optimism and sober, progressive meliorism.

Said Rabban Jochanan ben Zakkai, "if you hold a seedling in your hand and you hear the people shout, 'the Messiah has come,' plant the seedling first, and then go out to welcome the Messiah."

Except for the pseudo-messianic movements on the fringe of Jewish life, the advent of the Messiah was regarded as an extension of the values and norms of everyday life. The transition from this world into the "Days of the Messiah" was conceived either in the thunderous terms of a sudden and overwhelming catastrophe, or it was seen as a slow and painful climb. Also the resplendent image of the "Days of the Messiah" assumed varying guises in the fertile fancies of folk-pietists, poets and philosophers. But, never was the Messianic age represented in terms of an ethical break with the past. In the "future that is to come," the Torah was to be fulfilled, not transcended; God's law was to become a perfect reality, not replaced by a new reality; the people were to be judged, not the laws by which the lived.

(6)

As in his doctrines of the Kairos, Tillich's philosophy is determined throughout by the impetus of the Chistian "circle of ideas." Religion is for him, "ultimate concern"— that is, man's fundamental urge to discover the meaning of his destiny. Hermann Cohen followed the Jewish tradition in describing the essence of religion as being man's quest for his vocation, and his relative indifference to his own fate. To Cohen, concern with one's own soul and one's fate were marks of the mythological or pagan mentality, while the truly religious man asks only, "What is my role, my task, my duty?" Tillich, as a disciple of Kierkegaard, regards the individual's "anxiety" as to his own fate as being the essence of the faith. While the philosopher asks, What is being? the theologian inquires, What is being for us? . . . We may add parenthetically that the Jewish theologian is more likely to put the ultimate question in an inverted form, "What are we for being?"

Tillich analyzes the "existential" situation of modern man in terms of feeling. "Man experiences his present situation in terms of disruption, conflict, self- destruction, meaninglessness, and despair in all realms of life." ("Systematic Theology," I, p. 48)

433

Hence the answer to the basic question of man's existence can only be "a reality in which the self-estrangement of our existence is overcome." Hence, too the "norm" of theology is "the 'New Being in Jesus as the Christ." Needless to say that anyone grounded in Jewish tradition would reject not only the "norm," but the very concept of "new being" as well as the initial analysis of modern man's predicament as "meaninglessness."

A Jew might bemoan the moral failure of modern man, in the various areas of life, but he would find the very plaint of "meaninglessness" to be itself meaningless. Man knows himself to be called for a task, "chosen" for a role, and in the depths of his heart, he regrets his failure to achieve the fullness of his moral stature. Currents and cross-currents of feeling accompany every phase of our spiritual life, but the essence of the religious situation is God's call and man's response on the stage of life, not the alternation of moods and emotions.

(7)

From all the above, the Christological character of Tillich's seemingly general philosophy is manifest. In his painfully honest analysis of the contemporary intellectual scene, we behold the genius of Christian thought, as well as its peculiar bias and consequent limitations. Nor need we be surprised at this result, for unlike the great philosophers from Spinoza and Leibnitz to Dewey and Whitehead, he begins his analysis with a "preamble of faith." And this preamble he finds adumbrated symbolically in the story of the Gospels, which he takes to be "essentially" true. As Prof. Mollegen expresses his neo-Orthodox creed—"if there existed an absolutely accurate motion-picture film with color and sound effects of the words and acts of the Incarnate One, this picture would

434

support the Biblical pictures as to their Christian meaning." ("The Theology of Paul Tillich," p. 235)

To a Jew, the reading of Tillich's writings is stimulating and challenging, but unconvincing. For in the womb of the future, Jacob and Esau are still locked in a struggle that is also an embrace. And the two peoples derive strength from one another.[5]

[5] A rabbinic interpretation of Gen. XXV, 23.

Index

Note: This index was prepared by
Messrs. Daniel Litt and Norton
Shargell.